D0856519

AMERICAN MONEY AND BANKING

MAXWELL J. FRY
University of California, Irvine

RABURN M. WILLIAMS
University of Hawaii, Manoa

JOHN WILEY & SONS
New York
Chichester
Brisbane
Toronto
Singapore

Copyright © 1984, by John Wiley & Sons, Inc.

All rights reserved. Published simultaneously in Canada.

Reproduction or translation of any part of
this work beyond that permitted by Sections
107 and 108 of the 1976 United States Copyright
Act without the permission of the copyright
owner is unlawful. Requests for permission
or further information should be addressed to
the Permissions Department, John Wiley & Sons.

Library of Congress Cataloging in Publication Data

Fry, Maxwell J.
  American money and banking.

  Includes index.
  1. Money—United States. 2. Monetary policy—United
States. 3. Banks and banking—United States.
4. Finance—United States. I. Williams, Raburn M.
II. Title.
HG540.F79 1984   332.1'0973   83–21619
ISBN 0–471–86150–2

Printed in the United States of America

10 9 8 7 6 5 4 3 2

Preface

This book is designed for one-semester and one or two quarter under-
graduate courses in money and banking offered by economics departments
and business schools. The entire book can be covered rapidly in 10 weeks,
thoroughly in 15 weeks, and with supplementary readings in 20 weeks. We
provide suggestions on how to use this book for courses of different
lengths in the Instructor's Manual. In order to keep the book relatively
short, we concentrate exclusively on the nature and significance of money
in the U.S. economy. We start with the concept of money, analyze the
profit-maximizing behavior of depository institutions to explain multiple
deposit creation, emphasize the importance of the federal funds market at
the center of the money supply process in the United States, and examine
the Federal Reserve System and the way it implements monetary policy.
We use a three-stage analysis to explain exactly how monetary policy works,
what markets are affected, and how these markets move from one equilibrium to another. We analyze the effects of money on the macroeconomy
by building on a modern, yet simple, macroeconomic model of aggregate
demand and supply. Instead of devoting lengthy chapters to Keynes versus
the classics and the IS-LM model, we allot more space to gradual extensions
of the basic macroeconomic framework: money, inflation, and unemployment; money and government finance; money and interest rates (nominal
and real); money and the balance of payments; and the demand for money. This step-by-step development of the basic model allows us to cover
topics generally considered rather complex without confusing the student.
We then use the extended model to analyze, in a lively yet analytical style,
postwar domestic and international monetary policy.

We cannot nor do we wish to pretend that our book provides a comprehensive coverage of all the institutional details of the American financial

system. Instead, we equip the student with the basic analytical tools needed to understand changes in the financial system that may take place in the next 20 years. Wherever possible, institutional material is used to illustrate these analytical techniques. Simple yet thorough economic analysis is applied to each topic: defining money, monetary standards, present value calculations, fungibility of capital and government intervention in financial markets, interest-rate ceilings, demand for reserves under contemporaneous and lagged reserve requirements (the basic analysis of monetary policy implementation uses the post-February 1984 system of contemporaneous reserve requirements), search unemployment, adaptive and rational expectations, the political business cycle, money illusion in the tax system, the inflation tax, nominal and real interest-rate determination, inflation and savings decisions, inflation and the preference for nondepreciating assets, and disequilibrium in the market for money.

Many people helped us in writing this book. Clearly, our biggest debt is to our money and banking students at UCI and UH who were obliged to read our first draft. Our heartfelt thanks also go to Joseph Bisignano (Federal Reserve Bank of San Francisco), Andrew Crockett (International Monetary Fund), Charles Goodhart (Bank of England), John Judd (Federal Reserve Bank of San Francisco), Kevin Lang (University of California, Irvine), Charles Lave (University of California, Irvine), and Daniel Vencill (San Francisco State University) for information and suggestions; to Hank McMillan (University of California, Irvine), James Barth (The George Washington University), James R. Ostas (Bowling Green State University), Dennis McCornac (Manhattan College), and David Spencer (Washington State University) for reading the entire first draft; to Linda Babcock (University of Wisconsin, Madison) for research assistance; to John Ferguson (University of Miami, Ohio) and John Scadding (Federal Reserve Bank of San Francisco) for reviewing both the first and final drafts; to Sheen Kassouf (University of California, Irvine) for recommending cumulative distribution functions in preference to probability density functions and for reading the entire final draft; to Celia Fry for typing six sample chapters; to Cheryl Larsson (University of California, Irvine) for typing both drafts of the manuscript and drawing most of the figures; to our editor, Richard Esposito, for dangling carrots and waving sticks at the right moments; and to Edward Shaw (Stanford University) whose comments on our first draft encouraged us to complete what we had set out to do.

MAXWELL J. FRY

RABURN M. WILLIAMS

Contents

PART ONE

Money

Thomas Gresham was the first of a new breed—the merchant prince. Born about 1518, he graduated from Cambridge University at the age of 16. In 1543 he received his first commission as Royal Agent; in this capacity he was to buy gunpowder for King Henry VIII. While living in Antwerp, Gresham established a highly successful commercial business and also devoted considerable time and effort as Royal Agent to negotiating foreign loans for Henry VIII, Edward VI, Mary, and Elizabeth I.

As Gresham's private wealth increased, so did his concern with the Crown's mounting debts. He was determined to reduce the rate of interest on England's foreign loans. Gresham might well have become famous for his maxims on public finance. He put two of them successfully into effect while in Antwerp: it is better to borrow to repay debts than to reschedule them; interest must be paid punctually when due. The Crown's credit standing rose, except in the first year of Mary's reign, when Gresham, a Protestant, was relieved of his official duties. He managed to get the interest rate on foreign loans down from 14 to 10 percent. The prime rate in the mid-sixteenth century remained a fairly constant 7 percent. Royalty were not generally prime borrowers in those days!

After Queen Elizabeth acceded to the throne in 1558, Gresham's influence at court rose. He wrote a long letter to the new monarch in which he explained England's contemporary monetary problems:

It may please Your Majesty to understand that the first occasion of the fall of the Exchange [rate] did grow by the King's Majesty, your late Father, in abasing his coin from six ounces fine to three ounces fine. Whereupon the

> Exchange fell from 26s/8d to 13s/4d, which was the occasion that all your fine gold was conveyed out of this your realm.[1]

The last sentence in this quotation was Gresham's statement of Gresham's law. The bad or abased (debased) money drives the good money out of circulation. Alternatively, the overvalued money drives out the undervalued money.

Henry VIII's expenses had invariably exceeded his regular tax revenue. One of his solutions was recoinage. The coins that came in as tax payments were melted down with some scrap metal. By adding an equal weight of scrap metal to the old coins, Henry VIII could produce twice the amount of money—just what he needed. However, the quantity of money increased as he spent these new coins. Doubling the money supply in this way guaranteed inflation. Prices of everything, including silver, rose. The value of silver in an old, undebased coin soon exceeded the coin's face value. The same thing happened to gold coins; gold coins had not been debased.

Thomas Gresham explained clearly the outcome of Henry VIII's currency debasements. The new, bad money drove the old, good money out of circulation and the exchange rate fell. Good money was melted down for its silver content, hoarded, or, in the case of gold coins, used to buy goods abroad. Foreigners were unwilling to accept the debased currency, foreign trade was disrupted, and Gresham found it more difficult to raise foreign loans for Henry VIII. Potential lenders feared, with good reason, that they would be repaid in debased coins. Eventually, the rate of exchange fell from 180 old silver pennies to one gold sovereign to 360 new, debased pennies to the sovereign.

There are two ironic twists to the story of Gresham's law. First, Gresham persuaded Queen Elizabeth (who knighted him in 1559) to restore England's silver coins to their traditional sterling fineness of 925 parts of silver in 1000. In other words, he was responsible for the substitution of good money for bad money—the opposite of Gresham's law. The only way this could be done was to call in all the debased coins and exchange them for new, good coins. On September 27, 1560, Queen Elizabeth issued a proclamation on the currency reform. The proclamation established the rate at which the debased coins would be exchanged for the new issue of sterling silver coins and it threatened severe punishment for anyone discovered trying to profit from the reform. Old coins were to be accepted in exchange for the new coins during the following four months, after which they could no longer be used as money. Elizabeth's coinage reform not only turned Gresham's

---

[1]John William Burgon, *The Life and Times of Sir Thomas Gresham, Knt., Founder of the Royal Exchange* (London: Effingham Wilson, 1839), Volume 1, p. 484.

law on its head, but also yielded a small profit. In total, the old coins had been exchanged for new ones at a rate slightly below their silver content ratios.

The second twist is that Gresham's law had already been known for 2000 years. In *The Frogs*, first produced in Athens in 405 B.C., Aristophanes wrote:

I'll tell you what I think about the way
This city treats her soundest men today:
By a coincidence more sad than funny,
It's very like the way we treat our money.
The noble silver drachma, that of old
We were so proud of, and the recent gold,
Coins that rang true, clean-stamped and worth their weight
Throughout the world, have ceased to circulate.
Instead, the purses of Athenian shoppers are full of shoddy silver-plated
    coppers.
Just so, when men are needed by the nation,
The best have been withdrawn from circulation.[2]

---

[2]Aristophanes, *The Frogs and Other Plays* trans. David Barrett (Harmondsworth: Penguin, 1964), pp. 182–183.

1 Nature, Functions, and Value of Money

Today one can hardly open a newspaper or magazine without encountering at least one article on current monetary problems. Since the early 1960s American money has run amok, making monetary issues of central concern to economic policy. Money is blamed for the worst bout of inflation in America since the Civil War. Money makers are blamed for high interest rates. Some people hold OPEC, the Organization of Petroleum Exporting Countries, responsible for our monetary problems; others trace the problems back to the Vietnam War. Many believe that a balanced federal government budget is the cure. The cacophony of analyses, descriptions, and prescriptions for our monetary ills is deafening.

This book explains what money is and what money does. It looks at the market for money: the demand for money on one side and the supply of money on the other. Disequilibrium between this demand and supply has a pervasive effect on the economy, influencing the markets for other financial assets, goods, services, housing, and labor. This is why the study of what affects the supply of and demand for money is so important.

The Federal Reserve System (the Fed) is the central bank of the United States. The Fed, together with depository institutions such as commercial banks, mutual savings banks, savings and loan associations (S&Ls), credit unions, and some finance companies are the main suppliers, creators, or makers of American money. Hence, they receive considerable attention here. On the other side of the money market are individuals and business firms with demands for money. Consequently, individual and corporate decisions about how much money to hold are equally important in analyzing monetary disequilibrium.

Suppose people find themselves with too much money in their asset portfolios, given the levels of prices, incomes, interest rates, and wealth.

They can exchange those excess money balances for goods, services, common stocks, and/or bonds. In this process, demands for goods, services, stocks, and bonds increase. The immediate effect of these demand increases is either sales exceeding current production, which must involve inventory depletion, or an increase in prices brought about by quantity demanded exceeding the available supply, or a combination of inventory decumulation and higher prices.

It is no wonder, then, that controlling the money supply is considered to be so important. This is, in fact, the major concern of monetary policy. Basically, all Federal Reserve activities in the market for money—on the demand as well as the supply side—constitute monetary policy measures. The goals of monetary policy include economic growth, full employment, balance of payments equilibrium, and price stability. During the postwar period American monetary policy has failed to achieve any of these goals with any consistency. A considerable portion of this book analyzes what monetary policy can and cannot do, and gives the reasons for the apparent failure of monetary policy in recent times.

What Is Money?

Means of Payment   It is generally agreed that money's primary function is to serve as a means of payment or medium of exchange. Money can be exchanged without delay or difficulty for goods, services, stocks, and bonds. All final payments are made with money. But what is money and what is not? Why is one type of bank deposit classified as money while another type is not?

In value terms, less than 1 percent of transactions in the United States involve cash; credit cards are used for less than one-fourth of 1 percent. Checks, on the other hand, account for about 25 percent. The remaining 74 percent is accounted for by wire transfers! Although very few transactions are conducted via wire transfers, their average value is enormous. The wire transfer system consists of commercial bank computers all connected to one another through the Federal Reserve System's telegraphic network. Banks make these transfers for their clients and themselves in the same way that they clear checks. However, instead of sending checks through Federal Reserve banks, commercial banks transmit electronic impulses. (Chapter 6 explains how checks are cleared.)

It is a relatively simple matter to separate a crowd into two groups, one of people who are at least six feet tall and another of people under six feet. Provided accurate rulers were used, the same people would be placed in the same groups no matter who did the measuring. Splitting a crowd into clever and stupid groups poses much greater, if not insuperable, problems. Different evaluators would put the same people into different groups. Deciding what is money and what is not is analogous to the second problem of classification. What one person calls money another may not. The solution chosen by many economists nowadays is to agree to differ.

The Federal Reserve System's Definitions of Money

Since January 1982 the Federal Reserve has offered four alternative definitions of money—M1, M2, M3, and L (Tables 1.1 and 1.2). (M stands for money and L for liquid assets.) The M1 definition includes currency in circulation and deposits held for the purpose of making transactions. Hence, M1 is known as a *transactions-type monetary aggregate.* The other three definitions include components that are not generally held for making transactions. Hence, these definitions are called *nontransactions-type monetary aggregates.*

Table 1.1   The Federal Reserve's Definitions of Money

	M1	*M2*	*M3*	*L*
Currency in circulation	X	X	X	X
Commercial bank and thrift institution liabilities				
Demand deposits*a*	X	X	X	X
NOW accounts	X	X	X	X
Super NOW accounts	X	X	X	X
ATS accounts	X	X	X	X
Overnight RPs*b*		X	X	X
Savings deposits		X	X	X
Money market deposit accounts		X	X	X
Small time deposits*c* (<$100,000)		X	X	X
Large time deposits (>$100,000)			X	X
Term RPs			X	X
Other				
Overnight Eurodollar deposits of U.S. nonbank residents		X	X	X
Money market mutual funds shares		X	X	X
Term Eurodollars held by U.S. nonbank residents				X
Bankers' acceptances				X
Commercial paper				X
U.S. savings bonds				X
Liquid treasury securities				X
M2 consolidation component*d*		X	X	X

*a*Excluding deposits due to foreign commercial banks and official institutions.
*b*Repurchase agreements. A repurchase agreement is an acquisition of funds through the sale of securities, with a simultaneous agreement by the seller to repurchase them at a later date. Overnight RPs are extremely liquid since they will be repurchased the next day.
*c*Small time deposits are distinguished from large time deposits because interest-rate ceilings were imposed on the former but not the latter. With the complete abolition of ceilings, this distinction will be meaningless.
*d*To avoid double counting, thrift institution deposits with commercial banks and money market mutual funds' holdings of RPs are deducted.

Table 1.2 The U.S. Money Stock, 1959–1982 (average of daily figures during December of each year; billions of dollars)

Year	M1	M2	M3	L
1959	140.9	297.7	298.9	388.4
1960	141.9	312.3	314.3	403.4
1961	146.5	335.5	339.4	430.5
1962	149.2	362.8	369.7	465.9
1963	154.7	393.4	404.1	503.7
1964	161.9	425.1	440.2	540.5
1965	169.5	459.5	480.7	584.5
1966	173.7	481.3	504.9	616.5
1967	185.1	526.6	558.6	670.1
1968	199.4	569.4	608.4	733.9
1969	205.8	591.3	614.1	765.2
1970	216.5	628.8	675.2	816.5
1971	230.6	713.6	773.7	903.2
1972	251.9	806.4	882.8	1023.6
1973	265.8	863.2	981.4	1143.8
1974	277.4	911.2	1064.3	1249.8
1975	291.0	1026.9	1166.2	1376.6
1976	310.4	1171.2	1305.0	1531.4
1977	335.5	1297.7	1464.6	1724.3
1978	363.2	1403.9	1629.0	1938.9
1979	389.0	1518.9	1779.4	2153.9
1980	414.5	1656.2	1963.1	2370.4
1981	440.9	1822.7	2188.1	2642.8
1982	478.5	1999.1	2403.7	2896.8

Source: Economic Report of the President, 1983, p. 233.

Liquidity   The Fed uses a deductive or functional approach to defining money. Specifically, it attempts to rank possible candidates for inclusion in the definition of money by their liquidity. An asset's *liquidity* is assessed on the basis of the cost of converting it into a means of payment and the stability or predictability of its price. An asset is more liquid the lower is the transaction cost of selling it, which includes the speed at which it can be sold, and the more predictable is the price at which it can be sold.

Money's means-of-payment function gives it the attribute of perfect liquidity. Indeed, the desire to hold currency and checking account balances is, in large part, a preference for liquidity or a *liquidity preference*. As a means of payment, money can be exchanged immediately for goods, services, stocks, and bonds. Holding money provides flexibility and keeps all options open. Liquidity preference is generated by uncertainty about future income, prices, interest rates, and a myriad of noneconomic factors. If money yielded the same return as bonds, no one would want to hold bonds, because money would provide the same income *plus* liquidity.

Savings deposits are highly liquid because the cost of transferring them to a checking account or withdrawing them as currency is low and their value is completely predictable. Other financial assets such as stocks and bonds are fairly cheap and easy to sell, but their prices are unpredictable. Real estate, jewelry, and art work are illiquid assets because the costs of liquidation are substantial.

Components of M1   The Fed's M1 definition of money includes only components that are means of payment and so are perfectly liquid. Table 1.1 shows the variety of accounts included in M1. Curiously enough, the proliferation of different types of accounts is a result of the gradual abolition of interest-rate ceilings on deposits. The Automatic Transfer Service (ATS) and Negotiable Order of Withdrawal (NOW) accounts were both designed to avoid the prohibition of interest payment on checking accounts. The ATS account enables depositors to hold their balances in savings accounts and to write checks on demand deposits with no money in them—zero-balance accounts. Funds are transferred automatically by the bank from the saving to the checking account whenever a check arrives for payment. The NOW account avoids the zero-interest restriction on checking accounts by allowing holders to write negotiable orders of withdrawal instead of checks—a very fine legal distinction of no practical importance.

Both ATS and NOW accounts may pay up to $5\frac{1}{4}$ percent interest. Since the end of 1982, however, depository institutions have been allowed to pay any interest rate they choose on Super NOW and Money Market Deposit Accounts (MMDAs), provided a minimum balance of $2500 is maintained. Holders of Super NOW accounts can write an unlimited number of checks, whereas only six transfers (preauthorized or telephone transfer debits as well as checks) per month can be made from an MMDA, of which no more than three can be made by check. During the first half of 1983, MMDAs offered an annual rate of return $\frac{1}{4}$ to 1 percentage point higher than Super NOWs and attracted far more funds than Super NOWs. Because of the transfer restrictions on MMDAs, they are excluded from the Fed's M1 definition of money but are included in M2.

Abolishing Interest-Rate Ceilings   Interest-rate ceilings are to be eliminated completely by 1986. Then there will be no artificial distinctions between different types of deposits. Deposit variety can be expected to contract and all demand deposits may offer the same market-determined yield. Deposit holders will probably pay full costs of the bank services provided, such as check clearing and bookkeeping. The main variety will be in deposit maturity. Hence, depository institutions may offer time deposits with a range of maturities as they do now, but only one type of demand deposit. Clearly, demand deposits will be included in the M1 definition and time deposits in the M2 definition of money.

Money Market Mutual Fund Shares

Ironically, big spenders can get along rather well without holding any of the transactions-type deposits included in the Fed's M1 definition of money. Several large brokerage houses offer money market mutual funds (MMMFs) share accounts that enable account holders to write checks just as they can on ordinary checking accounts. The account balances are invested in short-term financial assets such as certificates of deposit and treasury bills, and so earn a market-determined yield. During the first half of 1983 the average yield on MMMFs was slightly below the MMDA yield but above the Super NOW rate. As a result, there was a substantial transfer of funds from MMMFs to MMDAs. As in the case of ATS accounts, checks on MMMF accounts are actually written against zero-balance checking accounts. Here, however, each check triggers an automatic sale of fund shares. The only drawbacks are that a substantial minimum opening balance is required (for example, $20,000 to open a Merrill Lynch cash management account) and deposits are not insured. Despite the absence of check-writing restrictions, the Fed treats MMMFs like MMDAs rather than Super NOWs and includes them in M2 but not M1.

Substitutability

The basic problem faced by anyone trying to decide just what is and what is not money concerns substitutability. Many nonmoney assets can perform some of the functions of money. In some respects, they are good substitutes for money. Some nonmonies are such good substitutes for money that they perform almost all the functions of money. As a matter of logic, a perfect substitute for money is indistinguishable from money and, hence, is money. The problem is where to draw the line. How much substitutability is enough?

The main difficulty here lies in measuring substitutability. Substitutability depends, in part, on people's subjective perceptions and not entirely on measurable attributes. For example, there probably exist red and green apples that are identical in every respect except color. If no one cares what color an apple is, then these particular red and green apples are perfect substitutes. Neither the store nor the shopper will mind whether this brand of apples turns up as red ones or green ones. In fact, however, color does matter. Lemons have been produced with exactly the same characteristics as regular lemons except that they are the color of oranges. Orange lemons just do not sell!

One implication of all this is that *if* MMMF account holders regard and treat their MMMF balances in exactly the same way as they would regard and treat ordinary checking account balances, then MMMF accounts are money. If, however, MMMF account holders regard and treat their MMMF balances quite differently from regular checking account balances, then MMMF accounts may not be money. Evidently, then, the problem of definition here is an empirical one. Although many MMMF account holders do use MMMFs as money, evidence suggests that most holders of MMMFs do not regard and treat their share balances like checking accounts:

> . . . [M]oney market mutual funds shares are viewed as substitutes for other non-transactions-type financial assets, despite the fact that owners of these shares are offered check-writing privileges. The fairly large minimum denomination requirement (usually $500 or more) for checks written on these accounts and the fact that these balances typically exhibit relatively slow turnover rates suggest that these accounts are used primarily as savings rather than transactions accounts.[1]

Again, it boils down to the empirical question of whether or not MMMFs are generally treated as money. Moreover, the way in which people view the moneyness of these assets may change over time. Indeed, many people did change their attitude towards MMMFs in the spring of 1980, a time when short-term interest rates hit record levels. (One MMMF earned dividends at an annual rate of $17\frac{1}{2}$ percent for the first quarter of 1981.) A substantial switch out of transactions-type deposits, such as demand deposits and ATS accounts, into MMMFs occurred in response to the newsworthy high yields on the latter. When short-term interest rates subsequently dropped that summer, no corresponding reverse substitution back into M1 money took place. Evidently, a large number of people started viewing MMMFs as a substitute not only for other nontransactions-type financial assets, but for M1-type transactions assets as well. Furthermore, within the past few years a number of brokerage houses have dropped the minimum denomination restriction on checks, making MMMFs even closer substitutes for regular checking accounts.

Empirical Approach to Defining Money   Although the Fed starts with a deductive or functional approach to defining money in terms of liquidity attributes of potential components, it supports its classification system by appeals to empirical evidence. This inductive or empirical approach can be used as an alternative way of defining money. It starts by asking: What use is to be made of the definition of money? Perhaps the most important use is monetary policy and, specifically, control over total income in the economy. In that case, the most useful definition of money might be that which is most closely related to income. It turns out that either M1 or M2 has the strongest association with income, depending on the time period analyzed and various technical factors such as the lags introduced.

The empirical approach has been taken a step further in an attempt to

---

[1]R. W. Hafer, "The New Monetary Aggregates," *Federal Reserve Bank of St. Louis Review*, 62(2), February 1980, p. 26.

measure substitutability. Recognizing that the issue of whether or not a particular asset should be included as money is not black and white, a number of studies have allowed some components to be included partially. This is done by deflating the component's dollar value by some proportion or coefficient. The actual value of the coefficient used is chosen on the criterion of best relationship with total income.

Credit Lines and Opportunity Costs

Overdraft arrangements and credit lines are excluded from all definitions of money. Although credit cards can be very useful for acquiring goods and services, there are two reasons why they are not money. The first reason is that a credit card transaction does not involve final payment. It creates a debt that is settled later. The second, and perhaps more important, reason is that holding money balances incurs a cost—an opportunity cost—whereas the line of credit does not.

An *opportunity cost* is an implicit or concealed cost in terms of the best alternative. The opportunity cost of being a student, for example, is the income that could otherwise have been earned from working instead of going to class, or the parties that could otherwise have been attended instead of studying. In the case of money, the opportunity cost also has two dimensions. First, the price or cost of *accumulating* one extra dollar in money balances is the goods and services that otherwise could have been purchased. If a pineapple is the next best alternative and costs $2, then the opportunity cost of adding an extra dollar to one's money balances is half a pineapple. If the price of pineapples goes up to $5, the opportunity cost of accumulating this money falls to one-fifth of a pineapple, and so does the value of the money. Second, the cost of *holding* a dollar from one year to the next is the difference between the market rate of interest and the return on money.[2] For example, currency earns zero interest and, hence, the opportunity cost of holding currency equals the market rate of interest.

Because both accumulating and holding money incur opportunity costs, the demand for money is finite. People accumulate and hold money up to the point at which the marginal benefits of accumulating and holding an extra dollar just equal the marginal costs. Marginal benefits decline as the quantity of money held rises. Hence, the quantity of money demanded increases as the marginal costs fall. Therefore, the money demand function is a normal downward-sloping demand curve, as illustrated in Figure 1.1.

The situation with respect to credit lines is entirely different. The only cost in demanding a higher credit limit is the time it takes to complete the application form. In some cases postage is prepaid, so one does not even have to buy a stamp. Of course, the marginal benefit of a larger and larger credit limit declines, but zero may well be as far as it can fall. When marginal benefit actually does equal marginal cost, demand is indeterminate or insatiable. Any extra supply will be absorbed at the same price, as shown in Figure 1.2, with no further reaction.

[2]Jurg Niehans, *The Theory of Money* (Baltimore: Johns Hopkins University Press, 1978), p. 77.

Figure 1.1   Demand for Money

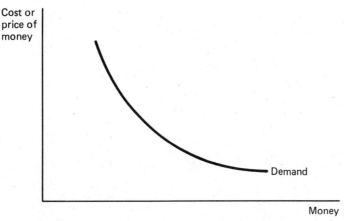

The demand for money is a standard downward-sloping demand curve. The cost or price of money actually has two dimensions. Here, it can be the inverse either of the general level of prices—a measure of how much one unit of money can buy—or the interest rate, which equals the cost of postponing consumption for a year.

This, then, is one good reason why credit and overdraft lines cannot be included in any definition of money. A change in the volume of credit lines may have no impact at all. The market can be in equilibrium at any volume; and a volume change need not necessarily throw this market into disequilibrium. On the other hand, if the money supply changes, as in Figure 1.3, the price of money in flow or stock sense must change to restore equilibrium between demand and supply. An increase in supply produces a fall in the price of money—through an increase in the general level of prices,

Figure 1.2   Demand for Credit Lines

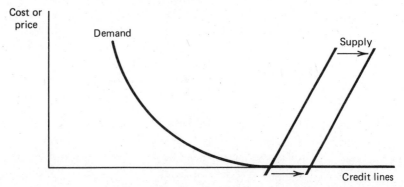

At a zero opportunity cost, the demand for credit lines may well become perfectly elastic. In this case a shift in supply has no effect at all. The additional quantity of credit balances is simply absorbed with no reaction.

Figure 1.3   A Shift in Money Supply

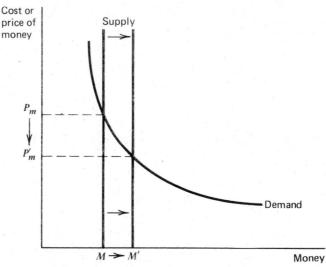

The shift in the money supply shown in this figure creates an excess supply of money at the original price of money, P_m. In an attempt to dispose of unwanted money balances, people offer more money in exchange for goods, services, equities, and bonds. This activity bids up prices and hence reduces the price of money.

or a decrease in interest rates, or both. The process by which equilibrium is restored in the money market is analyzed in detail later. The forces released by disequilibrium in the money market affect the rest of the economy. These effects are analyzed with the use of the macroeconomic model developed in Chapter 11.

The existence of credit and overdraft lines may certainly influence the demand for money. However, there is no evidence suggesting that a marginal change in the value of unused credit line balances has any noticeable effect on money demand. Using a credit card not only provides an interest-free loan for a month or more but also enables receipts and expenditures to be synchronized more easily. If an individual buys everything on credit and if payment of his or her credit card balance is due two days after payday, this person's average money balance over the month is likely to be considerably lower than would be the case if he or she made cash expenditures spread out evenly between one payday and the next.

Standard of Value   So far, most of the discussion in this section has focused on money as a means of payment, its primary function. Money also serves as a standard or measure of value. Without a common standard of value, people would be using different yardsticks for measuring and comparing relative values. For example, some people might measure value in terms of cattle, others might use salt as a measuring rod. Americans on vacation abroad usually translate franc, peso, lira, and yen prices into dollar prices. For Americans, the dollar is the standard of value. Although prices could be quoted in pounds sterling even in a country using the U.S. dollar as a means of payment, such practice would be inconvenient. Everyone would have to know the pound/dollar exchange rate to make a transaction. For this reason, the means of payment is invariably used as the standard of value.

A common standard of value allows people to compare prices of the same item sold at different stores. It also enables people to compare prices of different items. One might, for example, be shopping for a raincoat. After comparing raincoat prices in different stores, one could conclude that all raincoats were too expensive and buy an umbrella instead. Implicitly, the shopper is using the standard of value in both a relative and an absolute sense. Comparing raincoat prices uses it in the relative sense, while deciding that raincoats are, in general, too expensive uses it as an absolute standard of value. Relative and absolute prices are discussed later in the chapter.

Unit of Account The use of money as a standard or measure of value is related closely to its use as a unit of account. The unit-of-account function of money enables people to draw up accounts. These can range from a simple account showing the total amount owed at a grocery store to a corporate profit-and-loss statement. If receipts included ten fish, three sacks of wheat, and one cow, while expenditures consisted of one suit of clothes and a weekend in Las Vegas, no one could tell whether receipts were more or less than expenditures. Expressing all receipts and expenditures in a common unit of account allows people to compare total receipts with total expenditures. In a more elaborate framework, the unit-of-account function of money enables income statements and balance sheets to be prepared.

Store of Value Money also acts as a store of value. If ice cream was used as money, people would hold very little money. They would have to rush off and spend it before it melted away. The store-of-value function of money enables one to separate the timings of income and expenditure. In the United States the M1 definition of money is equal in value to about 17 percent of total income. To put it another way, money represents about two months' worth of aggregate expenditure on final goods and services. Some moneyholders are saving up for a relatively expensive purchase. Others maintain money balances just in case their income drops or they want to buy something in the future. Another group holds currency because their transactions are illegal or because they are evading taxes. In any event, money is held despite its opportunity cost because it is a store of value and can be used in the future to obtain goods and services.

Standard for Future Payment Finally, money performs an important function as a standard for future or deferred payment. When people borrow, they generally agree to repay the loan at some future date in money. Here, money is used as the standard in contracts concerning future payments.

Some monies perform their functions better than others. Even as a means of payment, some kinds of money are better than others. In addition, performance depends on the type of transaction. For example, Federal Reserve notes and treasury coins are generally the most acceptable means of payment in the United States. In Sweden, however, they would not be such a satisfactory means of payment as kronas. Even in the United States, $100 bills are not always acceptable because of the prevalence of forgery. Were forgery rampant, Federal Reserve notes would be a very poor means of payment; transactions would be more difficult to conclude and payments' efficiency would deteriorate. To prevent this from happening, considerable expense is incurred by the Federal Reserve System to deter forgery.

For some transactions, deposit money is the most satisfactory means of payment. Specifically, deposit transfer by check is invariably preferred to the use of currency when transactions are conducted by mail. A check can be made payable to the payee only, whereas currency cannot be earmarked in the same way. Hence, the use of checks provides some inbuilt insurance against loss or theft.

American money has been performing the functions of a store of value and standard for future payments less and less satisfactorily since the mid-1960s. This situation is, of course, due to accelerating inflation. American money has been a much poorer store of value than, say, German or Swiss money. This fact explains, in part, why the demand for German and Swiss money has been increasing relative to the demand for American money. With 10 percent annual inflation rates, money loses half its value in just over seven years. One hundred dollars stored today would be worth less than $1 in 50 years if inflation continued at 10 percent a year. Under such inflationary conditions, money's value is eroded, and therefore money serves as a poor store of value. Similarly, under relatively high and volatile inflation, money becomes an unsatisfactory standard for future payments.

The Value of Money and Price Indices

The value of money is its purchasing power or how much money can buy. Everyone knows that the dollar's value has been falling in recent years. One dollar buys less than half as much as it did ten years ago. Clothes, food, and housing all cost more: $1 buys less of these items. Nevertheless, $1 buys a lot more of an electronic calculating machine today than it did a decade ago. The value of the dollar has fallen against some things but risen against others.

A distinction can be made here between relative and absolute prices. A *relative price* is one item's price in relation to or compared with prices of other goods and services. The relative price of an apple is its price in comparison with the price of an orange, a pear, or a loaf of bread. The *absolute price* is simply the money price. If all money prices rise by 10 percent, relative prices remain unchanged. If only one money price rises by 10 percent, then the relative price of that item has increased by 10 percent too. It is now 10 percent more expensive in relation to all other goods and services. The absolute price is used when the comparison is between one item or a bundle of items and money. The value of money is the inverse of the absolute or money price level.

If everything increased in price by 1 percent, then you could say that the value of money had decreased by 1 percent. However, when different prices are changing by different amounts, some average measure for the change in money's value is needed. This is what price indices provide. The most popular price index in the United States is the Consumer Price Index (CPI) compiled by the U.S. Bureau of Labor Statistics.

Consumer Price Index As the first step, the Bureau of Labor Statistics conducted a sample survey of urban consumers to find out what their expenditures were. The interviewers asked how much these people spent on food, housing, clothing, transportation, medical care, entertainment, and other goods and services. Each of these broad categories is subdivided into a large number of specific items. Schematically, the information obtained from one interview in the base year or year 0 might be tabulated as follows:

Item	Expenditure $(p \cdot q)$	Price (p)	Quantity (q)
Food	$468.66	$ 6.42	73
Housing	426.00	426.00	1
Clothing	95.88	15.98	6
Transportation	68.60	2.45	28
Medical care	66.58	33.29	2
Entertainment	22.04	5.51	4
Other	74.16	8.24	9

Evidently, this hypothetical consumer spent $1221.92 during that particular month.

The aim of this exercise is to estimate changes in consumer prices or the cost of living for the average or typical urban consumer. Assuming that the tabulation above is the average expenditure pattern of the consumers sampled by the Bureau of Labor Statistics over the course of a year or two, the next step is to monitor price changes of all the items in the index or consumer basket. The Bureau might produce the following new price list a year later.

Item	Price (p)
Food	$ 7.39
Housing	477.12
Clothing	16.78
Transportation	3.06
Medical care	38.62
Entertainment	5.95
Other	7.66

The final step is to calculate the index. This is given by the following formula:

$$\text{CPI}_t = \frac{\sum_{j=1}^{7} p_{j,t} \cdot q_{j,0}}{\sum_{j=1}^{7} p_{j,0} \cdot q_{j,0}} \cdot 100 \qquad (1.1)$$

where Σ sums all the j items (there are seven items in this example: $p_{1,t} \cdot q_{1,0} + p_{2,t} \cdot q_{2,0} + p_{3,t} \cdot q_{3,0} + \cdots + p_{7,t} \cdot q_{7,0}$), p is the price, q is quantity, the first subscript refers to the item (food, clothing, and so on), and the second subscript denotes the period—t is the current year (in this case, year 1), and 0 is the base year. Hence, $p_{1,t}$ is the price of food in year t and $q_{3,0}$ is the quantity of clothing bought in the base year.

The calculation of the index can be done as follows.

Item	$p_{j,t} \cdot q_{j,0}$	$p_{j,0} \cdot q_{j,0}$
Food	$ 539.47	$ 468.66
Housing	477.12	426.00
Clothing	100.68	95.88
Transportation	85.68	68.60
Medical care	77.24	66.58
Entertainment	23.80	22.04
Other	68.94	74.16
Sum $\sum_{j=1}^{7}$	$1372.93	$1221.92

Hence, CPI_t equals 112.36—(1372.93/1221.92) $\cdot$ 100. Thus, consumer prices have increased on average by 12.36 percent—(1372.93/1221.92 − 1) $\cdot$ 100. If the CPI index for years 4 and 5 is 149.28 and 155.93, respectively, then consumer prices increased by 4.45 percent between these two years—(155.93/149.28 − 1) $\cdot$ 100.

The CPI is known as a base-weighted or Laspeyres index, because it always uses $q_{j,0}$ or the quantities purchased in year 0. However, the base year is changed about once a decade to allow for the changing pattern of consumer expenditures. The Bureau of Labor Statistics produces another base-weighted index known as the Producer Price Index or the Wholesale Price Index (WPI). This index measures price changes at the production or wholesale stage. It is useful in that it provides an early warning of likely changes in the CPI. A surge in producer prices this quarter is usually reflected in retail or consumer prices about two quarters later.

Prices and the Value of Money The price of money in terms of what it can buy can be defined as

$$P_m = \frac{1}{P/100} \cdot 100 \tag{1.2}$$

where P_m is the price or value of money and P is the price index, for example, the CPI. The two indices move inversely, perhaps like this.

Year	P	P_m
0	100.00	100.00
1	112.36	89.00
2	124.85	80.10
3	137.52	72.72
4	149.28	66.99
5	155.93	64.13

The P_m index indicates that $100 in year 5 buys only what $64.13 bought in year 0. Alternatively, the P index shows that one needs $155.93 in year 5 to buy the basket of consumer goods and services that $100 bought in year 0.

GNP Deflator The gross national product (GNP) is calculated by adding up all expenditures on the n different final goods and services in the economy. Expenditures on gross national product can also be broken down into price and quantity components. The gross national product can be measured using current prices $p_{j,t}$ (GNP at current prices) or using constant prices $p_{j,0}$ (GNP at constant prices, or real gross national product). Dividing gross national product at current prices $\sum_{j=1}^{n} p_{j,t} \cdot q_{j,t}$ by gross national product at constant prices $\sum_{j=1}^{n} p_{j,0} \cdot q_{j,t}$ provides another price index—the *implicit GNP deflator*, P_{GNP}. This index is a current-weighted or Paasche index.

$$P_{\text{GNP}} = \frac{\sum\limits_{j=1}^{n} p_{j,t} \cdot q_{j,t}}{\sum\limits_{j=1}^{n} p_{j,0} \cdot q_{j,t}} \tag{1.3}$$

Instead of base weights $q_{j,0}$, current year quantities $q_{j,t}$ are used.

All three price indices discussed here can be employed to calculate the value of money or P_m indices. None of them is perfect—each index has its own advantages and disadvantages.

CPI versus WPI　Over time, the CPI tends to show a greater price increase than the WPI because the CPI includes services and the WPI does not. Since productivity in service industries, such as legal advice, haircutting, and teaching, has tended to increase more slowly than productivity in goods industries, such as automobiles, electronic calculators, and ball-point pens, the costs of producing goods have tended to rise less rapidly than the costs of producing services. In fact, starting with both indices at 100 in 1967, the CPI and WPI were 289.1 and 280.6, respectively, in 1982. The difference would have been substantially greater had it not been for the rapid rise in the price of oil since 1973.

Base Weights versus Current Weights　The CPI also tends to rise faster than the implicit GNP deflator during periods of inflation because of the former's use of base weights and the latter's use of current weights. The CPI measures cost of living on the assumption that consumption patterns remain constant, but the law of demand says that as the relative price of a good rises (not necessarily its absolute or money price), the quantity demanded falls. Consumers will substitute cheaper goods for relatively more expensive ones. The following table elaborates the price–quantity tabulations presented earlier.

	Price		Percentage	Quantity	
Item	Year 0	Year 1	Change	Year 0	Year 1
Food	$ 6.42	$ 7.39	15.1	73	68
Housing	426.00	477.12	12.0	1	1
Clothing	15.98	16.78	5.0	6	9
Transportation	2.45	3.06	24.9	28	17
Medical care	33.29	38.62	16.0	2	2
Entertainment	5.51	5.95	8.0	4	5
Other	8.24	7.66	−7.0	9	15

The base-weighted price index calculated earlier gives a price increase between year 0 and year 1 of 12.36 percent. Using current year weights, the price increase is only 10.97 percent. The explanation is simple: the weights or quantities are smaller in the current-weighted index for items whose relative prices have risen. The relative prices of food and transportation, for example, increased. Hence, quantities of food and transportation demanded fell. The base-weighted CPI uses bigger weights than the current-weighted implicit GNP deflator for items whose prices have increased most. Clearly, therefore, the CPI will show a larger price rise than the implicit GNP deflator. With both indices at 100 in 1967, the CPI was 289.1 and the implicit GNP deflator 262.1, respectively, in 1982.

Old versus New CPI   The CPI has been strongly criticized for the way it treated housing costs. First, the data on housing costs are provided by the Federal Housing Administration. For CPI purposes, the sample is small and unrepresentative. Second, the weight given to the costs of home ownership is overstated and accounts for nearly 25 percent of the total index. An even more serious flaw, however, is the method of calculating mortgage costs. Under inflationary conditions, nominal interest rates tend to rise. The CPI includes the higher interest costs but fails to recognize that inflation tends to increase the value of the house.

Table 1.3   Year-to-Year Percentage Rates of Change in Consumer Prices

Year	Old CPI	New CPI
1968	4.7	3.7
1969	6.1	4.4
1970	5.5	4.9
1971	3.4	4.3
1972	3.4	3.1
1973	8.8	6.2
1974	12.2	10.1
1975	7.0	8.3
1976	4.8	5.7
1977	6.8	6.4
1978	9.0	6.8
1979	13.3	9.6
1980	12.4	11.2
1981	8.9	9.5
1982	3.9	6.1

Source: Economic Report of the President, 1983, p. 226.

For example, consider an individual who buys a house for $100,000 financed entirely by a mortgage at 10 percent interest. With 10 percent inflation, this individual might be able to sell the house for $110,000 a year later. The $10,000 capital gain would exactly meet the interest payments on the mortgage. In this particular case, therefore, housing costs are zero. However, the CPI would have included the $10,000 interest payments but ignored the $10,000 capital gain. Acknowledging this problem, in January 1983 the Bureau of Labor Statistics substituted a rental equivalence measure of housing costs for its old measure of homeownership costs. The old and new CPIs are compared over the period 1968–1982 in Table 1.3. Of particular note is the fact that the new CPI shows lower inflation rates in periods of rising nominal interest rates than does the old CPI. Conversely, as nominal interest rates fell sharply in 1982, the old CPI shows a substantially greater reduction in inflation than does the new CPI.

Summary

1. Gresham's law states that overvalued money will drive undervalued money out of circulation. This is a special case of the more general economic principle that any commodity will seek out its highest valued use. In equilibrium, values in all alternative uses are equated at the margin.

2. The Federal Reserve System defines money on the basis of liquidity. Liquidity means ease of conversion into a means of payment with low cost and predictable value. Money is perfectly liquid because it is by definition the means of payment.

3. Regulation of depository institutions has produced artificial distinctions between different types of deposits. This has increased the practical difficulties of defining money.

4. The main difficulty involved in defining money concerns substitutability. A perfect substitute for money *is* money. A close substitute for money is quasi-money. It performs some but not all of the functions of money, or it performs partially all of the functions of money.

5. Overdraft facilities and credit lines are not money. Credit transactions require final payment later. Credit lines do not incur an opportunity cost, whereas holding money does.

6. There are two opportunity costs of money. One is the cost of accumulating money and hence foregoing goods and services. The other is the cost of holding money and thereby foregoing interest that could otherwise be earned by holding other assets.

7. Money's main function is that of a means of payment. Money also acts as a standard of value, a unit of account, a store of value, and a standard for future payment.

8. American money has performed its store-of-value and standard-for-future-payment functions rather poorly since the mid-1960s because of large and erratic changes in its value.

9. The value of money is its purchasing power. Price indices provide measures of the price level. The inverse of the price level is the value of money.

10. Consumer and wholesale price indices use base weights, whereas the GNP deflator uses current weights. Because of different weights and different components, these three indices show different price movements. Revisions to the CPI indicate how sensitive the index is to the measurement of housing costs.

Questions

1. Explain Gresham's law.

2. What is money?

3. What is liquidity?

4. Why is substitutability important in defining money?

5. Why should credit card lines be excluded from the definition of money?

6. What are the costs of accumulating and holding money?

7. Outline the main functions of money.

8. Why has American money performed its store-of-value function unsatisfactorily since the mid-1960s?

9. What is the difference between relative and absolute price?

10. What is a price index and what information can it provide?

11. What distinguishes the CPI from the GNP deflator?

2 Monetary Standards

Emergence of Money

Uncertainty Money first made its appearance because of uncertainty, information costs, or transaction costs. These same factors explain money's continued use today. In a small, static, traditional society, there would be no demand for a means of payment. All transactions could easily be arranged by barter exchanges, that is, by swapping one commodity or service directly for another, or by barter credit. A fisherman could provide fish today in return for a sack of grain after the harvest. In such a world of virtual certainty and zero transaction costs, everyone would know where to send his or her products and when and where to collect the goods and services provided in exchange.

Even with uncertainty about other people's credit worthiness (a result of the positive costs of relevant information), there would still be no demand for money if all other transaction costs were zero. One could accept whatever was offered in exchange for his or her own goods or services to conclude each transaction without credit. A costless chain of transactions could be conducted to dispose of unwanted exchange goods to obtain what was wanted.

Transaction Costs In practice, transaction costs tend to be substantial. For example, retail margins generally range from 15 percent for groceries to over 50 percent for furniture, realtors' commissions are typically 6 percent of a house's sale price, and a travel agent gets 10 percent of the price of most airline tickets for domestic flights. These markups provide reasonable estimates of the seller's transaction costs in exchanging these categories of goods and services. So just imagine the total transaction costs of exchanging a diamond for a bundle of clothes, the clothes for groceries, and groceries for an airline ticket. Here, there are three sets of selling costs *plus* three sets of buying costs.

Using money economizes on transaction costs because it cuts out all but one intermediate transaction in exchange goods. That one exchange good, of course, is money. Once an item catches on as a medium of exchange (an exchange good that is generally acceptable as a means of payment), a snowball effect develops.[1] As people learn that a particular object can be exchanged easily for other goods, their willingness to accept it will increase. If you knew that a particular object could easily be exchanged for whatever was wanted, then you would be much more willing to accept it than you would if there were a high probability of being stuck with that object.

Varieties of Money

Because everyone's use of the same item as money reduces transaction costs and also produces this internal momentum towards greater and greater acceptability, the particular thing used as money is, to some extent, quite accidental. Indeed, before coinage was invented, many different things emerged as money in different places at different times. In America alone, beads, corn, tobacco, beaver skins, pins, wheat, barley, nails, and sandalwood were used as money at some time and place. Abroad, cattle, feathers, shells, and even rocks have been employed as means of payment.

Attributes of Commodity Money

Transactions or exchange goods that were found to be most suitable, and hence survived as money, possessed the following characteristics, all of which reduced transaction costs.

1. Durability
2. Divisibility
3. Portability
4. Homogeneity
5. Stable demand and supply

For money to serve as a store of value, it must possess the physical attribute of durability and the economic attributes of stable demand and supply. To permit payments of any particular value, money must be divisible. A relatively high ratio of value to weight or volume makes money portable so that it can be carried around easily. A uniform or homogeneous money saves time that would otherwise have to be spent in examining the particular bits of money offered to determine their value. Homogeneity is also crucial for money's unit-of-account function. By definition, non-homogeneous money can be neither compared nor added up without in-

[1]Karl Brunner and Allan H. Meltzer, "The Uses of Money: Money in the Theory of an Exchange Economy," *American Economic Review*, 61(5), December 1971, pp. 784–805.

troducing at least one more exchange rate for conversion into a common unit of account.

After a good deal of experimentation and a certain amount of technological progress, coins produced from precious metals evolved as the dominant form of money. The first known coins were made of electrum, a natural alloy of gold and silver, in the seventh century B.C. in Lydia, now part of Turkey.[2] Three or four centuries later the Greeks knew all about debasing the currency and had discovered Gresham's law, which states that overvalued money drives undervalued money out of circulation.

Government Involvement in the Provision of Commodity Money

Commodity or *full-bodied* money is, as its name implies, money taking the form of a commodity, such as silver or gold. (Cattle and tobacco were also commodity monies.) Commodity money emerged without government decree or interference when the benefits exceeded the costs. However, government tended to get involved with the development of coinage. Minting coins was seen to be a useful social service in that it provided information about the weight and purity of the metal very inexpensively. Transaction costs of using minted gold coins were lower than the costs of using plain lumps of gold, which had to be weighed and assayed. In some countries, government mints accepted gold or silver from anyone who brought it along and turned the metal into coins, charging a modest fee known as seigniorage for the service.

Under a system of unrestricted minting or, for that matter, under any monetary system that effectively enables anyone to produce money (so ensuring free convertibility), the exchange value of a commodity money equals its intrinsic or other-use value. Were gold worth more as money than as tooth fillings, the supply of gold for money would rise and the supply of gold for fillings would fall until gold's exchange value fell and its tooth-filling value rose to equal one another. Then and only then would there be no profit incentive to transfer gold from one use to another. If, on the other hand, gold for fillings was worth more than gold for money, gold coins would simply be melted down and used for fillings. Again, gold would be transferred from one use to another until values in all uses were equal.

Representative Money

Representative money can develop alongside a commodity money. It is, by definition, convertible into that commodity money on demand. The origins and development of representative money—bank notes and token coins—are closely related to banking and are described in Chapter 6. The issuers of representative money held reserves of commodity money to maintain convertibility. The guarantee of convertibility was essential to persuade people to hold representative money instead of commodity money itself. This convertibility tied the value of the representative money to that of the commodity money into which it was convertible.

[2]Philip Grierson, *The Origins of Money* (London: Athlone Press, 1977), p. 7.

Credit Money   Almost all money today is *credit* money. By definition, credit money is not convertible into any commodity money. There are two kinds of credit money: legal tender or fiat money, and fiduciary credit money. The issuers of *legal tender*—usually central banks—have no obligation to convert these currency notes into anything else. By law, legal tender must be accepted as a means of payment. Although legal tender is recorded as a liability in the balance sheet of its issuer, this is an accounting anachronism. The issuer is not liable for anything because legal tender is inconvertible. One of the largest items on the asset side of most central banks' balance sheets is credit to the government—hence, the term *credit money*. Effectively, legal tender currency notes are issued in exchange for purchases of government debt and other financial assets.

   The other kind of credit money is *fiduciary* money, money depending not on legal decree or fiat but on the public's trust and confidence in it. Deposit money is a fiduciary money. No one is obliged by law to accept your check in payment for goods or services. The payee does so only if he or she trusts both the payer and the depository institution on which the check is drawn. The bank is trusted to convert deposit money into legal tender currency on demand. This fiduciary money created by depository institutions is credit money because the assets backing it are, in the main, loans made to both the private sector and the government.

Monetary Standards

   The fundamental property of a monetary standard is its *convertibility* provisions. For example, under a gold standard the value of the unit of money, such as $1, is kept equal to the value of a predetermined weight of gold. Such a standard can be maintained only by guaranteeing convertibility.

Gold Standard   Suppose the monetary standard is a gold coin standard and the government holds a monopoly over minting coins. To maintain the value of a dollar coin at, say, one-twentieth of an ounce of gold, the mint must accept all gold offered and coin it for only a small seigniorage charge. Conversely, the mint must sell gold bars or bullion for gold coins or allow others to melt coins down. Such an arrangement is known as a *free coinage system*. There is unlimited convertibility between gold as money and gold for other uses. As was discussed earlier, this convertibility ensures that the value of gold for exchange (in coins) will always equal the value of gold for other uses.

Bimetallic Standard   The first federal gold and silver coins of the United States were struck under legislation enacted in 1792 that adopted a bimetallic standard. The monetary unit—the dollar—was valued at 24.75 grains of gold (480 grains to an ounce troy) and at 371.25 grains of silver. It is easy to calculate that a silver dollar would weigh 15 times more than a gold dollar. This weight ratio is known as the *mint ratio*. In fact, however, gold coins were minted only in $10, $5, and $2½ denominations until 1849, when the first gold dollars were issued.[3]

Bimetallism and Gresham's Law

To maintain the bimetallic standard, the U.S. mint produced both gold and silver coins in unlimited quantities free of charge for anyone supplying the bars of gold or silver. In addition, the mint had to stand ready to convert gold into silver, or vice versa, in unlimited quantities. However, vast stocks of both metals, which naturally the mint did not possess, were needed for this. By the beginning of the nineteenth century, people had discovered that one ounce of gold could be taken from the United States to France and there exchanged for 15½ ounces of silver because the mint ratio in France was 15½ to 1. If it was then brought back to the United States, only 15 ounces of silver were required in exchange for 1 ounce of gold. Clearly, the round trip yielded a profit of ½ ounce of silver for every ounce of gold exported to France. Exploiting such price differences for profit is called *arbitrage*. Arbitrageurs seek out the highest price for any given commodity. In the terminology of Gresham's law, silver coins were the "bad" money in the United States that drove the "good" gold money out of circulation, in fact drove the good money all the way to France. On the other hand, gold was the bad money in France and it drove out the good silver money.

This unsatisfactory state of affairs continued until 1834, when the mint ratio in the United States was raised to almost 16 to 1 (actually, 15.988 to 1). The new mint ratio overvalued gold coins relative to the prevailing market price ratio. Arbitrage then reversed the trans-Atlantic metal flows. Now gold was imported into the United States and silver was exported to Europe and to India. The United States was stripped of small change in the form of silver coins, causing considerable inconvenience. This problem was not rectified until 1853, when fractional coins, that is, coins of less than $1, were officially debased or declared token currency. Token coins, like gambling chips, have intrinsic values well below their face values. However, the silver dollar was still legal tender at a weight 16 times that of gold. Naturally, no silver dollars circulated, because they were worth about $1.04.

Effectively, the United States was on a gold standard after 1834. Since no one offered silver to the U.S. mint, no new silver dollars were produced. It was not surprising, therefore, that a coinage law of 1873 made no provisions for the production of silver dollars. Free coinage of silver was abandoned, since there was no demand whatsoever for this service. The United States had now adopted *de jure* its *de facto* gold standard.

Between 1870 and 1878, however, the production of silver in the United States more than doubled and the price of silver fell. In 1874 the market price of silver had dropped by so much that producers would now have found it profitable to sell to the mint at the 16 to 1 mint ratio. To their horror, they discovered that silver had been demonetized just a year earlier

---

[3]A. Barton Hepburn, *A History of Currency in the United States* (New York: Macmillan, 1903).

with no protest at all. Consequently, there was no support for silver from the U.S. mint because it was no longer authorized to exchange gold for silver at a ratio of 16 to 1. By 1889 the market price of silver had fallen to produce a weight ratio equivalence of 22 to 1 in the market.

1933 Suspension of Convertibility

The United States remained on a gold standard guaranteeing a price of $20.67 an ounce of gold until 1933. After President Franklin D. Roosevelt's inauguration in that year, transactions in gold were prohibited. All gold coins, bullion, and gold certificates had to be surrendered at Federal Reserve banks and exchanged for notes or deposits. Gold certificates were issued by the treasury as receipts for gold purchases. Until 1933 they could be redeemed on demand for gold at the official gold price. On January 31, 1934, the United States adopted a gold exchange standard at $35 an ounce. This meant that the dollar was convertible into gold for purposes of foreign transactions, but private gold ownership in the United States was still prohibited.[4] Even this limited convertibility was suspended in 1971.

Gold Clauses

Before 1933 the dollar's function as a standard for future payment was frequently overridden by a *gold clause* in loan contracts. The gold clause specified that the debt was to be repaid in gold coins of a predetermined fineness. Bonds and mortgages typically contained a phrase such as "to pay dollars in gold coin of the United States of the Standard and fineness existing on [date of contract]." Most federal government bonds contained this type of gold clause, a sure sign that few people trusted the government not to tamper with the money supply or the monetary standard. The temptation would have been greater had the government been able to sell bonds without gold clauses.

The government had the last laugh, however, by simply revoking the gold clause. In 1933 President Roosevelt suspended the convertibility of the paper dollar into gold. Subsequently, the government nationalized all gold holdings, except gold jewelry, and bought it up for paper notes at its statutory price. The gold clause was abrogated by further legislation. Then Roosevelt began to raise the price the government would pay for newly mined gold. In January 1934 the statutory price of gold was fixed at $35 an ounce, up from $20.67 an ounce less than a year earlier.

Raising the price of gold lowered the value of the dollar: more dollars were required to buy the same quantity of gold. Hence, Roosevelt changed the monetary standard of the United States by decreasing the quantity of gold in the unit of account. Had the price of gold in relation to all other goods and services remained unchanged, all prices expressed in dollars would have risen by almost 70 percent, which was the percentage increase in the dollar price of gold. In fact, prices did rise in 1934, but by less than 7

[4]M. L. Burstein, *Money* (Cambridge, Mass.: Schenkman, 1963), Chapter 2.

percent. Hence, the relative price of gold shot up and gold mining became a growth industry once more.[5]

This change in the monetary standard was precisely what gold clauses were designed to protect creditors against. However, the Joint Congressional Resolution of June 5, 1933, had pulled the rug from under lenders. This resolution abrogating gold clauses in all contracts made outstanding obligations to pay in gold coin payable in any legal tender. Many bondholders brought suits to test the resolution's constitutionality. One of these gold clause cases, *Norman* v. *Baltimore and Ohio Railroad Company*, finally reached the Supreme Court on appeal in February 1935. Mr. Norman wanted his $22.50 interest coupon on a B&O bond to be paid in terms of gold, which at that time would have been worth $38.10. Unfortunately for Mr. Norman and other creditors who hoped to profit from the increased price of gold or to be compensated for the reduced value of money, the Supreme Court ruled against the claim in a 5 to 4 decision reaffirming the resolution's constitutionality.

In the case of federal government debt, however, the Joint Congressional Resolution was held to be unconstitutional. However, since gold had been nationalized, government bondholders were no longer entitled to hold gold. Hence, the government was obliged, not too reluctantly, to repay in paper money! The 1933 Joint Resolution was itself revoked by Congress in 1977. Gold or any other indexation clauses that adjust the nominal or dollar values of debts for erosion in the value of the dollar are now legal, provided they do not violate state usury laws. However, federally chartered savings and loan associations are prohibited from offering indexed mortgages by the Federal Home Loan Bank Board's regulations. Since gold clauses were abrogated once before, the Federal Home Loan Bank Board may fear that such indexation clauses could be abrogated again in the future. Furthermore, the tax treatment of indexation is uncertain.

U.S. Paper Standard

In effect, the United States has been on a fiat paper monetary standard for over 20 years. The government holds a monopoly over the supply of paper currency notes and token coins designated as legal tender. A dollar is a dollar. The value of a dollar is fixed to nothing except another dollar. Therefore, the dollar's value or purchasing power is determined solely by the interaction of demand for and supply of dollars.

If the demand for dollars can be estimated (which it can), and the supply is under the government's control (which indirectly it is), then supply can be adjusted to maintain a constant value for the dollar, as shown in

[5]Milton Friedman and Anna J. Schwartz, *A Monetary History of the United States, 1867–1960* (Princeton, N.J.: Princeton University Press, 1963), Chapter 8; and Milton Friedman and Anna J. Schwartz, *Monetary Trends in the United States and the United Kingdom: Their Relation to Income, Prices, and Interest Rates, 1867–1975* (Chicago: University of Chicago Press, 1982), p. 124.

Figure 2.1   Maintaining the Dollar's Value

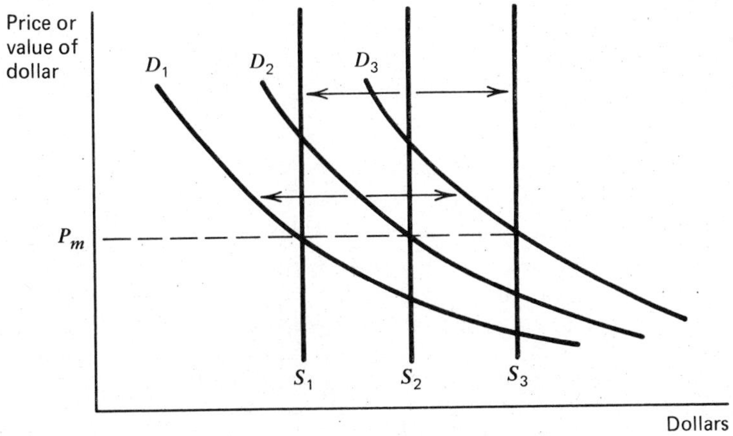

To maintain a constant value of the dollar, supply S must be shifted whenever the demand curve D moves, in order to ensure that the intersection of supply and demand always occurs at the same price level.

Figure 2.1. It would seem that maintaining a constant price level would be easier under a paper standard than under a gold standard. There can be random changes in both the supply of gold and the demand for gold for nonmonetary uses. However, the supply of paper money by a monopolist can be rigidly controlled, and demand (which is solely for monetary use) is fairly predictable.

In the real world, however, paper standards have generally had a poor record in terms of maintaining money's value. The great European hyper-inflations after both world wars and the postwar inflations in Argentina, Brazil, Chile, and Indonesia would have been impossible under any monetary standards other than paper ones. Why have so many governments supplied money that served its store-of-value function so badly? One answer is that money provides two sources of revenue for the government.

Seigniorage   The first source of revenue from monopoly supply of paper money is *seigniorage,* the term applied originally to the mint's charges for coinage. Seigniorage is also the difference between the face value and the intrinsic value of a monopoly-supplied money. For example, if gold dollars had been debased to only 40 percent of their original gold content but their supply held constant through monopoly control, then the seigniorage would have been 60 percent. The monopoly profit or seigniorage is all the gold left over after the recoinage. It could have been used, for example, to import guns and ammunition from abroad. Indeed, increased military expenditure was usually the reason for extracting more seigniorage. Greatest seigniorage accrues, of course, from substituting paper currency notes for precious metal coins. Provided the supply of paper money equals the quantity of coins withdrawn in exchange, the revenue from monopoly supply of paper notes equals the value of the gold acquired minus the relatively small costs of note production and forgery prevention.

Inflation Tax

The second source of revenue from monopoly supply of legal tender comes from increasing the volume of paper money. Extracting seigniorage is, for the most part, a once-and-for-all event. Increasing the supply of legal tender paper money can be continued indefinitely as a source of revenue. This kind of revenue is known as the *inflation tax*. The government increases the supply of money to procure more goods and services. The increase in the money supply raises the general price level and thus lowers the value of money. If an individual's money holdings decline in value by, say, 10 percent, he or she will have to forego expenditure on goods and services to build back the real value of those money holdings. The decline in the value of the individual's money holdings or the foregone expenditure needed to restore the purchasing power of his or her money balances can be regarded as a tax. The tax involves transferring the foregone expenditure on goods and services from moneyholders to the government. The higher the inflation rate, the higher is the tax rate.

Optimal Monetary Standard

From society's viewpoint, seigniorage increases the amount of goods and services available for nonmoney uses. Seigniorage need not damage any of money's attributes. Hence, social welfare can be maximized by maximizing seigniorage. This is achieved by substituting paper and bank deposit money for commodity money.

The inflation tax, on the other hand, reduces social welfare. As inflation increases, money loses its store-of-value attribute. People hold less money and devote more resources to synchronizing receipts and payments. More goods and services are consumed in the process of making transactions. Hence, the inflation tax reduces the amount of goods and services available for nonmoney uses.[6]

Ideally, then, society would be served best by a paper standard allowing maximum seigniorage, but a paper money that maintained its value over time. Can this ideal solution exist in practice?

Monetary Stability

Monetary Growth Rule

There are several proposals for stabilizing the value of American money. The one currently being implemented in the United States is a version of the monetary growth rule—expand the money supply at a fixed rate, such

---

[6]Martin J. Bailey, "The Welfare Cost of Inflationary Finance," *Journal of Political Economy,* 64(2), April 1956, pp. 93–110.

as 3 percent a year. This particular version aims at reducing the rate of monetary expansion steadily over several years until a constant, fairly low growth rate can be maintained. The main problem with this strategy concerns the choice of monetary aggregate. Which definition of money should be used and would that definition always be the best one?

Under a paper standard, control over any one definition of the money supply may not succeed in stabilizing money's value. Control always generates incentives for circumvention, in this case through proliferation of close money substitutes. Consequently, such induced financial innovations may produce unpredictable changes in the demand for any specific monetary aggregate. Some economists, therefore, have suggested that a preferable strategy would be to fix the value of money and to let its quantity adjust to demand. One way of doing this would be to return to the gold standard. However, that ties up a lot of resources and so incurs a high opportunity cost. Furthermore, gold prices themselves are not stable relative to the general price level.

Symmetallism

Another solution to this problem was developed about a century ago: symmetallism. Here, the standard is defined as a specified weight of gold plus a specified weight of silver. *Relative* prices of gold and silver are not frozen, as they are under a bimetallic standard. Were coins minted under this standard, they would be a mixture of gold and silver in the appropriate proportions. The idea of symmetallism can be extended: the standard can be defined in terms of any fixed basket of goods and services. The objective is to find a commodity basket whose relative price as a basket fluctuates less than the individual prices of any of its components. Representative money would be used instead of baskets of goods, but the representative money would maintain its value through the convertibility requirement. However, convertibility could be effected by conversion into only one commodity, such as gold. Suppose, for example, that the standard was defined as 1 ounce of gold plus 1 ounce of silver plus 1 ounce of platinum. If the relative price of gold to silver was 15 to 1 and the relative price of platinum to silver was 25 to 1, then one unit of money could be redeemed for 41 ounces of silver. If the relative price of gold rose to 17 to 1, then one unit of money could be redeemed for 43 ounces of silver.

Special Drawing Right

A close cousin to the commodity basket standard already exists in the form of the International Monetary Fund's unit of account—the Special Drawing Right (SDR). The SDR is defined as 0.46 of a Deutsche mark, 0.74 of a French franc, 34 Japanese yen, 0.071 of a Pound sterling, and 54 U.S. cents. The SDR's value in terms of the dollar is the dollar value of the SDR's components. For example, on August 5, 1982, the market exchange rates against \$1 were: DM2.4745, Ff6.885, ¥258.42, £0.579576. On this day DM0.46 was worth \$0.185896, Ff0.74 sold for \$0.107480, ¥34 fetched \$0.131569, and £0.071 was valued at \$0.122503. Summing the dollar values and then adding this total to 54 cents gives $1.087448—the SDR's value in terms of the U.S. dollar. So if you had SDR 1 million on deposit with the International Monetary Fund, you could withdraw it as $1,087,448, or as DM2,690,890.08, or as ¥281,018,312. This example shows that the idea of a standard composed of several or many items is not an impractical one. It works in the case of the SDR. The value of the SDR in relation to most commodity prices fluctuates less than the relative value of any one of its components. Hence, it provides a more stable standard of value than any of its individual currency components.

Competitive Money Supply

Government monopoly in the money supply process is not always necessary. The government could be responsible for defining the monetary standard but not for supplying any money under it. If the government defines the monetary unit in terms of gold, silver, or some foreign currency, the supply of money could be left entirely to the private sector. For example, Panama defines its monetary standard as one U.S. dollar. The supply of U.S. dollars in Panama is left entirely to the private sector. Panama has no central bank and the Panamanian government can collect no revenue from seigniorage or the inflation tax. Similarly, a gold standard might be established with government defining the dollar in terms of so many grains of gold. Then just as banks supply deposit money with guaranteed convertibility into paper dollars, so could the private sector supply deposit money with convertibility into gold.

From a gold standard, it is a simple logical step to a composite commodity standard. In practice, banks would not redeem deposits with a shopping basket containing the exact items in their specified proportions; however, if a generally acceptable price list was available, redemption could be made in one or a small number of commodities, such as gold and silver.

Summary

1. Money emerged because of uncertainty and positive transaction costs. Using money reduces costs of transactions.

2. The first kind of money to appear was commodity or full-bodied money. Convenient commodities for a means of payment have five attributes: durability, divisibility, portability, homogeneity, and stable demand and supply.

3. Representative money is convertible into the commodity money itself. Today, the means of payment is credit money—legal tender or fiat money (Federal Reserve notes), and fiduciary money (deposit money).

4. Credit money is not convertible into commodity money, but fiduciary credit money is convertible into legal tender. Credit money derives its

name from the fact that the main asset in the balance sheet of the suppliers of credit money (the Fed and depository institutions) is credit—loans made to both government and private sectors.

5. A monetary standard is determined by its convertibility provisions. A gold standard exists if and only if money is freely convertible into gold, and vice versa. This convertibility ensures that gold's value in terms of money remains constant.

6. A bimetallic standard provides for free convertibility into gold and silver at a fixed price ratio. The history of bimetallic standards illustrates Gresham's law because the fixed mint ratio invariably overvalued one metal and undervalued the other.

7. The present fiat paper standard involves convertibility only of deposit money into paper fiat money, that is, Federal Reserve notes. In theory, money's value could be kept stable under a paper standard. In practice, however, governments have tended to use money produced under paper standards as an additional source of revenue.

8. There are two sources of revenue from a paper monetary standard: seigniorage and the inflation tax. Seigniorage is extracted by substituting paper for commodity money—the intrinsic value of paper money is much less than its face value. This difference is monopoly profit or seigniorage. The inflation tax is imposed by increasing the supply of paper money to buy more goods and services. Since the increased money supply decreases money's value, the tax is paid by moneyholders.

9. The value of money can be stabilized by controlling its quantity or fixing its value in terms of one or more commodities. If the government defines the monetary standard in terms of commodities or foreign currencies, the supply of money can be left entirely to the private sector.

Questions

1. Why did money emerge?
2. Explain the five important characteristics of a good commodity money.
3. Distinguish representative from credit money.
4. Distinguish fiat from fiduciary credit money.
5. What is the difference between a bimetallic and a symmetallic standard?
6. How does the history of bimetallism illustrate Gresham's law?

7. How did the gold clause override the dollar's standard-for-future-payment function before 1933?

8. Explain the two sources of revenue from the monopoly supply of paper money.

9. Why does inflation create a welfare cost to society as a whole?

10. Explain the International Monetary Fund's unit of account, the Special Drawing Right.

PART TWO

Financial Claims and Financial Intermediation

The Franklin National Bank was established on Long Island by Arthur Roth in 1926. For almost 40 years it remained a Long Island retail bank, collecting small savings in the form of personal deposits and making small-scale loans to borrowers. Protected from competition from the big New York banks by state branching regulations, the Franklin National was able to intermediate between borrowers and lenders with little regard for efficiency or professional expertise. Rapid expansion of the rich Long Island commuter belt in the postwar period enabled Roth to increase his bank's assets from $71 million in 1950 to $1.2 billion in 1962. Roth proceeded aggressively, taking substantial risks and, in the process, acquiring many assets of dubious value. Nevertheless, with a loan portfolio earning one percentage point above the average for bank loan portfolios, he could absorb higher loan losses without undue difficulty.

This comfortable state of affairs was rudely disturbed in 1960 by a change in branching regulations. The 1960 New York State Omnibus Banking Act permitted New York banks to open branches on Long Island; it also allowed the Franklin National to operate in New York. With prospects for further rapid growth on Long Island gravely reduced, the Franklin National applied to open a branch in New York in September 1961. Its first New York branch opened in 1964 and Franklin National entered the field of wholesale banking.

The decision to meet the big New York banks head-on by setting up

From Robert Heller and Norris Willatt, *Can You Trust Your Bank?* (London: Weidenfeld and Nicolson, 1977); Joan Edelman Spero, *The Failure of the Franklin National Bank: Challenge to the International Banking System* (New York: Columbia University Press for the Council on Foreign Relations, 1980); and *New York Times*, December 27, 1982, p. 1.

for business alongside them was Roth's biggest gamble. It turned out to be an expensive mistake. To maintain its momentum in terms of asset growth, the Franklin National was forced to continue lending at the risky end of the spectrum, but it could no longer charge above-average interest rates. Indeed, it lent at prime rate to almost all its borrowers and required lower compensating balances than its major competitors. Since regular deposit growth was woefully insufficient to finance these new large-scale loans, Franklin National borrowed at market interest rates from other banks and through the sale of large certificates of deposit. By 1969 its assets had exceeded $3 billion.

Still inefficient and short on expertise, Franklin National soon found that its activities in the New York big league were not paying their way. Costs of funds had risen dramatically with recourse to other banks and sales of certificates of deposit, while earnings on assets were no longer above average. With above-average costs and bad debts, it was hardly surprising that the Franklin National posted a loss of $7.2 million in 1971. The next year, the bank was taken over by Michele Sindona, a well-known Sicilian financier with a somewhat dubious reputation in Europe.

Continuing to look out for new markets, Franklin National opened a branch in London in 1972. Its foreign business zoomed up but failed to have much impact on profits. Under Sindona and his foreign exchange department chief, the bank started speculating in foreign exchange. In about 1970 Franklin National's foreign exchange dealings averaged approximately $12 million a year. By 1974 they had increased to about $3.5 billion. It was this foreign exchange activity that eventually triggered the loss of confidence leading to the bank's failure.

However, confidence would have been of far less significance had Franklin National used insured deposits and capital to acquire its assets. Increasingly, however, short-term, high-cost funds were obtained from other banks and through sales of large certificates of deposit. Market rates of interest rose to exceptionally high levels in 1973 and 1974, yet a large portion of Franklin National's loan portfolio was locked up in long-term, fixed-interest loans. Interest costs of its liabilities therefore rose faster than interest earnings of its assets.

The last throe came in late 1973 and early in 1974, when Sindona and his new bank president gambled on a future fall in interest rates. The bank bought $200 million in long-term government bonds yielding about 3 percentage points *less* than the short-term money borrowed for their purchase. Had interest rates fallen, the twentieth largest U.S. bank might have survived—these long-term bonds would have appreciated in value. In fact, however, interest rates rose still higher. Low-yielding assets and higher-cost liabilities combined to produce an operating deficit of about $3 million a month in 1974. The spread between average asset earnings and average interest costs of its liabilities fell from

2.6 percentage points in 1971 to 1 percentage point in 1973. At one stage in 1974 the average yield on loans was below the cost of funds raised to cover them.

With its disastrous situation becoming transparent by the spring of 1974, Franklin National found that other banks would no longer lend to it, nor were there any buyers for its large certificates of deposit. The earnings squeeze turned into a liquidity crunch. On October 8, 1974, the Franklin National Bank was declared insolvent after five months of continuous crisis.

Sindona was indicted in March 1979 on federal charges of conspiring to conceal the transfer of $40 million from Italy to gain control of Franklin National, fraudulently removing $15 million from the bank, and speculating improperly in foreign currency at a cost to the bank of $30 million. He was convicted in 1980 and is currently (1984) serving a 25-year sentence at the federal prison in Otisville, New York. If he is released on parole in 1987, Sindona will face extradition to Italy, where he has been accused of conspiracy in a $200 million bank fraud case and of arranging the killing in 1979 of an official who was investigating Sindona's Italian assets.

3 Financial Claims

Credit money is one of many financial claims or financial instruments that exist today in the U.S. economy. This chapter concentrates on nonmoney financial claims for two reasons. First, nonmoney financial claims are the closest substitutes for money. Therefore, the demand for money is influenced by the yield on alternative financial claims, among other things. Second, banks and other financial institutions hold virtually all their assets in the form of financial claims and issue a number of nonmoney financial claims as liabilities. Understanding the behavior of financial institutions requires some knowledge of their assets and liabilities.

Nature and Functions of Financial Claims

Direct versus Indirect Claims Financial instruments or financial claims fall into one of two categories— direct and indirect. Direct financial claims are issued by nonfinancial units. Mortgages, corporate bonds, and treasury bills are direct claims issued by households, business firms and the federal government, respectively. Indirect claims, such as deposits and currency notes, are created by financial institutions. These claims are called indirect financial instruments because the depositor or lender supplies funds that are channeled indirectly to ultimate borrowers. In other words, financial institutions *intermediate* between lenders and borrowers or between savers and investors. They sell indirect financial instruments such as deposits and buy direct claims like mortgages and treasury bills.

Attributes of Financial Claims Financial instruments possess several characteristics that differentiate one type of claim from another. These characteristics include the duration of the contract, the marketability and riskiness of the instrument, the level and type of yield, and the kind of issuer. Finer distinctions can be drawn with respect to the rights of the issuer to make an early repayment of the loan (known as callability), the recourse available to the borrower for demanding premature repayment, the taxability of the yield, and so on. Competition ensures that disadvantages are balanced by advantages, such as a higher gross yield. Hence, a high-yielding financial claim invariably has at least one drawback.

Table 3.1 shows the magnitudes of direct financial claims in the United States. U.S. government securities consist of treasury bills, notes, and bonds; bills are issued for maturities of 1 year or less, notes for 1 to 10 years, and bonds for over 10 years. In general, notes and bonds issued by governments and corporations have fixed maturities, fixed interest rates, and no provisions for early repayment at the instigation of either the borrower or the lender. Mortgages, on the other hand, are usually repaid in installments over the duration of the loan and the borrower may, with or without penalty, repay the loan fully or partially at any time. Consumer credit and bank loans, like most bank deposits, are not marketable. On the other hand, common stock and bonds are marketable; ownership can be transferred at moderate cost through sales on a stock market. Stocks offer an uncertain yield in the form of both dividends and capital value fluctuations.

Financial Markets   In a broad sense, there are as many financial markets as there are financial instruments. There are, however, two distinct types of market. One is the centralized market such as the stock exchange on which stocks and bonds are traded. The other is the decentralized market like the market for deposits. The type of market is itself a differentiating characteristic of the financial instrument.

Table 3.1   Financial Claims in the United States (end of year, billions of dollars)

Type	1950	1960	1970	1980
U.S. government securities	218.3	243.1	343.0	1016.1
State and local government securities	24.4	70.8	144.4	312.5
Corporate and foreign bonds	39.2	90.2	202.4	503.8
Mortgages	72.8	208.9	473.1	1447.4
Consumer credit	21.5	65.1	143.1	385.0
Bank loans	28.2	56.8	151.2	456.3
Other	22.4	45.0	142.9	530.6
Total	426.8	779.9	1600.1	4651.7

Source: Board of Governors of the Federal Reserve System, *Flow of Funds Accounts, 1945–1972 and 1957–1980.*

For every financial claim in existence, there must be a demand and a supply. In some cases, such as stocks and bonds, demand and supply interact freely to determine price. In other cases, such as deposits, the prices or yields have been regulated by government agencies. Here, supply and demand may be equilibrated through nonprice competition, such as the provision of checking services at below cost. Alternatively, there may be disequilibrium in this market, necessitating some form of rationing.

Primary versus Secondary Markets   There is also a distinction between primary and secondary markets. Markets for newly issued financial claims are primary markets. Markets for "used" financial claims are secondary markets. The existence of an efficient secondary market increases a financial claim's liquidity because a secondary market facilitates liquidation. Financial claims serve the purpose of transferring purchasing power from the buyer to the seller. In the primary market, the transfer takes place from lender to borrower. This transfer increases the aggregate volume of credit and could be used, for example, to finance new investment. Transactions on secondary markets, on the other hand, take place between one lender and another lender. There can be no direct net increase in credit from secondary market activity. However, newly issued and used financial claims with identical characteristics are perfect substitutes. Hence, prices of identical new and used claims are always the same. Because secondary markets are so large in comparison to primary markets, they actually dominate the price determination process. For example, if demand in the secondary market increases, prices of financial claims rise and their yields fall. Borrowers can then issue new financial claims on the primary markets at lower rates of interest and borrowing becomes cheaper.

Price, Interest, and Yield

Present Value   If offered $100 now or $100 in a year's time, people would normally prefer $100 now. Aside from the risk of nonpayment or default in a year's time, $100 now could be invested to produce more than $100 a year later. In other words, a dollar in the future is worth less than a dollar now. This would be the case even if the price level remained stable, provided that interest rates were positive.

What is the value of $100 in a year's time? Today's value or the *present value* of $100 in a year's time is $100 *discounted* by the market rate of interest i. The present value of future receipts can be calculated from the general formula

$$PV = \frac{FV}{(1 + i)^n} \qquad (3.1)$$

where PV is the present value, FV is the future value or dollar amount to be received in the future, i is the market rate of interest expresssed as a proportion (0.05) rather than as a percentage (5 percent), and n represents the number of years before the receipt of FV. One hundred dollars to be received in one year's time is worth $90.91 today with a 10 percent interest rate ($100/1.1). Investing $90.91 at 10 percent today would yield exactly $100 in a year's time—$90.91 principal plus $9.09 interest.

The discounting technique described above is used to calculate the present value of commercial paper and treasury bills. These short-term financial claims offer no direct coupon or interest payments. (A few longer-term claims are also zero-coupon assets.) They simply possess a *face value* and a maturity date at which that value will be paid. Therefore, the face value is discounted by the market rate of interest to obtain the current market price. For example, with an annual rate of interest of 10 percent, a new six-month $1000 commercial note would be discounted by 5 percent to give its market value of $952.38 ($1000/1.05).

In fact, the market price of this commercial note would be somewhat higher than $952.38 with an *effective* annual rate of interest of 10 percent. This is due to the fact that interest is *compounded* when payments occur more than once a year. In this particular case, $952.38 invested in a six-month commercial note yields $1000 in six month's time. This $1000 could then be reinvested to produce $1050 at the end of the year. The growth of $952.38 to $1050 represents a yield of 10.25 percent over the year on the original investment—$100 · (1050/952.38 − 1). The 10.25 percent is known as the *effective annual rate of interest* (Box 3.1).

Comparing Yields

The present value formula provides a method for comparing alternative investments. Suppose investment A pays $10 a year for 10 years. Investment B, equivalent in all other characteristics such as risk and liquidity, pays $150 at the end of year 10. Which is the better investment if they both cost the same price?

The present value of $10 to be received at the end of every year for the next 10 years is

$$PV_A = \frac{\$10}{(1 + i)} + \frac{\$10}{(1 + i)^2} + \frac{\$10}{(1 + i)^3} + \cdots + \frac{\$10}{(1 + i)^{10}} \qquad (3.2)$$

or

$$PV_A = \sum_{n=1}^{10} \frac{\$10}{(1 + i)^n} \qquad (3.3)$$

BOX 3.1
COMPOUND INTEREST

The more frequently does the compounding of interest take place, the higher is the effective annual rate for any given nominal rate of interest. Suppose, for example, that the *nominal annual* rate is 12 percent but compounding takes place quarterly. An investment of $100 therefore yields $100 \cdot (1.03)$ or $103 at the end of the first quarter, $100 \cdot (1.03)^2$ or $103 \cdot (1.03)$ or $106.09 at the end of the second quarter, $109.27 at the end of the third quarter, and $112.55 at year's end. The *effective annual* rate in this case is 12.55 percent.

Suppose that the nominal annual rate is x percent. In this case, a $1 investment would be worth $\$(1 + x/n)^n$ at year's end, where n is the number of times that interest is compounded and x is expressed as a proportion (0.05) rather than a percentage (5 percent). This expression provides a general solution for converting nominal into effective annual rates of interest.

Consider the case in which x equals 1, or 100 percent. Any frequency of compounding can be incorporated in the expression $\$(1 + 1/n)^n$ to obtain the dollar value of a $1 investment yielding a nominal annual rate of 100 percent at year's end. With no compounding ($n = 1$), the investment yields $2 at the end of the year, with quarterly compounding ($n = 4$) it yields $2.44 or an effective annual rate of 144 percent, with monthly compounding (n equals 12) it yields $2.61 or 161 percent, with daily compounding (n equals 365) it yields $2.71 or 171 percent, and with *continuous compounding* (n is an infinitely large number denoted ∞) it yields $2.71828 or 171.828 percent.

Continuous compounding implies that interest is earned immediately and continuously right from the start of the investment. The interest earnings are added to the principal and earn interest too. The conversion from nominal to effective annual rates of interest with continuous compounding can be approximated by using a very large number for n in the expression $[(1 + x/n)^n - 1]$, where x is the nominal annual rate of interest expressed as a proportion. Alternatively, one can use the formula

$$i_E = e^{i_N} - 1$$

where i_E is the effective annual rate of interest expressed as a proportion, i_N is the nominal annual rate also expressed as a proportion, and e is the "natural" base equal to 2.718281828. If i_N equals 1, then i_E equals 1.71828 or 171.828 percent. In fact, e is calculated from the expression $(1 + 1/n)^n$ when n is an infinitely large number.

With an interest rate of 10 percent, PV_A equals $61.45 ($9.09 + 8.26 + 7.51 + 6.83 + 6.21 + 5.65 + 5.13 + 4.67 + 4.24 + 3.86). The present value of $150 to be received in 10 years time is

$$PV_B = \frac{\$150}{(1 + i)^{10}} \tag{3.4}$$

If i is 0.1 or 10 percent, PV_B equals $57.83. In this case, investment A is superior to investment B.

Now consider the investments when the market rate of interest is 5 percent. In this instance, equation (3.3) gives a present value for A of $77.22 and equation (3.4) can be used to obtain the present value for B of $92.09. Both investments have increased in value as a result of the lower interest rate, but now B is worth more than A.

At the 10 percent market rate of interest, investment A would be just worth buying at an asking price of $61.45. At that price, it would produce a *yield* of exactly 10 percent. If the cost of investment B was also $61.45, its yield would be below the market interest rate of 10 percent. Only at a price of $57.83 would B yield 10 percent. At $61.45, no one would invest in B because funds could earn a higher return or yield at the market rate of interest, the opportunity cost of investible funds.

If investments A and B cost $50 each, both would produce yields above 10 percent. If the market rate was 10 percent and supplies of A and B were fixed, demand for these relatively high-yielding investments would start to push up their prices. In equilibrium, prices would rise until A cost $61.45 and B $57.83. At lower prices, yields would be above 10 percent, thus creating an incentive to pay a little more for such investments. At higher prices, however, these investments would yield less than 10 percent. Were supplies fixed, prices would have to fall before any demand would be forthcoming. Indeed, prices would fall to $61.45 and $57.83, respectively, with a market interest rate of 10 percent, before anyone would buy these investments.

Mortgages The standard fixed-interest, level-payment, 30-year mortgage provides another illustration of the present value technique. Suppose one asks: How much can I borrow if I can just afford mortgage payments of $1000 a month? The answer is

$$PV_M = \sum_{n=1}^{360} \frac{\$1000}{(1 + i/12)^n} \tag{3.5}$$

In this case, the time period is one month, so the annual interest rate i is divided by 12. The lower is the interest rate, the more one can borrow for payments of $1000 a month:

$i(percent)$	PV_M
4	$209,461
6	166,792
8	136,283
10	113,951
12	97,218
14	84,397
16	74,363

Given the interest rate, the principal sum borrowed, and the monthly payment, one can then calculate the balance outstanding at any point during the mortgage's life. Consider a 12 percent mortgage rate and a loan of $97,218. The first month's interest on this loan is $972.18—the interest rate per month is 1 percent. Hence, the first month's payment of $1000 reduces the balance outstanding by $27.82. As the balance outstanding declines, a decreasing part of the $1000 constitutes interest payment and an increasing part represents repayment of principal. The last payment consists of $9.90 interest and $990.10 principal repayment.

Interest Rates and Bond Prices

Consider a 20-year corporate bond with a *coupon* rate of 15 percent. The coupon rate is the yield on the bond's *face* or *book* value. For example, a $1000 bond with a 15 percent coupon rate pays $150 in interest at the end of every year. If the market interest rate is also 15 percent, this bond's market price will be $1000 at the beginning of the year, but during the year the market price will rise as the interval remaining before interest payment shortens. Just before interest payment, the bond will be worth $1150.

If the market rate of interest were to fall to 10 percent, the market price of this same bond with the same 15 percent coupon rate would rise above its face value of $1000. Indeed, its market price at the beginning of the year would be $150/1.1 + $150/1.1^2 + $150/1.1^3 + \cdots + $1150/1.1^{20}$ or $1425.68. With the market interest rate at 20 percent, on the other hand, this bond would sell for only $756.52 in the market (Box 3.2).

The relationship between interest rates and bond prices can be illustrated most clearly in the case of a *consol*. A consol is a government bond (not issued by the U.S. government) with no redemption or repayment date. It continues to pay dividends indefinitely. The market value of a consol PV_C paying $25 a year forever with a market interest rate of 10 percent can be calculated from the expression

$$PV_C = \sum_{n=1}^{\infty} \frac{\$25}{(1 + i)^n}$$

(3.6)

BOX 3.2
TREASURY NOTES AND BONDS

Consider the following information taken from the *Los Angeles Times* (Business Section), September 28, 1981.

Treasury Bonds

Rate	Maturity Date	Bid	Ask	Yield	Bid Change
15.00	Mar 82 *n*	99.24	99.28	15.27	—
16.00	Sep 83 *n*	99.23	99.25	16.13	−.3
6.12	Nov 86	69.28	70.28	14.33	−.1
16.12	Nov 86	100.3	101.2	15.77	−1.

The first column gives the coupon rate on the treasury bond or treasury note. For every $100 face value, the interest on the first note is $15 per year, paid semiannually. The second column shows the maturity date, at which time the face value of the bond or note is repaid. The *n* stands for note; notes have initial maturities of 10 years or less. The third and fourth columns provide the bid and ask prices at the close of business on September 24, 1981. The fifth column shows the nominal annual yield to maturity, while the final column gives the change in bid price from close of business on September 23.

The figures to the right of the decimal point in the Bid, Ask, and Bid Change columns are *not* cents. They are thirty-seconds of a dollar. So, 99.24 or 99 24/32 is actually 99 dollars and 75 cents. The yield measures the nominal annual percentage rate of return on the ask price. It takes into account the semiannual interest payments and the repayment at face value or par value on maturity.

Janet Glazer bought a $10,000, March 1982 treasury note with a 15 percent coupon rate for $9987.50 (the ask price of $99 28/32 per $100 face value) on September 24, 1981. She will receive $10,000 in March 1982 together with the semiannual interest payment of $750, half of $15 per $100. Therefore, in six months she will receive $10,750. In this case, the yield on her investment is $100 \cdot (10{,}750/9987.5 - 1)$, or 7.635 percent. This is for half a year. The nominal annual yield, therefore, is $2 \cdot 7.635$, or 15.27 percent.

The calculation becomes more complicated when more than one six-month period is involved. Take, for example, the second treasury note listed above. This note will pay $8 per $100 par value at the end of March and September 1982 and 1983. The note will then be repaid at par. What is the nominal yield on $99,781.25 for a $100,000 note?

The yield must be above 16 percent, because the yield would be exactly

16 percent had $100,000 been paid for this particular note. The price is below $100,000, so the yield is above the coupon rate. In fact, the yield is calculated on a trial-and-error basis. The 16.13 percent nominal yield given above can be checked as follows:

1. Divide 16.13 by 2 to get the semiannual yield, which is 8.065 percent.

2. Calculate the present value *PV* of the $8000 coupon payment due in March 1982 using the 8.065 percent yield. This is done by dividing the future value *FV* by (1 + the yield expressed as a fraction). In this case, *PV* equals $8000/(1 + 0.08065), or $7402.95. Investing $7402.95 for six months at an annual rate of 16.13 percent yields exactly $8000 on maturity.

3. Calculate *PV* of $8000 due in September 1982. Using step 2 gives *PV* in March 1982. Therefore, $7402.95 must be discounted to *PV* in September 1981. Hence, $8000 is discounted twice, $8000/(1 + 0.08065)^2. The *PV* of $8000 this time next year is $6850.46.

4. Calculate *PV* of $8000 due in March 1983: $8000/(1 + 0.08065)^3, or $6339.21.

5. Calculate *PV* of $108,000 due in September 1983: $108,000/(1 + 0.08065)^4, or $79,192.40.

6. Finally, add up all four *PV*s: $99,785.02. The difference of $4 is explained by the fact that the purchase was actually made a few days before the end of the month. Hence, the first dividend will be received in just *over* six months. Its present value, therefore, is a little *less* than the present value of the same dividend received in exactly six months.

In practice, matters are not always quite this simple. Note above that the two bonds both maturing in November 1986 offer different yields. The reason for this is that the first bond has most of its return in the form of capital appreciation, while the second stands at a slight premium over par. Since capital gains are subject to a lower tax rate than interest income, there is a preference for the first bond. This bids up its price, hence reducing its yield about 1½ percentage points below the yield on the nonappreciating bond.

With a market interest rate of 10 percent, PV_C equals $25/1.1 + $25/1.1^2 + $25/1.1^3 + ⋯ + $25/1.1$^∞$. This infinite number of present values takes the form of an *infinite geometrically declining series*. The present values get smaller and smaller by the factor 1/1.1. Now the sum of any infinite geometrically declining series of this type can be expressed:

$$DIV/(1 + i) + DIV/(1 + i)^2 + DIV/(1 + i)^3 + \cdots + DIV/(1 + i)^\infty = DIV/i$$

$$(3.7)$$

In this case, therefore, with *DIV* equal to $25 and *i* at 0.1, the present value, and hence the market price, of this infinite stream of dividends is $250. For $250, one receives $25 a year, a yield of 10 percent. If the market interest rate is halved to 5 percent, the market price of this consol doubles to $500—25/0.05. With a doubling of the interest rate to 20 percent, the consol's price is halved to $125—25/0.2. In this particular case, market price and market interest are inversely related in simple fashion. A doubling of the interest rate halves the price, and vice versa.

Interest Rates, Bond Prices, and Maturities

Figure 3.1 shows market prices for a consol, a 20-year bond, and a one-year treasury note, all of which have a face value of $500 and a coupon rate of 5 percent. At a market interest rate of 5 percent, all three bonds have a market price of $500. A fall in the interest rate raises the market price of

Figure 3.1   Market Interest Rates and Bond Prices

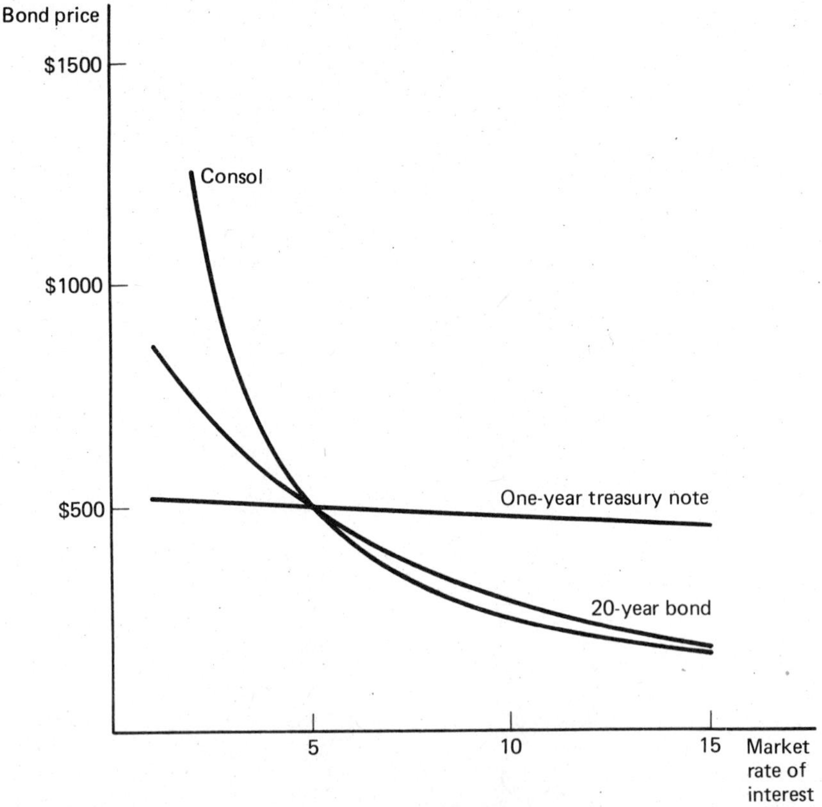

All three financial claims have a face value of $500 and a coupon rate of 5 percent. As the market interest rate rises, market prices fall. Longer-term bond prices fall by more than shorter-term bond prices. Conversely, when the market interest rate falls, longer-term bond prices rise by more than shorter-term bond prices.

the consol most and the price of the one-year note least. Similarly, a rise in the interest rate lowers the consol price most and the price of the one-year note least. The reason for the relative stability of the one-year note price is that the principal is repaid in one year's time. Thereafter, it can be invested again at the going market rate of interest. Hence, the change in market price of a one-year note caused by a change in the interest rate reflects only the difference between coupon and market rates for one year, in contrast to 20 years or indefinitely.

Fluctuations in market values of financial claims caused by changes in market rates of interest constitute *interest rate risk* or *market risk*. For the same change in interest rates, long-term financial claims are subject to greater interest rate risk than are short-term claims. There are, however, two additional factors to take into account before one chooses a short-term financial claim in preference to a long-term claim in an attempt to avoid such risk. First, long-term interest rates tend to fluctuate less than short-term rates. Hence, greater volatility of short-term rates offsets partially the lower interest rate risk associated with identical interest rate changes. Second, interest rate risk on an asset may be eliminated completely by incurring a liability of identical maturity. Then a change in the interest rate affects asset and liability values in the same way, leaving net worth unaffected. It is the mismatch of asset and liability maturities that gives rise to interest rate risk, as will be discussed in Chapter 4.

Summary

1. Direct financial claims are issued by nonfinancial units. Financial institutions sell indirect claims. New issues of financial claims are sold on primary markets, whereas used ones are traded on secondary markets.

2. Financial claims are differentiated from one another by characteristics such as maturity, callability, marketability, taxability, type of yield, and risk.

3. The market price of a financial claim is equal to the present value of all future payments—dividends plus principal—due under that claim.

4. The present value depends on the amount and timing of future payments and on the market rate of interest.

5. For any given nominal interest rate, the effective annual rate is higher the more frequently is interest compounded.

6. Level-payment mortgages involve gradual repayment or amortization of the loan principal throughout the mortgage's life. Early on the payment is mainly interest, but towards the end it is mainly principal repayment.

7. The market value of any financial asset with a fixed coupon rate or dividend moves inversely to the market rate of interest.

Questions

1. Distinguish between direct and indirect financial claims.

2. What are the main differences between a passbook savings account and a corporate bond?

3. How can activity on secondary markets affect primary markets?

4. What is the present value of $6000 to be received in one year's time when the interest rate is 20 percent?

5. What is the difference between the nominal and the effective annual rate of interest?

6. Explain what happens over time to the outstanding balance of a level-payment mortgage.

7. How can a financial claim for which the principal will never be repaid have a market value above zero?

8. Why do long-term bond prices fluctuate more than short-term bond prices for a given change in the market rate of interest?

4

Financial
Intermediation

Depository institutions, such as banks and savings and loan associations, are of particular importance because they create money. The amount of money they create depends in part on their ability to compete for business with other financial institutions. This competition takes the form of attracting both lenders by offering indirect financial claims and borrowers by buying their direct financial claims. In this way, financial institutions bring together or intermediate between borrowers and lenders. This chapter examines the general principles of financial intermediation, and Chapters 6, 7, and 8 concentrate on one subgroup of financial intermediaries, the depository institutions.

Nature and Functions
of Financial Intermediaries

Financial intermediation is the activity of obtaining funds from lenders to pass on to borrowers. What distinguishes financial intermediaries or financial institutions from all other business enterprises is that financial intermediaries' assets consist predominantly of financial claims. On the one hand, financial institutions buy direct financial claims, such as treasury bills, mortgages, and commercial notes, from borrowers. On the other hand, they offer their own indirect financial claims to lenders. Banks offer deposits—passbook entries or deposit receipts that represent claims against the bank. Other financial intermediaries offer insurance, pensions, or bonds. In the case of insurance, the claim or liability is contingent on special conditions—death or an accident. For pensions, the condition is reaching retirement age.

To survive, financial intermediaries must compete successfully with other borrowers to attract lenders, depositors, or savers. With funds thus obtained, they must then compete with other lenders to buy direct claims. In one way or another, financial intermediaries must offer indirect claims that are as attractive as or better than direct claims to lenders, while at the same time competing with lenders to buy direct claims. This is achieved through specialization and by reaping economies of scale in financial transactions, information gathering, and portfolio management.

Search Costs and Net Returns

If lenders had to seek out borrowers, and borrowers in turn had to search for lenders, the *net* return to lenders could be substantially lower than the *gross* cost to borrowers. Lenders would subtract these search costs from the interest payments in calculating the net return to lending, and borrowers would add them to find the gross cost of borrowing. A *broker* might be able to reduce the wedge between gross borrowing and net lending rates by reducing total search costs. He or she brings together borrowers and lenders. The broker's own costs are met from the spread between bid and ask or buy price and sell price of financial claims. A financial intermediary performs a function similar to that of a broker in reducing search costs through specialization and scale economies. In addition, it may engage in *denomination* and *maturity* intermediation, terms that are explained below in detail.

Uncertainty and Expected Value

Very rarely can an investor be completely certain about an investment's performance. The investor hopes that it will do well and yield a high return, but he or she recognizes the possibility of failure. Provided probabilities can be assigned to all possible outcomes, an investment's *expected value* can be calculated. Expected values can then be used as the basis for choosing between alternative investments.

Consider investment opportunities A and B, both costing $100. If everything goes well, A will yield $200 in one year's time. With a market interest rate of 10 percent, PV_A is $181.82 in this case. There is, however, only a 50 percent probability that everything will go well. Other future outcomes with different present values may occur. The alternative possible outcomes with their likelihoods or probabilities for both A and B can be set out as follows in terms of present values.

A		B	
Probability	PV_A	*Probability*	PV_B
.5	$181.82	.7	$127.27
.3	90.91	.2	118.21
.1	45.45	.1	100.00
.1	0		

Investment A has a 50 percent probability of future returns giving a present value of $181.82, a 30 percent probability of returning $100 in one year's time giving a present value of $90.91, a 10 percent probability of returning only $50, and a 10 percent probability of losing everything. Its expected value $E(PV_A)$ is

$$E(PV_A) = \sum_{j=1}^{4} \delta_j (PV_{Aj})$$

(4.1)

where δ_j represents the probability that the investment will produce PV_{Aj}. In other words, the expected value is the sum of the outcomes PV_{Aj} multiplied by their probabilities. In this case, $E(PV_A)$ is $[.5(181.82) + .3(90.91) + .1(45.45) + .1(0)]$, or $122.73. Similarly, $E(PV_B)$ is $[.7(127.27) + .2(118.21) + .1(100.00)]$, which also equals $122.73. In this particular case, therefore, both these investment opportunities will, on average, yield a return 22.73 percent above the market rate of interest. If the sole objective was to maximize expected profits, one would be indifferent between investments A and B.

Risk and Diversification
Most investors prefer to avoid or reduce uncertainty. In such case, investment B would be chosen in preference to A, because its range of uncertainty is substantially smaller than A's. Uncertainty can also be reduced without necessarily affecting expected return through portfolio diversification.

Suppose that there are three possible future states of the world, X, Y, and Z. Depending on which state of the world actually materializes, investments A and B will yield future returns with the following *present values*.

State of World	PV_A	PV_B
X	130	90
Y	110	110
Z	90	130

In this case, uncertainty can be eliminated completely by investing equal amounts in both A and B. Such a portfolio will yield 10 percent above the market rate of interest under all possible states of the world.

Consider a somewhat different pattern of yields from investments A and B.

State of World	PV_A	PV_B
X	170	90
Y	110	110
Z	50	130

In this case, uncertainty can be eliminated completely by holding a portfolio in which there are three times the number of Bs as As.

Suppose that state of the world X had a higher probability of materializing than Z. In that case, $E(PV_A)$ is greater than $E(PV_B)$. Hence, including B in the portfolio reduces the expected value of the portfolio as well as uncertainty. The investor is then faced with a tradeoff—less uncertainty but lower yield. Making this choice is examined in Chapter 19.

Denomination Intermediation

In general, portfolio diversification can reduce uncertainty without reducing expected return. Hence, risk-averse lenders have an incentive to lend small amounts to many borrowers in order to reduce uncertainty. Borrowers, on the other hand, prefer to make as few transactions as possible. In practice, a lot of lenders are unable to achieve adequate portfolio diversification through the purchase of direct claims alone because of relatively large minimum denominations and/or high unit costs of small transactions. By engaging in *denomination intermediation*, a financial intermediary can satisfy both lenders and borrowers. In effect, each lender lends very small amounts to a relatively large number of borrowers. Nevertheless, each borrower could borrow from just one financial intermediary. By providing more attractive lending and borrowing arrangements in this way, financial intermediaries increase the total volume of credit.

Credit Risk

Diversification of this kind by financial intermediaries reduces uncertainty with respect to the portfolio's yield but has no effect on the riskiness of each individual asset. Financial intermediaries assume *credit risk* whenever there is some chance of not being repaid. Suppose the default risk were 2 percent on each loan. In other words, there is a 2 percent probability that a loan will eventually have to be written off as a bad debt. Hence, if the return on riskless treasury bills is 10 percent, financial intermediaries would choose not to make any risky loans unless they could charge at least 12.245 percent interest. The expected present value of a $1 million loan portfolio would then be exactly $1 million—$1,122,450 discounted at 10 percent to a present value of $1,020,409, which is then inserted into the expected present value equation $[.98(1,020,409) + .02(0)]$. In other words, $1,122,450 to be received in one year's time with a probability of .98 has an expected present value of $1 million when the market interest rate is 10 percent.

Maturity Intermediation

Other things equal, lenders would prefer financial claims possessing more rather than less liquidity. In general, the shorter the maturity of a claim, the more liquid it is. Overnight loans are almost perfectly liquid because of the repayment the next day. Demand deposits are perfectly liquid because they are repaid on demand. By definition, a perfectly liquid financial claim is money. Borrowers, on the other hand, might prefer to sell claims with a maturity covering the earning period of the investment; they would find any obligation to repay a loan on demand quite impracticable.

Financial intermediaries also attract business through *maturity inter-mediation*. They can use the law of large numbers to offer short-term claims to lenders while buying longer-term claims from borrowers. In this case, the law of large numbers applies to the probability of lenders all wanting their money back at the same time. If deposits and withdrawals are random events and independent from one another, the more accounts a bank holds, the smaller the probability of any given percentage of net withdrawals. With a sufficiently large number of accounts subject to independent and random deposits and withdrawals, a financial intermediary need set aside only a small percentage of its assets to meet net deposit withdrawals. The rest of the deposits can be used to buy longer-term financial claims. From the lender's viewpoint, such maturity intermediation produces indirect claims that are more attractive than the direct claims bought by the financial intermediary. However, maturity intermediation necessarily exposes the financial intermediary to interest rate or market risk.

Transaction Cost Wedge

Consider a situation in which there are no financial intermediaries. Lending, represented by the supply curve in Figure 4.1, is a function of the net return on savings. The net return is the market interest rate adjusted for risk and illiquidity. For example, from a 10 percent yield on direct claims,

Figure 4.1 Effects of Financial Intermediaries on Borrowing and Lending

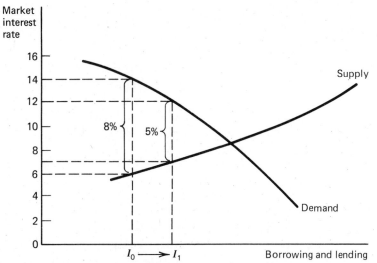

In the absence of financial intermediaries, lenders or suppliers of loans receive a net return on their savings of 6 percent while borrowers, investors, or demanders of loans pay a gross cost of 14 percent. This 8 percent wedge between gross cost and net return is reduced to 5 percent by financial intermediaries; they lower gross costs by eliminating borrowers' transaction costs and they raise net returns by reducing lenders' search and risk costs. The total volume of lending and borrowing rises from I_0 to I_1.

lenders might subtract a 3 percent risk premium and 1 percent for illiquidity, giving an adjusted yield of 6 percent. Borrowing, represented by the demand schedule in Figure 4.1, is a function of the gross cost of borrowing. Borrowers, for example, might add a 4 percent transaction cost of selling their direct claims to the 10 percent interest cost. In this way, a wedge of 8 percentage points is created between the gross cost to borrowers and net return to lenders; borrowers pay gross costs of 14 percent, while lenders receive a net return of 6 percent. As shown in Figure 4.1, the volume of lending and borrowing under such circumstances is I_0.

Financial institutions can reduce this wedge between gross costs of borrowing and net returns to lending. Through denomination and maturity intermediation, financial intermediaries might cut lenders' risk and illiquidity premia from a total of 4 to 1 percent, for example. Borrowers' transaction costs could be eliminated altogether. To cover their costs, financial intermediaries might offer loans at 12 percent and deposits at 8 percent. The wedge between the gross borrowing cost and the net return to lending is thereby reduced from 8 to 5 percentage points. In this example, borrowing increases as a result of the reduction in the gross cost from 14 to 12 percent. Lending rises too because of the increase in the net return from 6 to 7 percent. Figure 4.1 shows that the volume of borrowing and lending moves from I_0 to I_1.

Financial Intermediaries in the United States

Table 4.1 shows the main private-sector financial intermediaries in the United States by asset size. These financial intermediaries can be classified by their liabilities into four groups: depository institutions, contractual savings institutions, finance companies, and investment companies. Traditionally, depository institutions have been subdivided into commercial banks on the one hand and thrift institutions on the other. Thrift institutions consist of savings and loan associations, mutual savings banks, and credit unions.

Depository Institutions

At present, the depository institutions differ from one another much more on the asset than on the liability side of the balance sheet. Commercial banks' largest asset category consists of commercial and industrial loans. In contrast, savings and loan associations hold the bulk of their assets in the form of mortgage loans. Indeed, savings and loan associations were established originally to pool local savings in order to provide housing loans to the associations' members. A similar function was performed by mutual savings banks, which also hold most of their assets in mortgages. However, savings and loan associations and mutual savings banks, unlike credit

Table 4.1   Total Assets of Financial Intermediaries in the United States (end-of-year figures)

Type	1950 Billions of Dollars	1950 Percent	1982 Billions of Dollars	1982 Percent
Commercial banks	169	57	1972	43
Savings and loan associations	17	6	706	15
Life insurance companies	64	22	584	13
Private pension funds	7	2	336	7
State and local pension funds	5	2	253	5
Finance companies	9	3	230	5
Money market funds	0	0	207	4
Mutual savings banks	22	7	174	4
Credit unions	1	—	89	2
Investment companies	3	1	77	2

Source: United States League of Savings Associations, '83 Savings and Loan Sourcebook, p. 36.

unions, no longer confine their source of funds and their lending activities to members. Credit unions consist of members with some "common bond," such as working in the same organization. Credit unions obtain virtually all their funds from and specialize in making consumer loans to their members.

Contractual Savings Institutions

The contractual savings institutions are composed of insurance companies and pension funds. Funds are raised in the form of regular payments from policyholders. Liabilities consist of the expected insurance and pension payments to be made in the future. Life insurance companies hold most of their assets in the form of long-term debt, including corporate bonds, government securities, and mortgages. State and local pension funds have an asset composition similar to that of life insurance companies. Private pension funds, on the other hand, hold the majority of their assets in the form of corporate stock.

Finance Companies

Finance companies include business and commercial finance companies, mortgage companies, personal finance companies, and sales finance companies. Their liabilities consist of loans from banks and their own bills and bonds. Business and commercial finance companies specialize in business loans, particularly against or through the purchase of accounts receivable. Mortgage companies buy mortgages and also collect payments on mortgages they sell to other organizations, such as the Federal National Mortgage Association (Fanny Mae). Personal finance companies make small consumer loans at the high-risk end of the market. In other words, their loans have a relatively high probability of never being repaid. Hence the interest rates charged by personal finance companies are relatively high in order to produce an expected return on the loan portfolio comparable to the riskless return on government securities. Sales finance companies usually lend to retail stores which in turn sell to consumers on installment credit.

Investment Companies Most investment companies are open ended. This means that they buy and sell their own shares from and to the public all the time. Funds are invested in a diversified portfolio. Money market mutual funds are the fastest growing type of open-ended investment company at present. All shares have a value of $1, but investors receive additional shares out of the net investment earnings.

The diversity of financial institutions in the United States is due both to specialization and division of labor on the one hand and regulation on the other. Insurance, for example, is a specialized financial activity in which specialized expertise is needed for success. On the other hand, depository institutions are differentiated in large part because of regulatory constraints and special tax concessions. Credit unions, for example, operate tax free because of their nonprofit cooperative basis. Savings and loan associations receive special tax treatment on earnings from their mortgage loans. As regulatory constraints and special tax treatment are removed, as required by the Depository Institutions Deregulation and Monetary Control Act of 1980, depository institutions will probably become less specialized than they are at present.

Financial Intermediary Behavior

Marginal Cost Profit maximization always involves equating marginal costs with marginal revenues. In the case of financial intermediaries, the marginal cost is the cost of acquiring an extra dollar in liabilities. The extra dollar could come in the form of a deposit, in which case the marginal cost consists of both the explicit interest and the provision of banking services, such as clearing checks and maintaining the account, below their actual costs. Alternatively, the extra dollar could be borrowed from another financial institution or acquired through the sale of certificates of deposit. In all cases, however, there is a cost of obtaining an extra dollar. Profit maximization requires that funds be raised from all available sources until the marginal cost of each source equals marginal revenue.

Marginal Revenue Financial intermediaries' marginal revenue is the net return or net expected return from an extra dollar of assets. Part of that dollar may have to be held in the form of noninterest-earning reserves. All of the costs of managing the extra assets must be subtracted from the gross expected income from these assets. With a 10 percent reserve ratio, for example, a net return on earning assets of 10 percent would imply a revenue of 9¢ on an extra dollar of total assets. In this case, liabilities would be increased to the point where an extra dollar of liabilities also cost 9¢. The process of equating marginal cost with marginal revenue determines the overall size of any particular financial intermediary as well as the relative sizes of groups of intermediaries.

Balance Sheet Analysis   Consider, for example, the following combined balance sheet of all U.S. savings and loan associations as of December 31, 1982.

Assets			Liabilities		
	Billions of Dollars	*Percent*		*Billions of Dollars*	*Percent*
Cash and invest-			Deposits	566	80.2
ment securities	85	12.0			
Mortgage loans	482	68.3	Advances from Federal		
			Home Loan Bank[b]	98	13.9
Other assets[a]	139	19.7	Other liabilities	16	2.2
			Net worth	26	3.7
Total	706	100.0	Total	706	100.0

[a] Includes government-insured mortgage-type investments.
[b] Includes other borrowed money.
Source: United States League of Savings Associations, *'83 Savings and Loan Sourcebook*, p. 41.

The balance sheet figures make it immediately apparent that savings and loan associations are primarily in the business of accepting deposits and making mortgage loans. Denomination intermediation is exemplified by the fact that in 1980 savings and loan associations held 16,071 mortgages of an average face value equal to $31,311, but maintained 94,572 savings accounts with an average balance of $5410 each. Maturity intermediation is pronounced, since mortgage loans are generally extended for 25 years or more while liabilities consist mainly of savings accounts and medium-term time deposits. At the end of 1981, 64 percent of savings and loan deposits earned interest above the regular passbook rate of $5\frac{1}{2}$ percent, implying that they were fixed-maturity deposits.

Leverage   Another feature of financial intermediaries' activities illustrated by this balance sheet is the extent of *leverage*. Leverage is measured as the ratio of resources acquired to capital or net worth. In this case, leverage is 706 divided by 26, or 27.2 to 1. The principle of leverage can be illustrated by an individual investment. Suppose someone buys a $100,000 condominium as an investment. He or she puts up $25,000 and borrows the remaining $75,000. Leverage in this case is 4 to 1. The value of the asset is four times greater than the equity or net worth. If the property appreciates annually by 12 percent and the funds were borrowed at 10 percent, the investment appreciates by $12,000 during the first year and interest payments total $7500. The net return on the $25,000 equity is $4500, or 18 percent. Had this individual put up $10,000 and borrowed $90,000, interest payments would rise to $9000, but the net return on the $10,000 equity of $3000 now represents a yield of 30 percent.

Return to Equity   Provided the net return on assets exceeds the gross cost of borrowing, the greater the leverage, the higher is the rate of return to equity or net worth. In the case of savings and loan associations, the net spread between asset yield and liability cost averaged about one-half of 1 percent during the 1970s. With leverage of 15 to 1 and a net asset yield of 6 percent, the return to equity would be 13 percent. Each $1500 of assets produces a net income of $90. The interest on the borrowed $1400 is $77. Hence $13 is earned for every $100 of equity.

The situation changed dramatically in 1981. In that year, assets yielded a net return of 8.5 percent, but the average cost of deposits and other borrowed funds zoomed up to 9.5 percent. The leverage of 23.7 to 1 in 1981 implied a return on equity of −15 percent. Each $2370 of assets produced a net income of $201, while interest payments on the borrowed $2270 were $216. Each $100 of equity suffered a loss of $15.

Alternatively, the return on equity can be calculated as the product of the *return on assets* and the *equity multiplier*. Essentially, the return on assets is the net income or profit of the corporation divided by its total assets. Ignoring intermediation costs, this would be interest income minus interest cost for financial institutions. During the 1970s, commercial banks' return on assets averaged about 0.8 percent. The relationship between return on assets and return on equity depends upon the equity multiplier, which is just a measure of leverage. Since return on assets ROA equals net income NI divided by total assets A, and return on equity ROE equals net income divided by equity E, return on equity can also be expressed as return on assets times leverage:

$$ROE = ROA \cdot A/E \qquad (4.2)$$

This formulation shows clearly why leverage magnifies fluctuations in the return on assets.

Return on assets can be negative, as was the case for the savings and loan industry in 1981. Suppose, in the condominium example above, that the condominium actually appreciated by only 8 percent. With leverage of 4 to 1, return on equity would be 2 percent. But with 10 to 1 leverage, return on equity would fall to −10 percent. The higher the leverage, the greater is the risk—a fortune could be made but the attempt might be disastrous.

Interest Sensitivity Gap

One of the risks magnified by leverage is *interest risk*. One measure of this interest risk is called the *interest sensitivity gap*, expressed as a percentage of total assets. The gap is the dollar value of assets to be *repriced* during some specified time period minus the value of liabilities to be repriced during the same period. Repricing refers to changes in the interest rate on claims in order to reflect new market interest rates. It is assumed that all maturing claims are reinvested at the current market interest rate. In addition, certain nonmaturing claims may be repriced because their rate is tied to the current market rate. In fact, such claims are continually repriced.

A positive interest sensitivity gap means that more assets than liabilities will be repriced during the coming period. A negative gap implies that more liabilities than assets will be repriced. With a negative gap, a rise in market interest rates is accompanied by interest expenditure rising more than interest income. In this case, net income will fall, as happened to the savings and loan industry in 1981.

Consider the case where all market rates of interest increase by an equal amount, Δi. The change in the return on assets ΔROA equals Δi times the gap GAP divided by total assets A.

$$\Delta ROA = \Delta i \cdot (GAP/A) \tag{4.3}$$

For example, suppose interest rates rise by 2 percentage points and the interest sensitivity gap equals −8 percent of total assets. In this case, the change in the return on assets will be −0.16 percent [2(−0.08)]. With leverage of 20 to 1, the return on equity will fall by 3.2 percent [20(−0.16)].

Book versus Market Value

In fact, the rate of return on equity is an accounting concept measured in terms of *book value*, the original amount invested. The true worth of a corporation is its *market value*. If investors demand, say, a 16 percent return, the market value will equal book value only when the rate of return on equity is also 16 percent. If the rate of return on equity falls below 16 percent, the market value of the corporation would fall below its book value to the point at which the return on the market value of the corporation's equity is again 16 percent.

The market-value approach can be illustrated in an alternative way. A rise in interest rates produces a fall in the market values of fixed-interest financial claims, as was shown in Chapter 3. Because of maturity intermediation, financial institutions' interest sensitivity gap is often negative. Thus, the same rise in all market rates of interest will reduce the market value of assets by more than the market value of liabilities. Hence, the market value of the corporation or its net worth is reduced by a rise in interest rates. The market rate of return on the market price of the corporation would in fact increase with the rise in all other market rates of interest. Original stockholders, however, incur a capital loss from the fall in the market price of their stocks.

The combined balance sheet of savings and loan associations shown earlier gives the book or face value of mortgages that were extended. However, by 1982, with the rise in market interest rates, the market value of mortgages held by savings and loan associations had dropped about 15 percent below their book values. In other words, asset values of about $75 billion had been wiped out. Since some liabilities are long-term deposits, the book value of liabilities fell too, but only by about 3 percent. This removed about $15 billion in liabilities valued at market prices. Net worth, therefore, was reduced by the $75 billion fall in the value of assets but increased by the $15 billion drop in the value of liabilities. If assets and liabilities were calculated at market rather than book or face values, one would find that the net worth or equity of the savings and loan associations was negative, 1980–1982. Moreover, leverage magnified the effect of falling asset values on net worth. A 1 percent fall in asset values reduces net worth by 27.2 percent when leverage is 27.2 to 1.

Leverage and Credit Risk

Credit risk is also magnified by leverage. With a 27.2 to 1 leverage ratio, a 4 percent drop in asset values due to loan defaults would completely wipe out net worth. In other words, net worth is affected by 27.2 times the fluctuation in asset values arising from default or interest risk, provided liabilities remain unchanged.

Summary

1. Financial institutions sell indirect claims to lenders and buy direct claims from borrowers. Their assets consist predominantly of financial claims.

2. Financial intermediaries attract borrowers and lenders because they reduce search costs and offer denomination and maturity intermediation.

3. Denomination intermediation enables small savers to diversify their portfolios. Diversification reduces uncertainty.

4. Under uncertainty, the outcome of an investment is not definitely known. However, the investment's expected present value can be calculated, provided probabilities associated with all possible outcomes can be estimated.

5. Financial intermediaries can employ the law of large numbers to borrow short and lend long. The larger the number of accounts, the more predictable are net deposit withdrawals.

6. By reducing the wedge between gross costs of borrowing and net returns to lending, financial intermediaries increase the volume of both borrowing and lending.

7. Financial intermediaries tend to exhibit relatively high leverage. Leverage is measured by dividing total assets by net worth. Provided the net return on assets exceeds the gross cost of borrowed funds, higher leverage raises the return on equity. It also increases risk.

8. Maturity intermediation subjects financial intermediaries to interest risk. In such case, a rise in the market interest rate reduces the value of assets by more than the value of liabilities.

9. Financial intermediaries also face credit risk or the risk of loan default. They compensate for this by raising interest rates charged on riskier loans so that their expected yield equals or exceeds the yield on riskless government securities.

10. Interest risk occurs when asset maturities differ from liability maturities. The degree of risk is measured by the interest sensitivity gap.

11. Using book values, a negative interest sensitivity gap implies that a rise in interest rates reduces the return to equity. However, using market values, a negative interest sensitivity gap implies that a rise in interest rates reduces the net worth of the corporation. The fall in share prices actually *raises* the market return to equity.

Questions

1. How do financial intermediaries compete with direct claims?
2. How does maturity intermediation produce interest or market risk?
3. What is the expected return of an asset paying 20 percent interest with a default probability of 3 percent?
4. Explain diversification and denomination intermediation.
5. What is leverage and how does it increase risk?
6. Explain the distinction between book value and market value in relation to the savings and loan associations' balance sheet.

5

Government and Financial Markets

Federal and state governments, and their agencies, influence American financial markets in three important ways. First, they borrow in these markets through the sale of bonds, notes, and bills. Second, they buy financial claims, such as mortgages, to support both economic and political objectives—homeownership in the case of mortgage purchases. Third, the government regulates credit allocation through devices such as interest-rate ceilings and discriminatory taxation.

Interest-rate ceilings are one of the oldest and most pervasive forms of government involvement in financial markets. In early times, interest-rate ceilings were aimed primarily at preventing usury—lending money at an exorbitant rate. Usury laws, or more precisely anti-usury laws, are still on the books in many states to protect borrowers from being exploited. In recent times, interest-rate ceilings have also been used to influence the allocation of investible funds, to provide cheap credit for the government, and to promote economic stability. This chapter starts by analyzing the effects of this particular form of intervention. It then considers other forms of government involvement and intervention in U.S. financial markets. In general, government activities in the financial markets have had either no impact or the opposite effects to those intended.

Ceilings on Deposit Rates of Interest

Regulation Q Many of the regulations covering financial institutions in the United States originated in the banking acts of 1933 and 1935. Of utmost concern to legislators was the prevention in the future of the waves of bank failures that shook the economy in the early 1930s. As part of a package which

Table 5.1   Maximum Interest Rates Payable on Time and Savings Deposits
at Federally Insured Institutions, March 31, 1983
(percent per annum)

Type of Account	Commercial Banks	Thrift Institutions
Savings	5¼	5½
NOW accounts	5¼	5¼
Time accounts		
14–89 days	5¼	6
90 days to 1 year	5¾	6
1 to 2½ years	6	6½
2½ to 4 years	6½	6¾
4 to 6 years	7¼	7½
6 to 8 years	7½	7¾
8 or more years	7¾	8
Issued to governmental units (all maturities)	8	8
IRAs and Keogh plans (3 years or more)	8	8

Source: Federal Reserve Bulletin, April 1983, p. A9.

included deposit insurance, the Fed was given authority to set ceilings on
the deposit rates of interest that member banks could offer on savings and
time deposits. The Fed fixed the ceilings under its Regulation Q. Table 5.1
shows the deposit-rate ceilings in effect on March 31, 1983. The Federal
Deposit Insurance Corporation (FDIC) established the same ceilings as a
condition of deposit insurance for all insured banks that were not members
of the Fed. Hence, virtually all banks were effectively covered by Regulation Q.

**Objective of
Regulation Q**
Not only were ceilings fixed for interest rates on savings and time deposits,
but interest payments on demand deposits were prohibited. The main
purpose of this legislation was to reduce the risk of bank failure by lowering the costs of their funds and preventing cutthroat competition. Indeed,
the banking lobby arguing in favor of deposit-rate ceilings claimed that
excessive competition for deposits through unprofitably high deposit rates
had caused the bank failures of the early 1930s. Recent research lays this
assertion open to considerable doubt.

**Rising Market
Rates of Interest**
Initially, the maximum rate on savings and time deposit rates of interest
established under Regulation Q was 3 percent. At the time, this ceiling did
not constrain bank rate-setting behavior because it was above the level of
market rates of interest. In fact, the interest-rate ceiling on savings and
time deposits remained above market rates of interest and hence was not a
binding constraint until 1956. When market rates overshot the ceiling in

1957 and 1962, the ceiling was raised. From 1961, however, market interest rates in the United States increased steadily until they exceeded the 1962 ceiling rate of 4 percent towards the end of 1965. In 1966, interest-rate ceilings on thrift institution (such as savings and loan associations) deposits were introduced. Only occasionally, and then for brief periods, have market interest rates fallen below the deposit-rate ceilings since 1966.

Cheap Mortgages through Deposit-Rate Ceilings

The aim of the 1966 legislation covering thrift institutions differed from that of the 1933–1935 legislation dealing with the commercial banks. The main aim of the 1966 legislation was to restrict competition so that mortgage rates would not escalate any further. Thrift institutions were permitted to offer rates a full percentage point higher than banks could offer for certain deposits. This advantage, it was hoped, would attract plenty of relatively cheap deposits into the thrift institutions. Competition to lend this abundance of funds on the mortgage market would, in turn, keep mortgage rates low.

Although the ceiling differential between commercial banks and thrift institutions (thrifts for short) was reduced to half a percentage point in 1970 and to quarter of a percentage point in 1973, the differential was soon regarded as essential for expanding mortgage funds and increasing residential housing construction. These were important matters of public policy. To ensure that the differential was actually maintained, the ceiling on commercial bank deposit rates had to be binding. Hence, this ceiling had to be held below comparable market rates of interest. Since 1966 this has indeed been the case most of the time. Since 1979 the Regulation Q ceiling on passbook savings deposits at commercial banks has been $5\frac{1}{4}$ percent and the ceiling on passbook savings deposits at savings and loan associations and mutual savings banks has been $5\frac{1}{2}$ percent.

Ceilings and Disintermediation

The effects of below-market equilibrium deposit rate ceilings were not the ones intended. Funds available to thrift institutions from deposits for mortgage lending have fluctuated more rather than less as a result of the ceilings. When market interest rates rose, deposit growth decelerated or actually declined. Depositors switched out of deposits and into direct claims—a process known as *disintermediation*—when the return on direct claims became increasingly more attractive relative to the fixed return on deposits.

Exemptions from Regulation Q

Disintermediation was particularly prevalent among large deposits, for which close substitutes in the form of direct claims were readily available. Initial attempts to reduce disruptive disintermediation, therefore, focused on large-denomination deposits. For these, ceilings were either removed completely (in 1973 for large negotiable or marketable certificates of deposit of $100,000 or more) or tied to market rates (in 1978 for six-month money market certificates of $10,000 and longer-term deposits of smaller denominations).

**Elimination of
Deposit-Rate
Ceilings**

As market rates of interest almost tripled between 1976 and 1981 (the 3-month treasury bill yield rose from 5.0 percent in 1976 to 14.1 percent in 1981), more and more partial or complete exemptions from Regulation Q were introduced. It became increasingly apparent that these stopgap attempts to deter disintermediation simply discriminated against the small saver. Under mounting pressure, Congress finally passed the Depository Institutions Deregulation and Monetary Control Act of 1980. This legislates the gradual but complete elimination of all deposit-rate ceilings by 1986. The act established the Depository Institutions Deregulation Committee (DIDC)—composed of the secretary of the treasury; the chairman of the Fed's board of governors; the heads of the FDIC, Federal Home Loan Bank Board, and National Credit Union Administration; and the Comptroller of the Currency as a nonvoting member—to implement the phase-out of interest-rate ceilings. Initially, the DIDC moved cautiously and actually proliferated the regulations on deposit-rate ceilings. The Alice-in-Wonderland maze of new regulations imposed in the name of deregulation that existed in mid-1982 is set out in Box 5.1. Under congressional direction, however, the DIDC introduced Super NOW and Money Market Deposit Accounts at the end of 1982. Both are ceiling free but can be offered only for deposits with a minimum balance of $2500. On October 1, 1983, all time deposit ceilings were finally abolished, leaving ceilings only on ordinary demand, passbook savings deposits, and time deposits with maturities of 31 days or less.

BOX 5.1
EXEMPTIONS FROM REGULATION Q, MARCH 31, 1983

**Time Deposits
Subject to
Variable Ceiling
Rates**

91-day time deposits.   Effective May 1, 1982, depository institutions were authorized to offer time deposits that have a minimum denomination of $7500 and a maturity of 91 days. Effective January 5, 1983, the minimum denomination required for this deposit was reduced to $2500. The ceiling rate of interest on these deposits was indexed to the discount rate (auction average) on most recently issued 91-day treasury bills for thrift institutions and the discount rate minus 25 basis points for commercial banks (one basis point is 1/100th of a percentage point). The rate differential ended 1 year from the effective date of these instruments and was suspended at any time the treasury bill discount rate was 9 percent or below for four consecutive auctions.

Six-month money market time deposits.   Effective June 1, 1978, commercial banks and thrift institutions were authorized to offer time deposits with a maturity of exactly 26 weeks and a minimum denomination requirement of $10,000. Effective January 5, 1983, the minimum denomination required for this deposit was reduced to $2500. The ceiling rate of interest on these deposits was indexed to the discount rate (auction average) on most recently issued 26-week U.S. treasury bills. Interest on these certificates could not be compounded. Effective for all 6-month money market certificates issued beginning November 1, 1981, depository institutions could pay rates of interest on these deposits indexed to the higher of (1) the rate for 26-week treasury bills established immediately before the date of deposit (bill rate) or (2) the average of the four rates for 26-week treasury bills established for the 4 weeks immediately before the date of deposit (4-week average bill rate). Ceilings were determined as follows:

Bill Rate or 4-Week Average Bill Rate	Commercial Bank Ceiling
7.50 percent or below	7.75 percent
Above 7.50 percent	¼ of 1 percentage point plus the higher of the bill rate or 4-week average bill rate
	Thrift Ceiling
7.25 percent or below	7.75 percent
Above 7.25 percent, but below 8.50 percent	½ of 1 percentage point plus the higher of the bill rate or 4-week average bill rate
8.50 percent or above, but below 8.75 percent	9 percent
8.75 percent or above	¼ of 1 percentage point plus the higher of the bill rate or 4-week average bill rate

12-month all savers certificates.   Effective October 1, 1981, depository institutions were authorized to issue all savers certificates (ASCs) with a 1-year maturity and an annual investment yield equal to 70 percent of the average investment yield for 52-week U.S. treasury bills as determined by the auction of 52-week treasury bills held immediately before the calendar week in which the certificate was issued. A maximum lifetime exclusion of $1000 ($2000 on a joint return) from gross income was generally authorized for interest income from ASCs. The annual investment yield for ASCs issued in December 1982 (in percent) was as follows: December 26, 6.26.

2½-year to less than 3½-year time deposits.   Effective August 1, 1981, commercial banks were authorized to pay interest on any variable ceiling nonnegotiable time deposit with an original maturity of 2½ years to less than 4 years at a rate not to exceed one-quarter of 1 percent below the average 2½-year yield for U.S. treasury securities as determined and announced by the

Treasury Department immediately before the date of deposit. Effective May 1, 1982, the maximum maturity for this category of deposits was reduced to less than $3\frac{1}{2}$ years. Thrift institutions could pay interest on these certificates at a rate not to exceed the average $2\frac{1}{2}$-year yield for Treasury securities as determined and announced by the Treasury Department immediately before the date of deposit. If the announced average $2\frac{1}{2}$-year yield for treasury securities was less than 9.50 percent, commercial banks could pay 9.25 percent and thrift institutions 9.50 percent for these deposits. These deposits had no required minimum denomination, and interest could be compounded on them. The ceiling rates of interest at which they could be offered varied biweekly.

Between January 1, 1980, and August 1, 1981, commercial banks and thrift institutions were authorized to offer variable ceiling nonnegotiable time deposits with no required minimum denomination and with maturities of $2\frac{1}{2}$ years or more. Effective January 1, 1980, the maximum rate for commercial banks was $\frac{3}{4}$ percentage point below the average yield on $2\frac{1}{2}$-year U.S. treasury securities; the ceiling rate for thrift institutions was $\frac{1}{4}$ percentage point higher than that for commercial banks. Effective March 1, 1980, a temporary ceiling of $11\frac{3}{4}$ percent was placed on these accounts at commercial banks and 12 percent on these accounts at savings and loans. Effective June 2, 1980, the ceiling rates for these deposits at commercial banks and savings and loans were increased $\frac{1}{2}$ percentage point. The temporary ceiling was retained, and a minimum ceiling of 9.25 percent for commercial banks and 9.50 percent for thrift institutions was established.

Time Deposits Not Subject to Interest Rate Ceilings

Money market deposit accounts. Effective December 14, 1982, depository institutions were authorized to offer a new account with a required initial balance of $2500 and an average maintenance balance of $2500 not subject to interest rate restrictions. No minimum maturity period was required for this account, but depository institutions had to reserve the right to require seven days' notice before withdrawals. When the average balance was less than $2500, the account was subject to the maximum ceiling rate of interest for NOW accounts; compliance with the average balance requirement could be determined over a period of one month. Depository institutions could not guarantee a rate of interest for this account for a period longer than one month or condition the payment of a rate on a requirement that the funds remain on deposit for longer than one month. No more than six preauthorized, automatic, or other third-party transfers were permitted per month, of which no more than three could be checks. Telephone transfers to third parties or to another account of the same depositor were regarded as preauthorized transfers.

IRAs and Keogh (H.R. 10) plans (18 months or more). Effective December 1, 1981, depository institutions were authorized to offer time deposits not subject to interest rate ceilings when the funds were deposited to the credit of, or in which the entire beneficial interest was held by, an individual pursuant to an IRA agreement or Keogh (H.R. 10) plan. Such time deposits had to have a minimum maturity of 18 months, and additions could be made to the time deposit at any time before its maturity without extending the maturity of all or a portion of the balance of the account.

Time deposits of 7 to 31 days.   Effective September 1, 1982, depository institutions were authorized to issue nonnegotiable time deposits of $20,000 or more with a maturity or required notice period of 7 to 31 days. The maximum rate of interest payable by thrift institutions was the rate established and announced (auction average on a discount basis) for U.S. treasury bills with maturities of 91 days at the auction held immediately before the date of deposit or renewal ("bill rate"). Commercial banks could pay the bill rate minus 25 basis points. The interest-rate ceiling was suspended when the bill rate was 9 percent or below for the four most recent auctions held before the date of deposit or renewal. Effective January 5, 1983, the minimum denomination required for this deposit was reduced to $2500 and the interest rate ceiling was removed.

Time deposits of $3\frac{1}{2}$ years or more.   Effective May 1, 1982, depository institutions were authorized to offer negotiable or nonnegotiable time deposits with a minimum original maturity of $3\frac{1}{2}$ years or more that were not subject to interest-rate ceilings. Such time deposits had no minimum denomination but had to be made available in a $500 denomination. Additional deposits could be made to the account during the first year without extending its maturity.

Source: Federal Reserve Bulletin, April 1983, p. A10.

Effects of Deposit-Rate Ceilings

The elaborate structure of deposit-rate ceilings built up over the past 50 years produced three measurable effects: (1) it forced banks to substitute nonprice (such as free check clearing) for price competition; (2) it produced periods of violent and disruptive disintermediation; and (3) it discriminated blatantly against small savers who did not face any practical alternative for deposit accounts in which to hold their savings.

Noneffects of Deposit-Rate Ceilings

On the other hand, neither deposit-rate ceilings nor the ceiling differential between bank and thrift deposits had any measurable impact on mortgage interest rates or mortgage availability. Financial institutions face a wide range of closely substitutable assets. If mortgage yields fall, then financial institutions move into higher-yielding treasury bonds, for example. Since demand for mortgages is so sensitive to the mortgage yield in relation to other financial asset yields, the mortgage yield is tied closely to yields on comparable assets. If the mortgage rate were to fall, substitution of other financial assets would take place. The consequent fall in demand for mortgages would lower their market price and so raise their yield again. Clearly, thrifts would buy old, higher-yielding mortgages rather than new low-rate mortgages if such a choice existed. Hence, the yield on existing mortgages, which is closely tied to the yield on other comparable financial assets, determines the rate at which thrifts are prepared to extend new mortgages.

Given this asset substitutability, it is not at all surprising to find that the effective mortgage rate moved much more closely with, for example, the 10-year treasury bond yield than with the average cost of thrift institution funds.[1] To maximize profits, thrifts bought mortgages at the going market rate of interest. Deposit-rate ceilings did not provide any incentive to buy mortgages at subsidized rates. When market interest rates rose, thrifts increased their expenditure on attracting deposits through advertising and other forms of nonprice competition until the cost of attracting one more dollar in deposits just equaled the net return from the purchase of corresponding assets.

Government Mortgage Subsidies

The government offers subsidies of various kinds to encourage thrift institutions to hold mortgages. Thrifts are given a tax break on mortgage interest earnings. This subsidy takes the form of allowing thrifts to deduct a higher percentage of their income as bad debt reserves for tax purposes the higher is the percentage of mortgages in their portfolios. This tax advantage raises the net after-tax return on mortgages, hence encouraging thrift institutions to spend more to attract deposits with which to buy mortgages. As soon as thrifts start to raise mortgage prices and hence depress mortgage yields, however, other mortgage holders not receiving this tax advantage sell their mortgages and buy other higher-yielding financial claims. Since thrift institutions face an elastic supply of mortgages, the effect of this subsidy is simply to make the thrift institutions, as a group, larger than they otherwise would be. In other words, the subsidy encourages thrifts to attract more deposits with which to buy mortgages than they would in the absence of the subsidy. It does not affect the mortgage rate of interest because other mortgage holders supply any amount of mortgages the thrifts want as soon as the mortgage yield starts to fall below the yield on comparable financial assets.

Deposit-rate ceilings were rationalized on the grounds that it was essential to provide depository institutions with a source of low-cost funds in order to keep mortgage rates down. Higher deposit rates, it was argued, would necessitate higher mortgage rates, something no one wanted. Although an increase in deposit rates (and all other interest rates) may lead to higher mortgage rates, it is impossible to keep mortgage rates down by imposing deposit-rate ceilings.

---

[1]R. Alton Gilbert, "Will the Removal of Regulation Q Raise Mortgage Interest Rates?" *Federal Reserve Bank of St. Louis Review,* 63(10), December 1981, pp. 3–12.

Deposit-Rate Ceilings Can Raise Mortgage Rates of Interest

Loan rates of interest, including mortgage rates, are determined by the demand for and supply of funds. In other words, the interest rate finds the level at which demand equals supply. One source of supply comes from deposits. If deposit holding is deterred by deposit-rate ceilings, the supply of mortgage funds may be reduced. In this case, the mortgage rate of interest must *rise* to choke off enough demand to bring supply and demand back into equilibrium.

Consider Figure 5.1, in which supply represents the supply of funds from deposits and demand represents the demand for mortgage loans. In the absence of any interest rate controls or wedge between gross costs to borrowers and net return to lenders, the market clears at the interest rate i_1. If a deposit rate ceiling of i_0 is imposed, the quantity of mortgage loans that can be financed from deposits declines from q_1 to q_0. In other words, deposits are less attractive and people reduce deposit holding from q_1 to q_0. The reduced supply of mortgage funds raises the mortgage rate to i_2. The increase from i_1 to i_2 is needed to equate quantity demanded with the smaller quantity supplied. Hence, the imposition of a deposit-rate ceiling raises mortgage rates. Abolishing deposit-rate ceilings would *reduce* mortgage rates of interest in this case.

Figure 5.1   Effect of a Deposit-Rate Ceiling

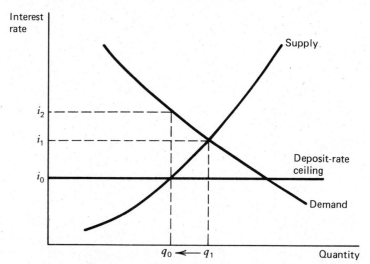

The imposition of a binding deposit-rate ceiling of i_0 reduces deposits and hence reduces the available supply of funds provided by deposits from q_1 to q_0. With a downward-sloping demand for funds, the mortgage rate rises from i_1 to i_2 to bring down quantity demanded to q_0. Only in this way is demand equated with the smaller quantity supplied.

Figure 5.2   Deposit Substitutability and a Deposit-Rate Ceiling

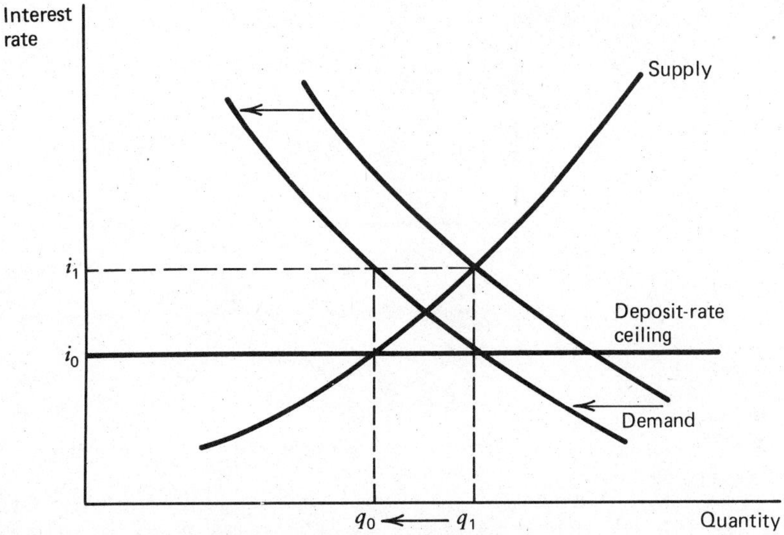

The deposit-rate ceiling reduces deposit holding but increases the supply of mortgage funds through other channels, as depositors shift funds into other financial claims. The increased availability of mortgage funds through other channels shifts the demand curve for mortgage funds from deposits. In this case, the mortgage rate remains at i_1, despite the fall in the deposit rate.

Deposit Substitutes and Mortgage Funds

Two complications must now be introduced. First, depositors who are deterred from holding deposits by the deposit-rate ceiling may supply funds to the mortgage market through other channels. Were the increase in funds through other channels exactly equal to the decrease in funds from deposits, the mortgage rate would be unaffected by a deposit-rate ceiling. This is shown in Figure 5.2, in which demand for mortgage funds *from deposits* is shifted by the greater availability of funds from other sources.

Mortgage Substitutes and Mortgage Funds

A similar situation would arise if mortgages were perfect substitutes for other financial assets in nondepositors' portfolios. Then, as soon as the mortgage rate began to rise after the imposition of the deposit-rate ceiling, nondepositors would switch funds into the mortgage market. If the mortgage market were small relative to other markets for financial assets, the mortgage rate would be forced back down to i_1, the general market rate of interest. This is shown in Figure 5.3, where the demand for mortgage loans from deposit funds is infinitely elastic at i_1. In this case the deposit ceiling reduces the deposit rate and hence the volume of deposits, but it has no impact on the mortgage rate. In practice, deposit substitution into alterna-

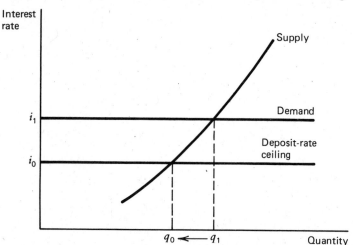

Figure 5.3   Nondeposit Substitutability and a Deposit-Rate Ceiling

Demand for mortgages from deposit funds is perfectly elastic in this case because there is a large supply of mortgage funds from other sources. In this case the deposit-rate ceiling reduces deposit holding but has no effect on the mortgage rate of interest.

tive funds for mortgages and nondeposit substitution into mortgages appear to be sufficiently strong to eliminate any impact of deposit-rate ceilings on mortgage rates of interest.

Fungibility of Capital

Financial capital is extremely *fungible*. This means that it can be used for a lot of different purposes. For example, financial capital can be invested in mortgages, corporate notes, treasury bonds, or any other financial claim. In that sense, fungibility is related to substitutability. Here, however, the importance of fungibility lies in the implication that specific liabilities or loans need not be used to buy specific assets. A home mortgage, for example, can finance the purchase of a Picasso painting.

Capital Fungibility and Household Sector Behavior

The fungibility of financial capital has made government efforts to promote home ownership impotent. Government action and initiative in spreading amortization, lengthening maturities, and providing mortgage insurance and subsidies have raised the ratio of mortgage debt to the value of the housing stock from about 10 percent at the beginning of this century to about 40 percent today. The ratio of mortgage debt to total liabilities rose substantially too. Mortgage debt was substituted for other forms of household borrowing. However, the ratio of housing to total assets of nonfarm households in the United States has remained virtually constant at 25 percent throughout this century.[2] In this case substitutability took place on the borrowing rather than the lending side.

The mortgage debt case exemplifies the fact that specific liabilities do not finance specific assets. Subsidized mortgages do not necessarily finance additional spending on housing. They do, on the other hand, encourage individuals to borrow funds by mortgaging their houses rather than taking loans on their cars. In either case, the additional expenditure financed by this borrowing may not involve cars or houses. Overall, subsidized mortgages may not affect the stock of houses or even the volume of construction, except in the short run, because financial resources are fungible.

Government Mortgage Purchases

The fungibility of financial capital on the lending side is illustrated by government mortgage purchases. Yet another form of government subsidy designed to encourage residential housing construction takes place through mortgage purchases by federal agencies. Availability of credit is increased by government mortgage purchases. However, credit availability is reduced back again through sales of the extra government bonds needed to finance the mortgage purchases. In effect, funds are drained from one side of the pool of savings and pumped back into the other side. The level of the pond—the aggregate supply of credit—and hence the market rate of interest, is unchanged. In this case, the subsidy takes the form of government expenditure on operating the mortgage-buying agencies. In terms of the pond example, the government meets part of the cost of running the pump.

All Savers Certificates

The concept of financial capital fungibility can also be used to analyze the impact of the All Savers Certificate program introduced by the federal government in 1981. The certificates had a maturity of 1 year and the interest rate was 70 percent of the yield produced at the most recent monthly 1-year treasury note auction. The first $1000 ($2000 for a joint return) of interest was free of income tax. All depository institutions could issue these certificates but were obliged to invest 75 percent of the proceeds in housing and agricultural loans.

Since depository institutions mounted advertising campaigns to attract funds into All Savers Certificates, one might infer that this source of funds was cheaper than others. Presumably, lenders substituted All Savers Certificates for other market-rate yielding financial claims. Had they substituted these certificates for regular fixed-interest $5\frac{1}{4}$ and $5\frac{1}{2}$ percent passbook savings deposits, the cost of funds to depository institutions would have risen, not fallen. In such case, depository institutions would have had no incentive to sell All Savers Certificates.

[2]Allan H. Meltzer, "Credit Availability and Economic Decisions: Some Evidence from the Mortgage and Housing Markets," *Journal of Finance*, 29(3), June 1974, pp. 763–777.

The tax break on All Savers Certificates subsidized both high-income individuals and depository institutions. The depository institutions spent their subsidy on attracting more funds until marginal cost equaled marginal return. On the liability side of their balance sheets, All Savers Certificates were substituted, in the main, for certificates of deposit and other market-rate liabilities. On the asset side, nothing happened. Fungibility ensured that depository institutions could earmark All Savers Certificate funds for the housing and agricultural loans they would have made in any case. Other sources of funds were thus freed for other purposes. In particular, mortgage interest rates maintained exactly the same relationship to the 10-year treasury bond yield—about one percentage point higher—as they had before the introduction of All Savers Certificates.[3] Even if depository institutions had increased mortgage and agricultural loans, interest rates on such loans would have been unaffected. Other lenders would have reduced their holdings of mortgage and agricultural loans as soon as depository institutions started offering higher prices and hence producing lower yields on these financial claims.

Usury Laws

Most states have enacted usury laws to set ceilings on loan rates of interest. As with deposit-rate ceilings, the aim has generally been to hold down the cost of borrowing, particularly for home ownership. In addition, usury laws are designed to protect the public from unscrupulous loan sharks. In general, however, the effect of loan-rate ceilings has been to prevent some groups of people from borrowing and to deter lending for some potentially high-yielding but risky investment projects.

Loan-Rate Ceilings Deter Riskier Lending

Consider Figure 5.4, in which less risky and riskier loan markets are depicted. The market is in equilibrium at an interest rate of i_1 for less risky loans and i_2 for riskier loans. The riskier loan rate incorporates expected losses from riskier lending and hence must be higher than the less risky loan rate. The imposition of a loan-rate ceiling of i_C eliminates the supply of riskier loans, because the ceiling is too low to compensate for expected loan losses. Funds released from the riskier loan markets are added to the supply of less risky loans, shifting this supply curve to the right. Nevertheless, the quantity of less risky loans supplied at i_C is reduced from q_1 to q_0. In this case the shift of funds out of both markets after the imposition of a loan-rate ceiling exceeds the shift of funds from the riskier to the less risky loan market.

There is another way of looking at this effect. Consider the following example of risky investment. Suppose all entrepreneurs face a $1 million 1-

[3]Gilbert, *op. cit.*, pp. 8–9.

Figure 5.4 Riskier and Less Risky Loan Markets: (a) Less Risky; (b) Riskier.

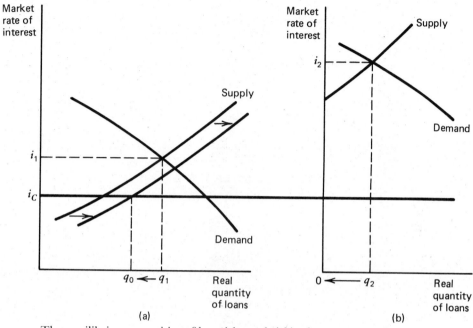

The equilibrium quantities of less risky and riskier loans are q_1 and q_2, respectively. The imposition of a loan-rate ceiling i_C eliminates risky lending and reduces the volume of less risky lending, despite a rightward shift in the supply function of less risky loans due to the shift out of risky lending.

year investment with an uncertain yield. Sixty percent of the time the investment will earn a 100 percent return. The other 40 percent of the time it will lose 50 percent of its value. Therefore, the investment's average or *expected return* is 40 percent—.6(100) + .4(−50).

Consider an entrepreneur who wants to borrow 100 percent of the required funds. If the investment fails, the entrepreneur would be able to repay only 50 percent of the loan principal and no accrued interest. To earn an expected return of 10 percent, the lender would have to charge 50 percent on such loans—.6(50) + .4(−50). Even if financial intermediaries had no aversion to risk, they would nevertheless turn down all loan applications of this kind if the loan-rate ceiling were anywhere below 50 percent and the riskless treasury bond yield were 10 percent.

Equity Participation and Moral Hazard

In this particular example the entrepreneur contributed no equity at all. Hence, the expected return on equity cannot be calculated. If the project succeeds, however, the investment yields $2 million, out of which $1.5 million must be repaid to the bank—the $1 million principal and the 50 percent interest. The entrepreneur retains $0.5 million. On the other hand, if the project fails, the bank loses $0.5 million but the entrepreneur loses nothing. Hence, even with an interest rate higher than the expected return on the investment, the entrepreneur expects to make a profit of $300,000—$.6(500,000) + .4(0).

Since the entrepreneur has nothing to lose, he or she may be more likely to take undue risks with the bank's money than would be the case if some of the entrepreneur's own capital were at stake. In technical jargon, this is known as the *moral hazard* problem. Its original application was to insurance, where full protection through insurance cover reduces the incentive to look after the insured property. So that a borrower is given an incentive to take care of the borrowed money, a bank normally insists that some equity be contributed to the project being financed. Not only does this requirement address the moral hazard issue, but it also reduces the loan's risk. For example, if the bank insisted on 25 percent equity participation, loss risk would be halved. With 50 percent equity finance, there would be no risk of principal loss although the project's failure would preclude any interest payment.

In practice, since probabilities of alternative outcomes are difficult if not impossible to assess, financial institutions develop rules of thumb with respect to equity, collateral, and even types of investments they may consider financing. Naturally, usury ceilings that keep the expected return from risky lending below the market yield on government securities discourage such lending. Funding for highly productive but risky investment projects may be impossible to obtain under these circumstances.

Loan-Rate Ceilings Discourage Small-Scale Lending

Most institutional lending rates of interest incorporate not only the pure return to the financial capital or savings, but also the costs of administering the loan. Such costs include periodic billing, bookkeeping, and other office expenses. Most of these expenses bear no relation to the size of the loan. Hence, in percentage terms the smaller the loan, the higher are the administrative costs. One would therefore expect to observe financial institutions charging higher rates of interest for small loans compared with large loans, other things being equal. To the extent that loan-rate ceilings prevent lenders from charging higher rates to reflect higher administrative costs for small loans, financial institutions simply stop offering small loans. Cheap but unavailable credit is no consolation to the small borrower.

Some Other Lending Constraints

Financial regulators have devised numerous techniques for regulating lending for one reason or another. To protect borrowers, several states prohibit lenders from charging interest on overdue interest payments. One of the side effects of this restriction is to prevent adoption of index-linked loans—debts whose remaining balances are adjusted for changes in the value of money.

Effective Maturity and Loan Indexation

Inflation reduces the effective maturity of all fixed-period loans. Take, for example, a 25-year mortgage of $100,000 at 3 percent interest under noninflationary conditions. The monthly payment is $474.21 and the remaining balance will be halved in just under 15 years.

Now suppose that inflation is running at a constant annual rate of 10 percent. In equilibrium, the nominal interest rate rises to offset this erosion in the value of money. Suppose, therefore, that the mortgage rate rises to 13 percent in such circumstances. Now the monthly payment on a 25-year, $100,000 mortgage rises to $1127.84, or by 138 percent. Clearly, such an enormous jump in the monthly payment makes it impossible for many households to borrow $100,000, despite the fact that such a sum would have been quite manageable under noninflationary conditions.

What happens is that, in real terms, the mortgage gets repaid much faster when there is inflation. In nominal terms, it now takes 20 years to halve the remaining balance. In real terms or at constant dollars, however, the remaining balance is halved in about $6\frac{1}{2}$ years. In other words, a much larger proportion of the monthly payment is, in effect, repayment of principal. The effective term of the mortgage has been greatly reduced by inflation and many households just cannot repay the mortgage that fast.

The ideal solution would be to substitute an indexed mortgage for the conventional level-payment mortgage. The remaining balance would be indexed to the price level and the interest rate would remain at 3 percent. Hence, the monthly payment again starts at $474.21. A fully indexed mortgage would have both the remaining balance and the monthly payment adjusted for inflation. Thus, after one year of 10 percent inflation, the monthly payment would have risen to $521.63 and the remaining balance ($97,272.16 before the inflation adjustment) would be $106,999.38.

Herein lies the legal problem. The nominal remaining balance of an indexed mortgage rises initially (although it always falls in real terms). If the concept of indexation is alien to the law, the only interpretation that can be placed on a rising remaining balance is that interest is being added to the principal. However, the law may prohibit interest being charged on interest owed. Hence, the legality of mortgage indexation may be dubious, despite its evident advantages.

Limitations on Loan Maturities

In 1967 the state of Maine enacted legislation limiting to 8 percent the interest rate that finance companies could charge on loan balances remaining unpaid after 36 months. In effect, this limited loan maturities to 36 months. In 1967 Maine had 116 offices operated by 28 finance companies. By 1972, 24 offices owned by 9 companies remained. By 1977 there were no finance companies doing business in Maine.

The primary reason for the sensitivity of finance company business to the maturity limitation lay in the implicit prohibition against loan refinancing. Rollover or refinancing is a standard device used by borrowers and lenders to avoid default. The remaining balance together with any unpaid interest is refinanced with a longer maturity in order to reduce the monthly payments.

Over the period 1960–1967 the net loss rate of Maine's finance companies averaged 2.2 percent annually. By 1970 the net loss rate had risen to 7.66 percent, and in 1971 it reached 8.41 percent. Borrowers in financial difficulties no longer had the opportunity of rolling over or refinancing their loans. Not only did the maturity limit put finance companies out of business, it also left many Maine residents with loan default records.[4]

Summary

1. The oldest and most pervasive government intervention in financial markets takes the form of interest-rate ceilings.

2. Ceilings on deposit rates of interest were imposed initially in the aftermath of the Great Depression to prevent waves of bank failures resulting from cutthroat competition.

3. The primary objective of deposit-rate ceilings was changed in the mid-1960s. At that time the main aim became one of keeping mortgage rates from rising.

4. When deposit-rate ceilings were binding, funds were withdrawn from depository institutions, a process known as disintermediation.

5. Deposit-rate ceilings did not prevent mortgage rates from rising but did discriminate against small savers.

6. Government subsidies to encourage thrift institutions to hold mortgages increased the size of thrifts in relation to other financial institutions but did not reduce mortgage rates.

7. The fungibility of financial capital implies that specific liabilities or loans may not be related to the acquisition of specific assets. Government efforts to increase the supply of mortgage funds have encouraged households to borrow against their homes. They have not, however, increased the proportion of houses in the household sector's asset portfolio.

8. Loan-rate ceilings can deter lending for some potentially high-yielding investment projects and can discourage financial institutions from offering small-scale loans. There is no evidence that loan-rate ceilings

[4]George J. Benston, "The Impact of Maturity Regulation on High Interest Rate Lenders and Borrowers," *Journal of Financial Economics*, 4(1), January 1977, pp. 23–49.

reduce the cost of borrowing. Rather, they may make that cost infinite. In other words, they may cut off loans entirely for some projects and some groups of the society.

9. Prohibition against charging interest on overdue interest payments may prevent adoption of index-linked loans, such as index-linked mortgages. The advantage of an index-linked mortgage in times of inflation is that it keeps initial monthly payments relatively low by preventing the effective mortgage term from shrinking.

10. Limitations placed on loan maturities can also cut off borrowing possibilities for poorer groups of the society.

11. In general, loan-rate ceilings and other limitations on terms and conditions of lending have one effect: they remove the borrowing option for at least some individuals.

Questions

1. Explain how deposit-rate ceilings caused disintermediation.

2. Explain why certain types of deposits began to be exempted from deposit-rate ceilings starting in the early 1970s.

3. How did Regulation Q discriminate against small savers?

4. Why did deposit-rate ceilings fail to reduce mortgage rates of interest?

5. Why did government subsidies to encourage thrift institutions to hold mortgages fail to reduce mortgage rates of interest?

6. Why did government mortgage purchases and government subsidies to mortgagees (people who borrow through mortgages) fail to increase the percentage of housing assets in households' asset portfolios?

7. Analyze the conditions under which the imposition of a deposit-rate ceiling could raise mortgage rates of interest.

8. Explain the concept of capital fungibility and apply it to the intended allocative effects of the All Savers Certificate program.

9. Analyze the effect of a loan-rate ceiling on financial institutions' lending behavior.

10. Why might loan-rate ceilings discourage small-scale lending?

11. How can loan indexation lengthen the effective term of a loan?

12. Who gains and who loses from binding loan-rate ceilings?

PART THREE

Depository Institutions and Money Creation

Amadeo Peter Giannini bought a safe for $750 in 1904 and, with minimal training and experience in banking, founded the Bank of Italy in San Francisco's Italian colony of North Beach. With three salaried employees—secretary, teller, and assistant cashier—the bank opened for business. Its main objective was to educate North Beachers as bank shareholders, depositors, and borrowers. Giannini became a banker to provide banking services for his compatriots in the North Beach neighborhood. His bank grew by collecting millions of small deposits and making thousands of small loans.

After satisfactory but undramatic progress, the Bank of Italy was burnt down in the fire following the 1906 earthquake. Five days later, with $80,000 in available cash reserves against deposits totaling $846,000, the bank reopened on the Washington Street wharf equipped with a plank for counter and a bag for safe. The aim was to finance reconstruction; loans were extended for rebuilding and checks for limited amounts were cashed.

Many North Beachers used a bank for the first time after the earthquake. They chose to deposit money with the Bank of Italy, money previously hidden in their homes now leveled to the ground. These new deposits were immediately lent out to finance the rebuilding. The bank's growth after the 1906 disaster was spectacular.

Having seen what benefits a neighborhood bank could bring to a community like North Beach, Giannini determined to set up branches of his bank all over California. The first out-of-town branch was opened at San Jose in 1909 and two branches were acquired by taking over a Los

From Marquis and Bessie James, *Biography of a Bank* (New York: Harper, 1954).

Angeles bank in 1913. By 1918 the Bank of Italy had 24 branches in 18 cities. By 1928 Giannini headed the second largest bank in the United States.

The bank's expansion, however, was not without its setbacks. In 1921 there was a run on the Bank of Italy's Santa Rosa branch. Many people still remembered the financial crisis of 1907, which had resulted in one bank failure in Santa Rosa. More recently, in 1918, the Santa Rosa National Bank had failed because of bad management. Deposits were not insured in those days. Unfounded rumors could—and did in this case—generate panic deposit withdrawals.

The Bank of Italy's Santa Rosa branch closed on Thursday, January 6, 1921, with $50,000 cash reserves in the vault and about $3 million deposits on the books. Next morning there was a crowd around the bank at opening time. The $50,000 cash reserves were soon exhausted and $400,000 was borrowed from the two other banks in Santa Rosa and from banks in nearby towns. That afternoon $1.5 million was brought in from the Bank of Italy's main office in San Francisco. Piles of gold coins were stacked ostentatiously in each teller's cage. The evident fact that the bank could and would meet all deposit withdrawals stopped the run by noon on Saturday, January 8.

The Great Depression of the 1930s saw the bank through two other setbacks. In 1931 Giannini's financial empire, which by now included several out-of-state banks owned by a holding company, was nearly split up and sold off by a board of directors which believed that retrenchment was the wisest part of valor. Giannini was brought back from semi-retirement by thousands of the original small stockholders to save the bank.

Disaster was again narrowly averted two years later when the bank was slated to remain closed after the March 1933 banking holiday on the recommendation of a prejudiced governor of the Federal Reserve Bank of San Francisco. The license needed to reopen was finally secured from Washington at 4:00 A.M. on March 13, just six hours before the end of the holiday.

From the Depression nadir in March 1932, deposits had doubled by 1937. In 1945 the bank's assets exceeded $5 billion, making it the largest bank in the world. The Bank of Italy was renamed the Bank of America in 1930.

6

Depository Institutions

Fractional Reserve Banking

The Bank of Italy's Santa Rosa branch held only $50,000 in cash reserves to back deposits of $3 million in 1921 because it was operating on the principle of fractional reserve banking. Under this system, a bank keeps only a fraction of its deposits in the form of cash reserves. The remaining part is used to buy income-earning assets. The Bank of Italy's most important earning assets were loans, except towards the end of World War II, when government bonds constituted its main assets. In 1921, for example, 66 percent of the Bank of Italy's deposits had been used to make loans.[1]

Origins of Fractional Reserve Banking

The origins of fractional reserve banking have been traced back at least as far as the twelfth-century Italian money changers or foreign exchange dealers in Genoa.[2] At one time, several historians believed that the Italians were taught banking by the Chinese, but there is no substantial evidence to support this theory.[3] In any event, the Genoese money changers (who were usually traders too) owned safes in which to keep their foreign currencies. It was a short step from possessing a safe to accepting deposits of others for safekeeping.

[1]Marquis and Bessie James, *Biography of a Bank* (New York: Harper, 1954), p. 142.

[2]Raymond de Roover, "New Interpretations of the History of Banking," *Journal of World History,* 2 (1954), pp. 38–76.

[3]Frank M. Tamagna, *Banking and Finance in China* (New York: Institute of Pacific Relations, 1942).

Investing Deposits With a sufficiently large number of deposits, the merchant-banker or money changer could predict quite accurately the maximum net volume of deposit withdrawals (withdrawals minus deposits) that would be made on any given day—the law of large numbers again. He could therefore use deposits to acquire income-earning assets, provided he kept sufficient cash reserves to meet possible net withdrawals. The Genoese bankers used their deposits to extend credit to customers and to participate in new trading ventures. Depositors were attracted by the offer of a share in the bank's profits. The only way bankers could make profits for their depositors was to invest a major portion of those deposits in income-earning assets.

Bank Balance Sheets

The combined balance sheet for all commercial banks in the United States on December 31, 1982, looked like this:

Assets			Liabilities		
	Billions of Dollars	*Percent*		*Billions of Dollars*	*Percent*
Cash items	201	10	Deposits	1410	71
Loans	1055	54	Nondeposit liabilities	426	22
Securities	375	19			
Other assets	341	17			
			Net worth	136	7
Total	1972	100	Total	1972	100

Source: Federal Reserve Bulletin, June 1983, p. A19.

Assets

Cash Items Cash items consist of cash held in the bank (vault cash), demand deposits held at Federal Reserve and correspondent banks by commercial banks (Box 6.1), and cash items in the process of collection. This last item consists of the value of checks deposited with the bank that are in the process of clearing. The check-clearing process is described in Box 6.2.

Secondary Reserves All cash items are highly liquid but earn no explicit income. Hence, holding cash reserves incurs an opportunity cost that has to be balanced against the liquidity benefits. To minimize holdings of non-income-earning assets

BOX 6.1
CORRESPONDENT BANKS

A bank that provides a service for another bank is called its correspondent bank. A major use of correspondent banks in the United States is for check clearing. A small bank may pay checks deposited by its deposit holders into its account with its correspondent bank. Hence, this bank maintains a deposit balance with its correspondent bank. The correspondent bank, usually a member of the Federal Reserve System, will then be responsible for clearing these checks in one of the ways described in Box 6.2. Correspondents are also used for bookkeeping services, stock market advice and dealings, representation abroad, and so on. Small bankers may use a handful of correspondent banks, while large banks may well have correspondent relationships with many banks all over the world.

while still maintaining some desired degree of liquidity, banks hold secondary reserves. These consist of very short-term loans and government securities such as treasury bills. Short-term loans take the form of bankers' acceptances, commercial paper, and call loans. *Bankers' acceptances* are drafts or bills of exchange representing short-term loans (often for foreign trade) accepted or guaranteed by the seller's bank to increase its marketability. The *draft* is an order from the buyer to pay the seller at some future date, such as the date when the shipment of goods arrives. The seller's bank may discount the draft to provide the seller with funds immediately. Then the bank can stamp "accepted" on the draft to guarantee repayment and sell it. *Commercial paper* are short-term bills issued by large corporations. *Call loans* are loans, mainly to brokers and securities dealers, that must be repaid whenever the bank demands.

Loans   Loans constitute by far the most important category of bank assets. The main types of loans are: (1) commercial and industrial loans; (2) mortgage loans; (3) loans to individuals; and (4) other loans (loans to farmers and securities dealers). On the asset side of the balance, this is where the bank's expertise is concentrated. Loans can be long term or short term, secured or unsecured, amortized or repaid fully at maturity. They may be extended in one lump sum for a specific purchase, such as an automobile loan, or may take the form of a line of credit, like credit card or overdraft balances. Bank management must choose a loan portfolio with appropriate liquidity and yield characteristics. Loan officers will then select individual loans meeting the overall management strategy that offer the highest expected return.

BOX 6.2
CHECK CLEARING

Eric Lee writes a check on his NOW account with Honolulu Federal S&L in favor of Larry Campbell, who also has an account with Honolulu Federal. Larry deposits Eric's check. Honolulu Federal, seeing that this is an "on us" check, simply credits Larry's account and debits Eric's. At the end of the month Eric gets that check back with his monthly bank statement.

Eric Lee writes another check out to Radio Shack to pay for a stereo set. Radio Shack deposits the check in its account with the Bank of Hawaii. The Bank of Hawaii takes the check to the Honolulu Clearing House, to which all depository institutions operating in Honolulu send representatives. There the check is handed over to Honolulu Federal's agent along with a lot of other checks. At the same time, Honolulu Federal will be presenting checks drawn on the Bank of Hawaii. When the clearing house closes, net balances are settled up.

Suppose that at the end of the day the clearing matrix looks like this:

Checks Payable by (thousands)	Checks Payable to (thousands)				
	American Security	Bank of Hawaii	Honolulu Federal S&L	UH Federal Credit Union	Total
American Security	—	526	313	102	941
Bank of Hawaii	475	—	258	89	822
Honolulu Federal S&L	292	333	—	55	680
UH Federal Credit Union	74	88	63	—	225
Total	841	947	634	246	2668

American Security Bank, for example, owes a total of $941,000 and is owed $841,000. The net payments picture looks like this:

	Due (thousands)
American Security	−100
Bank of Hawaii	125
Honolulu Federal S&L	−46
UH Federal Credit Union	21

Net balances can be settled in this case by American Security paying Bank of Hawaii $100,000, and Honolulu Federal S&L paying Bank of Hawaii $25,000 and paying UH Federal Credit Union $21,000. Reserves can be transferred either by trucking cash from one depository institution to another or by transferring balances held at a Federal Reserve bank (or held indirectly at a Federal Reserve bank through a Federal Home Loan bank, a correspondent bank, or the National Credit Union Administration Central Liquidity Facility).

Eric Lee writes out a third check to Angela Levin, who lives in New York. Angela deposits the check in her account with City Mutual Savings Bank. In this case, City Mutual might well deposit Eric's check in its own account with its correspondent, Chase Manhattan Bank. City Mutual has an account with Chase because this enables it to use the Federal Reserve System's national check-clearing system without being a member or holding an account with the Federal Reserve Bank of New York. City Mutual calculated the costs of alternative ways of collecting funds deposited by check into its customers' accounts and decided that, in most cases, the New York Clearing House was cheapest for local checks and the use of a correspondent, Chase, was cheapest for out-of-town checks.

Chase, in turn, deposits Eric's check in its account with the Federal Reserve Bank of New York. The Fed uses a contract air carrier to fly the check to San Francisco. At this point, the New York Fed is credited and the San Francisco Fed debited in the Interdistrict Settlement Fund, the Fed's internal bookkeeping arrangement. Now, the San Francisco Fed debits Wells Fargo's account and passes on Eric's check to the Wells Fargo Bank, because this bank is Honolulu Federal's correspondent. So Wells Fargo debits Honolulu Federal's account and sends Eric's check on to Honolulu Federal. Finally, Honolulu Federal debits Eric Lee's account and returns the check to him with his next monthly statement.

Apart from a lot of rubber stamp imprints on the back, Eric Lee's check will have the dollar amount typed in magnetic ink on the bottom right-hand corner below his signature. City Mutual did that before depositing the check with Chase. City Mutual also credited Angela Levin's account. These two operations were done manually. From then on, processing operations were carried out automatically. All the necessary information can now be read with magnetic ink character recognition equipment. Specifically, in the bottom left-hand corner of Eric's check printed in magnetic ink are Honolulu Federal's Federal Reserve District number, its correspondent bank's code number, its own code number, and Eric's account number.

Securities

Banks hold a considerable volume of securities mainly because of their liquidity attributes. The bulk of bank security holdings are U.S. treasury securities, securities of federal government agencies, and obligations of state and local governments. Unlike loans, securities can be sold quickly with small transaction costs on the stock market. Securities can be sold not only to meet deposit withdrawals, but also to extend new loans. Therefore, they act as a shock absorber against fluctuations in both deposits and loan demands of the bank's clients. As such, loans tend to increase in relation to total assets during an economic upswing and to fall during a recession.

Liabilities

Deposits   Over 75 percent of banks' liabilities consist of deposits. At the end of 1982, demand deposits represented 25 percent of total deposits, and savings deposits represented 18 percent, leaving 57 percent of deposits taking the form of time deposits. The variety of deposits offered by depository institutions has expanded rapidly since the introduction of large negotiable certificates of deposit (CDs) in 1961.

At present, depository institutions are free to offer whatever interest rate they wish on some types of deposits but not on others. This implies that banks have little influence over the volume of fixed-rate deposits, which is determined on the demand side. However, they do have a great deal of control over the volume of deposits such as large CDs, whose interest rate can be set freely by each bank.

Another distinction lies in negotiable versus nonnegotiable time deposits. Small time deposits are nonnegotiable: the deposit holder cannot transfer ownership of the deposit and may incur a penalty in asking the bank for the money back before the maturity date. Nonnegotiability makes such deposits fairly illiquid. It also ensures that the market is localized to the immediate vicinity of the bank.

CDs   Large CDs cannot be issued in denominations of less than $25,000. In practice, large CDs are usually sold in denominations of $1 million. They have fixed maturities ranging from 1 to 18 months, and most of them are negotiable. This simply means that the original buyer can sell the CD to someone else. Although the issuing bank sets the initial interest rate and is free to offer any rate it chooses, CD prices and hence yields vary as market rates move up and down.

Any bank can offer CDs if it wants to increase its resources. A profit-maximizing bank will offer CDs only if it can invest the proceeds in assets yielding a higher net return than the gross cost of the borrowed funds. Although small banks generally have to offer a slightly higher interest rate than large banks, there is a national market in CDs. Therefore, banks face a more-or-less elastic supply of funds through the CD market.

Nondeposit Liabilities

Banks raise about 25 percent of their resources from sources other than deposits. About 7 percent of the U.S. banking system's resources comes from equity capital or from shareholders. Another 7 percent is raised from short-term borrowing in the federal funds and repurchase agreement markets. The remainder is provided by lenders on the Eurodollar market and by the Federal Reserve System.

Federal Funds Market

The federal funds market was developed by Federal Reserve member banks in New York during the 1920s. Since borrowing and lending were effected by transferring deposits of member banks with the New York Fed, these loans became known as federal or fed funds. Today the federal funds market is used by over 14,000 commercial banks and by a large number of other financial institutions. Federal funds are transferred from lender to borrower through the Federal Reserve wire (Chapter 1). Most federal funds transactions are very short-term, overnight loans.

The largest banks in the United States are almost constant borrowers in the federal funds market, whereas the smaller banks are usually net lenders. Economies of scale enable large banks to arbitrage more efficiently than small banks. Hence, large banks tend to find more lending opportunities offering rates of return above the cost of borrowing money than do small banks. Large banks therefore lend until net lending and gross borrowing rates are equated at the margin, virtually unconstrained by the volume of their own resources. Excess lending is simply financed through nondeposit borrowing.

Market for Repurchase Agreements

The market for repurchase agreements (RPs) is another very short-term market. Whereas federal funds are unsecured loans, repurchase agreements are secured. The lender buys a government security from the borrower, who agrees to repurchase the security at a fixed price on a predetermined date. Commercial banks are the largest borrowers on the RP market, with the large banks again net borrowers and the small banks net lenders. The interest rate implicit in the difference between sale and repurchase prices is slightly below the federal funds rate. The lender has a secured loan, while the borrower incurs the cost of transferring the collateral. Hence, the lender is willing to accept a slightly lower yield in return for security, whereas the borrower would use the federal funds market unless compensated by a lower rate for the additional costs of providing the collateral in the RP market. Lenders in the RP market include large corporations, as well as state and local governments that are excluded from the federal funds market. For them, RPs are almost equivalent to interest-earning demand deposits.

The Eurodollar Market

Another way in which a bank can increase its resources is to borrow funds on the Eurodollar market. This market consists of dollar-denominated deposits held outside the United States. It developed in the main to avoid deposit-rate ceilings and reserve requirements imposed on deposits held in the United States. Banks abroad that accept dollar deposits generally prefer to match them with dollar-denominated assets in order to avoid the risk of exchange-rate fluctuations. Hence, U.S. banks can borrow these dollars in the Eurodollar markets at whatever the market interest rate happens to be.

Federal Reserve Discount Window

Finally, all depository institutions now have access to the Fed's discount window. Depository institutions may borrow from the Fed against eligible collateral, such as commercial paper. The interest rate charged by the Fed to the borrower is known as the discount rate.

Bank Profit-Maximizing Behavior

Fractional reserve banking enables banks to earn income from funds deposited with them. This necessarily involves *liquidity risk*, the risk of having insufficient reserves to meet deposit withdrawals. The Bank of Italy's Santa Rosa branch stopped the run (panic deposit withdrawals) on it by displaying large quantities of cash. Had the bank been unable to meet those deposit withdrawals, it would have been forced to close. The bank might then have been obliged to dispose of earning assets without delay. The less liquid assets might have been sold at substantial losses under such circumstances. Only after all depositors had been paid off would the remaining assets, if any, have been distributed among the shareholders.

Maintaining Depositor Confidence

Clearly, a bank needs to maintain the confidence of its depositors in order to maximize long-run profits (specifically, to maximize the present value of current and future profits discounted by an appropriate interest rate). The first way to sustain depositor confidence is to hold sufficient cash reserves to meet deposit withdrawals. The second way is to protect depositors from the adverse effects of credit and interest risks discussed in Chapters 3 and 4 by using the bank's own capital or equity. Actually, it is *uncertainty* about the future that explains the maintenance of a reserve/deposit ratio to meet uncertain deposit withdrawals and of an equity or net worth/asset ratio to protect depositors against the uncertain quality of the bank's loan portfolio and unanticipated changes in interest rates.

Establishing a Bank

Giannini's first task in establishing the Bank of Italy was to sell 3000 shares for $100 apiece, $50 to be paid right away, the other half in just over a year's time. His board of directors bought 905 shares, six other investors bought 475 shares. Giannini sold the remaining 1620 shares to a cross section of North Beachers—bakers, barbers, fishmongers, and grocers. In total, 160 shareholders had put up $150,000 before the bank accepted a single dollar in deposits.[4]

[4]James and James, *op. cit.*, pp. 14–15.

The Bank of Italy opened its doors on October 17, 1904, with a balance sheet position that looked something like this:

Assets		Liabilities	
Cash reserves	$133,484		
Other assets (premises, etc.)	16,516		
		Net worth (capital accounts)	$150,000
Total	150,000	Total	150,000

The sale of shares had raised $150,000, shown under net worth or capital accounts on the right-hand side of the balance sheet. Part of this sum—$16,516—had been used to buy a safe, some account books, and a counter over which banking business could be transacted. The remaining $133,484 constituted cash reserves. A small part of this was kept in the safe, but most of it was deposited with one of the larger San Francisco banks. In this balance sheet, deposits and loans—the business of banking—are both noticeable by their absence.

Depositor Protection

The situation had changed by December 31, 1904:

Assets		Liabilities	
Cash reserves	$ 89,484	Deposits	$134,000
Loans	178,000		
Other assets	16,516		
		Net worth	150,000
Total	284,000	Total	284,000

Depositors were extremely well protected at this stage. First, the Bank of Italy had cash reserves equal to 67 percent of deposits. The ratio of reserves to deposits or the reserve/deposit ratio rd was 0.67. Second, the bank's capital or net worth equaled 84 percent of its loans. This meant that the market value of the loan portfolio would have to have fallen by 84 percent before depositors' funds would have been impaired. Under normal circumstances, banks expect to lose through credit risk well under 1 percent of their loans as completely uncollectible. After all, most personal and many business loans are secured against collateral which the bank can sell if the borrower defaults. However, interest or market risk in the form of unanticipated increases in market rates of interest can reduce (and recently have reduced) market values of fixed-rate assets by substantially more than 1 percent.

The combined balance sheet of all commercial banks in the United States shown at the beginning of this chapter also suggests that, on average, depositors can be reasonably confident about the security of their money, even without deposit insurance. That balance sheet indicates that banks maintained a reserve/deposit rd ratio of 14 percent and a ratio of capital or net worth to their total assets of 7 percent at the end of 1982. Both these ratios are far smaller than were the Bank of Italy's in 1904, but they are nonetheless larger than they would be in the absence of the current regulations to which all depository institutions are now subject.

Bankers' Incentives

To maximize the overall return on its assets, a bank would try to reduce its reserve/deposit ratio to as small a fraction as possible. It would attempt to invest the maximum possible percentage of its asset portfolio in income-earning assets. With a positive spread between the net yield on assets and gross cost of borrowed funds, a bank would also try to increase its leverage as much as possible in order to maximize the return on its equity.

Depositors' Preferences

Depositors, on the other hand, would prefer their bank to maintain a reasonably high reserve/deposit ratio to meet deposit withdrawals and a rather low leverage ratio to protect them against credit and interest risks. Were liquidity risk too high or equity protection too low, depositors would move their funds to a safer depository institution in the absence of deposit insurance. Such a reaction could produce a run on the bank, one of the last things the banks' shareholders want.

Marginal Cost and Benefit of Reserves

The marginal cost of holding reserves is the foregone net marginal return from an income-earning asset i_L. In other words, the marginal cost of holding reserves is its opportunity cost in terms of foregone interest earnings. The marginal benefit is more difficult to measure because of the uncertainty about deposit withdrawals. Actually, the bank is concerned only about *net* deposit withdrawals—total withdrawals minus total deposits.

Probability of Net Deposit Withdrawals

Figure 6.1 depicts a cumulative distribution function showing the probability of net deposit withdrawals falling somewhere in the range from minus infinity to x. The probability is measured on the vertical axis and the range of net deposit withdrawals is measured on the horizontal axis. In this particular case, the probability of net deposit withdrawals falling in the range $-\infty$ to 0 ($x = 0$) is .5. In other words, there is exactly 50 percent probability of a net increase in deposits. There must therefore be a 50 percent probability of a net decrease in deposits, that is, of positive net deposit withdrawals.

Figure 6.1 illustrates the case in which expected net deposit withdrawals are zero. Were the vertical axis shifted to point A, however, ex-

Figure 6.1   Cumulative Distribution Function of Net Deposit Withdrawals

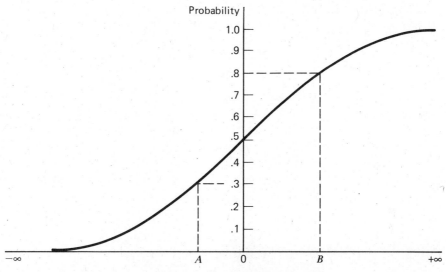

This diagram shows the probability of net deposit withdrawals falling in the range $-\infty$ to x. If $x = A$, the probability of net deposit withdrawals falling in the range $-\infty$ to A is .3 or 30 percent. If $x = 0$, the probability is .5 or 50 percent. With $x = B$, the probability is .8 or 80 percent.

pected net deposit withdrawals would be positive because there is only 30 percent probability of negative net withdrawals. Conversely, if the vertical axis were moved to B, expected net deposit withdrawals would be negative, since there is 80 percent probability of a net increase in deposits.

Reserve Holdings and Reserve Shortfalls

If the bank held no reserves at all, according to Figure 6.1, the probability of a reserve shortfall or running out of reserves on any particular day would be .5 or 50 percent ($x = 0$). If a reserve shortfall occurred, the depository institution would be forced to borrow reserves at some interest rate i_F. If the depository institution held reserves equal to B dollars in Figure 6.1, however, the probability of a reserve shortfall would fall from 50 to 20 percent. Eighty percent of the time net deposit withdrawals would fall in the range $-\infty$ to B ($x = B$) and hence could be met without the bank's having to borrow.

The expected cost of $1 shortfall in reserves equals the borrowing rate i_F multiplied by the probability of a reserve shortfall. The greater are reserve holdings (the larger is B), the smaller is the probability of a reserve shortfall and, hence, the lower is the expected cost of reducing reserves by $1. Profits are maximized when the opportunity cost of holding an extra dollar of reserves equals the expected cost of a reserve shortfall. If, for example, i_L is 15 percent, i_F is 20 percent, and the probability of a reserve shortfall is 80 percent, the opportunity cost of holding an extra dollar of reserves (15 percent) is less than the expected cost of a reserve shortfall (20 × .8, or 16 percent). In this particular case, reserves should be increased until the probability of a reserve shortfall is reduced to 75 percent (20 × .75, or 15 percent).

Condition for Zero Reserve Holdings

Today the marginal return to lending i_L and the marginal cost of borrowing i_F are virtually identical, particularly for large banks. Were i_L above i_F, banks would borrow at the low rate i_F in order to lend at the higher rate i_L. Arbitrage would (and in fact does) equate i_L and i_F, where i_F can now be defined as the federal funds rate.[5] Hence, banks hold virtually no cash reserves in excess of legal requirements to meet net deposit withdrawals. The profit-maximizing strategy is to borrow when a net deposit withdrawal occurs, rather than to hold excess cash reserves for this purpose.

Liability Management

Until the early 1960s, banks tended to concentrate on managing their assets, taking the resources at their disposal as given. That is, for the most part, they accepted deposits in a fairly passive manner. Such behavior began to change after the introduction of large certificates of deposit (CDs) in 1961.

Determinants of Bank Size

The description of the combined balance sheet of the U.S. banking system given above indicates that banks are now as active in arranging their liabilities as they are in choosing their assets. Since banks face an elastic supply of funds on such national markets as the CD market, bank size is not constrained by any fixed deposit base. Rather, it is the availability of profitable lending opportunities that limits the size of any individual bank.

In fact, a number of regulations discussed in the next chapter are designed to constrain bank size in the interests of maintaining a competitive banking industry. In the main, these regulations increase the marginal cost of raising resources as bank size grows. Hence, larger banks may require a higher marginal net return on their assets than smaller banks to remain profitable. However, economies of scale, particularly with respect to information costs, tend to offset the higher marginal costs imposed through regulation.

Portfolio Mix

Banks can actively increase their available resources by selling CDs, borrowing in the Eurodollar market, negotiating repurchase agreements, or going to the federal funds market. These constitute a bank's managed

[5]Paul DeRosa and Gary H. Stern, *In the Name of Money* (New York: McGraw-Hill, 1981), Chapter 2.

liabilities. The mix of liabilities is as crucial to a bank's profitability as the composition of its assets. If a bank believes that market rates will rise, it will sell longer-term CDs and borrow at the longer end of the Eurodollar market. Conversely, if it expects rates to fall, a bank will move to short-term RPs and borrowing in the federal funds market.

The opposite reaction takes place on the asset side of the balance sheet. If interest rates are expected to rise, the bank will buy short-term assets in the expectation that it will be able to invest these funds at higher rates when they mature. Conversely, if the bank anticipates a fall in rates, it will buy longer-term assets to lock into the present relatively high return. Hence, expectations about the future path of interest rates can affect the degree of maturity intermediation that a depository institution performs.

Summary

1. Fractional reserve banking means that banks keep only a fraction of their deposits in the form of reserves. The rest is used to acquire income-earning assets.

2. Bank assets fall into four major categories: cash items, loans, securities, and other assets. Loans represent about 55 percent of the assets of the American banking system.

3. Managing a bank's asset portfolio entails balancing liquidity, risk, and return. Liquidity incurs an opportunity cost in terms of a lower return. Higher returns may involve greater risk.

4. Over 75 percent of bank liabilities are deposits. Liability management consists of decisions about the composition and volume of a bank's liabilities. Banks can choose to sell CDs or RPs and can borrow on the federal funds and Eurodollar markets.

5. The federal funds market is used by financial institutions to borrow and lend among themselves. Immediately transactions are concluded, the loans are transferred over the Fed's wire system. Most federal funds transactions consist of overnight loans.

6. Depository institutions can maintain depositor confidence—vital for survival—by holding a sufficiently large cash reserve to meet deposit withdrawals and maintaining an equity/asset ratio high enough to protect depositors from loan defaults.

7. Depository institutions determine profit-maximizing reserve/deposit and equity/asset ratios at which marginal costs (earnings foregone) of higher ratios equal marginal benefits. With the borrowing rate i_F equal to the loan rate i_L, the profit-maximizing reserve/deposit ratio is zero. Under these circumstances, banks would always borrow reserves when required to meet net deposit withdrawals.

8. If a bank expects interest rates to rise, it will tend to shorten the maturity of its asset portfolio and lengthen the maturity of its liabilities. In this process, the extent of maturity intermediation is reduced.

Questions

1. Explain the concept of fractional reserve banking.
2. Why are cash items in the process of collection an asset?
3. How are correspondent banks used in the check-clearing process?
4. Trace the progress of an out-of-state check back to a debit from the payer's account.
5. What factors influence a bank's choice of asset portfolio?
6. What are the two main reasons that banks hold securities?
7. Why is the distinction between negotiable and nonnegotiable certificates of deposit important?
8. What is the federal funds market?
9. Why do depository institutions need to maintain depositor confidence and, in the absence of deposit insurance, how can they do so?
10. What factors determine the optimum level of cash reserves a bank should hold to meet net deposit withdrawals?
11. What is liability management?
12. What would a bank that expects interest rates to rise do to its asset and liability portfolios?

7

The Regulated Deposit Industry

Bank Failures in the 1930s

The New York stock market crashed on October 29, 1929. Industrial production, which had started to decline in August of that year, fell 26 percent in the ensuing 12 months, wholesale prices declined 14 percent, and personal income decreased 16 percent. By October 1930 the Great Depression had already been one of the most severe recessions on record. Of course, it did not end there. Indeed, that month witnessed the start of the first banking crisis. In November 1930, 256 banks with $180 million of deposits failed. There followed in December the failure of 352 banks with $370 million of deposits. In total, 7763 banks failed between 1930 and 1933. From 1921 to 1929, 5067 banks had failed. The annual average rate of bank failures more than quadrupled during the first four years of the Depression. The most serious effect of the Depression's three banking crises (1930, 1931, and 1933), however, was the reduction in the money supply.

Regulatory Response The reduction in the number of banks in the United States from 24,000 in 1929 to under 15,000 at the end of 1933, three specific banking crises during that period, disruption of financial markets, together with the disastrous monetary contraction, persuaded Franklin D. Roosevelt to "do something" moments after his inauguration. His first action was to close all the banks in the country. He then called Congress together to pass the Emergency Banking Act, which gave the president wide powers to regulate banking and foreign exchange transactions. It was under this legislation that the Bank of Italy came near to staying closed after the bank holiday ended on March 13, 1933. More than 5000 banks were not allowed to open—3000 were opened later, but over 2000 were closed for good.[1]

The ensuing two years saw a flurry of legislative activity concerned with banks and other depository institutions. Much of the present regulatory system was set up at this time. Of greatest significance was the establishment of the Federal Deposit Insurance Corporation (FDIC).

Regulations on Entry

Dual Banking System

The United States possesses what is called a *dual banking system*. A charter must be obtained from either the Comptroller of the Currency or a state chartering authority to open a new bank. Similar federal and state agencies exist to charter mutual savings banks, savings and loan associations, and credit unions. The dual nature of the banking system—national (federally chartered) alongside state banks—is largely illusory because of the FDIC.

Federal Power over State Chartering

At the federal level, the Comptroller of the Currency is required under the Banking Act of 1935 to examine capital adequacy, earnings prospects, and ". . . the convenience and needs of the community to be served . . ." before chartering a new bank. The same criteria are also to be used by the FDIC before it may insure a new state-chartered bank. Since deposit insurance, at an effective premium of $\frac{1}{30}$th of 1 percent of total deposits, is particularly attractive for a new depository institution, this condition gives the federal authorities an effective veto over the chartering policies of individual states. Indeed, prior to 1935 there was no practical restriction on entry because federal and state chartering authorities competed with each other to hand out charters. Since 1935 the number of new banks formed each year has been halved by the legal restrictions on entry.[2]

Market Value of Charter

If effective, limited entry into any industry creates a positive value for the charter or license. The chartering or licensing authority could therefore charge a market clearing price for the restricted number of licenses offered. This is sometimes done, for example, in the case of taxi licenses. Alternatively, nonprice rationing criteria can be used and the license provided free or at a price below the market clearing level. This is how bank charters are allocated.

Restricted Entry Raises Price

Irrespective of the allocation criterion, the holder of the charter or license possesses something whose value would be eroded by free entry. It is there-

[1]Milton Friedman and Anna J. Schwartz, *A Monetary History of the United States, 1867–1960* (Princeton, N.J.: Princeton University Press for the National Bureau of Economic Research, 1963), p. 425.

[2]Samuel Peltzman, "Entry in Commercial Banking," *Journal of Law and Economics*, 8(1), October 1965, pp. 11–50.

fore predictable that operators in a limited-entry industry will be strong advocates for the benefits of restrictive entry—"orderly market conditions" (whatever that may mean), higher-quality product (an argument favored by the professions), regular service (used by the transport industry), elimination of cutthroat competition and so reduced risk of failure (the standard argument of the deposit industry), and so on. The fact that restricting entry must always reduce supply and raise price is studiously ignored by both the regulators and the regulated. In the case of the deposit industry, restricting entry has indeed lowered output, raised returns, and reduced failures.[3] From 1941 to 1981 there were 20 or fewer bank failures per year. In 1940, 43 banks failed, and 42 failed in 1982.

Deposit Insurance

In an amendment of the Banking Act of 1933, Congress initiated deposit insurance, in opposition to Roosevelt and most large banks (at first Giannini was against it, but he had changed his mind after he saw its effect on depositor confidence). Insurance coverage started on January 1, 1934, and was then limited to $2500 per depositor. The ceiling was raised to $5000 in the middle of 1934 and since then has been increased in stages to $100,000 in 1980. Insurance coverage is obligatory for national banks but optional for state banks. By mid-1934, however, over 90 percent of all the banks in the country (accounting for 97 percent of total deposits) had taken out insurance coverage. By 1980 over 98 percent of the country's banks (accounting for $99\frac{1}{2}$ percent of deposits) were insured. Most of the uninsured banks are mutual savings banks chartered by Massachusetts and covered by their own state scheme.

Insurance not Based on Actuarial Principles

Deposit insurance has undoubtedly achieved its major objective—the prevention of banking panics. Indeed, deposit insurance has contributed much more to monetary stability than the establishment of the Federal Reserve System.[4] Nevertheless, it is a far from perfect system because the premium is assessed at a uniform effective rate of $\frac{1}{30}$th of 1 percent against *total* deposits. In other words, the FDIC is not run like private insurance on actuarial principles, assessing premia in accordance with risk and coverage. A large bank with a portfolio of low-risk assets and perhaps less than 50 percent of its deposits covered (because of large uninsured business and government deposits) pays a higher premium on its *insured* deposits than does a small bank with a portfolio of riskier assets and over 90 percent of its deposits insured.

[3]Samuel Peltzman, "The Costs of Competition: An Appraisal of the Hunt Commission Report," *Journal of Money, Credit and Banking*, 4(4), November 1972, pp. 1001–1004.

[4]Friedman and Schwartz, *op. cit.*, pp. 434–442.

Insurance Encourages Banks to Take Risks

The FDIC's method of assessing insurance premia actually encourages banks to acquire riskier assets than they otherwise would. Consider the following bank balance sheet:

	Assets		Liabilities	
Loans	$100	Deposits		$90
		Net worth		10

This bank can choose between two alternative loan portfolios. Portfolio A gives a 95 percent probability of a 20 percent return and 5 percent probability of -100 percent. Portfolio B has an 80 percent probability of a $42\frac{1}{2}$ percent return and 20 percent probability of -100 percent. The expected return on both portfolios is exactly 14 percent (Chapter 4).

Expected Returns on Equity

Now suppose that the deposit rate of interest (gross cost of borrowed funds) is 10 percent. If portfolio A is held, the return on equity would be 110 percent with a .95 probability and -100 percent with a .05 probability. If the portfolio yields 20 percent, it earns $20 from which $9 goes to pay deposit interest. The $10 equity earns $11 or 110 percent. If the loans default (-100 percent), equity is wiped out (-100 percent). However, -100 percent is the worst that can happen. Hence, the expected return on equity for portfolio A is $99\frac{1}{2}$ percent—$.95(10) + .05(-10)$.

The same calculation can be performed for portfolio B. The return on equity is 335 percent with a .8 probability—$100 \cdot (42.5 - 9)/10$—and -100 percent with a .2 probability. In this case, therefore, the expected return on equity is 248 percent. Clearly, risk-neutral shareholders would prefer portfolio B to portfolio A. However, portfolio B is a riskier loan portfolio than is portfolio A.

Depositor Choice without Deposit Insurance

Without deposit insurance, depositors would deposit their money in bank A holding loan portfolio A rather than in bank B holding portfolio B. For the same 10 percent deposit rate, the risk of deposit loss is 5 percent with bank A but 20 percent with bank B. Uninsured depositors would require a deposit rate of at least 30.6 percent from bank B to offset the higher probability of deposit loss. Such higher cost of borrowed funds would now reduce the expected return on bank B's equity to $99\frac{1}{2}$ percent, exactly equal to the expected return on bank A's equity. In other words, without deposit insurance, there is no incentive to hold a higher-risk loan portfolio if the expected return on that portfolio is the same as the expected return on a lower-risk loan portfolio.

Depositor Choice with Deposit Insurance   All this changes with deposit insurance. Depositors are no longer at risk and so are indifferent as to whether their money is held in bank *A* or bank *B*, provided both banks offer the same deposit rate. In this case, shareholders are no longer indifferent regarding loan portfolios *A* versus *B*. Loan portfolio *B* provides a higher expected return *to equity* than does portfolio *A*, despite the fact that both portfolios yield the same expected return. Hence, deposit insurance encourages more risk taking than is efficient. Shareholders would prefer a riskier loan portfolio *even if* its expected return were slightly lower than the expected return of a less risky portfolio.

Insurance Premia Based on Risk   Under competitive private insurance arrangements, the riskier the loan portfolio, the higher would be the deposit insurance premium. Even with a uniform deposit rate, the incentive to choose the riskier loan portfolio with the same expected yield would be offset exactly by the higher deposit insurance premium. In fact, bank soundness or solvency has been assured not by correcting the method of deposit insurance assessment but rather by imposing restrictions on the composition of bank asset portfolios and explicit payment of interest on deposits, and on "capital adequacy" requirements. Bank deregulation raises questions about the appropriate future role of the FDIC. Simulating the competitive private deposit insurance solution would be no easy task.[5]

Sound Banking

Capital Adequacy   Minimum capital requirements are imposed by the chartering authorities. Thereafter, banks are inspected regularly by the Comptroller of the Currency (national banks), the Federal Reserve System (state banks that are members of the Fed), the FDIC (state banks that are members of the FDIC), and state bank examiners (all state banks). In all cases, bank examination is aimed at maintaining "sound banking conditions." In practice, bank examiners look out for fraud (by auditing the bank's account books and adding up cash reserves), weak management (by analyzing the bank's assets, liabilities, and income statements), and capital adequacy. Assessing management and capital adequacy is based on several rules of thumb developed by bank examiners over the years.

Loan Ceilings   With minor exceptions, banks are prohibited from holding corporate stocks and real estate. They may, however, make loans and acquire bills and bonds. Loans are the least regulated bank asset simply because of the individual nature of each loan. However, there are ceilings imposed on the

[5]John H. Kareken, "The First Step in Bank Deregulation: What About the FDIC?" *American Economic Review*, 73(2), May 1983, pp. 198–203.

ratio of loans to capital or net worth for a single borrower and the ratio of real estate loans to savings deposits. Given regulators' innate caution, it is perhaps surprising to find that the bulk of bank loans is unsecured. Banks may hold U.S. treasury bills, notes, and bonds. They are also permitted to invest in "substandard" bonds—bonds rated AAA, AA, A, or BBB by the Standard and Poor's, and Aaa, Aa, A, or Baa by Moody's. Bonds issued by state and local governments as well as those issued by corporations are all "substandard" in comparison to U.S. government securities, which are considered completely safe from default risk.

Capital Adequacy versus Deposit Insurance

Because loans, whose soundness is difficult if not impossible for regulators to assess, constitute about 55 percent of banks' assets, bank regulation has emphasized capital adequacy as a substitute for detailed evaluation of loan portfolios. The method of deposit insurance assessment is responsible here too for banks' incentive to reduce their equity capital or net worth/asset ratios and, hence, to increase their leverage indefinitely. Deposit insurance is a very satisfactory substitute for equity as protection against loan defaults from the viewpoint of insured depositors. They no longer demand a higher return to compensate for a lower equity/asset ratio. They are protected at any equity/asset ratio by deposit insurance. Evidence suggests that banks have managed to respond to the incentive to substitute deposit insurance for equity capital as protection for depositors, despite regulatory attempts to ensure "capital adequacy." It seems that banks hold about 60 percent less equity capital against their insured deposits than they do against their uninsured deposits.[6] Therefore, it is not surprising that the problem of capital adequacy is of great concern to the FDIC.

Deposit-Rate Ceilings

The 1933–1935 banking legislation prohibited banks from paying interest on demand deposits. This prohibition was effectively removed in 1979 by the cumbersome procedure of the automatic transfer service (ATS), which permitted banks to transfer funds automatically between savings and checking accounts such that checking account balances were always zero. All funds available in the tandem accounts earned the maximum $5\frac{1}{4}$ percent interest allowed under Regulation Q, which sets a maximum interest-rate ceiling for savings deposits. These deposit-rate ceilings applied to all FDIC-insured banks.

On January 1, 1981, banks were allowed to offer NOW accounts—a checking account whose balance earned $5\frac{1}{4}$ percent interest—in place of the ATS. At the same time, mutual savings banks, savings and loan associations, and credit unions were also permitted to offer interest-earning checking accounts. The maximum interest-rate ceiling was $5\frac{1}{4}$ percent for mutual savings banks and savings and loan associations, but 7 percent for

[6]Samuel Peltzman, "Capital Investment in Commercial Banking and Its Relationship to Portfolio Regulation," *Journal of Political Economy*, 78(1), January/February 1970, pp. 1–26.

credit unions. It was at this point that these financial institutions, which had previously been deliberately differentiated by specific regulations, moved more rapidly towards greater homogeneity. At the end of 1982, Super NOW and money market deposit accounts with minimum balances of $2500 on which banks could offer any interest rate they chose were introduced (Chapter 1). Under the Depository Institutions Deregulation Act of 1980 all interest-rate ceilings are to be phased out completely by 1986.

Welfare Loss from Deposit-Rate Ceilings

Substitution of Services for Interest In fact, banks were able in effect to evade the prohibition against paying interest on demand deposits by offering other banking services free or priced below cost. One bank service that was typically provided at no charge in the 1970s was check clearing. Box 6.2 on check clearing makes it clear that check processing is far from costless. Indeed, a local check cost about 20¢ to process, whereas an out-of-state check cost about 50¢ in 1982. If a depositor maintains an average balance of $600 and writes four out-of-state and 20 local checks a month, the implicit return on that balance is 12 percent a year in the form of free check-clearing services alone (Box 7.1).

BOX 7.1
ELECTRONIC FUNDS TRANSFER SYSTEMS

Checks are the dinosaurs of the deposit industry. Both volume and costs have exploded over the past three decades. Sheer size makes checks unwieldy. Their function—transfer of deposit balances—is being taken over by electronic funds transfer systems (EFTS). The simplest EFTS device is the automatic teller. By inserting a card (possibly disguised as a credit card) and punching in a number code, the depositor accesses his or her account and can then withdraw funds in cash, transfer funds from savings to checking account and vice versa, ascertain balances in both accounts, or make a deposit.

Automatic tellers are now being linked up all over the country so that customers can get at their own accounts wherever they happen to be. For example, the Bank of America has joined forces with other banks throughout the United States to set up the PLUS system. It handles all normal automatic teller transactions, except deposit taking. Nationwide automatic teller systems work like this. Suppose Nancy Crockett, who has an account with Riggs National Bank in Washington, D.C., is vacationing in Hawaii. Wanting to withdraw some cash, she finds one of the First Hawaiian Bank's automatic tellers, inserts her automatic teller card, punches in her access code, and receives cash. Instantaneously, four balances are changed—her balance at Riggs is debited, Riggs' balance at the Richmond Fed is debited,

Wells Fargo's balance at the San Francisco Fed is credited, and the First Hawaiian Bank's balance with Wells Fargo is credited. (Wells Fargo is First Hawaiian's correspondent bank.) Clearly, the process is exactly the same as check clearing, but it is done with electronic impulses rather than paper. It is much cheaper and infinitely faster than check clearing.

Another EFTS device is the point-of-sale terminal. The terminal is installed by a retail store, for example, and linked up to the same system as automatic tellers. Now when Eric Lee buys his stereo set from Radio Shack, his EFTS card is inserted into Radio Shack's terminal and he punches in his access code (or, possibly, identifies himself by allowing his fingerprint to be scanned and identified electronically). Eric's account at Honolulu Federal is debited and Radio Shack's account with the Bank of Hawaii is credited. Funds are transferred from Honolulu Federal to the Bank of Hawaii through the Honolulu Clearing House or their correspondents, both of whom maintain accounts with the the San Francisco Fed. Point-of-sale terminals are likely to be commonplace by the mid-1980s.

The third EFTS facility is the automated clearing house. It works in the opposite direction to the regular clearing house. Instead of going to the automatic clearing house to collect on checks deposited with it, the depository institution takes a computer tape on which is written instructions to make payments. The automatic clearing house is therefore a computer terminal linked up to the same system as automatic tellers. It is already in extensive use for paying salaries, utility bills and installment loan repayments. To use the automatic clearing house, the payer or the payer's depository institution has to know the payee's account number; this information together with the amount due is encoded on the computer tape.

EFTS has been surprisingly slow to catch on. However, with the abolition of deposit-rate ceilings, depositors may well be faced with the full costs of check clearing. Their response is likely to be rather rapid adoption of EFTS, a method of transferring funds at a small fraction of the cost of transferring funds by check.

Welfare Cost of Interest Prohibition

Substitution of nonprice for price competition or free banking services for a competitive interest payment, as a result of restrictions on interest payments, is inefficient from the social viewpoint. In other words, it reduces social welfare. In the case of free check-clearing services, many more checks are written than would be the case if costs were charged to the check writer. Individuals are encouraged to write checks in situations where they value the check-clearing service less than its cost. Therefore, the cost of check-clearing services exceeds its value. Society would increase its welfare by reducing the resources (labor, capital, and materials) used up in processing checks and allocating them to other, higher-valued activities. This, of course, happens automatically when competitive pricing of check clearing deters check writers from writing checks for whose processing costs they are unwilling to pay.

Demand for Check Clearing

Every time a check is used, the check writer implicitly makes a demand on the banking system's check-clearing facilities. As with other demands, the demand for check clearing is a function of its price. Figure 7.1 represents the aggregate demand curve for check clearing, showing that as the price declines, the quantity demanded increases.

If the check-clearing service is offered free of charge to depositors, they will write a volume of checks equal to Q_1 in Figure 7.1. If the cost of clearing each check is 25¢, the banking system incurs a total cost of $\$Q_1(.25)$. If banks charged 25¢ per check, the demand for check clearing and hence the number of checks written would fall to Q_0.

Figure 7.1 shows that people demand check-clearing facilities of Q_0 if they are charged 25¢ per check. Evidently, the benefits of writing more than Q_0 checks are not worth 25¢ per check. Indeed, the value of additional check clearing falls along the demand curve as quantity rises from Q_0 to Q_1.

Figure 7.1 Welfare Effect of Below-Cost Checking

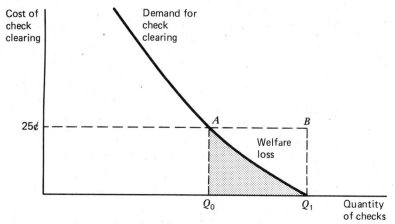

This diagram illustrates the welfare loss from providing check-clearing facilities at zero cost to the user. When the price is zero, demand for check clearing is Q_1. If the cost of clearing each check is 25¢, the marginal value of additional check clearing falls below cost from Q_0 to Q_1. Depositors would be better off, and the banks no worse off, if banks paid depositors $\$Q_1(.25)$—the cost of clearing Q_1 checks—and, at the same time, charged 25¢ per check. Then depositors would gain $\$(Q_1 - Q_0)(.25)$ or $A B Q_1 Q_0$ and lose only the smaller shaded area under the demand curve. This shaded area represents the user value of check clearing between Q_0 and Q_1.

Welfare Gain from Switch to Cost Pricing

When banks offer free check-clearing facilities instead of charging 25¢ a check, the volume of checks to be cleared rises from Q_0 to Q_1. The extra cost incurred by the banks equals $\$(Q_1 - Q_0)(.25)$. Suppose that the banks gave $\$Q_1(.25)$ to their depositors and at the same time imposed a 25¢ charge for each check cleared. Depositors would receive $\$Q_1(.25)$ and spend $\$Q_0(.25)$, giving a net cash gain of $\$(Q_1 - Q_0)(.25)$, the rectangular area represented in Figure 7.1 as $A\,B\,Q_1\,Q_0$. They would lose the benefits of additional check clearing represented by the shaded area under the demand curve between Q_0 and Q_1. Hence, they are better off with $\$Q_1(.25)$ and a 25¢ per check charge than they were with free check clearing. The banks, on the other hand, are unaffected. The welfare loss of free check clearing, therefore, is $\$(Q_1 - Q_0)(.25)$ minus the shaded area under the demand curve between Q_0 and Q_1.

Advantage to Banks

In the absence of tax distortions, depository institutions would cost-price their services when allowed to compete freely for deposit balances. Nonprice competition is inefficient from the depository institution's viewpoint too. As was shown above, free check clearing is valued below cost by depositors precisely because they are encouraged to overuse the service to the point where marginal utility is zero. Banks, therefore, could offer less than $\$Q_1(.25)$ to depositors as interest payment but charge 25¢ per check and still attract depositors from banks offering free check clearing and no deposit interest.

Tax Distortion

In fact, however, interest income on household sector deposits is subject to income tax, whereas the nonmoney or nonpecuniary benefits of free banking services are not. Therefore, even in a completely unregulated world, some banks would offer some banking services at below cost and reduce interest payments. The substitution of below-cost services for interest income could attract individual depositors to the point at which they valued $1 spent on these services at the *after-tax* yield from $1 in interest.

Costs Unrelated to Size of Balances

Nonprice competition in the form of free check-clearing services is inefficient from the depository institution's viewpoint for a second reason. The cost of the services provided are quite unrelated to the size of the balance held. Depository institutions want to encourage customers to hold larger balances so that they have more resources with which to acquire income-earning assets. Providing free check-clearing services simply encourages more check writing, however. The relationship between average balances held and number of checks written is tenuous at best. Hence, direct interest payment can be used to encourage what the depository institutions want—deposit balances—rather than what they do not want—a greater number of checks to process.

Reserve Requirements

Pre-MCA Differential Treatment

Before the Monetary Control Act (MCA) of 1980 becomes fully effective, reserve requirements will continue to differ among depository institutions. Member banks of the Federal Reserve System are obliged to maintain vault cash plus zero-interest-earning deposits with the Fed equal to various minimum proportions of deposits and certain managed liabilities. These proportions rise with deposit size but are lower for time than for demand deposits. Nonmember state banks follow state regulations with respect to reserve requirements, and minimum reserve requirements imposed by states are typically lower than those imposed on member banks. Furthermore, such requirements can often be satisfied by holding interest-earning assets such as treasury bills.

Uniform Imposition of Reserve Requirements

Under the Monetary Control Act of 1980, however, all depository institutions will be obliged to maintain required reserves in the form of vault cash and zero-interest-earning deposits with or passed through to the Federal Reserve banks. At the end of the phase-in period, reserve requirements will be imposed uniformly across all depository institutions, as shown in Table 7.1. The Monetary Control Act of 1980 empowers the Fed to fix the precise ratios of reserves to transactions balances—checking, NOW, and share draft—and transferable time deposits held by corporations that depository

Table 7.1 Uniform Reserve Requirements to Cover All Depository Institutions by 1993

	Initial Level	Legal Range
Regular Reserves[a]		
1. Transactions accounts		
First \$X million[b]	3	3
Over \$X million	12	8 to 14
2. Nonpersonal time deposits		
under $2\frac{1}{2}$ years maturity	3	0 to 9
3. Eurocurrency liabilities	3	0 to 9
Supplementary reserves[c]		
1. Checking accounts	0	0 to 4

[a] Vault cash and zero-interest deposits with or passed through to a Federal Reserve Bank by a pass-through agent.

[b] The cutoff started at \$25 million, but is changed annually by 80 percent of the change in total transaction deposits. For 1983, for example, the cutoff had risen to \$26.3 million.

[c] These reserves will receive an interest rate set in relation to the average yield on the Fed's own asset portfolio.

Source: Federal Reserve Bulletin, various issues.

institutions must hold. Under the same legislation, all Federal Reserve bank services, such as check clearing and borrowing from the discount window, were made available to all depository institutions. Fees for such services are the same for members and nonmembers of the Federal Reserve System.

Reserve Shortfalls and Federal Funds Borrowing

The existence of required reserves alters the analysis of the optimal reserve/deposit ratio discussed in Chapter 6. Now, instead of having to borrow on the federal funds market at an interest rate i_F only when reserves are fully exhausted, depository institutions must borrow when actual reserves fall short of their required levels.

Deposit Rates and the Reserve Requirement Tax

Required reserves impose a cost or tax on depository institutions. If these institutions face an elastic demand for loans at an interest rate i_L, the reserve requirement tax is borne by depositors (and, to some extent, bank stockholders). If the banks' borrowing rate in the event of reserve shortfalls i_F equals i_L, then banks have no incentive to hold any excess reserves at all, as shown in Chapter 6. In this case, the competitive deposit rate of interest i_D with a required reserve ratio of rrd is

$$i_D = (1 - rrd) \cdot i_L - ic, \tag{7.1}$$

where ic represents the marginal costs of financial intermediation per unit of deposits. For example, with rrd equal to 0.1, i_L 10 percent, and ic 3 percent, i_D would be 6 percent. The higher is rrd, the lower is i_D for any given i_L.

Balance Sheet Illustration

This result is illustrated by the following bank balance sheet:

Assets	Liabilities
Required reserves $100	Deposits $1000
Loans 900	

If loans earn 10 percent, the bank makes $90 from its loan portfolio each year. Intermediation costs are 3 percent of deposits, or $30. Hence, the bank has $60 to distribute as interest and so depositors receive a deposit rate of interest of 6 percent.

Reserve Requirement Tax and Inflation

The reserve requirement tax rises with the nominal market rate of interest and hence, in equilibrium, with the inflation rate. Suppose ic is zero, i_L is 3 percent under noninflationary conditions, and rrd is 0.1. Then, equation (7.1) shows that i_D is 2.7 percent. The tax rate is 10 percent.

Now consider the situation with 10 percent inflation and i_L equal to 13 percent. Then i_D is 11.7 percent. Of this, 10 percent is required simply to maintain the deposit's original purchasing power. Hence, the real deposit rate has fallen from 2.7 to 1.7 percent, or the tax on the real return has risen from 10 percent to 43.3 percent. In real terms, the reserve requirement drives an increasing wedge between the gross cost of borrowing and the net return to lending as inflation accelerates.

Reserve Requirements to Reduce Bank Failures

The original aim of minimum reserve/deposit ratio regulations was to reduce the risk of bank failures. However, if the required (minimum) reserve/deposit ratio is 10 percent and there is a deposit withdrawal of $100, only $10 can be taken from required reserves to meet the withdrawal. All other required reserves are needed to maintain the 10 percent required reserve ratio against the remaining deposits. Unless the required reserve ratio is 100 percent, required reserves are not a depository institution's most readily available (liquid) assets to meet deposit withdrawals.[7] As was discussed earlier, reserve shortfalls are met by the bank's borrowing in the federal funds or RP markets.

Reserve Requirements to Prevent Concentration

Required reserves are also used to promote competition in the deposit industry. Most regulations discussed so far are designed to restrict competition and hence to reduce the probability of bank failures. Two sets of regulations, however, are aimed at increasing competition or, more precisely, at preventing excessive concentration in the deposit industry. The required reserve ratio is higher the larger the volume of deposits. This would mean that, in the absence of any economies of scale, bigger depository institutions would not be able to offer as high a deposit rate of interest i_D as smaller ones, as seen from equation (7.1). The higher the required reserve/deposit ratio *rrd,* the lower is the competitive deposit rate of interest i_D.

Scale Economies in Banking

In fact, there do appear to be economies of scale in the deposit industry. Factor inputs are used in the process of accepting deposits and acquiring income-earning assets. One empirical study found that a 10 percent increase in size is accompanied by only a 9 percent increase in cost.[8] Bigger depository institutions would therefore be able to offer higher deposit rates than smaller institutions because *ic* is lower, were it not for the higher required reserve ratios to which they are subject. This device of increasing

[7]Marvin Goodfriend and Monica Hargraves, "A Historical Assessment of the Rationales and Functions of Reserve Requirements," *Federal Reserve Bank of Richmond Economic Review,* 69(2), March/April 1983, pp. 3–21.

[8]Ernst Baltensperger, "Economies of Scale, Firm Size, and Concentration in Banking," *Journal of Money, Credit and Banking,* 4(3), August 1972, pp. 467–488.

marginal reserve requirements enables the smaller depository institutions to survive and hence deters concentration in the deposit industry.

Since smaller institutions are less efficient than larger ones because of the phenomenon of economies of scale, the end result of differential reserve requirements is to foster a less concentrated but also a higher-cost industry than would otherwise emerge. However, differential reserve requirements themselves tend to create apparent scale economies. Large banks subject to higher reserve requirements have to be more efficient than smaller banks maintaining lower reserve ratios in order to survive. Nevertheless, international comparisons also tend to support the view that banking is subject to economies of scale.

Reserve Requirements and Monetary Control

Reserve requirements also constitute one of the instruments of monetary policy. As will be shown in Chapter 8, an increase in the required reserve ratio reduces the money supply. However, reserve requirements have not actually been used for this purpose to date, because of their differential impact on member and nonmember banks. For some time the Fed has worried about loss of membership caused by the reserve requirement burden. In terms of bank numbers, Fed membership declined from 50 percent in 1950 to 40 percent in 1976. Over the same period membership measured in terms of gross deposit volume fell from 86 to 74 percent.[9] With uniform treatment of all depository institutions under MCA, the Fed may make more active use of this potential instrument of monetary policy.

Branching Regulations

The second set of regulations to prevent excessive concentration concerns branching. States can be divided into three roughly equal groups: those permitting statewide branching (mainly in the west), those permitting limited branching, such as within the same city or adjacent counties (mainly in the east), and those allowing a bank to operate only one banking office, also called unit banking (mainly in the midwest). Federally chartered banks are subject to state regulations concerning branching. There are also state-imposed restrictions against interstate banking. However, there have been a number of major exemptions to or breaches in these regulations in recent years (Box 7.2). Starting in 1975 with Maine, several states have enacted legislation to permit interstate branching. Nationwide branching will probably be fairly common by the end of the 1980s.

Concentration versus Competition

Concentration of the deposit industry in large urban areas is much lower in unit banking than in branch banking states. This fact is used in support of the argument that restricting branching promotes competition. Unit bank-

[9]Goodfriend and Hargraves, *op. cit.,* p. 9.

BOX 7.2
FIRST INTERSTATE AND FIRST NATIONWIDE

Interstate branching was prohibited under the McFadden Act of 1927. However, this law does not prohibit a bank holding company from owning banks in more than one state. The Transamerica Corporation, for example, was established in 1928 by A. P. Giannini to circumvent the McFadden Act. By 1956 Transamerica owned banks in 11 western states.

The 1956 Bank Holding Company Act prohibits the interstate acquisition of banks by holding companies, except for acquisitions specifically permitted under the laws of the acquired bank's state. A growing number of states now allow such acquisition. In addition, the 1956 law restricted the activities in which bank holding companies could engage through their affiliates. The 1956 Bank Holding Company Act contained a "grandfather" clause permitting existing bank holding companies to continue in business.

As a result of the 1956 Bank Holding Company Act, Transamerica was split into two companies, one of which owned nothing but banks. The new bank holding company was called Firstamerica when it started business in 1958. This name was changed to Western Bancorporation in 1961. Finally, on June 1, 1981, Western Bancorporation and all of its 21 banks became known as First Interstate—the holding company is First Interstate Bancorp and each bank is First Interstate Bank (Los Angeles), First Interstate Bank (Denver), and so on.

In general, the Federal Home Loan Bank Board, which charters federal savings and loan associations, does not permit interstate branching. There is, however, a "limited exception" to this policy which was clarified in 1981. When an interstate takeover would prevent the failure of a savings and loan association whose accounts are insured by the Federal Savings and Loan Insurance Corporation, interstate branching may be permitted.

Citizens Savings of California acted under the "limited exception" policy in 1981 to acquire two failing savings and loan associations on the east coast. One was West Side Federal S&L of New York, the other Washington S&L of Florida. On January 1, 1982, Citizens changed its name to First Nationwide Savings.

ing also means that loan application decisions must be made on the spot locally and not in some remote head office miles away. This is also used in support of unit banking: there is less discrimination against customers living far from the big urban centers.

On the other hand, there are about 50 percent more bank offices per capita in statewide branching than in unit banking states. A branch can be operated profitably in a community too small to sustain a complete bank.

There may be more competition in smaller towns in statewide banking states; two or more branches may coexist whereas only one (if any) unit bank could survive there. Finally, the success of a branch banking network, as Giannini knew so well, depends on knowing and catering to local conditions. It necessitates considerable autonomy for the local branch manager and his or her loan committee. The best advertisement a bank has is its local lending activities.

Summary

1. Entry into the banking industry is regulated by licensing. Restricted entry has lowered output, raised price, and reduced bank failures.

2. Deposit insurance is perhaps the most significant financial innovation in the United States this century. However, the uniform premium encourages banks to hold riskier assets than they otherwise would. If insurance costs are based on failure risk, this incentive would be removed.

3. Regulations to promote sound banking include capital adequacy, ceilings on loan to capital ratios for individual loans, and deposit-rate ceilings.

4. Deposit-rate ceilings encourage substitution of nonprice for price competition. Providing free check-clearing facilities to depositors is a typical form of nonprice competition. It results in a welfare loss because it encourages depositors to write more checks than they would if they had to pay the resource costs.

5. Reserve requirements against deposits impose a tax on depositors. The tax rises with the required reserve ratio and with the inflation rate.

6. The required reserve ratio is higher for deposits over a total given value than for deposits of a smaller total size. This differential reserve ratio is designed to prevent concentration in the banking industry. It raises intermediation costs for large banks and hence protects small banks.

7. Restrictions on branching are also designed to prevent concentration in the banking industry. Although these restrictions have been successful at the national level, they do not necessarily produce more bank competition at the local level.

Questions

1. Analyze the effects of restrictions on entry into the banking industry.

2. How does the present system of deposit insurance encourage excessive risk taking by banks?

3. How would the absence of deposit insurance influence banks' attitudes towards risk?

4. What is capital adequacy and how can deposit insurance be a substitute for it?

5. In what ways can banks substitute nonprice for price competition when ceilings on deposit rates of interest are binding?

6. Demonstrate that the provision of free check-clearing facilities is suboptimal from the social welfare viewpoint.

7. How could a tax distortion encourage banks to offer services at below-cost prices rather than interest on deposits?

8. How do reserve requirements impose an implicit tax on depositors?

9. How does the reserve requirement tax rise as inflation accelerates?

10. How can reserve requirements be used to prevent concentration in the banking industry?

11. What are the purpose and the effect of branching regulations?

12. How and why would you expect the balance sheet of a unit bank to differ from that of a multi-branch bank?

8 Bank Creation of Money

Goldsmith-Bankers

Banks create money through fractional reserve banking. To understand the essential elements of this process, consider the activities of the London goldsmith-bankers who rose to prominence in the second half of the seventeenth century.[1] Goldsmith-bankers became recognized deposit takers following the general insecurity accompanying England's Civil War (1642–1649), which had been preceded in 1640 by Charles I's requisitioning merchants' deposits with the Mint in the Tower of London. Naturally, the king's action destroyed the reputation of the Mint as a safe custodian of surplus cash. In the future, merchants employed the somewhat less fortified facilities of the goldsmiths.

Deposit Receipts as Bank Notes

Bank notes originated from goldsmiths' deposit receipts. By 1660, goldsmiths' receipts, promissory notes, or bank notes circulated freely as a medium of exchange. To the extent that one gold coin was deposited in exchange for one receipt or bank note, goldsmiths had no effect on the overall amount of money in circulation. Paper money was simply substituted for the gold that was withdrawn from circulation. However, fractional reserve banking enabled the goldsmiths to issue more bank notes than there were gold coins to back them, thus *creating* money.

Fractional Reserves and Money Creation

Suppose that goldsmith-bankers had discovered that a ratio of gold reserves to deposits or notes of 10 percent was sufficient to meet virtually any net deposit withdrawal or note redemption into gold. After receiving new

[1]Richard D. Richards, *The Early History of Banking in England* (London: King, 1929).

deposits of £100 in gold coin, a banker would be holding more reserves than necessary. Hence, he might have loaned out £90 of the initial deposit. At this point, the money stock was increased. The new deposits simply changed the composition of the money stock —£100 more bank notes or deposit money and £100 less gold currency in circulation. Of course, the gold coins still existed, but, as bank reserves, they were no longer counted as part of the money supply, since they no longer constituted currency in circulation. The goldsmith-banker created money not by accepting deposits, but rather by putting a fraction of these deposits back into circulation. He did this by making loans and buying other earning assets.

Multiple Money Creation

Suppose that the £90 loan was spent and that these gold coins were re-deposited with another banker. This second banker neither knew nor cared that these particular gold coins had already been deposited once before. This banker simply realized that he now had excess gold reserves. Hence, he might have extended a loan of £81, keeping £9 as a reserve against the £90 deposit. The second goldsmith-banker increased the money supply by an additional £81.

These two bankers created £171 in new money against the initial £100 deposit. The process known as multiple creation of money had begun. A total of £190 in new bank notes had been issued and £19 in gold coins had been withdrawn from circulation and held as reserves. In this particular example, therefore, the banking system multiplied money tenfold by issuing £190 in bank notes against £19 in gold coin reserves.

Multiple Money Contraction

Had those new depositors withdrawn their £100 in gold coins, the bank would have found its reserve ratio falling below 10 percent. This bank held only £10 of the deposits as reserves and so would have had to use £90 of reserves backing other deposits to meet these withdrawals. The bank could have increased its reserve ratio back to 10 percent by calling in the £90 loan. If this produced a deposit withdrawal of £90 from the second bank, that bank might have called in its £81 loan too. Deposits and loans would have been contracted by £190 and £171, respectively. Furthermore, the money supply would have been reduced by £171. Deposit withdrawal, therefore, can produce a multiple contraction in the money supply.

Deposit Money

The main purpose of depositing gold with a goldsmith-banker was to reduce the risk of loss or theft. If the gold was exchanged for an equal value of bank notes, however, the only advantage was a reduction in the weight of a given sum of money. Loss and theft of bank notes was just as likely as loss and theft of gold coins. Hence, many depositors preferred to receive nonnegotiable deposit receipts, whose loss or theft did not necessarily involve deposit loss, rather than bank notes payable on demand to the bearer. If bank notes were not issued in exchange for deposits, however, other ways of withdrawing or transferring deposits had to be devised.

Origin of Checks

Checks were used first in fourteenth-century Italy, although they were not called checks until the eighteenth century. In those days depositors normally had to visit their bank to make a withdrawal or a transfer to someone else's account. The transfer order was given orally. However, if a customer was unable to visit the bank because of absence or illness, a written transfer order could be used. The transfer order became known as a check after the Bank of England began providing its customers with special printed order forms with a counterfoil, stub, or "check" as a safeguard against fraud. Today, some checks have counterfoils, but many do not.

Advantage of Checks

The check has one important advantage over deposit receipts or bank notes as a means of transferring the ownership of a deposit. It can be made payable to a specific individual or company. Only after it has been endorsed by the payee (person or company being paid) does it have any value to a third party. Hence, it is a convenient and safe method of making payments by mail. Of course, the drawback from the recipients' viewpoint is that there is always a possibility that there may be insufficient funds in the payer's account.

Checks and Bank of England Monopoly over Note Issue

Checks became the most popular way of transferring ownership of deposits held in London banks after the Bank of England was granted a monopoly of note issue in the London area in 1844. The switch-over from deposit receipts in the form of bank notes to deposit receipts in the form of a bookkeeping entry and transferability of ownership by check was not traumatic. The deposit balance and the checkbook fulfilled much the same functions as bank notes had. The checking account balance was and still is money. In the United States at the present time not only commercial banks but also mutual savings banks, savings and loan associations, and credit unions create money by offering checking deposits.

Multiple Deposit Creation

Federal Reserve Notes

Today Federal Reserve notes perform much the same function as gold did in the days of the goldsmith-bankers. Suppose that the Federal Reserve buys treasury bills from an individual for $100,000 in newly printed Federal Reserve notes. That individual now deposits the notes in his or her checking account at a bank. The bank has an increase in assets (the notes) and in liabilities (the checking account balance) of $100,000. Had this bank been satisfied with its reserve/deposit ratio rd of, say, 0.1 or 10 percent before the new deposit, it would now have too high a ratio of reserves to deposits. This reserve/deposit ratio includes both required reserves and any (possibly zero) excess reserves held solely to meet net deposit withdrawals. The first reaction of a bank holding $90,000 in excess reserves is to lend these reserves out or to buy an interest-earning asset.

In either case, the $90,000 excess reserves are drawn down and this particular bank is in equilibrium again. However, almost immediately, another bank takes a deposit from whoever received the $90,000. This second bank may now have excess reserves of $81,000 which it, in turn, lends out or uses to buy interest-earning assets.

Lending-Depositing-Lending Sequence In theory, this lending-depositing-lending sequence could be repeated indefinitely after the initial injection of Federal Reserve notes, with the sum declining by 10 percent, the reserve/deposit ratio rd, each round. In this case, the total increase in deposit money ΔD generated by an injection of Federal reserve notes equal to ΔR can be expressed

$$\Delta D = \Delta R \cdot [1 + (1 - rd) + (1 - rd)^2 + \cdots + (1 - rd)^\infty] \quad (8.1)$$

Equation (8.1) is another infinite geometrically declining series, similar to equation (3.7). In this case, however, the sum of an infinite geometrically declining series of this form can be expressed

$$R + R \cdot x + R \cdot x^2 + R \cdot x^3 + \cdots + R \cdot x^\infty = R/(1 - x) \quad (8.2)$$

Here, x equals $(1 - rd)$. Hence, ΔD equals $\Delta R/[1 - (1 - rd)]$, or $\Delta R/rd$. With ΔR of $100,000 and rd equal to 0.1, ΔD equals $1 million. In other words, the $100,000 injection of Federal Reserve notes produces an increase in deposits of $1 million.

Bank Behavior and Multiple Deposit Creation The same result can be derived in another way. Suppose all depository institutions wish to maintain the following relationship between their reserves R and their deposits D:

$$R = (rd) \cdot D \quad (8.3)$$

Since the banks cannot fix the overall level of reserves, they can satisfy the relationship in equation (8.3) only by expanding deposits through the lending-depositing-lending process until

$$D = R/rd \quad (8.4)$$

In this example, the change in R is $100,000 and rd equals 0.1. Consequently, D is expanded by $1 million.

High-Powered Money   Federal Reserve banks actually supply reserve money, also known as *high-powered money H,* in two forms. Federal Reserve notes are one form of reserve or high-powered money. Another kind is bank deposits with Federal Reserve banks. As was discussed in Chapter 7, reserve requirements can be satisfied by holding Federal Reserve notes as vault cash or deposits with the Fed. For the purpose of satisfying reserve requirements, they are perfect substitutes.

High-powered money also consists of reserves deposited by depository institutions indirectly with the Fed through correspondent banks, the Federal Home Loan banks (for mutual savings banks and savings and loan associations), and the National Credit Union Administration Central Liquidity Facility (for credit unions' deposits). These institutions are known as pass-through agents. The depository institutions' reserves, then, consist of their vault cash and balances maintained in a Federal Reserve bank or a pass-through agent.

For most analytical purposes, however, it is more useful to define high-powered money H as reserves R (depository institution deposits with the Fed and pass-through agents plus vault cash) and currency in circulation CC:

$$H = R + CC \qquad (8.5)$$

Currency in Circulation and Money Creation

Currency Leakages   Each time a deposit is made, there is a leakage from the circular flow of lending, depositing, and lending that takes place between the banks and the nonbank private sector. Part of each deposit leaks out of this circular flow into reserve holdings. There is, in practice, a second leakage in the form of currency holdings by the nonbank private sector. Money is not held solely in the form of deposits. Indeed, almost 30 percent of M1 is currency in circulation. Hence, the ratio of currency to deposits cd is about 0.4. This implies that, on average, only 60 percent of loans made from transactions-type M1 deposits are returned to the banking system as additional deposits.

Currency Leakage Reduces Deposit Creation   The leakage into currency holdings reduces the magnitude of deposit creation from a given increase in high-powered money. Currency in circulation CC is high-powered money which is not available to the banking system for multiple deposit expansion. Suppose that the public maintains a ratio of currency to deposits cd of 0.2 and that depository institutions have a reserve/deposit ratio rd of 0.1. Now the Federal Reserve System injects $100,000 of high-powered money into the economy by buying government bonds from the public. Of this $100,000, only $83,333 is deposited, while

$16,667 remains as currency in circulation. Hence, the banks start the process of deposit creation with fewer reserves. Furthermore, each round of the lending-depositing-lending process produces additional leakages into currency holdings.

Currency and Deposit Creation The public's preference for currency holding in relation to its deposits can be expressed by the equation

$$CC = (cd) \cdot D \tag{8.6}$$

Depository institutions maintain a relationship between reserves and deposits that can be written

$$R = (rd) \cdot D \tag{8.7}$$

Adding equations (8.6) and (8.7) produces

$$CC + R = H = (rd + cd) \cdot D \tag{8.8}$$

Equation (8.8) can be rearranged after dividing both sides by $(rd + cd)$:

$$D = H/(rd + cd) \tag{8.9}$$

The greater the value of cd and/or rd, the smaller is D for any given H.

High-Powered Money and the Money Stock The money stock M consists of currency in circulation CC plus various types of deposits D, depending on the particular definition of money chosen:

$$M = CC + D \tag{8.10}$$

Since CC equals $(cd) \cdot D$ from equation (8.6), equation (8.10) can be rewritten

$$M = (1 + cd) \cdot D \tag{8.11}$$

Finally, substituting equation (8.9) into equation (8.11) gives

$$M = H \cdot (1 + cd)/(rd + cd) \tag{8.12}$$

Money Supply Multiplier

The ratio of money to high-powered money is known as the *money supply multiplier m:*

$$m = M/H \qquad (8.13)$$

which can be rewritten

$$M = m \cdot H \qquad (8.14)$$

Substitute the right-hand side of equation (8.12) into the left-hand side of equation (8.14):

$$H \cdot (1 + cd)/(rd + cd) = m \cdot H \qquad (8.15)$$

which can be rearranged to express the money supply multiplier in terms of the reserve/deposit and currency/deposit ratios:

$$m = (1 + cd)/(rd + cd) \qquad (8.16)$$

Determinants of the Currency/Deposit Ratio

Further understanding of the money supply process entails analysis of the determinants of cd and rd. The currency/deposit cd ratio is determined by the factors that affect the demands for currency in circulation CC and deposits D. One might reasonably assume that currency and deposits are substitutes. This means that demand for currency will be influenced positively by its own yield i_C (invariably zero) and negatively by the return on deposits i_D. Conversely, the demand for deposits will increase with a rise in i_D but will decrease with a rise in i_C. In the absence of deposit insurance, the demand for deposits will also decrease with a rise in the probability of depository institution failure F.[2] In addition, both demands may be affected by other variables such as the rate of return on bonds (which is closely related to the bank lending rate i_L), the level of income, and population density (and, hence, proximity to a bank branch). The demand for currency is also influenced positively by the income tax rate t. This is so because tax evasion is facilitated by cash transactions, and the incentive to evade taxation is related positively to the tax rate. Since cd equals CC/D, cd is itself determined by factors affecting CC and D. Hence, cd might be expressed

$$cd = f(\overset{+}{i_C}, \overset{-}{i_D}, \overset{+}{F}, \overset{+}{i_L}, \overset{+}{t}) \qquad (8.17)$$

General Functional Form

The way the relationship is expressed in equation (8.17) is known as the *general functional form* $f(...)$. Unlike the other equations used so far, this one does not specify the precise form of the relationship. It could be linear:

$$cd = b_0 + b_1 i_C + b_2 i_D + b_3 F + b_4 i_L + b_5 t \qquad (8.18)$$

[2]Arthur E. Gandolfi, "Stability of the Demand for Money during the Great Contraction—1929–1933," *Journal of Political Economy*, 82(5), September/October 1974, pp. 969–983.

with b_1, b_3, b_4, and b_5 taking positive signs and b_2 a negative sign. Alternatively, the relationship might be logarithmic. If the true functional form is unknown or irrelevant for the purpose at hand, the general functional form may be used. The signs above each variable denote the direction of influence of an increase in the particular variable on the dependent variable cd. For example, an increase in the probability of bank failure F increases the currency/deposit ratio cd in the absence of deposit insurance.

Determinants of the Reserve/Deposit Ratio

In general, the reserve/deposit ratio is a function of the bank lending rate i_L, the bank borrowing rate i_F, and the required reserve ratio rrd, as discussed in Chapters 6 and 7. If i_F exceeds i_L by a sufficient margin, the profit-maximizing reserve/deposit ratio rises with an increase in i_F and falls with a rise in i_L. Hence, rd can be expressed in general functional form:

$$rd = f(\overset{-}{i_L}, \overset{+}{i_F}, \overset{+}{rrd}) \tag{8.19}$$

Determinants of the Money Supply Multiplier

The money supply multiplier m increases as both cd and rd fall, as can be seen from equation (8.16). It is clear that m declines with a rise in rd, since rd appears in the denominator of the right-hand side of (8.16). Provided rd is less than one, m also declines with a rise in cd, despite the fact that cd appears in both the denominator and the numerator. Given rd less than one, an increase in cd must raise the denominator by a larger percentage amount than it raises the numerator. Hence, m must decline. Equations (8.17) and (8.19) can be substituted into (8.16) to produce the following expression for m:

$$m = f(\overset{-}{i_C}, \overset{+}{i_D}, \overset{-}{i_L}, \overset{-}{i_F}, \overset{-}{F}, \overset{-}{t}, \overset{-}{rrd}) \tag{8.20}$$

Money Supply in Functional Form

Finally, equation (8.20) can be substituted into equation (8.14):

$$M = f(\overset{-}{i_C}, \overset{+}{i_D}, \overset{-}{i_L}, \overset{-}{i_F}, \overset{-}{F}, \overset{-}{t}, \overset{-}{rrd}) \cdot H \tag{8.21}$$

In other words, more money is created in the lending-depositing-lending sequence, given the volume of high-powered money, the higher is i_D, and the lower are i_C, i_F, F, t, and rrd.

Lending-Depositing-Lending Sequence

The result given in equation (8.12) can also be derived from the lending-deposit-lending sequence illustrated earlier. With the leakage into currency in circulation, deposits increase in the lending-depositing-lending process as follows:

$$\Delta D = [\Delta H/(1 + cd)] \cdot [1 + (1 - rd)/(1 + cd) + (1 - rd)^2/(1 + cd)^2$$
$$+ \cdots + (1 - rd)^\infty/(1 + cd)^\infty] \tag{8.22}$$

or

$$\Delta D = [\Delta H/(1 + cd)]/[1 - (1 - rd)/(1 + cd)] \qquad (8.23)$$

or

$$\Delta D = \Delta H/(rd + cd) \qquad (8.24)$$

Equation (8.22) shows that the initial injection of high-powered money suffers an immediate currency leakage $[\Delta H/(1 + cd)]$ before any of it gets into the lending-depositing-lending sequence. Thereafter, it suffers a reserve leakage $(1 - rd)$ and a currency leakage $1/(1 + cd)$ each time round the circle.

At the same time, currency in circulation is building up through these leakages in the following way:

$$\Delta CC = [\Delta H \cdot cd/(1 + cd)] \cdot [1 + (1 - rd)/(1 + cd) + (1 - rd)^2/(1 + cd)^2$$
$$+ \cdots$$
$$+ \cdots + (1 - rd)^\infty/(1 + cd)^\infty] \qquad (8.25)$$

or

$$\Delta CC = [\Delta H \cdot cd/(1 + cd)]/[1 - (1 - rd)/(1 + cd)] \qquad (8.26)$$

or

$$\Delta CC = \Delta H \cdot cd/(rd + cd) \qquad (8.27)$$

Now $\Delta D + \Delta CC$ is ΔM. From (8.24) and (8.27),

$$\Delta M = \Delta H \cdot (1 + cd)/(rd + cd) \qquad (8.28)$$

which is identical to equation (8.12).

Money Supply in the United States

Table 8.1 shows the U.S. M1 money stock and its determinants over the period 1959–1982. During these years, M1 increased by 240 percent, high-powered money H rose by 295 percent, and the money multiplier decreased by 14 percent. The decrease in the money multiplier does not completely offset the difference between the rates of growth in M1 and high-powered money. However, when the rates of change are expressed in continuously compounded form, the difference between the rates of growth in money and high-powered money exactly equals the rate of change in the money supply multiplier:

Table 8.1 U.S. Money Stock and Its Determinants, 1959–1982 (average of daily figures for December; billions of dollars; seasonally adjusted)

Date	M1	H[a]	m	CC	cd	rd
1959	140.9	44.3	3.18	28.9	0.26	0.14
1960	141.9	44.5	3.19	29.0	0.26	0.14
1961	146.5	45.7	3.21	29.6	0.25	0.14
1962	149.2	47.1	3.17	30.6	0.26	0.14
1963	154.7	49.4	3.13	32.5	0.27	0.14
1964	161.9	51.9	3.12	34.3	0.27	0.14
1965	169.5	54.7	3.10	36.3	0.27	0.14
1966	173.7	56.8	3.06	38.3	0.28	0.14
1967	185.1	60.5	3.06	40.4	0.28	0.14
1968	199.4	64.8	3.08	43.4	0.28	0.14
1969	205.8	67.9	3.03	46.1	0.29	0.14
1970	216.5	72.0	3.01	49.1	0.29	0.14
1971	230.6	77.1	2.99	52.5	0.29	0.14
1972	251.9	84.2	2.99	56.8	0.29	0.14
1973	265.8	90.3	2.94	61.5	0.30	0.14
1974	277.4	98.3	2.82	67.8	0.32	0.15
1975	291.0	104.5	2.78	73.8	0.34	0.14
1976	310.4	112.0	2.77	80.6	0.35	0.14
1977	335.5	121.4	2.76	88.6	0.36	0.13
1978	363.2	132.2	2.75	97.4	0.37	0.13
1979	389.0	142.5	2.73	106.1	0.38	0.13
1980	414.5	155.0	2.67	116.2	0.39	0.13
1981	440.9	162.7	2.71	123.1	0.39	0.12
1982	478.5	175.1	2.73	132.6	0.38	0.12

[a]Adjusted for changes in reserve requirements.

Source: Economic Report of the President, 1983, pp. 233, 234, and 239.

$$\Delta\ln(M1) = \Delta\ln(H) + \Delta\ln(m)$$
$$(122\%) \quad (137\%) \quad (-15\%) \tag{8.29}$$

Increase in *H*, Decrease in *m*

Equation (8.29) shows that M1 increased solely as a result of the increase in high-powered money. Indeed, had there been no change in H, the money supply would have fallen because of the decline in m. The general point to note, however, is that the change in m over this period was small relative to the change in H. Changes in high-powered money were far more important than changes in the money supply multiplier.

Changes in the Money Supply Multiplier

The money supply multiplier fell on average by two-thirds of a percentage point a year over the period 1959–1982. As can be seen from Table 8.1, the relatively small change in the money supply multiplier was a result of opposing movements in the currency/deposit and reserve/deposit ratios. The currency/deposit ratio increased gradually until 1973, after which it rose more rapidly until 1980. The reserve/deposit ratio was virtually constant until 1976, after which it declined from 14 percent to 12 percent by 1982.

Since 1973 nominal interest rates have increased dramatically. With respect to the currency/deposit ratio, the rise in market yields i_L on close substitutes for demand deposits, such as money market mutual funds shares, produced substitution out of M1-type deposits. Hence, cd rose. On the other hand, the increase in i_L spurred technological innovations to economize on excess cash reserve holdings on the part of the depository institutions. Higher market rates of interest also increased the reserve requirement tax. There was also, therefore, a greater incentive to avoid or reduce this burden by substituting nondeposit for deposit liabilities and dropping membership in the Federal Reserve System. Hence, rd fell.

Stability of Money Supply Multiplier

Given high and volatile market rates of interest, numerous regulatory changes, and important innovations in the deposit industry over the past decade, it is perhaps somewhat surprising to find that the money supply multiplier has been so stable. The long-run stability of the money supply multiplier makes the Fed's task of controlling the money supply that much easier. If m is predictable, the Fed can control the money supply provided that it has control over high-powered money. The next part of the book focuses on the Federal Reserve System and monetary policy techniques designed to affect the money stock.

Summary

1. Fractional reserve banking involves multiple deposit creation because reserves deposited in one depository institution are used to acquire income-earning assets and eventually become deposits in other institutions.

2. Originally, banks issued bank notes in exchange for deposits of gold coin. At a later stage, nonnegotiable deposit receipts or passbook entries were used. Checks then developed as a means for transferring or withdrawing deposit balances.

3. The process of money creation can be viewed as a circular sequence of lending-depositing-lending. Each time round the circle there is a leakage into reserve holdings.

4. High-powered money is created by Federal Reserve banks in the form of Federal Reserve notes and depository institutions' deposits (directly or indirectly) with the Fed. It is held by the public as currency in circulation and by depository institutions as reserves.

5. A second leakage in the circular lending-depositing-lending process involves holdings of currency in circulation. If individuals choose to hold some given fraction of their money in currency form, the process of deposit expansion will increase demand for currency in circulation. This, in turn, creates a leakage of high-powered money from the deposit industry.

6. The money supply multiplier m is the ratio of the money supply to high-powered money M/H. It is determined by the public's currency/deposit cd ratio and the depository institutions' reserve/deposit rd ratio, since $m = (1 + cd)/(rd + cd)$.

7. The currency/deposit ratio is determined by returns on currency, deposits, and other financial assets, the risk of bank failure, and tax rates. In practice, cd has risen rather smoothly in the United States since 1959.

8. The reserve/deposit ratio is determined in the main by the required reserve ratios. It is also determined by the return on income-earning assets and the cost of borrowing funds to meet net deposit withdrawals. Since 1959 the reserve/deposit ratio adjusted for reserve requirement changes has been remarkably stable.

9. The money supply M is related to high-powered money H in the relationship $M = H \cdot (1 + cd)/(rd + cd)$.

10. Over the period 1959–1982, M1 increased 240 percent and H increased by an even larger percentage amount. Hence, m fell. This can be deduced from the relationship $\Delta \ln(M1) = \Delta \ln(H) + \Delta \ln(m)$.

Questions

1. Explain how banks can create money.

2. What are the advantages and disadvantages of checks vis-à-vis bank notes as a means of transferring claims against a deposit?

3. How does the lending-depositing-lending sequence illustrate the process of multiple deposit creation?

4. What is high-powered money, where does it come from, and who holds it?

5. Explain how high-powered money can leak out of the banking system during the process of deposit creation.

6. Derive the relationship between deposits and high-powered money, taking the reserve/deposit and currency/deposit ratios as stable behavioral relationships.

7. What is the money supply multiplier and what determines its size?

8. Derive the relationship between the money stock and high-powered money, taking the reserve/deposit and currency/deposit ratios as stable behavioral relationships.

9. What variables might be expected to influence the currency/deposit ratio?

10. What variables might be expected to influence the reserve/deposit ratio?

11. What might explain the concomitant increase in the currency/deposit ratio and decline in the reserve/deposit ratio in the United States over the past decade?

12. Explain the general functional form expression for the money supply.

PART FOUR

The Federal Reserve System and the Implementation of Monetary Policy

Alexander Hamilton was born in 1757 on Nevis, a tiny island in the Caribbean. His father deserted the family when Hamilton was 9. His mother died three years later. At the age of 12, Hamilton set up his own trading business. Most of his fellow freshmen entering New York's Columbia University in 1772 had somewhat more sheltered childhoods. Just five years later Hamilton was George Washington's chief of staff.

The American Revolution was responsible for Hamilton's meteoric rise through the military. That revolution, like the French Revolution of 1789, the Russian Revolution of 1917, and the Chinese Revolution of 1949, was paid for with paper money. With no powers to levy taxes, the Continental Congress issued $242 million in paper money between 1775 and 1779. Individual states issued a combined total in paper money of $210 million over the same period. The ensuing inflation was spectacular. In 1778 a pair of shoes cost $5000, a complete set of new clothes ran over $1 million.

Much of the paper money had been printed specifically to pay the troops. With both Continental Congress and state paper money rapidly becoming worthless (this is the origin of the phrase "not worth a Continental"), Alexander Hamilton and others became increasingly concerned about disaffection spreading through the ranks. It was in 1779 that Hamilton—entrepreneur, scholar, and soldier—wrote a treatise on public finance which addressed the problem of stabilizing the currency of the United States. His proposed solution was to establish a national bank, the Bank of the United States. The bank would take over the paper money as both its capital and its liabilities. It would then run itself

From John Kenneth Galbraith, *Money: Whence It Came, Where It Went* (Boston: Houghton Mifflin, 1975); Gail E. Makinen, *Money, Banking, and Economic Activity* (New York: Academic Press, 1981); Forrest McDonald, *Alexander Hamilton: A Biography* (New York: Norton, 1979).

on principles of sound banking. How convertibility of paper money into gold would ever be restored was given little thought. Hamilton's proposal was shelved.

For the next ten years American money remained in shambles while Hamilton involved himself in state and local politics. By 1786, however, he knew where he was going—to be the first U.S. minister of finance. He got that job—Secretary of the Treasury—in 1789. By now the Constitution prohibited both national and state governments from issuing paper money. In an effort to tidy up some of the financial debris still left over from the Revolution, Hamilton assumed the debts of the states and the Continental Congress and paid out one cent in specie or "hard" money (gold and silver coins) for every Continental paper dollar surrendered. Hamilton was also responsible for the establishment of a mint in Philadelphia to produce the $10 gold eagle containing $247\frac{1}{2}$ grains of gold and a $1 coin of $371\frac{1}{4}$ grains of pure silver. Thus was the official mint ratio of 15 to 1 adopted.

Hamilton's bank was finally set up in 1791. Some very significant changes had been made to his earlier proposal. Modeled closely along the lines of the Bank of England, the Bank of the United States was chartered for 20 years with an authorized capital of $10 million, of which $8 million was to be privately subscribed in hard money and only $2 million to be contributed by the federal government in the form of bonds. The Bank's head office was in Philadelphia, but it established ten branches mainly on the eastern seaboard, where they collected import duties.

The establishment of the Bank of the United States ushered in a 20-year period of monetary stability. The bank was a useful fiscal agent for the federal government. It promoted capital mobility through its branch network. It developed correspondent relationships with European banks, thereby facilitating capital inflows from abroad. Finally, and most important, it imposed the tenets of sound banking on the relatively few state-chartered banks, preventing them from overissuing bank notes. It did this by presenting such notes for conversion into hard money on a regular basis. Furthermore, the bank refused to accept notes of any bank that did not pay out specie on demand. It also acted as a lender of last resort to "good" state banks.

In this light, it seems surprising indeed that the bank's charter was not renewed in 1811. The explanation lies in the age-old political conflict between creditors and debtors. But that is another tale taken up in the introduction to Part 7. Suffice it here to say that the demise of the Bank of the United States was followed by more than a doubling of the supply of paper money within five years, the suspension of convertibility by banks outside New England, proliferation of state-chartered banks and counterfeit bank notes—in other words, monetary chaos. In 1816, the Second Bank of the United States was chartered under virtually the same legislation as its predecessor.

9

Central Banking and the Federal Reserve System

Central Banking Functions

Origins of Central Banks

Central banks are relative newcomers on the financial scene. The oldest is the Riksbank of Sweden, established in 1656. However, the Swedish Riksbank has performed a full range of central banking functions only since 1897. Essentially, central banking was pioneered by the Bank of England, founded in 1694. The Bank of England's development has had an important influence on the form and functions of most other central banks, including the Swedish Riksbank, the Bank of the United States, and the Federal Reserve System. The Bank of England's influence has been due, in large part, to the writings by Walter Bagehot on the subject of central banking and, in particular, the Bank of England's "proper" role. One of Bagehot's most important books is *Lombard Street,* which was first published in London in 1873.

Establishment of the Bank of England

The Bank of England, like most other central banks established before the twentieth century, was set up to raise funds for the government to finance a war. In return for a loan to the government of £1.2 million, the Bank of England was granted a charter giving it a monopoly of joint stock banking with limited liability. No other bank in England was permitted the legal protection of limited liability, nor could any other bank incorporate as a joint stock company, even with unlimited liability, until 1826. This restriction meant that all the other English banks remained rather small sole proprietorships or partnerships.

Acceptability of Bank of England Notes

The Bank of England was not empowered or obliged to carry out specific central banking functions, as they are recognized today. To be sure, it could issue bank notes, but so could all other banks. Indeed, the Bank of England did not acquire a monopoly over the supply of currency notes until 1844. Even then, the monopoly held only in the immediate vicinity of London. Nevertheless, its privileged position as a joint stock company, banker to the government and hence holder of the government's gold reserves gave Bank of England notes widespread acceptance and liquidity. These notes were used for virtually all large transactions in London during the eighteenth century. By the second half of that century almost all the other banks in London had stopped issuing their own notes.

Banker to Government and Commercial Banks

Herein lies the origin of two central banking functions—banker to the government and banker to the commercial banks. Because of the general acceptability of Bank of England notes, the other banks found it convenient to open accounts with the Bank of England. These smaller banks could then withdraw their deposits in the form of Bank of England notes, which their own customers preferred increasingly to gold for making payments. An additional advantage was that the smaller banks could deposit their gold, which was costly to store and guard, with the Bank of England for safekeeping.

Note Issue Monopoly in 1844

In the first half of the nineteenth century there was much discussion about the government's responsibility over the money supply. The special status of the Bank of England was also brought into question. After a number of banking panics, these debates culminated in the Bank Charter Act of 1844. In effect, this legislation gave the Bank of England a monopoly, albeit a limited one, over note issue.

Lender of Last Resort

It was also, not coincidentally, during the first half of the nineteenth century that the Bank of England assumed another central banking function—lender of last resort. The Bank of England first discounted, or bought at less than face value, bills issued by the smaller banks in 1797. The banking panics of 1825 and 1837, which resulted in many bank failures, generated considerable criticism against the Bank of England. Why, it was asked, could not the Bank of England help the smaller banks at such times? In response, it began to assist other financial institutions during crises by rediscounting, or buying *again* at a discounted price, bills of exchange which the smaller banks had discounted for merchants and traders. By selling these bills—their earning assets—to the Bank of England, the smaller banks were able to meet depositors' cash withdrawals. Panics were averted at no cost to the Bank of England. Indeed, the bank made a profit!

Expansion of Bank of England Notes

But how did the Bank of England get the money to rediscount bills at such times? In practice, deposit withdrawals from the smaller banks were typically satisfied by the provision of Bank of England notes; there was still confidence in the Bank of England, even if none in the smaller banks. Some of the extra supply of cash could come from the notes held in reserve by the Bank of England itself. However, the 1844 Bank Charter Act set a limit to the amount of new notes which the Bank of England was allowed to print. Nevertheless, during two subsequent banking panics, the Bank obtained special permission from Parliament to print extra notes.

Maintaining Gold Cover and Bank Rate

Had the Bank of England done nothing except print up more notes, confidence in Bank of England notes would soon have eroded. That bank, like all other banks, needed to maintain a reserve ratio or *gold cover* such that convertibility of notes into gold could be maintained. The Bank of England maintained convertibility of its bank notes into gold, even during a banking panic, through interest rate manipulation. If the Bank of England needed more gold, it raised its *bank rate,* the rate at which it lent to the other banks. As a market leader, the Bank of England's interest rate influenced all other interest rates in London. Higher interest rates in London attracted gold inflows from abroad. Most of this gold seeking out a higher return on savings eventually found its way into the Bank of England in the form of deposits.

Maintaining Confidence in the Monetary System

By now the Bank of England had assumed the broader central banking function of preserving confidence in the country's money and banking systems. On the one hand, it ensured that its bank notes could almost always be converted into gold. On the other hand, it came to the rescue of the smaller banks to prevent runs developing into panics. As was discussed in Chapter 6, banks can never meet all deposit withdrawals of panic dimensions under a fractional reserve system. Yet, to avert a panic, banks *must* meet all deposit withdrawals. Central banks can provide the necessary reserves by buying commercial banks' income-earning assets. Today, few central banks are seriously restricted in the amount of currency they may print for such rescue operations.

Central Bank Lending to the Government

Today, most central banks are bankers of their governments and of the commercial banks. As the government's banker, the central bank normally maintains government deposits and lends to the government, either by making advances, or by buying treasury bills or longer-term government securities in the *open* market. *Open market operations* by the central bank serve two functions. First, the central bank can lend to the government by buying government debt. Second, open market operations change the stock of high-powered money H in an amount equal to the value of government securities purchased. Hence, open market operations constitute one of the instruments of monetary policy.

Central Bank Lending to Commercial Banks As banker to commercial banks, the central bank holds the banks' deposits and lends to the commercial banks by discounting (still called rediscounting in a number of countries) bills and by extending advances or overdrafts. The central bank can make loans directly at its official discount rate or it can provide cash reserves indirectly to the commercial banks through open market operations. If banks are selling government securities in order to increase their cash reserves, the central bank can buy such securities in the market to increase the aggregate supply of reserves.

Establishment of the Federal Reserve System

The Fed was established as the central bank of the United States under the Federal Reserve Act of 1913 and started operations in 1914. Its original functions were to provide an "elastic" currency, facilities for discounting commercial banks' holdings of commercial bills, and better bank supervision. Membership in the Federal Reserve System was made obligatory for nationally chartered banks but voluntary for state-chartered banks. Of the 14,436 insured banks in the United States at the end of 1982, 5618 were members of the Federal Reserve System. Of the 5618 member banks, 4579 were nationally chartered banks and 1039 were state-chartered banks.

Elastic Currency Banking panics occurred periodically in the United States throughout the nineteenth century and in 1907. Typically, the crisis originated in the loss of bank reserves that occurred regularly at harvest time each year. Then the demand for currency rose and demand for bank deposits fell. About once a decade this seasonal increase in the currency/deposit ratio over strained the banking system. A few banks would run short of reserves and panic deposit withdrawls would follow.

Under its mandate to provide an elastic currency, the Fed was expected to supply reserves to the banking system when deposits were withdrawn and to remove them when currency was subsequently redeposited. Apart from forestalling runs on the banking system, the provision of reserves when the currency/deposit ratio rose stabilized the money supply. The increase in high-powered money offset the decline in the money supply multiplier.

Discounting The elastic currency was provided through the discounting facilities offered by the Fed to its members. At harvest time, the Fed discounted bills for member banks, in this way performing its "lender-of-last-resort" function

tion. The bills were bought with new Federal Reserve notes. Hence, high-powered money was increased to replenish the banks' reserves. To reduce high-powered money later, the Fed simply stopped replacing maturing bills with new ones. In this way, loan repayments produced a reduction in outstanding Federal Reserve notes.

Supervision The Fed had some self-interest in supervising member banks. When it discounted a bill for a member bank, that bank guaranteed repayment (as it does in the case of bankers' acceptances). Therefore, even if the borrower went broke, the Fed got paid, provided the bank was still sound. This, then, was one of the reasons behind giving supervisory powers to the Fed. A great deal of attention was focused on ensuring that the Fed would always be amply protected against possible loss.

Organization and Functions of the Federal Reserve System

The Fed has changed considerably since it started business in 1914. Today, for example, all depository institutions have access to the Fed's services, such as its check-clearing system, discount facilities, and so on. The Fed's functions have also evolved. Its main task now is to implement monetary policy aimed at keeping prices or the value of money stable. There is, however, considerable disagreement over the proper function of the Fed. Recently, for example, some members of Congress proposed that the Fed should implement policies aimed at bringing down real or inflation-adjusted rates of interest. Indeed, Congress has legislated a smorgasbord of incompatible, if not unattainable, objectives for the Fed.

Structure of the Fed The Fed consists of twelve Federal Reserve banks spread around the United States, and the Board of Governors in Washington, D.C., as shown in Figure 9.1. The Fed is a unique central bank in this respect. All other central banks have one head office in the nation's capital city and perhaps small branches in other major urban centers. In other countries, monetary policy is formulated in and executed by head office. In the United States, monetary policy is formulated in Washington but executed primarily in New York.

The Board of Governors Between 1914 and 1933 there was little centralized authority in the Federal Reserve System, despite the existence of a Board of Governors from the very beginning.[1] Indeed, until 1928 the New York Fed under its governor

[1]On the status ladder of Washington hierarchy, President Wilson placed the Board "right after the fire department."

Figure 9.1   Geography of the Federal Reserve System

January 1978

Source: Federal Reserve Bulletin, April 1983, p. A88.

(now known as president) Benjamin Strong exerted much independence. Today, however, power is centralized in Washington under the seven members of the Board of Governors. The members of the Board are nominated for 14-year, nonrenewable terms by the president of the United States and confirmed by the Senate. The chairman of the Board, also nominated by the president and confirmed by the Senate, serves as chairman for only four years, not necessarily coincident with the president's term of office. This four-year term is renewable and, in any event, exchairmen are entitled to serve out their full 14-year Board membership. The chairman of the Board of Governors wields considerable power.

Indeed, it has been said that the chairman of the Fed is the most powerful individual in America after the president of the United States. Certainly, the current (1984) chairman, Paul Volcker, has at least as much influence over macroeconomic policy as the Secretary of the Treasury and is a considerably more prominent public figure. Volcker definitely leads his Board in the directions he thinks appropriate.

The power of the Board of Governors springs from three sources. First, the Board determines reserve requirements and margin requirements, as shown in Figure 9.2. Until 1980 the Board also determined deposit-rate ceilings. Second, the Board constitutes a majority on the Federal Open Market Committee (FOMC), which is charged with determining and implementing the nation's monetary policy. Finally, the Board exercises general supervision over the Federal Reserve banks.

Federal Open Market Committee   The Federal Open Market Committee or FOMC consists of the seven governors plus five presidents of Fed banks. The president of the New York Fed is automatically a member of the FOMC, since the New York Fed

Figure 9.2   Monetary Policy Making in the Federal Reserve System

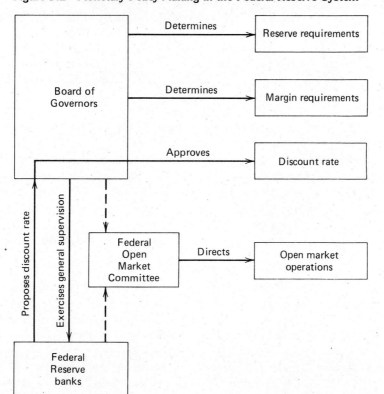

Source: Federal Reserve System, *Purposes and Functions*, 1974, p. 50.

implements the Fed's open market policies. The other four positions rotate among the remaining eleven Fed bank presidents. The FOMC meets about once a month in Washington, D.C., and sometimes holds emergency meetings by conference calls. The FOMC's main task is to set the monetary targets and then to determine the appropriate path for reserves. The FOMC might well be regarded as the apex of the Federal Reserve System. The FOMC's policies are implemented primarily through purchases and sales of government securities by the Federal Reserve Bank of New York. These transactions in government securities constitute open market operations and are by far the most important instrument of monetary policy.

The Federal Reserve Banks

The Federal Reserve Act split the country into twelve districts, each with its own Federal Reserve bank. Every Fed bank has a board of nine directors—three bankers elected by the member banks, three nonbank business people also elected by the member banks, and three people appointed by the Board of Governors. The chairman and vice-chairman of a Fed bank's board are selected by the Board of Governors from among the Board's appointees. In practice, the Fed bank itself often proposes candidates for the six elected directors. The board of directors selects the president of the Fed bank, with the approval of the Board of Governors. Informally, the Board frequently suggests names of candidates.

As well as participating in the making of monetary policy, the Fed banks carry out the housekeeping chores of central banking. They have primary responsibility for the supervision of financial institutions under their jurisdiction, run a national check-clearing system and the Fed's wire service, replace worn currency with new notes, collect vast quantities of statistics, and act as fiscal agent for the U.S. government.

Discount Policy

The Fed banks also implement monetary policy. Each Fed bank sets its discount rate, the rate at which it will lend to depository institutions in its district. However, the Board of Governors has the ultimate authority over the discount rate through its veto power. All Fed banks' discount rates move to new uniform levels within two weeks of any change. In reality, the Fed banks give advice on the discount rate and can delay a change for up to two weeks.

More important is the fact that each Fed bank administers its own discount window and decides on each individual application. Since there is a considerable amount of nonprice rationing at times, the Fed banks do influence monetary policy directly through their behavior towards borrowers at the discount window.

New York Fed

Each Fed bank offers advances, discounts, and check-clearing facilities to the depository institutions in its district, thus acting as the bankers' bank. The New York Fed, however, is the only Fed bank that engages in open market operations. It also conducts most of the Fed's foreign exchange business. The New York Fed holds about 25 percent of the system's total assets. Another 25 percent is held by the Chicago and San Francisco Feds.

Fed Bank Research Each Fed bank has a research department staffed mainly by economists. Their primary function is to prepare briefing papers for the FOMC meetings and for the Fed Board's committee meetings. However, these research departments also undertake basic research on a range of monetary issues. The Board of Governors also has a large staff of economists. Among various other channels, research findings can influence policy through the staff briefings prepared for each member of the FOMC before the monthly meeting. The St. Louis Fed has probably exerted more influence on monetary policy over the past two decades than any other Fed bank, through the policy-oriented research work conducted in its research department.

Central Bank Independence

Central bank functions described above are performed not with the objective of maximizing profit, but rather in the public interest. In this sense, therefore, one could argue that the central bank is a part of the central government just like the ministry of finance or department of the treasury.

On the other hand, there is a strong tradition behind the independence of the central bank. The case for central bank independence rests on the belief that governments would be tempted to use the central bank to create an excessive amount of cash if they possessed unrestricted control over it. It was for this reason that the Bank of England remained a privately owned joint stock company until 1946.

Independence of the Fed Central bank independence was strongly supported at the time the Fed was established. Monetary history attested to the view that government involvement in the money supply process invariably resulted in debasements and inflation. For the United States, the Civil War provided a relatively recent case in point. Hence, the Federal Reserve Act of 1913 gave the Fed a considerable degree of independence.

First, members of the Board of Governors are appointed for 14-year, nonrenewable terms. The terms overlap so that it is almost impossible for one president to appoint a majority in less than eight years. Second, the Fed has its own budget not subject to congressional appropriation or outside audit. Indeed, the Fed makes a sizable profit from its income-earning assets that is transferred to the Treasury.

Congressional Control In fact, however, the Fed cannot behave just as it pleases. Congress established the Fed and could amend the Federal Reserve Act if it wished. Indeed, Congress requires the Fed to report to it twice a year on past and future monetary policy. Hence, the objectives and performance of monetary policy are subjected to congressional scrutiny at least twice a year.

Administration Control

The administration exerts even more influence on the Fed than does Congress. For one thing, the president will appoint at least one Fed chairman during each four-year term. However, that power may be severely constrained by the possibility of adverse reactions in the financial markets. Although appointed by President Carter, Paul Volcker was never a Carter man. His reappointment as Fed chairman in 1983 by President Reagan again suggests that the extent of effective presidential choice is constrained. Nevertheless, the historical evidence indicates that monetary policy is strongly influenced by the incumbent administration.[2] Indeed, the history of postwar monetary policy presented in Chapter 21 leaves little doubt that the independence of the Fed is more a pious hope than a reality.

The Fed's Balance Sheet

For analytical purposes, it is convenient to consolidate the Board of Governors and the twelve Fed banks into one big institution—the Fed. The Fed's balance sheet is basically the twelve Fed banks' balance sheets added together, since the Board possesses virtually no assets. The main items in the Fed's balance sheet are shown in Table 9.1.

Gold and SDRs

The first asset item, gold and SDRs, consists of gold certificates ($11 billion), which are claims against the country's official gold stocks owned by the Treasury (the values of gold certificates and the official gold stock are always identical) and Special Drawing Rights (SDRs), which are Fed deposits with the International Monetary Fund. Under the gold standard, the Treasury bought and sold gold at a fixed price ($35 an ounce from 1933 to 1971), and the Fed automatically bought or sold an equal amount of gold certificates from or to the Treasury. For analytical purposes, gold and gold certificates are interchangeable. One can think in terms of the Fed holding gold and ignore the Treasury.

Foreign-Currency Assets

Together with assets denominated in foreign currencies, gold and SDRs can be used to influence the value of the dollar directly in foreign exchange markets. The Fed would sell gold, SDRs, and foreign exchange (obtained by selling foreign-currency assets) if it wanted to raise the price of the dollar, since this would increase the supply of foreign currencies and at the same time raise the demand for dollars.

Loans

Fed loans are mainly credit provided to depository institutions through the discount window. Originally, the Fed banks rediscounted eligible paper

[2]Sherman J. Maisel, *Managing the Dollar* (New York: Norton, 1975), pp. 146–148.

Table 9.1   The Fed's Balance Sheet, December 31, 1982 (billions of dollars)

Assets		Liabilities	
Gold and SDRs	16	Federal Reserve notes	142
Foreign-currency assets	6	Depository institution deposits	26
Loans to depository institutions	1	U.S. Treasury deposits	5
Securities	150	Other deposits	1
Cash items in process of collection	10	Deferred availability of cash items	7
Other assets	4	Other liabilities	3
		Total liabilities	184
		Net worth	3
Total	187	Total	187

Source: Federal Reserve Bulletin, February 1983, Table A12.

(commercial bills) for their member banks. Today, the same purpose is achieved by their providing advances or loans secured by collateral such as government bonds. Since 1980 all depository institutions have been entitled to borrow from the Fed banks. The rate at which these loans are furnished is the discount rate.

Securities   Virtually all the Fed's security holdings consist of U.S. government bonds, notes, and bills. The Fed banks also hold a small amount of securities issued by federal agencies and a tiny volume of bankers' acceptances bought under repurchase agreements or RPs. (Some government securities are also bought as RPs.) All the Fed's securities are bought and sold on the open market. The size of this balance sheet item gives an accurate indication of the relative importance of open market operations as an instrument of monetary policy. In essence, open market operations dominate all other policy instruments.

Cash Items in the Process of Collection   The fifth balance sheet item is the trickiest. Cash items in the process of collection constitute the value of all checks accepted for clearing by the Fed banks. Suppose the San Francisco Fed accepts a check for $500 in favor of Julian Dilks with an account at the Bank of America written by Jeremy Faulkner with an account at Citibank, New York. When that check arrives at the San Francisco Fed, two balance sheet entries are made. First, cash items in the process of collection are increased by $500, because the Fed System will eventually collect through the New York Fed $500 from Citibank by debiting Citibank's account with the New York Fed.

Deferred Availability of Cash Items   Second, however, the San Francisco Fed owes the Bank of America $500. Therefore, the liability item called deferred availability of cash items goes up $500. The availability of cash is deferred from the viewpoint of the Bank of America, because the Bank of America has not yet had its own account with the Fed credited. The San Francisco Fed consults the Deferred Availability Schedule, which will indicate how many days the Bank of America must wait under the "fixed availability" scheme until its account is credited. At present, this would be one or two days, depending on the location of the bank on which the check has been drawn. In this example, the San Francisco Fed will delay for a maximum of two days before crediting $500 to the Bank of America's account, thereby increasing depository institution deposits and reducing deferred availability of cash items by that amount.

Float At this stage, however, Jeremy's check may not yet have reached New York. If it has not, cash items in process of collection will record Jeremy's $500 check for a while after it has been removed from the deferred availability items. The difference between the Fed's cash items asset and deferred availability liabilities is called the *float*. In the present example, the New York Fed might debit Citibank's account on the fourth day. Cash items are then reduced by $500 and the float is eliminated. The decline in this asset item is matched by a $500 reduction in depository institution deposits, a liability item. The Fed's balance sheet remains balanced throughout this series of transactions.

Float Charges Until 1983 the float was invariably a positive non-income-earning asset of the Fed. Since 1979, however, when the daily average float was $6.7 billion, the Fed has been taking measures to reduce the float. In 1982 the float averaged only $2.3 billion a day. In 1983 charges were levied on the float. In the example above, the Bank of America is charged interest on its $500 credit until Citibank is debited. If it chooses, the Bank of America could opt for the "fractional availability" scheme. In this case, partial credit is given based on the Fed's actual past clearing-period experience. The introduction of float charges reduced the daily average float substantially, as depository institutions could no longer obtain interest-free credit in this way.

Other Assets Other assets include bank premises, coins issued by the Treasury, equipment, and an assortment of miscellaneous assets of small values. None of them changes noticeably from year to year. They are not bought or sold to implement monetary or exchange-rate policies.

High-Powered Money Two liability items in Table 9.1—Federal Reserve notes and depository institution deposits—constitute high-powered money. Together they account for over 90 percent of the total liabilities of the Fed. Federal Reserve notes are held as currency in circulation by the public and as vault cash by depository institutions. Depository institution deposits are held both to satisfy reserve requirements and to make transactions, such as a wire transfer of funds following an operation on the federal funds market.

Other Deposits The U.S. Treasury maintains with the Fed banks substantial deposits with which to make payments, such as tax refunds, employee salary payments, and purchases of goods and services. The Fed acts as banker to the government in this respect. However, the federal government does not deposit tax receipts directly into its Fed accounts. Instead, it deposits all its receipts in tax and loan accounts at many depository institutions throughout the country. As it draws on its account at the Fed, the Treasury transfers funds from its various tax and loan accounts.

Other deposits include accounts of foreign central banks and governments, some federal agencies, and international organizations such as the International Monetary Fund and the World Bank. These accounts are very small in comparison with depository institution deposits.

Other Liabilities A variety of small items are lumped into the category "other liabilities." They include such things as expenses incurred but not yet paid for.

Balance Sheet Analysis

Analysis of the Fed's balance sheet starts from the accounting identity: Assets $\equiv$ Liabilities + Net Worth. If the focus of analysis is high-powered money H, the balance sheet items can be rearranged:

$$H \equiv \text{Assets} - \text{Other Liabilities} - \text{Net Worth} \qquad (9.1)$$

In the absence of any changes in other liabilities or net worth, an increase in the Fed's assets must be matched by an increase in high-powered money. If assets and net worth remain constant, an increase in other liabilities will be offset by a reduction in high-powered money.

Open Market Purchases Purchases and sales of government securities in the open market constitute the main method by which the Fed deliberately changes the size of its assets and liabilities. When the New York Fed buys government securities, depository institution deposits (and hence high-powered money) increase by the same amount. If the Fed buys the securities directly from a depository institution, it simply credits that institution's account or the account of its correspondent through a wire transfer. If the security is bought from a dealer or any nondepository institution, the Fed credits the account of the seller's depository institution. In turn, that depository institution credits the seller's account. Thus, whenever the Fed buys government securities in the open market, high-powered money increases by an equal amount through an immediate increase in depository institution deposits.

Normally the Fed does not buy government securities directly from the U.S. Treasury. Even if it did, however, the balance sheet changes would be identical, since the Treasury would have the proceeds paid into its tax and loan accounts. Hence, the Fed would still credit depository institution deposits with the value of securities bought.

Open Market Sales

When the New York Fed sells government securities on the open market, high-powered money is reduced immediately by the value of the sale. If a depository institution buys these securities, its balance with the Fed is debited. Depository institution deposits and hence high-powered money both decline. If a nondepository institution buys the securities, that institution instructs its bank to pay the Fed. The bank, in turn, authorizes the Fed to debit its account. Hence, the bank debits the buyer's account by, say, $2 million and has its own account with the Fed debited by $2 million. The bank's cash reserve assets fall by $2 million, as does its deposit liabilities.

Discount Window Operations

If the Fed makes a loan to a depository institution through the discount window, it credits that institution's account with the value of the loan. Hence, depository institution balances and high-powered money increase instantaneously by the value of the loan. When the loan is repaid, depository institution balances and high-powered money are reduced.

A loan from the Fed also shows up on the depository institution's balance sheet. Its cash reserves have increased because of the credit to its account at the Fed. At the same time, it has increased its managed liabilities in the form of the loan from the Fed.

Float and High-Powered Money

An increase in the float also increases high-powered money through depository institution deposits. Suppose weather conditions impede the interdistrict transfer of checks. In such case, the Fed's cash items in the process of collection will rise. Checks pile up waiting to be flown to the appropriate Fed banks as soon as weather permits.

On the other side of the Fed's balance sheet, however, there may be no change in the value of deferred availability of cash items. Under the fixed availability scheme, depository institutions are credited for checks deposited according to a predetermined schedule. Hence, accounts of check depositing banks are credited on time.

Until the weather clears, however, there will be no corresponding debits for depository institutions on which the checks are drawn. Hence there is a net increase in depository institution balances equal to the increase in the float. Until the checks are actually cleared through the Fed, the institutions that were credited automatically are charged interest equal to the federal funds rate on the value of the uncleared checks.

U.S. Treasury Deposits

The system of tax and loan accounts is designed mainly to prevent U.S. Treasury activities from affecting high-powered money. If the Treasury maintained exactly the same balance in its deposits with the Fed, then this would indeed ensure that the Treasury could have no effect on high-powered money.

Suppose, however, that the Treasury makes some payments without transferring an equal value of funds from its tax and loan accounts. In such case, depository institution balances and high-powered money will increase by the same amount that the Treasury deposits decrease. The Treasury checks are debited to the Treasury accounts and credited to the deposits of the payees' depository institutions. The check-clearing process here is identical to the process used for all other checks. The effect on high-powered money arises only from the fact that a depository institution deposit is credited while a Treasury deposit (not included in the definition of high-powered money) rather than another depository institution deposit is debited.

Control over High-Powered Money

The balance sheet analysis presented above might give the erroneous impression that high-powered money is the residual balance sheet item that just rises or falls with changes in any asset or other liability item. In fact, the Fed does not view changes in high-powered money as a residual outcome of everything else. Specifically, if the Fed wants to achieve some target with respect to high-powered money, it can offset all other asset- and liability-induced changes through appropriate open market operations.

Given the Fed's huge holdings of U.S. government securities, relatively small percentage changes in this asset item swamp relatively large percentage changes in other balance sheet items. Even if changes in other balance sheet items were completely beyond the Fed's control, they could always be counteracted by open market operations. Hence, the Fed can and does use open market operations to determine the quantity of high-powered money.

In equation form:

$$\Delta H = \Delta OMO + \Delta NOA \qquad (9.2)$$

where ΔH is the change in high-powered money, ΔOMO is the change in the Fed's holdings of government securities, and ΔNOA is "net other assets" (all other assets minus all other liabilities and net worth). On December 31, 1982, H equaled $168 billion, OMO equaled $150 billion, and NOA equaled $18 billion. If NOA rises by $5 billion and the Fed wants H to increase by $3 billion, it must sell $2 billion of government securities in open market operations. Then:

$$\Delta H = \Delta OMO + \Delta NOA$$
$$\$3b = -\$2b + \$5b \qquad (9.3)$$

Summary

1. Today most central banks perform the following functions: (1) being banker to the government, (2) being banker to commercial banks, (3)

preserving confidence in the country's money and banking systems. The third function is carried out through monetary policy and bank supervision.

2. The Federal Reserve System started operations as the central bank of the United States in 1914. Its original functions were to provide an elastic currency, rediscounting facilities for member banks, and improved bank supervision.

3. The Fed consists of a seven-member Board of Governors in Washington, D.C., and twelve regional Federal Reserve banks. The Federal Open Market Committee (seven governors plus five Fed bank presidents) is the most important policy-making organ of the Fed.

4. The Fed's dominant asset is U.S. government securities. It is the sale and purchase of these securities in the open market that constitute open market operations, by far the most important instrument of monetary policy.

5. Traditionally, it has been argued that the central bank should be independent from the government to ensure the conduct of prudent and responsible monetary policy. The Fed was established in the light of this view. However, it has not exerted much independence from government policy in the postwar period.

6. The Fed banks provide loans to depository institutions at the discount rate through the discount window.

7. The Fed's check-clearing arrangements give rise to the float—the difference between the value of checks being cleared (cash items in the process of collection) and the value of checks to be credited to depository institution accounts (deferred availability of cash items). The float is positive when checks are credited before they are debited.

8. The main liability of the Fed is high-powered money—Federal Reserve notes plus depository institution deposits.

9. If the Fed buys U.S. government securities in the open market or extends loans to depository institutions, high-powered money rises by an equal value through an immediate increase in depository institution deposits.

10. The Fed can offset the effects of other asset and liability changes on high-powered money through open market operations. Hence, the Fed can achieve a target level of high-powered money if it wishes to do so.

Questions

1. How did the Bank of England emerge as a bankers' bank?
2. Explain the three original functions of the Fed.

3. From where does the Fed's Board of Governors obtain its power?

4. What is the FOMC and what does it do?

5. What are open market operations and which organ of the Fed conducts them?

6. What is the discount window and how does it work?

7. How can Congress and the administration influence Fed behavior?

8. Explain the two balance sheet changes resulting from Fed sales of foreign exchange.

9. Explain the two balance sheet changes resulting from Fed open market sales.

10. Explain the two balance sheet changes resulting from a Fed loan to a depository institution.

11. What is the float and how do changes in it affect high-powered money?

12. How does high-powered money appear in the Fed's balance sheet?

13. How can changes in U.S. Treasury deposits affect high-powered money?

14. How can the Fed actually control the amount of high-powered money?

10

Implementing Monetary Policy

Goals

Legislative Mandates

The Federal Reserve System was established to stabilize the nation's banking system by providing an elastic currency, discounting facilities, and improved bank supervision. Today, the Fed is expected, in conjunction with the administration, to pursue a much broader range of goals. Under the Employment Act of 1946 the government was given the responsibility for promoting maximum employment, production, and purchasing power. The Full Employment and Balanced Growth Act of 1978 legislates the following goals of monetary and other macroeconomic policies: full employment, reasonable price stability, more investment, a balanced budget, reduced government spending, an improved trade balance, freer international trade, and a stable international monetary system. Twice a year the Fed is obliged to report to Congress on its monetary policy objectives aimed at achieving these goals.

Feasible Short-Run Goals

The subsequent four parts of this book present a macroeconomic model of the economy. In it, monetary policy consists solely of controlling the money supply. *Unanticipated* changes in the money supply affect real (inflation adjusted) interest rates, investment, the levels of production and employment, the balance of payments, and inflation. However, even in this short-run situation when monetary policy has real effects only because it is unanticipated, changes in the money supply cannot at the same time reduce both inflation and real interest rates or unemployment. In other words, unanticipated changes in the money supply have effects that come in packages. Some parts of the package are desired, others are not. There is therefore an inevitable conflict of goals. Monetary policy may be used to reduce unemployment in the short run, but only by producing an unanticipated increase in the inflation rate.

Feasible Long-Run Goal

In the long run, however, the macroeconomic model indicates that there is no conflict of goals. This is due to the fact that in the long run the money supply affects only the price level. Hence, the only feasible long-run goal of monetary policy is price stability. In the long run, changes in the money supply are *anticipated*. In fact, this is one definition of the long run. The macroeconomic model shows that anticipated changes in the money supply have no "real" effects.

Targets

Real Bills Doctrine

For most of its existence the Fed has been concerned not so much with money as with credit. Until the 1930s the discount rate was the primary instrument of monetary policy. Member banks increased their borrowing from the discount window during an economic upturn as the "needs of trade" grew. This borrowing decreased again in the subsequent downturn. According to the real bills doctrine, these procyclical movements in Fed loans were entirely appropriate. So long as the increased lending was used to finance an increase in "real" inventories, credit policy was sure to be noninflationary. The extra credit was needed to match the increased real level of economic activity.

The fact that Fed loans increased high-powered money and hence produced a multiple expansion in the money stock was not appreciated. That the increase in the money stock would itself cause a multiple rise in nominal spending was quite alien to the real bills doctrine. Nevertheless, a $1 Fed discount to finance a $1 increase in real output could produce a $3 increase in the money supply, leading in turn to a $12 increase in nominal spending. When nominal spending rises by more than real output, the difference is met by higher prices.

Anticyclical Discount Rates

The real bills doctrine still has its supporters,[1] but the Fed discarded it as the basis for monetary policy in the 1920s. Still concerned primarily with credit conditions, the Fed adopted a general strategy of raising the discount rate to deter part of the increased credit demand during a boom and lowering the discount rate in a recession. The general aim was to smooth out, to some extent, fluctuations in the quantity of credit.

In practice, this anticyclical interest rate policy was constrained by balance of payments considerations. Specifically, the Fed kept the discount rate high during the recession of 1920–1921 and actually raised it in Octo-

[1]Thomas M. Humphrey, "The Real Bills Doctrine," *Federal Reserve Bank of Richmond Economic Review,* 68(5), September/October 1982, pp. 3–13.

ber 1931 during the Great Depression to attract gold inflows from abroad. In these instances, it was following a policy similar to that pursued by the Bank of England in the nineteenth century (Chapter 9).

Cheap Money

In both World War I and World War II the Fed maintained low discount rates in order to hold down the interest costs of federal government deficits. During World War II this was achieved not only by keeping the discount rate low but also through open market purchases of government securities. The national debt was so large by the end of the war in 1945 that the Fed was persuaded to continue its low-interest-rate policy and to support government bond prices until 1951. During the 1940s the discount mechanism decreased in importance as open market operations emerged as the primary instrument of monetary policy.

Money Market Conditions

After abandoning its support of government bond prices in March 1951, the Fed turned for about the next 15 years to money market conditions as the appropriate target for monetary policy. Concentrating on short-term markets, the Fed employed open market sales and purchases of treasury bills to influence interest rates. The Fed sold bills to raise rates at times of accelerating inflation and bought bills to lower rates when unemployment was high. Again, the focus was on credit rather than money. Credit was tightened to reduce expenditure during a boom and eased to stimulate expenditure, particularly investment expenditure, in a recession.

Money market conditions were not too difficult to interpret, provided that nominal interest rates did not diverge significantly from real interest rates. As inflation accelerated during the 1960s, however, the Fed's reading of money market conditions became increasingly misleading. What appeared to be tight money market conditions turned out to be simply an inflation premium built into nominal interest rates. Even at apparently high rates of interest, demand for credit surged and inflationary pressures mounted. Higher nominal interest rates no longer succeeded in cutting back credit demand and expenditure.

Monetary Aggregates

Early in 1970 the Fed began using the money supply as its primary target. Since then the Fed has established annual target ranges for the growth rates of M1, M2, and M3, and a monitoring range for the growth rate of bank credit. The experience suggests that hitting the targets has been no easy task. In an attempt to improve its performance in this respect, the Fed changed its methods of controlling the money supply in October 1979. The Fed switched to monetary targeting for two reasons. First, nominal interest rates were providing increasingly misleading signals about money market conditions. Second, a growing body of empirical evidence indicated that the demand for money in the United States was stable. The importance of and evidence on money demand stability are discussed in Chapter 20.

Operating Targets

Short-Term Interest Rates The Fed does not and cannot control the money supply directly. It therefore selects variables that both influence the target variable in a stable and predictable way and can be affected directly by Fed activities. Between 1970 and 1979 the Fed used the federal funds rate as its main operating target.

The choice of the federal funds rate as its operating target was based on two factors. First, the Fed staff believed that there was a stable and predictable relationship between the money stock and short-term interest rates. This view was supported by a huge volume of studies on the demand for money, some of which is reviewed in Chapter 20. The empirical evidence suggested that demand for money is related inversely to the level of interest rates, as illustrated in Figure 10.1. The interest rate is the opportunity cost of holding money (Chapter 1). Hence, the higher the cost, the smaller is the quantity demanded.

Perfectly Elastic Supply of Money In essence, the Fed made the money supply perfectly elastic at its chosen interest rate. At this rate, it would buy or sell unlimited amounts of government bonds. These transactions, in turn, would enable high-powered money to adjust automatically to support the money stock forthcoming at the selected interest rate.

Figure 10.1 Demand for Money

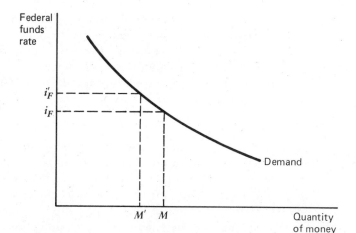

If money demand is related stably to the interest rate and if demand always equals supply, then any target money stock can be achieved by producing the appropriate rate on the federal funds market through open market operations.

If the Fed wanted an expansion in the money supply, it bought government securities, thus bringing down interest rates. Lower interest rates would increase the quantity of money demanded. The open market purchases had already increased high-powered money to support the higher money stock.

Open Market Operations and the Federal Funds Rate

To implement monetary policy in the way described above, the Federal Open Market Committee (FOMC) provided directives to the New York Fed's open market account managers. The directive would instruct the managers to buy or sell government securities to achieve a given federal funds rate.

An open market purchase has two immediate effects. First, it affects the price and hence the yield of government securities. Second, it increases depository institution deposits with the Fed. In aggregate, depository institutions now have more reserves than they previously held. Hence, demand for reserves on the federal funds market shifts to the left and supply shifts to the right, as will be shown below. The federal funds rate must decline to equate the new demand and supply.

The open market account managers' aim under this system is to conduct open market operations in order to bring demand for and supply of federal funds into equilibrium at the stipulated interest rate. The historical evidence indicates that the account managers generally succeeded in hitting this operating target. Unfortunately, however, the interest rate set by these open market operations rarely produced the target money stock.

Money and Interest Rates

There are at least three possible explanations for the failure of interest-rate setting to achieve monetary targets. First, demand for money might have been unstable. The empirical evidence on the demand for money is analyzed in Chapter 20. Second, there may have been lags between interest-rate movements and corresponding money stock changes. Lags are discussed in more detail later in this chapter.

Demand for Money versus Demand for Credit

Third, what the Fed was really doing was providing an elastic supply of credit. The demand for credit and the demand for money are, however, two entirely different things. Hence, a surge in credit demand would have produced open market purchases to hold interest rates constant. High-powered money and hence the money supply would have increased without any change in money demand. For a time, therefore, the market for money would have been in disequilibrium with excess money supply. The evidence on money market disequilibrium is also considered in Chapter 20

Post-1979 Operating Procedures

Reserves as an Operating Target

On October 6, 1979, the Fed changed its operating target from the federal funds rate to bank reserves. Under the Monetary Control Act of 1980 the operating target is depository institution reserves. The reserve targeting procedure can be viewed as a three-stage process.[2]

Short-Run Monetary Target

The first stage involves choosing the appropriate short-run paths for M1 and M2. At the end of each quarter the FOMC chooses three-month growth targets for these monetary aggregates for the next quarter. Since the money stock is frequently outside its long-run or annual target range, the short-run paths often necessitate a decision about the optimal speed of reentry.

Slow Reentry Rate

In 1981, M1 was outside the annual target range established in November 1980 for the entire year, except for a couple of weeks in April. Hence, reentry paths had to be chosen each quarter. The FOMC opted consistently for relatively slow reentry (4 or 5 months) in the belief that faster reentry would produce unacceptably large fluctuations in interest rates.[3]

Reserve Aggregates

The second stage in the post-1979 operating procedure is to estimate the path for total reserves consistent with the short-run money stock path. This involves projecting each component of depository institutions' reservable liabilities and then multiplying them by their required reserve ratios. The projections are based on the short-run money supply path. In addition, excess reserve holdings are forecast. The sum equals the projected aggregate reserves that the Fed will have to supply to achieve its short-run monetary target. This stage also includes projecting changes in currency in circulation that will leak from or add to reserves and hence require appropriate modifications to the reserve supply estimates.

Open Market Operations to Affect Reserves

The third and final stage in this process of monetary control is to set the appropriate level of reserves. Were open market purchases the sole source of reserves, the Fed could produce appropriate reserve changes on a dollar-for-dollar basis through open market operations. For example, a reduction in reserves of $500 million could be achieved through open market sales of $500 million.

---

[2]John P. Judd, "An Examination of the Federal Reserve's Strategy for Controlling the Monetary Aggregates," *Federal Reserve Bank of San Francisco Economic Review*, Fall 1982, pp. 7–18.

[3]Judd, *op. cit.*, p. 15, concludes that the Fed could attempt to reenter the long-run M1 target range within 2 to 3 months rather than 4 to 5 months, without creating greater interest-rate volatility.

Federal Funds Market

**Aggregate Demand
for Federal Funds**

The federal funds market lies at the heart of the money supply process. Market equilibrium in this market is depicted in Figure 10.2. The demand for federal funds is generated by depository institutions with shortfalls in their required reserves. The demand curve is downward sloping to the right because depository institutions face a larger volume of profitable lending opportunities the lower is the cost of their borrowed funds. As the federal funds rate i_F declines, depository institutions extend more loans. The extra loans are financed in part from increased borrowing on the federal funds market. If depository institutions in aggregate increase their lending, the money supply increases through the lending-depositing-lending sequence analyzed in Chapter 8. In equilibrium, the money supply rises and so absorbs (through increased required reserves) the increased quantity of reserves that produced the decline in the federal funds rate in the first instance.

**Aggregate Supply
of Federal Funds**

The supply of federal funds comes from depository institutions with excess reserves and some nondepository institutions. The supply curve shown in Figure 10.2 is upward sloping to the right because depository institutions find fewer profitable lending opportunities and/or substitute federal funds lending for other assets as the federal funds rate rises.

Figure 10.2   Demand for and Supply of Federal Funds

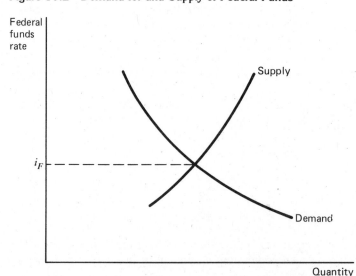

Demand for and supply of federal funds are equated at a federal funds rate of i_F.

Market Equilibrium Figure 10.2 shows that the demand for federal funds is equated with the supply of federal funds at an interest rate of i_F. At this rate, the deposit industry as a whole will have adjusted its size such that on the asset side there are no more profitable lending opportunities available. On the liabilities side, reservable liabilities such as deposits will have reached a level that exactly absorbs depository institutions' unwanted reserves.

Expansion in Profitable Lending Opportunities Suppose that an economic upturn increases the volume of profitable lending opportunities that face the deposit industry. In such case, the demand curve for federal funds will shift to the right and the supply curve will move to the left, as shown in Figure 10.3. The federal funds rate will rise until the volume of profitable lending opportunities is reduced to its original level. The size of the deposit industry remains unchanged.

Shift in Composition of Deposits Consider what happens if there is an exogenous shift in the composition of deposits from demand to time deposits. Now required reserves to support this aggregate volume of deposits fall. Hence, on the federal funds market the demand curve shifts to the left and the supply curve moves to the right. The federal funds rate falls, depository institutions expand loans, and deposits increase in the subsequent lending-depositing-lending sequence.

Figure 10.3   Impact of Increase in Profitable Lending Opportunities on the Federal Funds Market

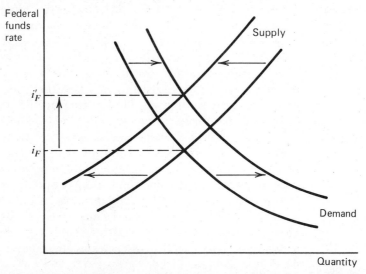

An exogenous increase in profitable lending opportunities facing the deposit industry shifts the demand for federal funds to the right and the supply of federal funds to the left. The equilibrium federal funds rate is raised from i_F to i_F'.

Reserve Drain   Suppose, finally, that the Fed removes reserves from the deposit industry through open market sales. The net drain of aggregate reserves shifts the demand curve to the right and the supply curve to the left. These effects are identical to those produced by the increase in profitable lending opportunities shown in Figure 10.3. In this case, however, the deposit industry contracts. As the federal funds rate rises, the volume of profitable lending opportunities facing depository institutions declines. Curtailed lending reduces deposits through the unraveling of the lending-depositing-lending sequence. The smaller level of deposits reduces required reserves to the lower volume of reserves now available to the deposit industry as a whole.

Aggregate Reserves

Borrowed and Nonborrowed Reserves   Reserves consist of *nonborrowed reserves* created primarily through open market purchases and *borrowed reserves* produced through Fed loans from its discount window. If the Fed reduces reserves through open market sales, depository institutions can replenish them by borrowing at the Fed's discount window. In fact, therefore, it takes more than $500 million in open market sales to achieve a $500 million reduction in aggregate reserves. To some extent, the reduction in nonborrowed reserves will be offset by an increase in borrowed reserves.

Supply of Borrowed Reserves   Were depository institutions able to borrow unlimited quantities of reserves at the discount window with no conditions or nonpecuniary costs imposed, borrowed reserves would be perfect substitutes for nonborrowed reserves. In such case, the federal funds rate would never exceed the discount rate. Depository institutions would borrow at the discount window to relend on the federal funds market whenever the federal funds rate exceeded the discount rate. The arbitrage would completely counteract the effects of open market operations on the level of reserves.

In fact, however, banks are reluctant to use the discount window because the Fed imposes restrictions on the quantity and frequency of loans that it is willing to extend to individual depository institutions over given time intervals.[4] When the Fed conducts open market sales to reduce the supply of nonborrowed reserves, increased use of the discount window will occur only if the federal funds rate rises relative to the discount rate. Hence, the supply of borrowed reserves is not perfectly elastic at the discount rate. The effective cost rises as the quantity supplied increases, as illustrated in Figure 10.4.

---

[4]Judd, *op. cit.*, p. 10.

Figure 10.4   Supply of Borrowed Reserves

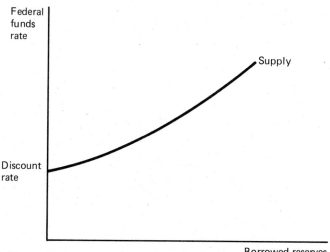

Although the discount rate is fixed, the effective cost of borrowing at the Fed's discount window rises as the quantity borrowed increases. Hence, the supply of borrowed reserves can be depicted as an upward-sloping curve.

Supply of Aggregate Reserves

The supply of nonborrowed reserves is interest inelastic. The Fed determines that quantity through open market operations. Hence, the total supply of reserves—borrowed plus nonborrowed—can be depicted as the kinked supply curve shown in Figure 10.5.

Equilibrium in the Market for Reserves

By superimposing an aggregate demand curve for reserves on Figure 10.5, the equilibrium federal funds rate i_F can be determined from the intersection of the aggregate supply of and demand for reserves. The aggregate demand for reserves equals reserves not obtained through the federal funds market plus reserves borrowed on that market. Similarly, the aggregate supply of reserves equals reserves not placed on the federal funds market plus those that are lent on that market.

Reserve Market and Federal Funds Market

Since aggregate demand for reserves equals aggregate supply of reserves, and aggregate demand for federal funds equals aggregate supply of federal funds, reserves *not* obtained through the federal funds market must equal reserves *not* placed on that market. Hence, the demand and supply curves for reserves are the demand and supply curves for federal funds, both shifted to the right by the volume of reserves not obtained from or placed on the federal funds market. Both sets of demand and supply curves must therefore intersect at exactly the same federal funds

Figure 10.5   Demand for and Supply of Aggregate Reserves

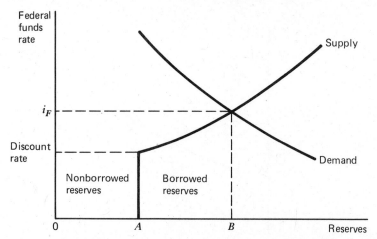

The supply of aggregate reserves consists of nonborrowed reserves produced by the Fed through open market operations and reserves borrowed by depository institutions at the discount window. The interest-inelastic supply of nonborrowed reserves is added to the interest-elastic supply of borrowed reserves to obtain the aggregate supply of reserves. Supply intersects demand at a federal funds rate i_F

rate. In other words, analyzing the determinants of the federal funds rate can be conducted by examining either the demand for and supply of federal funds or the demand for and supply of reserves. In fact, they are simply two sides of the same coin.

Changing Supply of Reserves through Open Market Operations

Suppose that the Fed wants to reduce total reserves by $500, from B to B' in Figure 10.6. In this case the federal funds rate will increase from i_F to i'_F. To produce the intersection of supply and demand at B', the Fed must reduce nonborrowed reserves from A to A'. In this particular example, nonborrowed reserves must be reduced by $900 million to achieve a reduction of $500 in aggregate reserves. Depository institutions will borrow $400 million more at the discount window at the higher federal funds rate i'_F.

Reserves versus Federal Funds Rate as Operating Target

Figure 10.6 shows that in theory the Fed could use either reserves or the federal funds rate as its operating target. The open market account managers could be instructed either to raise the federal funds rate from i_F to i'_F or to reduce reserves from B to B'. In practice, however, the effects would be quite different because of fluctuations in the demand curve. In terms of reserves, a rise in the federal funds rate from i_F to i'_F could be more than offset by a rightward shift in the demand curve. In such case, an increase in the federal funds rate would not be accompanied by the desired decrease in the money stock. A target money stock can, however, be achieved irrespective of reserve demand fluctuations by using reserves as the operating

Figure 10.6 Changing Reserves through Open Market Operations

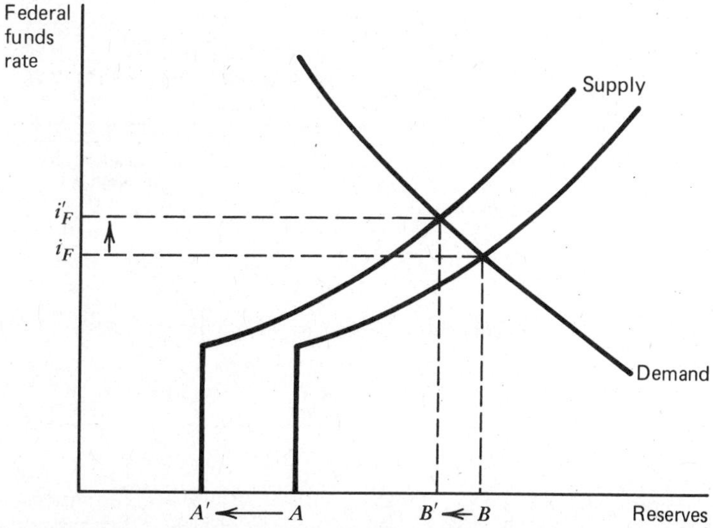

If the Fed wants to reduce reserves by $500 million from B to B' it must conduct open market sales to reduce nonborrowed reserves by $900 million from A to A'. The increase in the federal funds rate from i_F to i'_F induces depository institutions to increase their borrowing at the Fed's discount window by $400 million.

target. Then, demand shifts change only the federal funds rate. These rate changes will, in turn, produce variations in the quantity of reserves borrowed at the discount window. Open market operations, therefore, must offset variations in borrowed reserves to achieve any given aggregate reserve target. The open market account managers need to know the aggregate reserve target and be kept informed on a continuous basis of changes in borrowed reserves. Then from any initial level of aggregate reserves they can calculate the appropriate amount of open market sales or purchases.

Reserve Accounting

Lagged Reserve Requirements

From 1968 to 1984, depository institutions subject to the Fed's reserve requirement rules followed a system known as *lagged reserve accounting*. Under this arrangement, a depository institution's required reserves were calculated against reservable liabilities that were on the books two weeks earlier, as shown in the top half of Figure 10.7. Over the seven-day reserve maintenance period (Thursday to Wednesday) the depository institution was obliged to maintain average daily reserves equal to or exceeding its required reserves. The required reserves were calculated against average

Figure 10.7   Timing of Lagged and Contemporaneous Reserve Accounting Systems

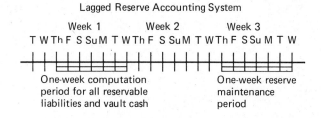

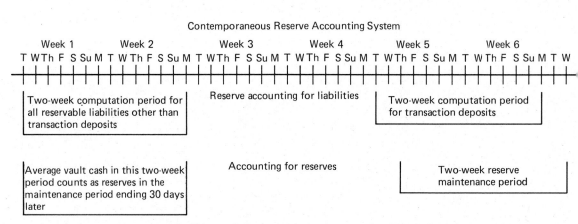

Note: A "reserve maintenance period" is a period over which the daily average reserves of a depository institution must equal or exceed its required reserves. Required reserves are based on daily average deposit liabilities in "reserve computation periods."

Source: R. Alton Gilbert and Michael E. Trebing, "The New System of Contemporaneous Reserve Requirements," *Federal Reserve Bank of St. Louis Review,* 64(10), December 1982, pp 3–7.

daily deposits over the seven-day period two weeks before (the computation period). However, the daily average vault cash held in the computation period was counted as reserves for the reserve maintenance period. Hence a depository institution had to hold an average daily balance on deposit at the Fed during the reserve maintenance period equal to its required reserves minus the daily average vault cash held during the computation period.

Reserve Demand under Lagged Reserve Accounting

Lagged reserve accounting implied that required reserves were fixed absolutely for any given reserve maintenance period. No amount of current or contemporaneous change in deposits could change the level of required reserves. Hence, the demand for reserves was interest inelastic. In Figure 10.6 this demand curve would be a vertical line at, say, *B*. In this case therefore, the Fed was obliged to supply whatever amount of reserves was demanded. In the reserve maintenance period, the Fed could affect only the federal funds rate.

Over the period October 1979 to February 1984 the Fed could not actually use reserves as its day-to-day operating target, because the level of reserves in the short run was determined by demand. Therefore, the Fed estimated the medium-term demand function for reserves, which was interest elastic like the demand curve in Figure 10.6. The Fed would then produce a federal funds rate i_F' corresponding to the reserve target B'. If reserve demand was stable, the quantity of reserves would shift from B to B' in the medium term. If, on the other hand, reserve demand shifted, the Fed could find itself chasing behind a volatile demand for reserves. Indeed, this is the main explanation for the poor performance of monetary control during these years. Only since February 1984 has it been possible for the Fed to use aggregate reserves as its day-to-day operating target.

Lagged Reserve Requirements and Monetary Control

The difficulty of controlling reserves and hence the money supply by manipulating the federal funds rate, the only method available to the Fed under lagged reserve accounting, has been described as follows by Milton Friedman:[5]

> Is it really conceivable that the Fed produced these gyrations on purpose, given its repeated protestations that it was committed to a steady and moderate rate of monetary growth? . . . A better explanation is that the Fed is, as it were, driving a car with a highly defective steering gear. It is driving down a road with walls on both sides. It can go down the middle of the road on the average only by first bouncing off one wall and then off the opposite wall. Not very good for the car or the passengers or bystanders, but one way to get down the road.

Contemporaneous Reserve Requirements[6]

The new system of contemporaneous reserve accounting introduced in February 1984 is represented schematically in the bottom half of Figure 10.7. Both the reserve computation period and the reserve maintenance period are increased to 14 days. The reserve computation period ends two days before the reserve maintenance period. Hence, there is a 12-day overlap.

Lagged Accounting for Vault Cash and Nonmoney Reservable Liabilities

There are, however, two important lags. First, required reserves against liabilities other than transaction deposits (nonpersonal time deposits and Eurodollar liabilities) are calculated against average daily liabilities over 14 days ending 30 days before the end of the current maintenance period. Second, average daily vault cash holdings in the 14-day period ending 30

[5]Milton Friedman, "The Wayward Money Supply," *Newsweek*, December 27, 1982, p. 58.

[6]This description is taken from R. Alton Gilbert and Michael E. Trebing, "The New System of Contemporaneous Reserve Requirements," *Federal Reserve Bank of St. Louis Review*, 64(10), December 1982, pp. 3–7.

days before the end of the current maintenance period count as required reserves for the current maintenance period.

Improved Monetary Control

These two accounting lags are designed to strengthen control over aggregate reserves and to tighten the link between reserves and transaction-type deposits. The Fed does not know the value of depository institutions' vault cash until reports are filed. Lagged vault cash accounting eliminates errors in estimating current vault cash, which would, in turn, produce errors in the quantity of reserves supplied by the Fed. Similarly, lagged reserve accounting for nontransaction-type deposits eliminates error in estimating their current level, which would again produce errors in supplying the appropriate quantity of reserves to support a target volume of transaction deposits. Since depository institutions can reduce transaction deposits to reduce reserve requirements in the form of deposits at the Fed during six-sevenths of the reserve maintenance period, the demand for reserves is interest elastic as shown in Figure 10.6. Hence, the Fed can now use reserves as its operating target and can calculate quite accurately the reserve changes needed to achieve a target level of transaction balances.

Lags and Rules

So far in this chapter it has been assumed that the Fed knows what money supply target to achieve. In fact, however, the Fed itself has to set the annual target ranges for money stock growth. The main debate has focused around the question of whether the Fed should adopt a money growth rule or pursue countercyclical monetary policy. Both sides generally agree that monetary policy can influence real variables, such as the level of output, at least in the short run. Hence, the dispute revolves around the issue of whether or not monetary policy should attempt to stimulate economic activity in a recession by accelerating the rate of monetary growth and to dampen the economy in a boom by cutting back monetary growth.

Recognition Lag

The proponents of the monetary rule would like to make the Fed responsible for achieving a steady rate of growth in M1 of, say, 3 percent a year. Their case rests largely on the fact that there are long and variable lags in the monetary policy process. First, there is the *recognition lag*. It takes time for information on the state of the economy to be generated. Figures for several months or even quarters may be needed before any trend deviation of, say, output from its full-employment level can be detected. Only then can policy be formulated to counteract the perceived deviation.

Implementation Lag

Having decided that policy action should be taken, the Fed then has to decide exactly what to do. The time taken to discuss alternative strategies produces an *implementation lag*. The FOMC may postpone monetary policy measures, waiting for stronger evidence of the problem to appear or for additional assessments of alternative policy measures to be made.

Impact Lag Even after the new monetary policy measures have been implemented, there is an *impact lag* between the policy changes and the economic response to them. For example, a policy to expand monetary growth to counteract a recession can affect the money supply relatively quickly. However, there is then a lag between the monetary expansion and its effect on spending. Initially, the main effect of a change in monetary policy is felt in the financial markets. Even if these changes affect *plans* to spend, such as investment plans, it takes time for these plans to result in actual additional spending. For example, today's new plan to build a house will result in only small expenditures until foundations are actually laid in 9 to 18 months' time. In the meantime, the blueprints have to be prepared, a geological survey conducted, and planning permission obtained.

Right Policy at the Wrong Time The existence of these three lags gives rise to the possibility that today's monetary policy measures designed to counteract today's perceived problems will exert their main effects on an economy facing the opposite set of difficulties. Indeed, proponents of a monetary rule suggest that far from dampening economic fluctuations, monetary policy has accentuated them. Expansionary monetary policy has its predominant impact during booms, whereas contractionary policies formulated during the boom exert their full power in the subsequent recession. Therefore, this argument goes, the economy would suffer less instability were contracyclical monetary policies abandoned in favor of a monetary rule. Since the Fed's performance with respect to monetary control under the new system of contemporaneous reserve accounting has yet to be tested, this debate will probably continue for some time to come.

Summary

1. The Full Employment and Balanced Growth Act of 1978 specifies the goals of monetary and other macroeconomic policies. In practice, monetary policy produces a package of effects resulting in an inevitable conflict of goals in the short run. In the long run, however, monetary policy can affect only the price level.

2. The targets of monetary policy have changed since 1914. In the 1950s and 1960s the primary target of monetary policy was money market conditions. Since 1970 the target has been the money supply.

3. Since the Fed cannot control the money supply directly, it uses operating targets which it can control to influence its target variable. From 1970 to 1984 the federal funds rate was the chief day-to-day operating target. Since February 1984 the Fed has used reserves as its operating target to control the money supply.

4. Monetary policy is conducted primarily through open market operations. These have an immediate effect on the federal funds market. Open market purchases increase reserves, which, in turn, shift the supply of federal funds to the right and move the demand to the left. These changes in supply and demand reduce the federal funds rate and expand depository institution lending. Increased lending raises the level of deposits.

5. Prior to February 1984 the system of lagged reserve requirements made demand for reserves completely interest inelastic. In the short run, therefore, the Fed could affect the federal funds rate but not the level of reserves. Fluctuations in the medium-term demand for reserves impeded monetary control implemented with the federal funds rate as the operating target.

6. The present (1984) system of contemporaneous reserve requirements enables depository institutions to alter their required reserves by changing the level of their deposits. Hence, it ensures that reserve demand is interest elastic. Therefore, reserves can now be used as the operating target.

7. There are long and variable lags between monetary policy measures and their impact on the economy. Hence, an appropriate policy for present economic conditions may be inappropriate by the time it exerts its effect. For this reason, a number of people have advocated a monetary rule whereby the Fed's task would be to ensure a steady rate of monetary growth.

Questions

1. How can goals of monetary policy conflict?

2. Why does implementation of the real bills doctrine produce destabilizing monetary policy actions?

3. What was the main problem in using money market conditions as the monetary policy target?

4. How did the Fed attempt to control the money supply in the period 1970–1979?

5. Explain why the demand for federal funds is influenced by the interest rate.

6. Explain why the supply of federal funds is influenced by the interest rate.

7. How is the federal funds market linked to the market for reserves?

8. Explain why the supply curve for reserves is upward sloping.

9. Why does the existence of borrowed reserves make reserve targeting more difficult?

10. Explain the effect of lagged reserve requirements on the demand for reserves.

11. Why did lagged reserve requirements hinder monetary control?

12. What is the case for a monetary rule?

PART FIVE

Money, Income, and Prices

The 1920s were an Elysian era for the Federal Reserve System. Since the international gold standard was gone and the United States was the only large trading country still maintaining gold payments, it was clear that the old rules of the gold standard were no longer relevant to the conduct of monetary policy. At last the Federal Reserve System could use its power to promote internal economic stability. The principal architect of the Federal Reserve's new monetary policy was Benjamin Strong, governor of the Federal Reserve Bank of New York. As a member of the Committee of Governors on Centralized Execution of Purchases and Sales of Government Securities, and later on the Federal Open Market Committee which replaced it, Strong was an advocate of the use of open market purchases and sales to stabilize economic activity. Never before had the Fed banks bought or sold government securities for the purpose of regulating economic conditions. This increased importance of open market operations gave considerable power to the New York Fed, since it acted as the agent for the Federal Reserve System in executing the purchase or sale of securities. Because of the position of the New York Fed and the persuasiveness of Benjamin Strong's logic, Strong was able on most occasions to determine the policy of the whole Federal Reserve System, much to the displeasure of some of the members of the Federal Reserve Board who were jealous of their prerogatives.

From Lester V. Chandler, *American Monetary Policy, 1928–1941* (New York: Harper and Row, 1971); Lester V. Chandler, *Benjamin Strong, Central Banker* (Washington, D.C.: Brookings Institution, 1958); and Milton Friedman and Anna J. Schwartz, *A Monetary History of the United States, 1867–1960* (Princeton, N.J.: Princeton University Press for the National Bureau of Economic Research, 1963), Chapters 6, 7, and 8.

Under Strong's leadership, the Fed reacted quickly to economic conditions in a countercyclical manner. In early 1923 the Fed became concerned about inflation and switched to a policy of monetary restraint. Very soon after the economy entered a mild recession, the Fed reversed its policy and stimulated the economy. In the summer of 1926 the Fed again switched to a policy of mild restraint and the economy entered another recession in October 1926. Like the previous one, this recession was extremely mild because the Fed reacted quickly to reverse its policy of restraint. Starting in May 1927 the Open Market Investment Committee, under the influence of Governor Strong, started to purchase government securities in open market operations. In late July the discount rate was reduced from 4 to $3\frac{1}{2}$ percent. With this easing of monetary conditions, the economy started to recover in late 1927. Accompanying this recovery was an incredible stock market boom.

Benjamin Strong's policies contributed to an unparalleled era of economic growth and stability, but his forceful leadership ended in 1928. During the first seven months of the year Strong was ill and spent most of his time in Europe. When he returned to the United States in early August, he informed the directors of the New York Fed that he would have to retire soon. The directors asked him to delay his resignation until the end of the year, even though he would be unable to work. He was never to resign. On October 6, 1928, he underwent surgery for an abscess caused by diverticulitis. The operation appeared to be a success, but on October 15 Strong suffered a relapse in the form of severe secondary hemorrhaging and died the next morning, not yet 56 years old. The New York Fed directors elected George Harrison to replace him on November 22, 1928. Harrison was well qualified for the job but lacked the prestige that Strong had accumulated during his 14 years at the Fed. Moreover, the passing of Strong created a power vacuum which prevented effective action. There had been rising opposition to the power and influence of the New York Fed within the System. The Federal Reserve Board had been especially jealous of Strong's influence and moved to reassert its authority.

Meanwhile, the Fed became increasingly worried about the spectacular stock market boom. The objective of promoting economic growth was sacrificed to that of restraining stock market speculation. During the first seven months of 1928, the New York Fed raised its discount rate in three equal steps, from $3\frac{1}{2}$ to 5 percent, the highest it had been since 1921. These restrictive measures caused the money supply to decline slightly during 1928 and early 1929, but stock market speculation continued. Stock prices rose 25 percent during the second half of 1928 and another 30 percent during the first nine months of 1929. The persistence of the stock market boom led the New York Fed to raise the discount rate a full percentage point to 6 percent in August. This increase, together with the onset of a business recession, broke the speculative bubble. The stock market reached its peak on September 9, 1929, when the Standard & Poor's composite price index of 90 common stocks hit 254. After falling to 228 on October 4, the market rallied to 245 on October 10. Then a selling panic hit the market. On October 24, 1929, known as Black Thursday, huge blocks of stocks were dumped on the market. Thirteen million shares of stock were traded as compared with a typical daily volume of about four million. On October 29, $16\frac{1}{2}$ million shares were traded and the Standard & Poor's price index fell to 162.

The stock market crash created the danger of a banking crisis because of the size of broker loans, particularly from the New York banks, which might have been in default. To ease the strain on New York banks, the New York Fed voted to reduce the discount rate from 6 to $5\frac{1}{2}$ percent on October 24, but the Federal Reserve Board disapproved the request unanimously. In order to prevent the sharp decline in stock prices from turning into a rout, the New York Fed purchased $50 million government securities on October 29 and another $65 million over the next two days. These open market purchases were far in excess of the amount authorized by the Open Market Investment Committee—$25 million in any given week. Some members of the Board were furious when Governor Harrison informed them of the action he had taken without the prior approval of the Open Market Investment Committee. The Board passed a unanimous resolution calling for the suspension of further purchases by the New York Fed. However, the Board did approve a reduction in the discount rate to 5 percent on October 31, 1929.

Governor Harrison of the New York Fed continued to argue for more purchases of securities and reductions in the discount rate in order to stimulate business, but the Federal Reserve Board in Washington resisted. The Board disapproved a reduction in the discount rate to 4 percent on January 30, 1930. Again, on August 24, the Board disapproved a reduction to 3 percent. Harrison encountered similar resistance to his advocacy of open market purchases in the Open Market Policy Committee. Although the discount rate did ultimately drop from 6 to $2\frac{1}{2}$ percent during 1930, this decline in the discount rate was not as rapid as the decline in market rates of interest. Hence, discounting became less attractive and borrowing from the Fed declined. From August 1929 to October 1930 the money supply fell 2.6 percent.

During the autumn of 1930 the economic situation worsened dramatically. Commercial banks started failing in the midwest and the south. A banking panic started as the public attempted to withdraw deposits. By December the banking panic had spread to New York City, and on December 1, 1930, the Bank of the United States failed. Not only was the Bank of the United States a member of the Federal Reserve System, it was also the largest bank ever to have failed in this country up to that time. The New York Fed tried to forestall a financial crisis by proposing a plan to merge the Bank of the United States with other banks. Unfortunately, the New York Clearing House banks decided at the last minute not to go along with the plan, partly because of anti-Semitic prejudice. The Bank of the United States was owned and managed by Jews.

The failure of the Bank of the United States led to runs on other banks and deposit withdrawals of more than $150 million. The New York Fed tried to alleviate the banking crisis by injecting reserves into the banking system through open market purchases of $45 million for its own account and an additional $80 million for the System's account. Although the Open Market Policy Conference (which replaced the Open Market Investment Committee in 1930) ultimately approved the New York Fed's actions at its January 1931 meeting, it authorized no future purchases and actually recommended that the System dispose of some of its holdings of government securities when an opportunity presented itself to do so without tightening monetary conditions. By February 1931 the Fed's security holdings had fallen by $130 million even though there was some tightening in money markets. Following a second wave of bank failures in March, the Board did approve a reduction in the discount rate to $1\frac{1}{2}$ percent on May 7, but the Open Market Policy Conference delayed new purchases of government securities until mid-June and then they were extremely modest. These actions were nowhere near sufficient to offset the decline in the money supply multiplier. The money supply dropped $5\frac{1}{4}$ percent during the five months from March to August, the same decline that had occurred during the previous 19 months.

The Fed then turned very restrictive in September 1931, when Britain left the gold standard. Fearing an outflow of gold, it raised the discount rate from $1\frac{1}{2}$ to $2\frac{1}{2}$ percent on October 9, and to $3\frac{1}{2}$ percent on October 16. This was the sharpest increase in the discount rate ever experienced to date. The result was one of the most violent deflations in U.S. history. In the five months from August 1931 to January 1932, the stock of money fell by 12 percent, equivalent to an annual rate of over 31 percent. From January to March 1932 the stock of money continued to decline, but at a slower annual rate of 13 percent.

The Fed did not attempt to stop the drastic declines in both economic activity and prices until late February 1932. When the Fed did act, it was primarily because of indirect pressure from Congress. Congress was considering legislation which would force the Fed banks to issue Federal Reserve notes for making substantial payments to veterans of World War I. Federal Reserve officials opposed the legislation and thought they might prevent its passage by taking more expansionary actions. In order to forestall this radical legislation, they lowered the discount rate from $3\frac{1}{2}$ to $2\frac{1}{2}$ percent and the Open Market Policy

Conference approved a dramatic program of government security purchases. During the period from February 24 through July the Fed
bought more than $1 billion government securities, the largest purchases
ever made by the Federal Reserve System up to that time. Unfortunately, soon after Congress adjourned on July 16, the purchases stopped.
After August 10 no net purchases were made until 1933.

The final wave of bank failures started in the last quarter of 1932.
As the banking panic spread to New York, Governor Harrison of the
New York Fed tried to persuade President Hoover to close all the banks
for a banking holiday. The president refused, but Harrison did succeed
in getting New York Governor Lehman to declare a statewide banking
holiday on March 4, 1933, the day Franklin Roosevelt was inaugurated.
The day after he assumed office, Roosevelt invoked the questionable
authority of a 1917 Trading with the Enemy Act to close the banks.
When Congress reconvened on March 9, it passed the Emergency
Banking Act that extended the banking holiday. Thus ended one of the
most disastrous monetary collapses in American history.

When the banking holiday ended on March 15, fewer than 12,000
banks reopened, less than half of the 25,000 banks that had been in
operation in mid-1929. From August 1929 to March 1933 the stock of
money had declined by 35 percent. Nominal income had fallen by more
than 50 percent, prices by 25 percent. The seemingly boundless prosperity of 1928 turned into the breadlines of the 1930s. The unemployment rate, which was only 3.2 percent in 1929, would soar to over 25
percent of the labor force in 1933.

11

Aggregate Demand and Supply

Macroeconomics

The monetary history of the Great Contraction of 1929–1933 is a dramatic illustration of the relationship between the money supply and total spending. This chapter will develop the macroeconomic aspects of this relationship.

Circular Flow of Income

Macroeconomics is the branch of economics that deals with inflation and unemployment. The central concept around which macroeconomic theory is organized is called the *circular flow of income and product.* The basic concept is very simple. When goods and services are sold, receipts from the sales become the income of individuals in the economy. A business firm's sales revenue becomes the wages, salaries, rent, interest, or profits earned by individuals who supplied the services or raw materials used in producing the firm's output. These payments to individuals are the sources of income used to purchase goods and services. This completes the circular flow.

Flows and Stocks

Economists use the word *flow* to mean a process that occurs continuously through time. For this reason, flows are measured in units per time period. Total spending on goods and services, income, and gross national product are all flows and thus are measured in terms of dollars per year. A *stock* can be measured at any point in time. The money supply is a stock and so it is measured in terms of dollars, not dollars per year.

Closed Economy Model

This chapter analyzes a simple closed economy, that is, an economy with no foreign trade. The model is extended to include foreign trade and the balance of international payments in Chapters 17 and 18. The model in this chapter also excludes government expenditure and taxation. The importance of government expenditure and the alternative ways it can be financed—taxation, bond sales, and creation of high-powered money—are addressed in Chapters 13 and 14.

Flow Equilibrium

Income and Product Flows

Consider a hypothetical economy consisting only of households and business firms. In this simple economy, each transaction involving final goods and services gives rise to two important flows. (To simplify the analysis even further, intermediate transactions, such as the sale of steel to an automobile manufacturer, are not considered explicitly here.) The first is the dollar value of all the final goods and services produced during one year, called *gross national product,* or GNP for short. Since all revenue from the sale of final goods and services becomes someone's income, production always generates an equivalent amount of income, the second flow. Of course, some output may not be sold but could be held by producers as inventories. Even though no actual sale occurs, production held as inventories by producers still generates income because producers are really using someone's income to purchase their own production.

Inventories

For analytical purposes, it is necessary to distinguish between *planned* and *unintended* inventory accumulation. The efficient marketing of production in the face of uncertain demand usually requires the holding of substantial stocks of inventories. The planned accumulation of these stocks by producers in anticipation of future sales should properly be considered a component of desired expenditures on goods and services. However, some inventory accumulation may occur because expected sales fail to materialize and consequently production is not sold. Clearly, this sort of unintended inventory accumulation should not be treated as a component of *desired* expenditures on goods and services.

Disequilibrium and Unintended Inventory Changes

Flow equilibrium in this simple economy would require individuals in the aggregate to desire to spend on goods and services an amount that is exactly equal to gross national product. In this equilibrium, there will be no unintended inventory investment in the aggregate. However, when individuals in the aggregate desire to spend more or less than gross national product, there will be an imbalance between aggregate demand and supply causing unintended changes in inventories.

Excess Demand and Inventory Depletion

Suppose, for example, that individuals in the aggregate desire to spend more than gross national product. Desired expenditures on goods and services will exceed the value currently being produced. This excess of expenditures over production causes an unintended drop in the stock of inventories:

Unintended change in the stock of inventories
= Gross national product − Desired expenditures on goods and
          services (including planned inventory
          accumulation)   (11.1)

Deficient Demand and Inventory Accumulation

On the other hand, if desired expenditures on goods and services fall short of gross national product, business firms cannot find enough buyers to purchase their output. In this case, some production becomes unintended inventory accumulation.

Business Reaction to Deficient Demand

When desired expenditures on goods and services are less than gross national product, business firms will not be able to sell all of their current production. Initially, this unsold output will simply go into inventories, but sooner or later business firms will react to the unplanned buildup of inventories by reducing prices or production. Since gross national product is equal to output valued at current prices, a reduction in output or prices will reduce the dollar value of income and production. Because the dollar value of current production falls, so too does income generated by the sale of that output.

Business Reaction to Excess Demand

On the other hand, when desired expenditures on goods and services are greater than gross national product, the excess of expenditure over production can be realized only if there is an unintended reduction in the stock of inventories. Although spending on goods and services in excess of production can be satisfied temporarily by reducing inventories, sooner or later business firms will raise their prices or increase production in response to the unplanned drop in inventories. This in turn will raise gross national product.

Money Stocks and Spending Flows

Money Demand

The *demand for money* is of central importance to macroeconomic analysis. The public has a certain desired stock of money that it wants to have on hand as a general source of purchasing power. As was discussed in earlier chapters, the money stock consists of all currency in circulation plus some types of deposits at depository institutions. Moreover, the stock of money that individuals and businesses desire to hold has been closely related to gross national product. Since the early 1960s, for example, individuals and businesses have desired to hold, on average, a stock of M2 money balances equal to about 42 percent of national income. If depository institutions supply either too much or too little money, the *stock disequilibrium* between the demand for and the supply of money quickly leads to a *flow disequilibrium* between expenditures on goods and services and current production. Indeed, this is the main cause of flow disequilibrium.

Individual Budget Constraints

Each individual can adjust his or her money balances to any level desired by spending more or less than he or she receives. If people desire to increase their current money balances, they can spend less than they receive and their money balances will rise. On the other hand, they can reduce their money balances by spending more than they receive. Each individual's budget constraint for any given time period can be represented by the following equation:

$$\text{Changes in the stock of money held} = \text{Flow of receipts} - \text{Flow of expenditures} \qquad (11.2)$$

Excess Money Supply and Flow Disequilibrium

When the public finds itself with a larger stock of money than it collectively desires to hold, each individual will attempt to spend it or loan it to someone else who will spend it. However, the public as a whole cannot get rid of its excess money balances, because someone's expenditure is someone else's receipt. Although the public cannot reduce the existing stock of money, its attempts to reduce individual money balances create a flow disequilibrium between production and expenditures on goods and services. Aggregating all the individual budget constraints in this hypothetical economy (which has no government sector), the following budget constraint for the household sector can be defined:

$$\text{Desired changes in money balances held} = \text{Gross national product} - \text{Desired expenditures on goods and services} \qquad (11.3)$$

Excess Money and Inventory Depletion

When individuals find themselves with excess money balances, they will attempt to reduce those balances by spending more than they receive. In the aggregate, the attempt to reduce money balances means that individuals are desiring to spend more than gross national product on goods and services. However, if desired expenditures on goods and services exceed gross national product, the household sector is trying to purchase more goods and services than are currently being produced. Initially, inventories will drop, but sooner or later businesses will respond to this excess demand for goods and services by raising prices and/or increasing output.

GNP Rises to Eliminate Excess Money Supply

It is the increase in gross national product resulting from the increase in prices or output that eliminates the excess supply of money. Since the demand for money is closely related to gross national product, the rise in gross national product resulting from the excess supply of money will increase the demand for money until the public's demand for money balances is equal to the existing stock. Collectively, individuals cannot reduce their money balances, but their attempts to do so will increase gross national product until the demand for money is raised to equal the supply of money. At that equilibrium level of gross national product, individuals in the aggregate no longer want to reduce their money balances. Consequently, they desire to spend on output an amount exactly equal to gross national product, producing flow equilibrium between production and expenditures.

Excess Demand for Money and Flow Disequilibrium

When the public finds itself with a smaller stock of money than it wants to hold, the process described above works in reverse. The attempts by individuals to increase their money balances will cause desired expenditures on output to fall short of current production. Initially, this will cause unplanned increases in inventories, but sooner or later business firms will act to stop this accumulation of unplanned inventories by reducing output or prices. When that occurs, gross national product will fall, reducing the demand for money until the demand for money is equal to the existing stock of money. At that level of gross national product, the economy will again be in flow equilibrium.

The Cambridge Equation and M2 Money Demand

The process described above implies that the equilibrium level of gross national product is determined by the stock of money created by the banking system and a demand-for-money function. One of the simplest demand-for-money functions is called the Cambridge equation. The Cambridge equation is based on the assumption that desired money balances M^d are a fraction k of gross national product:

$$\text{Desired money balances} = k \cdot (\text{Gross national product}) \quad (11.4)$$

The public currently wishes to hold M2 money balances equal to about 42 per cent of gross national product. This fraction has been virtually constant for over 20 years. The fact that the ratio of M2 money supply to gross national product (the Cambridge k) has been almost constant implies that the M2 money supply and gross national product grow at approximately the same rate.

The Cambridge Equation and M1 Money Demand

The ratio of M1 money supply to gross national product, however, has fallen in the postwar period. Table 11.1 shows that over the past two decades the ratio of M1 money balances to gross national product fell, on average, by about 3 percent a year. This implies that gross national product increases about 3 percentage points faster each year than does M1.

Table 11.1   Three-Year Average Annual Percentage Rates of Change in Nominal Gross National Product, the M1 Money Stock, and the Cambridge k

| | Average Annual Percentage Change in[a] | | |
Period	Nominal Gross National Product	M1	Cambridge k
1962–1964	6.51	3.31	−3.20
1965–1967	7.54	4.46	−3.08
1968–1970	7.21	5.25	−1.96
1971–1973	9.66	6.87	−2.79
1974–1976	8.62	5.17	−3.45
1977–1979	11.39	7.52	−3.87
1980–1982	7.82	6.90	−0.92

[a]Continuously compounded rates of change.

Source: Economic Report of the President, 1983, pp. 163 and 233.

Short-Run Fluctuations in Cambridge k

Although relatively stable in the long run, the percentage change in the Cambridge k varies substantially from one quarter to the next. The money supply series typically leads gross national product at turning points. An acceleration (or deceleration) in the rate of monetary growth tends to increase (or reduce) the rate of growth in gross national product about six months later, thus causing a temporary rise (or fall) in the Cambridge k during the first six months. The reason for this lag is that the initial impact of changes in the rate of monetary growth is on unplanned inventories. Gross national product is affected only when businesses react to changes in unplanned inventories and alter their output or pricing plans about six months later.

Long-Run Stability of Cambridge k

The variance of the Cambridge k falls substantially as the unit of time lengthens, because this adjustment period is smoothed out in longer-period data. In the seven 3-year periods shown in Table 11.1, the average percentage fall in the Cambridge k ranged from −0.9 to −3.8 percent. However, except for the 1980–1982 period, a time of rapid institutional and regulatory change, the average annual rates of change in k deviated from the 20-year average by only a little over 1 percentage point.

The Aggregate Demand Schedule

Nominal versus Real GNP

So far, this analysis has concentrated on the determination of the *nominal* value of gross national product. Nominal gross national product is the value of production expressed in current prices and so is the product of the quantity of output and the price level. Changes in the quantity of output, commonly called *real* gross national product, are measured by comparing final outputs valued at their prices of some base year. The gross national product price deflator or, simply, the GNP deflator (the applicable price index for final output) is then found by dividing current dollar nominal gross national product by real gross national product:

Nominal gross national product
$$= \text{(Real gross national product)} \cdot \text{(GNP deflator)} \quad (11.5)$$

or

$$Y = y \cdot P \quad (11.6)$$

where Y is nominal gross national product, y is real gross national product, and P is the GNP deflator.

Money Supply and Aggregate Demand

The equilibrium level of nominal gross national product that makes the demand for money equal to the supply of money can be thought of as an *aggregate demand schedule*. For example, the Cambridge equation assumes that desired money balances are a fraction k of nominal gross national product:

Money supply $=$ Demand for money $= k \cdot$ (Nominal gross national product) $\quad (11.7)$

or

$$M = k \cdot \text{(Real gross national product)} \cdot \text{(GNP deflator)} \quad (11.8)$$

or

$$M = k \cdot y \cdot P \quad (11.9)$$

Given any money supply M, there can be various combinations of output and prices which equate demand for and supply of money. Figure 11.1 shows all the combinations of output and prices that will make the demand for money equal to a given supply of money $\overline{M}$.

Excess Money Demand

In Figure 11.1 point A is a disequilibrium level of gross national product because here the demand for money is greater than the supply of money. When individuals in such a situation attempt to increase their money balances, desired expenditures on goods and services will be less than gross national product. Initially, this excess demand for money will cause unanticipated increases in inventories, as spending on goods and services is not sufficient to take current production off the hands of suppliers. Sooner or

Figure 11.1   Aggregate Demand Schedule

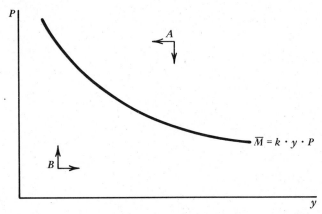

The vertical axis represents the price level as measured by the GNP deflator, P. The horizontal axis represents output as measured by real gross national product, y. The schedule depicted in the diagram represents all the combinations of output and prices that would make the demand for money $k \cdot y \cdot P$ equal to the supply of money $\overline{M}$.

later, however, producers will react to the accumulation of unwanted inventories by reducing production or prices.

Excess Money Supply

Point B is also a disequilibrium level of gross national product because here the supply of money is greater than the demand for money. When individuals attempt to reduce their money balances, desired expenditures on goods and services will exceed gross national product. Initially, this excess supply of money will cause unwanted reductions in inventories as the public purchases more goods and services than are currently being produced. Sooner or later, however, producers will react to these unwanted drops in inventories by increasing production or raising prices.

Money and Nominal GNP

This aggregate demand schedule shows the relationship between the money supply and the corresponding equilibrium level of nominal gross national product. It does not say anything about the relationships between the money supply and prices or the money supply and output. There are many combinations of output and prices that would produce the same equilibrium level of nominal gross national product. The level of real output that producers supply must be known before the equilibrium level of nominal gross national product can be separated into real output and the price level. This requires the derivation of an aggregate supply schedule.

The Aggregate Supply Schedule

Profit Maximization   The aggregate supply schedule shows the quantity of output that producers want to supply at various price levels. Since producers are attempting to maximize their profits, each producer would want to expand output
only if the cost of producing one additional unit of output is less than the
additional revenue generated by the sale of that additional output.

Production Function   To simplify the derivation of the aggregate supply schedule, assume that,
in the short run, plant and equipment cannot be increased. Additional
output can be generated only by using more labor or working the existing
labor force overtime. Figure 11.2 shows a simple short-run production
function representing the relationship between output and hours of labor
employed. As employment of labor increases, output increases, but at a
diminishing rate. The increase in output Δy generated by a small increase
in hours of labor ΔL is called the *marginal product of labor* $\Delta y/\Delta L$. With a
fixed capital stock, this marginal product of labor decreases as the employment of labor increases. As more labor is added to a fixed capital stock,
each worker has less capital to work with and is thus less productive. Consequently, the slope of the production function (equal to $\Delta y/\Delta L$) becomes
flatter as employment increases.

Figure 11.2   Short-Run Production Function

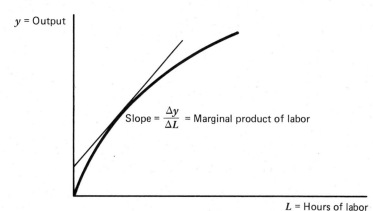

This diagram shows the relationship between output and hours of labor employed
in the economy. The capital stock is constant in the short run. As employment of
labor increases, output increases, but at a diminishing rate because of the law of
variable proportions. The slope of the production function, $\Delta y/\Delta L$, is called the
marginal product of labor. It represents the change in output that occurs when
there is a marginal addition to hours of labor employed.

Change in Profit from Increase in Labor

Profit Π is equal to total revenue minus total costs (labor costs plus the fixed costs of financing the existing capital stock). When a producer hires one additional worker, the change in profit $\Delta\Pi$ equals the increase in revenue minus the increase in cost. If all producers are price takers, their output decisions have no effect on the price at which they can sell output. Consequently, the additional revenue generated by the addition of one hour of labor is the price P at which output is sold times the marginal product of labor, $\Delta y/\Delta L$. The wage rate, W, represents the cost of acquiring one additional hour of labor. Hence, the change in profit produced by a small increase in hours of labor $\Delta\Pi/\Delta L$ is

$$\frac{\Delta\Pi}{\Delta L} = P \cdot \frac{\Delta y}{\Delta L} - W \tag{11.10}$$

Thus, profits will be maximized when price times the marginal product of labor equals the wage rate:

$$P \cdot \frac{\Delta y}{\Delta L} = W \tag{11.11}$$

If $P(\Delta y/\Delta L)$ is greater than W, producers could increase their profits by hiring additional workers, because the increase in output would generate an increase in revenue greater than the increased costs of hiring additional labor. On the other hand, if W is greater than $P(\Delta y/\Delta L)$, producers could increase their profits by laying off workers and reducing output, because the savings in labor costs would exceed the loss of revenue.

Aggregate Supply with Constant Wage Rate

If the wage rate is held constant at $\overline{W}$, an aggregate supply schedule can be derived that shows the level of output supplied by profit-maximizing producers at different price levels. The condition for profit maximization can be rewritten as

$$\frac{\Delta y}{\Delta L} = \frac{\overline{W}}{P} \tag{11.12}$$

Hence, as the price level rises, $\overline{W}/P$ will fall because the wage rate is held constant. Profit-maximizing producers will then increase output and employment until the marginal product of labor, $\Delta y/\Delta L$, falls to the new level of $\overline{W}/P$.

Supply Schedule Derived from Production Function

Consider the production function depicted in Figure 11.3a. At a price level P_0, equilibrium occurs at an output of y_0 and an employed labor force of L_0, because that is the point on the production function where the slope $\Delta y/\Delta L$ is equal to $\overline{W}/P_0$. If the price level rises to P_1, producers will hire additional labor and expand output to y_1, because that is the point where

Figure 11.3 The Relationship between (a) the Production Function and (b) the Aggregate Supply Schedule

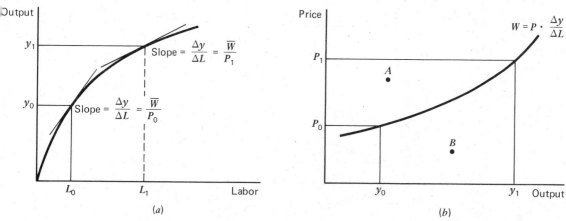

(a)   (b)

Figure 11.3a represents the production function. At a price level P_0, profit-max-imizing producers will choose to produce an output of y_0 and employ L_0 hours of labor, because that is the point where the slope of the production function $\Delta y/\Delta L$ is equal to $\overline{W}/P_0$. At a price P_1, profit-maximizing producers would employ L_1 hours of labor and produce an output of y_1, because that is the point where $\Delta y/\Delta L$ is equal to $\overline{W}/P_1$. These combinations of output and prices are then transposed to Figure 11.3b. The aggregate supply schedule represents all combinations of output and prices that make $\overline{W} = P(\Delta y/\Delta L)$.

$\Delta y/\Delta L$ is equal to $\overline{W}/P_1$. These equilibrium points can then be transposed to Figure 11.3b, which shows the derived *aggregate supply schedule*. This aggre-gate supply schedule shows the equilibrium outputs of profit-maximizing producers if they can acquire labor at a wage rate of $\overline{W}$. Point A represents a disequilibrium level of gross national product because $\overline{W}$ is less than $P(\Delta y/\Delta L)$. Producers would have an incentive to increase employment and output because the additional revenue generated exceeds the increase in labor costs. Point B also represents a disequilibrium level of gross national product because $\overline{W}$ is greater than $P(\Delta y/\Delta L)$. Producers would have an incentive to lay off workers and reduce output because the savings in labor costs exceed the loss of revenue.

Equilibrium Price Level and Output

Aggregate Demand Equals Aggregate Supply By combining the aggregate demand and aggregate supply schedules, the equilibrium price level and output for any given wage rate and money supply can now be derived. Consider Figure 11.4, which shows the aggre-gate supply schedule for a wage rate of $\overline{W}$. The equilibrium price level is P_0 and the equilibrium output is y_0, because this point lies on both the aggre-gate demand and the aggregate supply schedules. The economy is in *flow*

Figure 11.4 The Equilibrium Price Level and Output

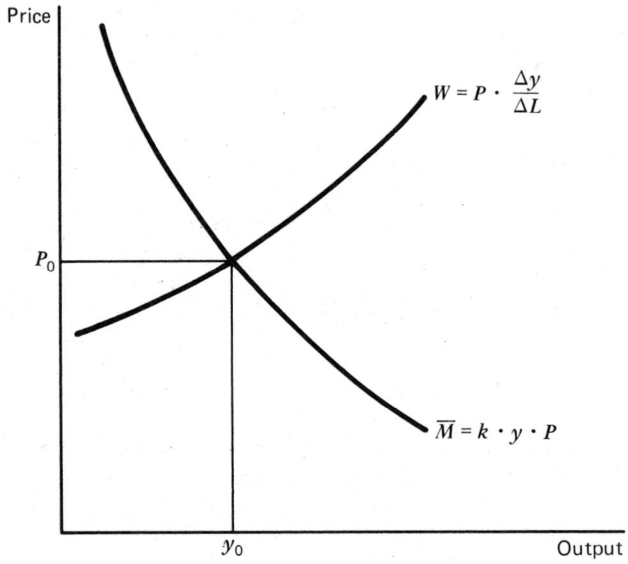

The diagram shows the aggregate demand schedule for a money supply of $\overline{M}$ and the aggregate supply schedule for a wage rate of $\overline{W}$. The equilibrium price level is P_0 and the equilibrium output is y_0.

equilibrium because $\overline{M} = k\cdot y_0\cdot P_0$. Since individuals in the aggregate are satisfied with their money balances, they desire to spend on goods and services an amount exactly equal to gross national product. Profit-maximizing producers also have no incentive to alter their production plans because $\overline{W} = P(\Delta y/\Delta L)$. Any change in employment or output would reduce profits because producers are currently operating at the profit-maximizing point on their production function.

Money, Prices, and Wages Double

Now consider what happens to the equilibrium values of output and the price level when the money supply doubles, as shown in Figure 11.5. The new aggregate demand schedule becomes $2\overline{M} = k\cdot y\cdot P$. A doubling of the money supply eventually leads to a doubling of nominal gross national product. Without knowledge of the supply response, though, the equilibrium values of output and the price level cannot be derived. If all potential workers are already employed, the doubling of the money supply simply doubles the price level, because additional production is impossible. As the price level rises, each producer would like to hire more labor at a wage rate of $\overline{W}$. However, producers can succeed in attracting additional labor only by bidding labor away from other producers. Consequently, competitive bidding by producers for a fixed labor force eventually raises the wage rate to $2\overline{W}$. This shifts the aggregate supply schedule upward until the economy is again in equilibrium at an output of y_0 and a price level of $2P_0$

Figure 11.5   Output and Price Level Effects of a Doubling of the Money Supply

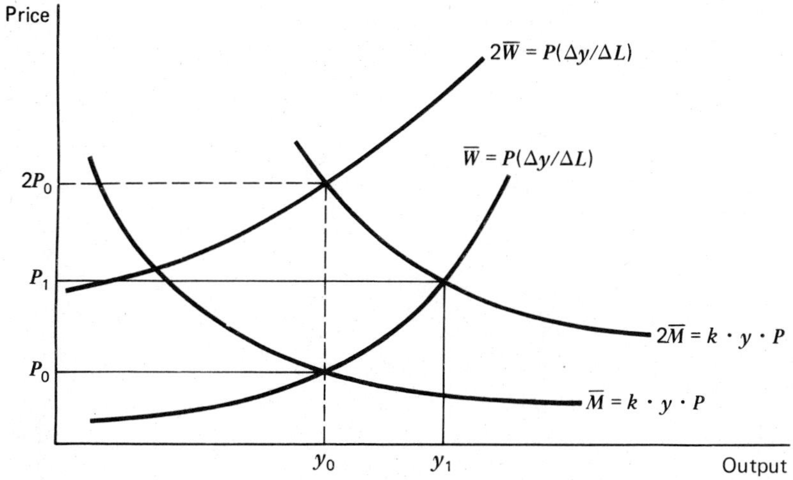

The economy is initially in equilibrium at y_0, P_0. A doubling of the money supply will shift the aggregate demand schedule upward to $2\overline{M} = k{\cdot}y{\cdot}P$. If output cannot increase because all potential workers are already employed, competitive bidding for the fixed supply of labor will raise wage rates to $2\overline{W}$, shifting the aggregate supply schedule upward to $2\overline{W} = P(\Delta y/\Delta L)$. The new equilibrium will be y_0, $2P_0$. If a net supply of labor is forthcoming at the wage rate $\overline{W}$, a doubling of the money supply will increase output to y_1 and prices will rise to P_1.

Money Doubles and Output Rises

On the other hand, if there are unemployed workers who are willing to work at a wage rate of $\overline{W}$, a doubling of the money supply would increase employment and output. Since the wage rate remains at $\overline{W}$, output rises to y_1 and the price level increases to P_1, but it does not double. In the situation where wages and prices both double, nothing happens to the *real wage rate* W/P. However, in the case where output rises to y_1, the real wage rate falls because the nominal wage rate remains constant at $\overline{W}$ while the price level rises to P_1. In fact, this fall in the real wage rate is the reason why employment and output increase as a result of the increase in the money supply.

Money Supply Is Halved

Figure 11.6 shows the effects of reducing the money supply by 50 percent. Suppose the economy is initially in equilibrium at a price level of P_0 and output of y_0 when the money supply is $\overline{M}$. If the money supply falls by 50 percent, the new aggregate demand schedule is $\overline{M}/2 = k{\cdot}y{\cdot}P$. Nominal gross national product falls by the same proportion as the money supply. Whether this affects output or not depends critically upon the behavior of wage rates. If workers agree to cut their wage rates by 50 percent, output will not be affected. Both prices and wages fall by 50 percent, leaving the real wage rate unchanged. However, if workers refuse to cut their wage rates and continue to demand wage rates of $\overline{W}$, producers will lay off

Figure 11.6   The Output and Price Level Effects of Reducing the Money Supply by 50 Percent

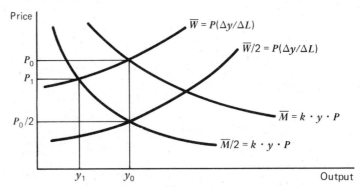

Assume the economy is initially in equilibrium at an output of y_0 and a price level of P_0. If the money supply falls by 50 percent, the aggregate demand schedule will shift down to $\overline{M}/2 = k \cdot y \cdot P$. If workers agree to cut their wage rates by 50 percent, the aggregate supply schedule will shift down to $\overline{W}/2 = P(\Delta y/\Delta L)$. Output remains at y_0 but prices and wages rates fall by 50 percent. On the other hand, if workers refuse to cut their wage rates, output will fall to y_1 and the price level will decline to P_1.

workers and reduce output to y_1. Prices fall, but by less than 50 percent. The real wage rate of those workers who continue to be employed increases. In fact, it is precisely this increase in the real wage rate that produces a decline in employment.

Summary

1. The economy is in flow equilibrium when individuals in the aggregate desire to spend an amount exactly equal to gross national product.

2. Flow disequilibrium implies unplanned changes in inventories.

3. Deficient aggregate demand causes unplanned inventory accumulation. Business firms react by reducing production.

4. When money supply exceeds money demand, individuals in the aggregate spend more than GNP and inventories decline. Business firms react by raising output and/or prices.

5. The Cambridge equation holds that desired money balances M^d are a fraction k of nominal gross national product—$M^d = k \cdot y \cdot P$. Here, M^d is money demand, y is output (real gross national product), and P is the price level. From this relationship, a demand curve relating price and quantity (P and y) combinations for a given M and k can be constructed.

6. Over the period 1962–1981, the Cambridge k for M1 declined

smoothly by about 3 percent a year. In the short run, however, k has fluctuated considerably.

7. If the money supply is doubled, aggregate demand shifts to the right so that the same quantity is demanded at twice the old price level or the same price level induces twice the quantity previously demanded.

8. The aggregate production function indicates that the marginal product of labor declines, given the stock of capital, as more labor is employed. Profits are maximized at the point where the value of labor's marginal product exactly equals the wage rate.

9. The aggregate supply curve is derived from the aggregate production function. An increase in the price level raises the value of labor's marginal product. With a constant wage rate, business firms will employ more labor to produce more output until the value of labor's marginal product is again reduced to the wage rate.

10. If all potential workers are employed, an increase in the money supply will lead to a proportional increase in wages and in the price level, leaving the level of output unchanged.

Questions

1. What is flow equilibrium in the economy?
2. What happens initially when excess demand appears in the economy?
3. How do business firms react to deficient aggregate demand?
4. How does the public react to a smaller stock of money than it collectively wants to hold?
5. How does disequilibrium in the money market create disequilibrium in the market for goods and services?
6. What is the Cambridge equation?
7. Draw a diagram showing aggregate demand for a given money stock $\overline{M}$. What happens to that demand curve when the money stock is reduced to $\overline{M}/2$?
8. Given a fixed price level, how does output vary with changes in the wage rate?
9. How does the marginal product of labor affect the aggregate supply function?
10. Derive an aggregate supply curve from a production function.
11. If the money supply is increased when the labor force is fully employed, what happens to wages, prices, and output?
12. If there are unemployed workers and the wage rate remains constant, what happens to prices and output when the money supply is increased?

12 Inflation and Unemployment

Unemployment and Wage Rigidity

Fixed Wages in Keynes's Theory

The failure of wage rates to adjust to changing price levels is one of the principal causes of fluctuations in the unemployment rate. The assumption that nominal wage rates are relatively rigid with respect to changes in the price level is a central feature of economic theories relating employment to changes in nominal aggregate demand. In his *General Theory of Employment Interest and Money,* John Maynard Keynes made wage rigidity one of the central features of his theory of employment. An increase in total spending would cause prices to rise but wages would remain unchanged. When the prices of finished goods rise and wages do not, employers have an incentive to increase employment and output. Keynes argued that the unemployment rate could be reduced by expansionary monetary and fiscal policies because he assumed that wage rates would rise less rapidly than the prices of goods and services. Real wage rates would fall, and that would stimulate employment and output.

Output Prices Rise before Costs

Basically the same reasoning was also used by Irving Fisher to explain the relationship between price level changes and unemployment many years before Keynes's *General Theory:*[1]

> When the dollar is losing value, or in other words when the price level is rising, a business man finds his receipts rising as fast, on the average, as that general rise of prices, but not his expenses, because his expenses consist, to a large extent, of things which are contractually fixed. Employment is then stimulated—for a time at least.

[1]Irving Fisher, "A Statistical Relationship between Unemployment and Price Changes," *International Labour Review,* 13(6), June 1926, pp. 787–792.

Expectations and Anticipated Inflation

An important feature of any theory of the relationship between unemployment and inflation is the method people use to form their expectations about future prices. Inflation affects employment levels largely because workers make errors in forecasting future inflation. Were the rate of inflation always anticipated with complete accuracy, real wage rates would be unaffected by changes in the inflation rate. In such a world of perfect foresight, a change in the rate of monetary growth has no effect on real output and employment. All that changes is the rate of inflation.

Minimum Wage Floors and Unemployment

In reality, changes in the rate of inflation have had significant effects on output and employment because of wage rigidity. Long-term union wage contracts, the minimum wage, and other institutional arrangements account for some of this rigidity. These minimum wage floors prevent certain segments of the labor market from reaching equilibrium. A minimum wage floor above the market equilibrium or market clearing monetary wage rate causes a shortage of jobs at that wage rate. Unemployed workers are willing to take jobs at those wage rates, but no job offers are forthcoming. However, very few unemployed workers are in the position of having no job offers. Typically, workers are unemployed because current job offers do not meet their wage expectations.

The Theory of Search Unemployment

Frictional Unemployment

Unemployment is always present because of the dynamic nature of a market economy. At any moment in time, some industries are declining and laying off workers while others are expanding and hiring new workers. The workers who are laid off or quit their jobs will normally be unemployed for several months before they find new jobs. This unemployment—known as *frictional unemployment*—is part of the cost of shifting resources from less valued to more valued uses.

Job Search

Unemployment plays an important role in the search for a new job. Once workers become unemployed, the duration of their unemployment depends on the costs of and the returns to obtaining additional information about job opportunities by remaining unemployed and continuing to search for job offers. Were unemployed workers willing to accept low enough wages, they could find employment almost immediately. However, they usually do not accept job offers if they expect to receive better ones by remaining unemployed and continuing the job search a little longer.

Reservation Wage

Consider some workers who have just become unemployed. They can always get jobs if they are willing to accept any wage offers, but rational workers will usually set some *reservation wage* below which they will reject all wage offers. The expected duration of unemployment will depend critically upon that reservation wage. Figure 12.1 shows the distribution of

Figure 12.1   Cumulative Distribution Function of Wage Offers

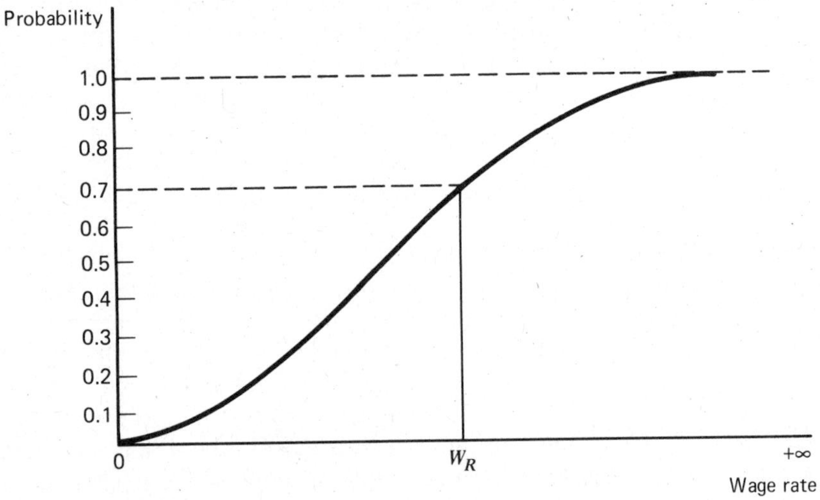

The diagram shows the cumulative distribution function of wage offers facing an unemployed worker. If the unemployed worker has a *reservation wage* W_R below which he or she will reject all wage offers, the probability of receiving an acceptable wage offer on any random selection will be .3. The expected number of random offers before an acceptable wage offer will be received is $1/.3$ or $3\frac{1}{3}$. More generally, if x is the probability of receiving an acceptable offer, the expected number of offers made before an acceptable one is $1/x$.

wage offers facing one unemployed worker as a cumulative distribution function (Chapter 6, Figure 6.1). If the individual sets his or her reservation wage at W_R, the probability that any random wage offer will fall short of the individual's reservation wage is .7 or 70 percent. In other words, there is only a 30 percent chance that any particular wage offer will be acceptable. If the probability of receiving an acceptable wage offer is x, then the expected number of offers that will be received before an acceptable one is made is $1/x$ (Appendix, proof 12.1). Consequently, the higher the reservation wage, the greater the expected number of offers that have to be obtained before an acceptable offer will be received.

Unemployment Duration and Unemployment Rate

The length of time unemployed individuals spend in searching for job offers is an important factor in determining the unemployment rate. This is so because the unemployment rate equals the percent of the labor force that becomes unemployed each week times the average duration of unemployment in weeks (Appendix, proof 12.2):

Unemployment rate = (Percent of the labor force that becomes unemployed each week) · (Average duration of unemployment in weeks)   (12.1)

Figure 12.2 The Relationship between the Unemployment Rate and the Average Duration of Unemployment

*Duration of unemployment represents the average length of time (arithmetic mean) during which those classified as unemployed have been continuously looking for work.

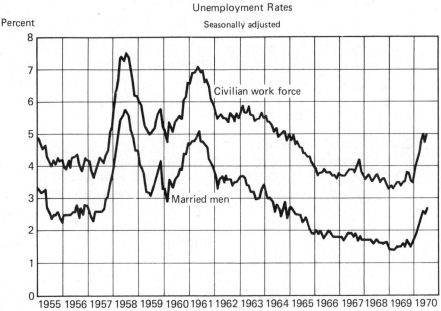

Source: Federal Reserve Bank of St. Louis Review, 52(8), August 1970, pp. 14–15.

The percent of the labor force that becomes unemployed each week from quits, layoffs, firings, and new entrants into the labor force has been a fairly stable fraction of the labor force during most of the postwar period. Over the business cycle, layoffs move inversely to quits. During recessions, when layoffs are high, people who have jobs hesitate to quit; when times are better, quits rise and layoffs fall. As a result of these offsetting movements in quits and layoffs, the number of people who become unemployed each week has been a fairly constant 0.5 percent of the labor force. Consequently, as an approximate rule of thumb, the unemployment rate is equal to this 0.5 percent of the labor force that becomes unemployed each week times the average duration of unemployment in weeks. An average duration of unemployment of 10 weeks, for example, is generally associated with an unemployment rate of about 5 percent, as shown in Figure 12.2.

The Natural Rate of Unemployment

Optimal Search Unemployment Given the distribution of wage offers, each individual will continue to remain unemployed as long as the expected value of further search is greater than its expected cost. The expected value of continuing to remain unemployed is the expected present value of the higher lifetime wages that further search may make possible. The cost of remaining unemployed is the income lost from further unemployment (net of any unemployment benefits). The higher is the current wage offer, the smaller will be the expected value of further search and the larger will be the foregone earnings from unemployment. Consequently, there will be some optimal reservation wage that will divide wage offers that are acceptable from those that are not.

Unemployment Benefits One of the important factors determining this reservation wage is the level and duration of unemployment benefits. The unemployment compensation system in the United States mitigates the economic hardships of families suffering from unemployment. However, this financial aid also reduces the cost of remaining unemployed and therefore encourages unemployed workers to set higher reservation wages, thus increasing the average duration of unemployment. Recent changes in the level and duration of benefits under the unemployment compensation system have contributed to substantial variations in the average duration of unemployment. For example, the duration of unemployment benefits has often been extended during periods of high unemployment. During the 1974–1975 recession Congress passed two measures which increased the duration of unemployment benefits significantly and extended the coverage. The Federal Supplemental Benefits Act of 1975 extended unemployment compensation for eligible workers to an unprecedented 65 weeks from the previous 26 weeks. In addition, the Special Unemployment Assistance Act offered 39 weeks of benefits to workers not previously covered by unemployment compensation. Although motivated by humanitarian considerations, these additional unemployment benefits had the undesirable effect of increasing the unemployment rate. By some estimates, these two pieces of legislation added almost one percentage point to the unemployment rate.

Optimal Search Produces a Natural Rate of Unemployment
If unemployed individuals know the relevant wage offer distribution and the costs of search, the reservation wages they choose will lead to a *natural rate of unemployment.* By definition, the natural rate of unemployment is the rate that occurs in equilibrium when workers estimate their wage offer distributions correctly. Of course, this rate is not constant over time. In the 1950s the natural rate of unemployment was about 4 percent. Liberalized unemployment benefits, the elimination of the military draft, and an increase in new entrants to the labor force raised the natural rate of unemployment to over 6 percent in the 1970s.

Fluctuations Around the Natural Rate of Unemployment

Reservation Wages Set Too High
So far, the discussion has assumed that individuals know the distribution of relevant wage offers. In reality, workers frequently make mistakes in estimating their distribution of wage offers, and these errors produce deviations from the natural rate of unemployment. Figure 12.3 shows the ex-

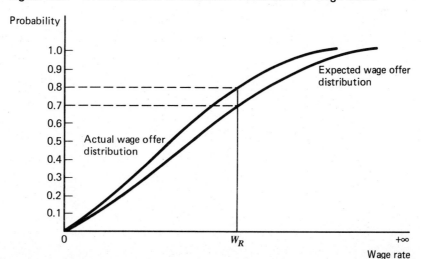

Figure 12.3   Overestimation of Cumulative Distribution of Wage Offers

The diagram shows the actual and expected wage offer distributions of individuals who overestimate their wage offer distribution. They will set their reservation wage W_R too high. As a result, the average duration of unemployment will be too high because these people are holding out for wage offers that do not exist.

pected and actual wage offer distributions for individuals who overestimate their wage offer distributions. These individuals set their reservation wages too high and, consequently, spend too much time searching for wage offers which they have a very small probability cf receiving. When unemployed workers overestimate their wage offer distributions, the average duration of unemployment will be too high. This produces an unemployment rate above the natural rate.

Reservation Wages Set Too Low

Individuals who underestimate their wage offer distributions tend to set their reservation wages too low. Although they may think they are holding out for only the best wage offers, in fact their reservation wages are lower than the optimal level. Hence, they may well end up accepting inferior wage offers. On average, these individuals have a very short duration of unemployment because they accept most job offers that are made to them, as shown in Figure 12.4. These errors in estimating wage offer distributions, in the aggregate, produce fluctuations in the unemployment rate around the natural rate. When unemployed workers underestimate their wage offer distributions, the average duration of unemployment will be too low and this produces an unemployment rate below the natural rate.

Unemployment and Welfare

One should not conclude that such a reduction in the unemployment rate raises economic welfare. In the long run, labor can increase its real wages only by increasing its marginal productivity. One important source of pro-

Figure 12.4   Underestimation of Cumulative Distribution of Wage Offers

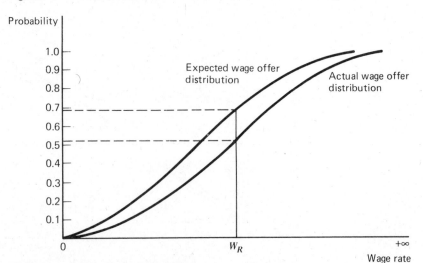

This diagram shows the actual and expected wage offer distributions for workers who underestimate their wage offer distribution. They set their reservation wage W_R too low and hence spend too little time searching for better-paying jobs.

ductivity improvement is the redistribution of labor from sectors of the economy where labor's marginal productivity is low to sectors where it is high. In situations where workers, in the aggregate, underestimate their wage offer distribution, they also underinvest in the search for job offers. The additional employment and production created when workers accept jobs too soon are worth less than the job-seeking time displaced. The rate of labor's productivity growth is reduced because a larger percentage of the labor force gets stuck in low-productivity sectors of the economy as a result of not investing enough time in the search for the highest-paying jobs. If workers, in the aggregate, overestimate their wage offer distribution, they invest too much time in *search unemployment* and this causes the unemployment rate to rise above the natural rate. This condition, of course, is also suboptimal because time is wasted searching for job offers that do not exist.

Expectational Errors and the Unemployment Rate

Figure 12.5 summarizes these effects of forecast errors on the unemployment rate. When workers, in the aggregate, underestimate the wage offer distribution, the unemployment rate lies below its natural rate. Conversely, when workers, in the aggregate, overestimate the wage offer distribution, the unemployment rate lies above its natural rate.

Figure 12.5 The Relationship between Errors in Estimating the Wage Offer Distribution and the Unemployment Rate

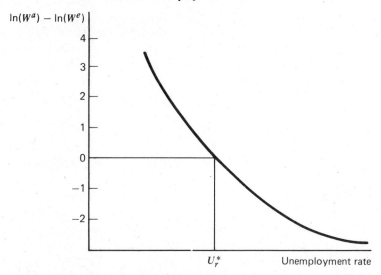

The vertical axis is the natural logarithm of the actual wage offer mean $[\ln(W^a)]$ minus the natural logarithm of the expected wage offer mean $[\ln(W^e)]$. Mathematically, the difference in the natural logarithm of a variable is a percentage difference. Consequently, the vertical axis is interpreted as the percentage *underestimation* of the wage offer distribution. When this variable is zero, unemployed workers correctly estimate their wage offer distribution and the unemployment rate is at its natural level, U_r^*.

Unanticipated Inflation and Unemployment

Expectations Formation

Past distributions of wage offers are public information, but workers may be unaware of current labor market conditions. For this reason, they may make errors in estimating their current wage offer distribution. Since employers offer only wage rates equal to the price of final output times the marginal product of labor, one can expect nominal wage offers to rise through time at a rate equal to inflation plus the rate of increase in labor's marginal product. It might be assumed that, in forming their estimates of current wage offers, rational workers extrapolate the known past distribution of wage offers into the present, adjusting for expected increases in prices and the marginal product of labor. Thus, errors in estimating the current wage offer distribution are of two types: errors in estimating the rate of inflation and errors in estimating the rate of change in labor's marginal product (Appendix, proof 12.3).

Tradeoff between Unanticipated Inflation and Unemployment

If workers can forecast correctly the increase in their marginal product of labor and thus the distribution of real wage offers, the only source of error left is incorrect estimates of the rate of inflation. In this case, Figure 12.5 can be reinterpreted as a tradeoff between unanticipated inflation and unemployment. When workers underestimate the rate of inflation, they also underestimate the current wage offer distribution. When they overestimate the rate of inflation, they also overestimate the current wage offer distribution. Consequently, deviations from the natural rate of unemployment are positively related to the difference between the expected rate of inflation π^e and the actual rate of inflation π. This relationship is illustrated in Figure 12.6.

Employers React Faster than Workers

Of course this description of the effects of unanticipated inflation on unemployment rests on the assumption that employers adjust to changes in the rate of inflation very rapidly in making wage offers but employees adjust more slowly in altering their reservation wages. One important reason for this difference in response is the difference in the relative costs of gathering the relevant information. An employer's wage offer depends only on one price, the price of the producer's final output, which the producer knows. The distribution of wage offers facing an unemployed worker, however, depends on the prices of hundreds of goods and consequently is much more difficult to forecast. It should not be surprising, then, that actual wage offers adjust to changes in inflation more rapidly than the distribution of expected wage offers used by workers to set their reservation wage.

Figure 12.6   Unemployment Rate and Unanticipated Inflation

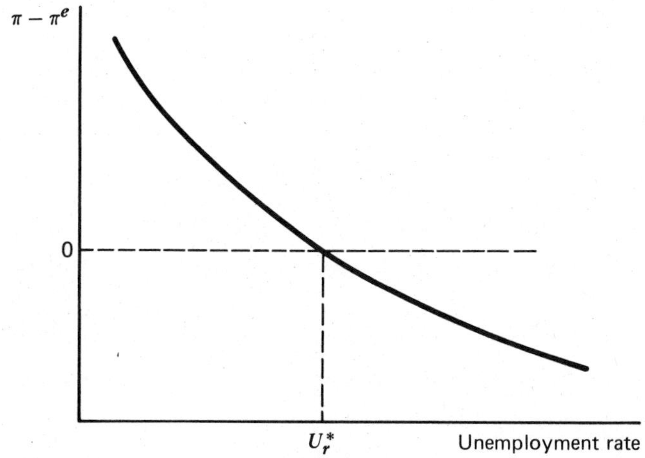

The diagram shows the tradeoff between unanticipated inflation and the unemployment rate. The vertical axis is the difference between the actual rate of inflation π and the expected rate of inflation π^e. When the expected rate of inflation is exactly equal to the actual rate of inflation, workers make no errors in estimating their wage offer distributions and the unemployment rate is at its natural level U_r^*. When the actual rate of inflation exceeds the expected rate of inflation, workers underestimate their wage offer distribution and the unemployment rate is less than its natural rate. When the actual rate of inflation is less than the expected rate, workers overestimate their wage offer distribution and the unemployment rate is above the natural rate.

The Tradeoff between Inflation and Unemployment with Fixed Expectations of Inflation

The exact relationship between inflation and unemployment depends critically upon the public's expectations of inflation. If the public held fixed expectations of inflation, there would be a stable tradeoff between inflation and unemployment. For example, if the public expected prices to rise at 3 percent a year, the unemployment rate would be at its natural rate when the actual rate of inflation was 3 percent a year. If prices rose at a rate greater than 3 percent a year, workers would underestimate the rate of inflation and the unemployment rate would drop below the natural rate. Conversely, rates of inflation below 3 percent a year would be associated with unemployment rates greater than the natural rate.

Money and Unemployment under Fixed Expectations

With fixed inflationary expectations, the rate of monetary growth determines both the rate of inflation and the unemployment rate in the long run. The monetary authorities in this situation would be faced with the dilemma of trading a higher rate of inflation for less unemployment. This tradeoff between inflation and unemployment is illustrated in Figure 12.7.

Okun's Law   In order to derive the rate of monetary growth associated with each point on the tradeoff schedule, the relationship between the rate of change in output and the unemployment rate must be developed. In 1962 Arthur Okun estimated this relationship, now known as Okun's Law. First, Okun calculated the rate of growth in output necessary to keep the unemployment rate constant. Each year the labor force increases and each worker's productivity rises. In order to keep a constant fraction of the labor force employed, output has to grow at a rate equal to the sum of the growth in the labor force (in work hours) and the growth in output per hour. Okun called this the rate of growth in *potential output:*

Rate of growth in potential output
    = Rate of growth in the labor force (in work hours)
    + Rate of growth in output per work hour   (12.2)

Okun found that, for every percentage point that actual output growth falls below potential output growth, the unemployment rate rises by one-third of a percentage point a year. Okun's Law may be described by the following equation:

Figure 12.7   **Tradeoff between Inflation and Unemployment with an Expected Rate of Inflation of 3 Percent a Year**

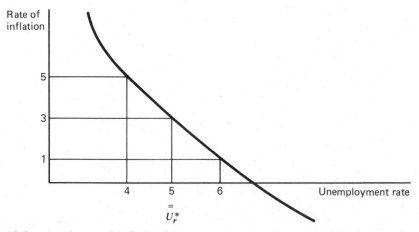

If the actual rate of inflation is 3 percent a year, the unemployment rate is at its natural level (assumed to be 5 percent). An actual rate of inflation of 5 percent would push the unemployment rate below its natural rate to 4 percent.

The change in the unemployment rate (in percentage points per year)
= [Annual rate of growth in potential output
− Annual rate of growth in actual output]/3   (12.3)

Required Growth of Nominal GNP Suppose the tradeoff between inflation and unemployment is represented by Figure 12.7. In order to validate the public's inflationary expectations, prices would have to increase at an annual rate of 3 percent. This would produce an unemployment rate of 5 percent, which is the natural rate. If the rate of growth in potential output is 4 percent a year, real output would also have to increase at a rate of 4 percent, in order to keep the unemployment rate constant. In addition, since prices would have to increase at 3 percent to validate the public's inflationary expectations, nominal gross national product would have to increase at an annual rate of 7 percent:

$$\Delta\ln(y \cdot P) = \pi + \Delta\ln(y)$$
$$(7\%) = (3\%) + (4\%) \qquad (12.4)$$

Required Growth of Money Supply One can determine the rate of monetary growth required to keep the unemployment rate at 5 percent by using the Cambridge equation model of the demand for money. If the Cambridge k (the ratio of desired money balances to nominal gross national product) is constant, the money supply would have to grow at an annual rate of 7 percent to keep the unemployment rate at 5 percent:

$$\Delta\ln(M) = \Delta\ln(k) + \Delta\ln(y \cdot P)$$
$$(7\%) = (0\%) + (7\%) \qquad (12.5)$$

Monetary Acceleration under Fixed Expectation Now assume that the Fed, which has been increasing the money supply at an annual rate of 7 percent, suddenly accelerates the rate of monetary growth to 9 percent a year. The annual rate of increase in nominal gross national product would then increase to 9 percent a year:

$$\Delta\ln(M) = \Delta\ln(k) + \Delta\ln(y \cdot P)$$
$$(9\%) = (0\%) + (9\%) \qquad (12.6)$$

Given the initial rate of inflation of 3 percent a year, an annual rate of growth in nominal gross national product of 9 percent a year implies a 6 percent a year growth in output:

$$\Delta\ln(y \cdot P) = \pi + \Delta\ln(y)$$
$$(9\%) = (3\%) + (6\%) \qquad (12.7)$$

This rate of growth exceeds the potential rate of growth in output of 4 percent a year, causing the unemployment rate to decline. A decline in the unemployment rate represents an upward movement along the schedule represented in Figure 12.7 to higher and higher rates of inflation. Eventually, a new equilibrium point will be reached at 5 percent inflation and 4 percent unemployment. With prices rising at 5 percent a year, the 9 percent a year growth in nominal gross national product will produce a 4 percent a year growth in output:

$$\Delta\ln(y \cdot P) = \quad \pi \quad + \Delta\ln(y)$$
$$(9\%) \quad = (5\%) + \quad (4\%) \tag{12.8}$$

Since this 4 percent a year growth in output is exactly equal to the growth in potential output, the unemployment rate will stop declining and come to rest at a rate of 4 percent.

This tradeoff between inflation and unemployment occurs only if expectations of inflation are constant. However, this assumption of rigid expectations implies that no one learns from past forecasting errors. Every year prices would rise 5 percent, but the public would continue to expect 3 percent inflation.

Adaptive Expectations and the Tradeoff between Inflation and Unemployment

Adaptive Expectations of Inflation

If past rates of inflation are used to form expectations of inflation, this permanent tradeoff between inflation and unemployment can no longer exist. Models of expectations formation in which past forecasting errors are used to revise current forecasts are called *adaptive expectations* models. The simplest adaptive expectations model assumes that individuals modify their forecasts by the error experienced during the past time period. If individuals experienced 5 percent inflation during the last time period and they forecast only 3 percent inflation, they would have underestimated the rate of inflation by 2 percentage points. Consequently, they raise their expectation of inflation by 2 percentage points for the next time period. As a result, the expected rate of inflation π^e is the actual rate of inflation experienced during the last time period π_{t-1}:

$$\pi_t^e - \pi_{t-1}^e = \pi_{t-1} - \pi_{t-1}^e \tag{12.9}$$

which can be rearranged in the form

$$\pi_t^e = \pi_{t-1} \tag{12.10}$$

In the more general case, individuals may modify their forecast by only a fraction of the error experienced during the last time period:

$$\pi_t^e - \pi_{t-1}^e = \lambda(\pi_{t-1} - \pi_{t-1}^e) \qquad (12.11)$$

or

$$\pi_t^e = \lambda\pi_{t-1} + (1 - \lambda)\pi_{t-1}^e \qquad (12.12)$$

By writing π_{t-1}^e in terms of π_{t-2} and π_{t-2}^e, and π_{t-2}^e in terms of π_{t-3} and π_{t-3}^e, and so on, π_t^e can be expressed solely in terms of past actual inflation rates:

$$\pi_t^e = \lambda\pi_{t-1} + \lambda(1 - \lambda)\pi_{t-2} + \lambda(1 - \lambda)^2\pi_{t-3} + \cdots \qquad (12.13)$$

Dynamic Relationship between Inflation and Unemployment

If expectations of inflation are indeed formed in this way, the monetary authorities can still trade less unemployment for more inflation in the short run. However, a once-and-for-all increase in the rate of monetary growth cannot permanently reduce the unemployment rate. To illustrate the dynamics of the relationship between inflation and unemployment when individuals adapt their expectations to recent experience, consider Figure 12.8. Suppose the economy is initially in equilibrium with an unemployment rate of 5 percent (which is the natural rate) and an inflation rate of 3 percent. Since potential output is increasing at 4 percent a year, nominal gross national product has to increase by 7 percent a year to keep the unemployment rate at its natural rate. If the Cambridge k is constant, the money supply has to increase at 7 percent a year to accommodate the increase in the demand for money generated by that increase in nominal income. This equilibrium is shown as A in Figure 12.8.

Monetary Acceleration under Adaptive Expectations

Now consider what happens if the rate of monetary growth accelerates to an annual rate of 9 percent. This acceleration in the rate of monetary growth will raise the growth of nominal aggregate demand to 9 percent a year. Given the initial rate of inflation of 3 percent a year, output would start to increase at 6 percent a year, 2 percentage points faster than the potential rate of 4 percent. Any output growth rate exceeding the potential rate reduces the unemployment rate. As long as expected inflation remains constant at 3 percent, the economy moves up the short-run schedule from A to B in Figure 12.8. However, since inflationary expectations are based upon past experience, this short-run schedule between inflation and unemployment starts to move upwards as individuals experience inflation higher than 3 percent a year.

Figure 12.8   Effects on Unemployment and Inflation of a Given Acceleration in the Rate of Monetary Growth with Adaptive Expectations

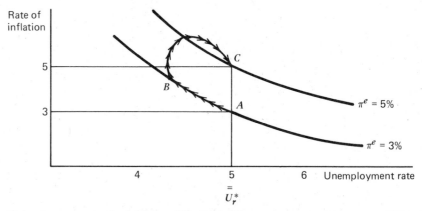

Point *A* represents the initial equilibrium of 5 percent unemployment and 3 percent inflation. An acceleration in the rate of monetary growth of 2 percentage points will initially lower the unemployment rate as the economy moves up the short-run schedule relating inflation to unemployment with an expected rate of inflation of 3 percent. However, since inflationary expectations are based on past experience, eventually expectations of inflation will adjust to any steady state rate of inflation, and the unemployment rate will return to its natural rate of 5 percent. In the long run, the rate of inflation will simply accelerate to 5 percent, percentage point for percentage point with the acceleration in the rate of monetary growth. However, during the period when the unemployment rate is rising back to its natural rate, the rate of inflation will temporarily rise above the long-run equilibrium rate of 5 percent.

Long-Run Neutrality of Money

In the long run, the expected rate of inflation adjusts to any steady state rate of inflation and the unemployment rate returns to its natural rate of 5 percent. With the 9 percent growth rate in nominal gross national product associated with the 9 percent increase in the money supply, the long-run equilibrium rate of inflation is 5 percent. Output must rise at 4 percent a year to keep the unemployment rate constant at its natural rate of 5 percent. Therefore, the long-run rate of inflation equals the 9 percent growth in nominal gross national product minus the 4 percent growth in output. However, as the unemployment rate rises back to its natural rate of 5 percent, the rate of inflation will temporarily overshoot this long-run equilibrium rate. Since the unemployment rate must rise in order to return to its natural rate, output has to increase at a rate *less* than the potential rate of 4 percent during the transition period. With nominal gross national product increasing continuously at 9 percent a year, inflation must temporarily increase at more than 5 percent a year.

Empirical Evidence
on the Relationship
between Inflation and Unemployment

Changing Postwar Relationship The precise relationship between inflation and unemployment depends critically on how individuals form their expectations about inflation. Rigid inflationary expectations generate a stable tradeoff between inflation and unemployment. Adaptive expectations models, on the other hand, produce no permanent tradeoff between inflation and unemployment. Empirical evidence on the relationship between inflation and unemployment indicates that this relationship has changed radically during the postwar period. Prior to the 1960s there appeared to be a fairly stable tradeoff between inflation and unemployment, indicating that individuals did have relatively rigid expectations about inflation. Beginning in the 1960s, however, this seemingly stable relationship became unglued. Studies of the relationship since the early 1960s indicate that individuals have begun to use adaptive expectations in forming their estimates of future inflation.

The Phillips Curve Postwar analysis of the relationship between inflation and unemployment can be divided into two stages. The first stage was the apparent discovery of an inverse relationship between inflation and unemployment. One of the first studies of this relationship was published by A. W. Phillips in 1958.[2] Phillips examined the data for the United Kingdom from 1861 to 1957 and found that the rate of change in nominal wage rates could be explained very well by the unemployment rate. Wages tended to rise at a faster rate when unemployment rates were relatively low. The relationship was quite stable over the whole period, despite changing institutional characteristics of the wage-determining process. Figure 12.9 shows one of the curves Phillips constructed. The curve shown in the diagram represents the average relationship between unemployment and the rate of increase in nominal wage rates during the period 1861 to 1913. The dots represent data for the years 1948–1957. Amazingly, the data for these postwar years lie very close to the curve constructed from data during the 1861–1913 period, suggesting that the relationship had changed very little.

U.S. Data on the Phillips Curve Although Phillips's study actually examined the relationship between the rate of increase in nominal wage rates and the unemployment rate, economists were quick to realize that it also implied a tradeoff between *inflation*

---

[2]A. W. Phillips, "The Relationship between Unemployment and the Rate of Change of Money Wage Rates in the United Kingdom, 1861–1957," *Economica*, 25(4), November 1958, pp. 283–299.

Figure 12.9   The Original Phillips Curve

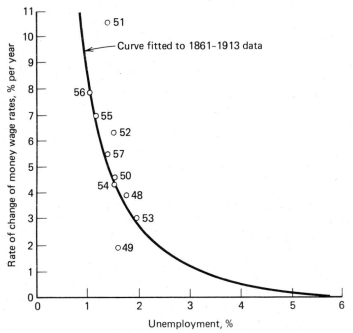

The diagram shows the relationship between unemployment and the rate of increase in nominal wage rates for the United Kingdom. The curve represents the average relationship between the unemployment rate and the rate of increase in nominal wages for the period 1861 to 1913. The dots represent data from 1948 to 1957.

Source: A. W. Phillips, "The Relationship between Unemployment and the Rate of Change of Money Wage Rates in the United Kingdom, 1861–1957," *Economica*, 25(4), November 1958, pp. 283–299.

and unemployment. In fact, since the publication of Phillips's article, these tradeoffs between inflation and unemployment have been called *Phillips curves*. One of the first studies of that tradeoff for the U.S. economy was presented to the American Economic Association by Paul Samuelson and Robert Solow in 1960. They pointed out that prices tend to rise at about the same rate as unit labor costs. Unit labor costs increase at a rate equal to the rise in hourly labor compensation minus the rate of increase in output per work hour. Consequently, one can simply subtract the trend rate of growth in output per hour from the annual increase in nominal wage rates to get a measure of the underlying rate of inflation. They then used this relationship to translate Phillips's relationship into a tradeoff between inflation and unemployment, as shown in Figure 12.10. Samuelson and Solow described

Figure 12.10   The Tradeoff between Inflation and Unemployment as Estimated by Samuelson and Solow for the United States Economy in 1960

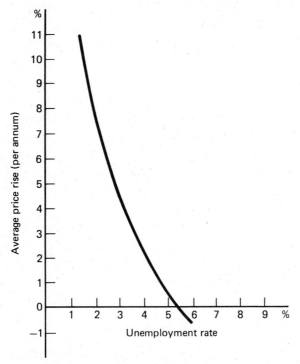

The curve represents the average relationship between inflation and unemployment for the 1935–1960 time period.

Source: Paul Samuelson and Robert Solow, "Analytical Aspects of Anti-Inflation Policy," *American Economic Review,* 50(2), May 1960, pp. 177–194.

the tradeoff between inflation and unemployment for the United States economy as follows:[3]

> 1. In order to have wages increase at no more than the $2\frac{1}{2}$ percent per annum characteristic of our productivity growth, the American economy would seem on the basis of twentieth century and postwar experience to have to undergo something like 5 to 6 percent of the civilian labor force's being unemployed. That much unemployment would appear to be the cost of price stability in the years immediately ahead.

[3]Paul Samuelson and Robert Solow, "Analytical Aspects of Anti-Inflation Policy," *American Economic Review,* 50(2), May 1960, pp. 177–194.

Figure 12.11   Inflation and Unemployment, 1960–1982

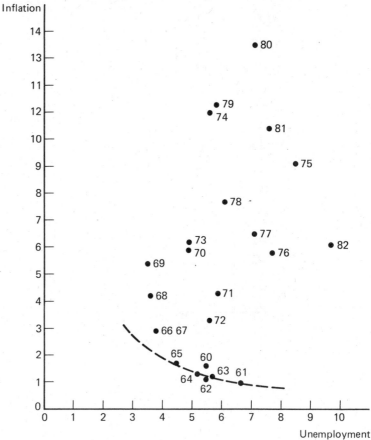

Source: Economic Report of the President, 1983, pp. 201 and 225.

2. In order to achieve the nonperfectionist's goal of high enough output to give us no more than 3 percent unemployment, the price index might have to rise by as much as 4 to 5 percent per year. That much price rise would seem to be the necessary cost of high employment and production in the years immediately ahead.

The Unstable Phillips Curve   The stable relationship between inflation and unemployment that economists thought they had detected began to fall apart as the decade of the 1960s neared its end. It became clear that even higher rates of inflation were required to keep the unemployment rate low, as seen in Figure 12.11. An explanation for the diminishing usefulness of the relationship Phillips had discovered was advanced by Milton Friedman and several other economists in the late 1960s.[4] Friedman's analysis stressed the importance of inflationary expectations mentioned earlier. If workers can forecast correctly current and future prices, there should be no tradeoff between inflation and unemployment. Fluctuations around the natural rate of unemployment occur only because expectations about current and future prices are incorrect. The stable tradeoff between inflation and unemployment that Phillips found reflects the fact that individuals held relatively rigid expectations of inflation during the period he studied. During the late 1960s, however, individuals no longer held fixed expectations of inflation.

Rational Expectations

The change in the way individuals formed expectations of inflation in the 1960s is explained by the concept of *rational expectations*. Because information is costly to obtain, individuals use crude rules of thumb to form their expectations of future price changes. However, they do not continue to use rules of thumb that yield consistently biased forecasts. For two centuries before World War II in the United Kingdom, and for a century and a half in the United States, prices varied around a roughly constant level. They rose substantially in times of war, then declined in postwar periods to roughly prewar levels. During peacetime, fluctuations around the mean rate of inflation were to a large degree random and fairly small. In such a world it is not irrational for individuals to hold fixed expectations of inflation. Since changes in the inflation rate is a "white noise" series (random fluctuations with zero mean), last year's rate of inflation provides no new information about this year's rate of inflation. Consequently, there is no reason why individuals should use information about last year's rate of inflation to modify their forecast of this year's rate.

Rational Inflation Expectations since the 1960s

Starting in the mid-1960s, however, inflation began to accelerate. The average annual rate of inflation for the 1966–1978 period was over 6 percent. More important, the deviations from the average annual rate of inflation had a pattern that differed strongly from the pattern that had prevailed earlier. Instead of deviating from the average in a random manner, inflation rates since the early 1960s have been positively correlated. This means that, if last year's change in the inflation rate was positive, this year's change in the inflation rate will probably be positive too. When inflation rate changes are strongly correlated, past rates of inflation contain a lot of information about future rates of inflation. Because of this change in the pattern of inflation rates, the public's adherence to fixed expectations of inflation was no longer rational, and people started using past rates of inflation as a forecast of future inflation.

[4]Milton Friedman, "The Role of Monetary Policy," *American Economic Review*, 58(1), March 1968, pp. 1–17. Also Milton Friedman, "Nobel Lecture: Inflation and Unemployment," *Journal of Political Economy*, 85(3), June 1977, pp. 451–472.

Money under Gold Standard Rules

This change in the behavior of the inflation series is no accident but springs from the fact that the United States effectively abandoned the rules of the gold standard in the 1960s. Under a gold standard, domestic inflation led to balance of payments deficits which, in turn, reduced the money supply. Consequently, inflation could not continue for long. During the 1960s, however, the U.S. money supply was effectively insulated from balance of payments disequilibrium. This shift from a gold standard to a dollar standard is discussed in greater detail in Chapters 17 and 18.

Accelerationist Phillips Curve

The switch from fixed to adaptive expectations of inflation destroyed the apparent stability of the Phillips curve. Once individuals use past rates of inflation to form their forecasts of future inflation, there is no long-run tradeoff between inflation and unemployment. In order for an unemployment rate below the natural rate to be maintained, the actual rate of inflation must exceed the expected rate of inflation. However, since expectations eventually adjust upwards because of past experience, an accelerating rate of inflation is required to maintain the gap between actual and expected inflation. For this reason, the new relationship between inflation and unemployment is known as the *accelerationist Phillips curve.*

Economic Policy and the Tradeoff between Inflation and Unemployment

Isovote Curves

The precise relationship between inflation and unemployment has important implications for economic policy. The evidence indicates that individuals prefer low unemployment rates and stable prices to high unemployment rates and high rates of inflation (or deflation, for that matter). When unemployment rates lie below the natural rate, individuals are pleasantly surprised because wage offers tend to exceed expectations. Only later will they realize that those wage offers are not as good as anticipated because the rate of inflation was underestimated. The higher the inflation and the unemployment rates, the greater will be the number of votes against the party in power. These preferences of the electorate for low unemployment rates and stable prices are represented by the *isovote curves* in Figure 12.12. These curves represent combinations of inflation and unemployment rates which will elicit the same amount of support for the incumbent party (measured as a percentage of the total electorate).

Vote-Maximizing Policy under Perfect Foresight

The accelerationist Phillips curve permits no long-run tradeoff between inflation and unemployment. In the long run, individuals correctly anticipate any given rate of inflation, and the unemployment rate returns to its natural rate. If the electorate had perfect foresight about the long-run consequences of economic policies, the vote-maximizing combination of

Figure 12.12   The Aggregate Voting Function

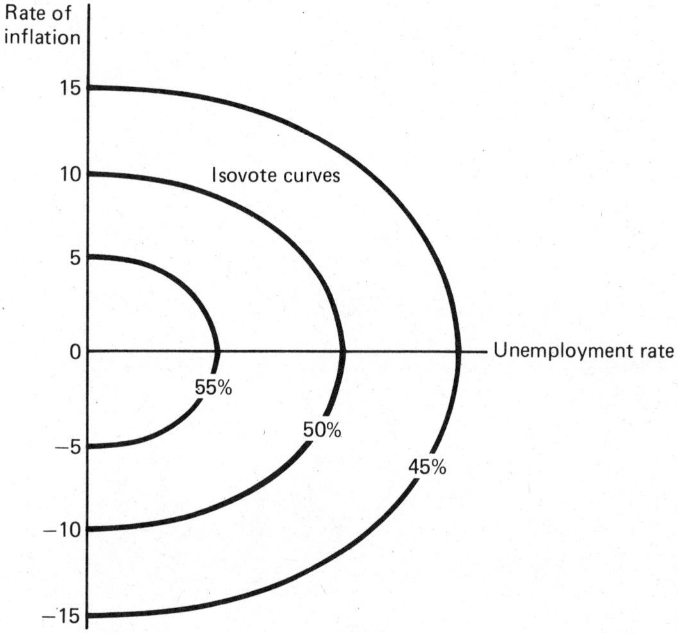

This diagram shows the electorate's preferences for inflation and unemployment. The electorate is assumed to prefer low unemployment rates and stable prices to high unemployment rates and high rates of inflation (or deflation). The isovote curves represent the combinations of unemployment and inflation (or deflation) that will yield the same support for the incumbent party. The closer the unemployment and inflation rates are to zero, the higher will be the percentage of the electorate that votes for the party in power.

inflation and unemployment rates would be at point A in Figure 12.13. Since the unemployment rate always returns to its natural rate U_r^*, politicians should concentrate on economic policies that produce stable prices.

Vote-Maximizing Policy with Myopic Electorate

In practice, the electorate is not usually sophisticated enough to be aware of the future consequences of economic policy. It is more realistic to assume that the electorate is myopic in the sense that it is unaware of the future consequences of monetary policy and has a decaying memory of past events. On election day, the influence of economic factors on voting behavior is determined primarily by recent economic conditions. Faced with a myopic electorate, politicians are understandably more concerned with economic policies that will yield low inflation and unemployment rates on election eve than they are with the long-run consequences of such policies. After all, the time horizon for political decision making is no further ahead than the next election. As the election nears, politicians become less and less concerned about the long-run consequences of their economic policies.

Figure 12.13   The Long-Run Accelerationist Phillips Curve and the Aggregate Voting Function

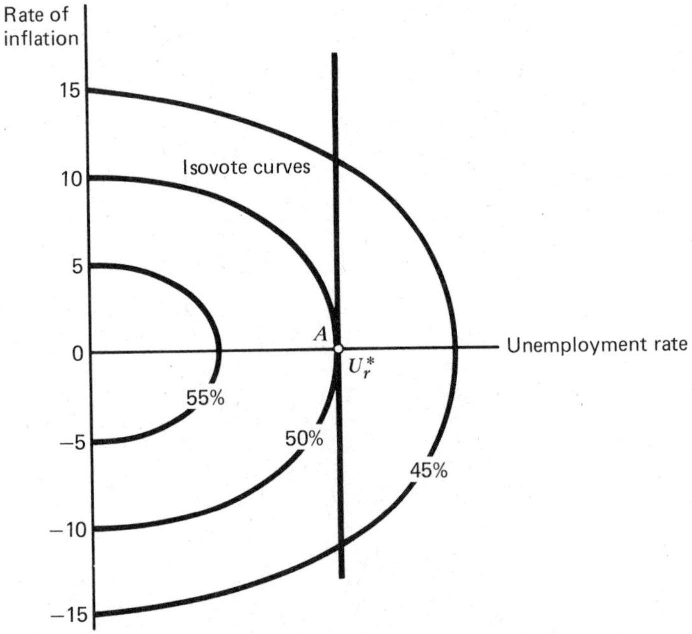

This diagram shows the long-run accelerationist Phillips curve superimposed on the aggregate voting function. Since the unemployment rate is always at its natural rate U_r^* in the long run, the vote-maximizing economic policy would be to produce stable prices.

Location of the Short-Run Phillips Curve

Although the accelerationist Phillips curve implies that there is no long-run tradeoff between inflation and unemployment, it is still possible to buy less unemployment by paying the price of more inflation in the short run. The short-run tradeoff is determined by past inflation rates. A low rate of unemployment can be obtained by generating higher rates of inflation this year. However, this will worsen the tradeoff between inflation and unemployment next year. Conversely, high rates of unemployment will improve the future tradeoff between inflation and unemployment. This relationship is illustrated in Figure 12.14.

Shifting the Short-Run Phillips Curve

Suppose the economy is initially in equilibrium at point A in Figure 12.14. If the monetary authorities accelerate the rate of monetary growth, the economy moves up the short-run Phillips curve to point B, trading a higher rate of inflation for less unemployment. This unemployment rate lies below its natural rate because individuals are temporarily underestimating the rate of inflation. However, in subsequent periods the public will raise its expectations of inflation, shifting the short-run Phillips curve upwards. If, instead, the monetary authorities decelerate the rate of monetary growth,

Figure 12.14   The Effects of Current Unemployment on Future Short-Run Tradeoffs between Inflation and Unemployment

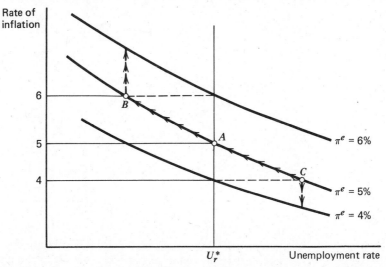

Suppose the economy is initially in equilibrium at point A. If the monetary authorities accelerate the rate of monetary growth, the economy moves up the short-run Phillips curve to point B. At point B, the unemployment rate lies below its natural rate of U_r^*, because workers underestimate the rate of inflation. In the next time period the public will raise its expectations of inflation, shifting the short-run Phillips curve upwards. If the monetary authorities reduce the rate of monetary growth, the economy moves down the short-run Phillips curve to point C. The unemployment rate lies above the natural rate of U_r^*, because individuals overestimate the rate of inflation. In the next time period the public will reduce its expectations of inflation, shifting the short-run Phillips curve downwards.

the economy moves down the short-run Phillips curve to point C, trading a higher unemployment rate for less inflation. This unemployment rate lies above its natural rate because individuals are temporarily overestimating the rate of inflation. In future time periods the public will reduce its expectations of inflation, shifting the short-run Phillips curve downwards.

The Political Business Cycle   Many social scientists have become convinced that politicians have consciously manipulated the economy in order to produce low rates of inflation and unemployment in years of presidential elections. Politicians know that high rates of inflation and unemployment are politically disastrous for incumbent administrations. Because of these political considerations, some economists, notably William Nordhaus, have hypothesized that there is a four-year *political business cycle*, as depicted in Figure 12.15.[5] A successful

[5]William Nordhaus, "The Political Business Cycle," *Review of Economic Studies*, 42(2), April 1975, pp. 169–190.

Figure 12.15   The Political Business Cycle

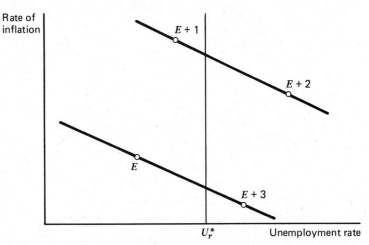

Assume that the incumbent president inherits an inflation-unemployment combination of $E + 1$. According to the political business cycle, the president immediately restricts monetary expansion, so moving the inflation-unemployment combination down the short-run Phillips curve to $E + 2$. Then the payoff begins. The short-run Phillips curve starts to shift down because the public reduces its expectations of inflation. The year before the election the inflation-unemployment combination has moved to $E + 3$. During the year before the next election, the rate of growth in the money supply is accelerated and the inflation-unemployment combination on election day is at E. By superimposing the isovote curves from Figure 12.13, one can see that only E produces an election-winning vote.

strategy necessitates a reduction in the rate of monetary growth in the early years of an incumbent president's term, thus pushing the unemployment rate above its natural level in order to reduce the rate of inflation. This temporary rise in the unemployment rate will buy the incumbent an improved tradeoff between inflation and unemployment in future years. As the election approaches, monetary policy should be redirected towards accelerating the rate of monetary growth. Then, by election eve, the unemployment rate would lie below the natural rate. However, the inflation rate would also be quite low because the public has very low expectations of inflation. Because the public now underestimates the rate of inflation, next year's tradeoff between inflation and unemployment will worsen. However, the incumbent need not be concerned with this subsequent upward shift in the short-run Phillips curve because there are four more years before the electorate can exert its will in the voting booth. The U.S. elections of 1948, 1952, 1956 (a borderline case), 1964, and 1972 all had this basic pattern of unemployment rates and inflation. The elections of 1960, 1968

1976, and 1980, which do not fit this pattern, were years in which the incumbent party lost the election.

Monetary Policy and the Fed

The successful implementation of a politically motivated business cycle depends on whether or not the Fed will cooperate with the incumbent administration's game plan. The fact that monetary policy is controlled by the Fed, rather than by Congress or the president, may weaken the ability of the president to follow a successful strategy. The governors of the Federal Reserve System are insulated from immediate political pressures by their 14-year appointments, which span the terms of several presidents. This independence has, in fact, caused several bitter disagreements between incumbent administrations and the Fed over the conduct of monetary policy. But the president does have persuasive powers which he can bring to bear on the members of the Federal Reserve Board and he does appoint at least one chairman of the Board during his term.

Deception and Democracy

The use of expansionary demand policies to manipulate the unemployment rate raises some serious philosophical questions in a democracy. Remember that expansionary demand policies lower the unemployment rate by tricking individuals into underestimating the rate of inflation and thus causing them to work for lower real wage rates than they would otherwise accept. Gordon Tullock makes the following comment about the ethics of such policies:[6]

> This whole discussion of deception as a government policy raises most interesting political problems. . . . The voters cannot adopt a policy of deceiving the workers because they are largely the same people. [The argument in favor of using inflationary demand policies to reduce the unemployment rate] . . . must be addressed to some group which is thought of as politically powerful and capable of carrying on a policy of deceiving the workers without telling the voter-workers what it is. It is only on this elitist interpretation that it makes any sense at all. . . . Open discussion of the desirability of fooling the worker must be based on a quite unjustified contempt for his intelligence.

Increased Economic Understanding

The growing sophistication of the electorate may be changing the old political rule that keeping unemployment rates low on election day is always good for votes. The rule was certainly broken in Britain with the reelection of Margaret Thatcher's conservative government in June 1983. The political business cycle hypothesis is based upon the assumption that voters cannot perceive the long-run consequences of expansionary demand policies. However, voters are learning to anticipate the long-run consequences of monetary policy and, as they learn more, they will become less impressed with unsustainable booms on election day.

[6]Gordon Tullock, "Can You Fool All of the People All of the Time?" *Journal of Money, Credit and Banking*, 4(2), May 1972, pp. 426–427.

Appendix

Proof 12.1   The expected number of wage offers before an acceptable offer is received

$$= \sum_{t=1}^{\infty} (t = \text{Offer number}) \cdot (\text{Probability that it will take } t \text{ offers before receiving an acceptable wage offer})$$

$$= x + 2x(1 - x) + 3x(1 - x)^2 + \cdots$$

$$= 1/x$$

Proof 12.2   Assume that an unemployed worker receives one wage offer each time period. F equals the percent of the labor force that becomes unemployed each time period. The unemployment rate will be equal to the percent of the labor force that has become unemployed during the current time period, plus the percent of the labor force that became unemployed during past time periods and still has not received an acceptable wage offer, and so on. Hence,

$$\text{Unemployment rate} = F + F(1 - x) + F(1 - x)^2 + \cdots = F/x$$

$$= F \cdot (\text{Average number of time periods before receiving an acceptable wage offer})$$

This is another example of an infinite geometrically declining series.

Proof 12.3   Let

$$\ln(W^e) = \ln(\overline{W}) + \pi^e + \Delta\ln\left(\frac{\Delta y}{\Delta L}\right)^e$$

where

$$W^e = \text{expected wage offer mean}$$

$$\overline{W} = \text{known past wage offer mean}$$

$$\pi^e = \text{expected rate of increase in the price level}$$

$$\Delta\ln\left(\frac{\Delta y}{\Delta L}\right)^e = \text{expected change in labor's marginal product.}$$

Now,

$$\ln(W^a) = \ln(\overline{W}) + \pi + \Delta\ln\left(\frac{\Delta y}{\Delta L}\right)$$

where

$$W^a = \text{the actual wage offer mean}$$

$$\pi = \text{the actual rate of increase in the price level}$$

$$\Delta\ln\left(\frac{\Delta y}{\Delta L}\right) = \text{the actual increase in labor's marginal product.}$$

Consequently, $\ln(W^e) - \ln(W^a) = [\pi^e - \pi] + \left[\Delta\ln\left(\frac{\Delta y}{\Delta L}\right)^e - \Delta\ln\left(\frac{\Delta y}{\Delta L}\right)\right]$

Summary

1. If prices rise faster than wages, the cost of labor in real terms falls and more labor is employed.

2. The duration of unemployment is affected by the minimum or reservation wage set implicitly by those searching for jobs.

3. The unemployment rate equals the percent of the labor force that becomes unemployed each week multiplied by the average duration of unemployment (in weeks).

4. Reservation wages are determined on the basis of an expected wage offer distribution. If the wage offer distribution is overestimated, reservation wages will be set too high, and the duration of unemployment and hence the unemployment rate will increase. When the wage offer distribution is estimated correctly, unemployment will be at its natural rate. If the wage offer distribution is underestimated, unemployment will be below the natural rate.

5. Workers will overestimate the wage offer distribution when expected inflation exceeds the actual rate of inflation and vice versa. If expected inflation is constant, there will be an inverse relationship between inflation and unemployment—the Phillips curve.

6. With fixed inflationary expectations, an acceleration in the rate of growth in the money supply will increase the inflation rate and lower permanently the unemployment rate.

7. If expected inflation adapts to recent actual rates of inflation, there will be no tradeoff between inflation and unemployment in the long run. A relationship will exist only between unanticipated inflation and unemployment—the accelerationist Phillips curve.

8. Over the periods 1861–1957 in Britain and 1935–1960 in the United States the inflation-unemployment relationship (the Phillips curve) was stable. This stability was due to fixed expectations of inflation.

9. Since the mid-1960s, inflationary expectations have adapted to the new experience of accelerating inflation rates that have been strongly correlated. Adaptive expectations unglued the Phillips curve relationship.

10. The accelerationist Phillips curve is the basis for the theory of the political business cycle. The new incumbent president starts off with a tight money policy which reduces inflation but raises unemployment. Expected inflation starts to decline. A year before the next election the money supply is expanded to lower unemployment under a favorable short-run inflation-unemployment tradeoff.

Questions

1. How did Keynes argue that expansionary monetary policy could reduce the unemployment rate?

2. Outline the theory of search unemployment.

3. What is the reservation wage and how is it determined?

4. How does the average duration of unemployment determine the unemployment rate?

5. What is the natural rate of unemployment and when does it occur?

6. When will unemployment be below its natural rate? Explain.

7. What is Okun's law?

8. What is the accelerationist Phillips curve?

9. What has happened to the Phillips curve in the United States since the 1950s? Why?

10. How can an incumbent president win the political business cycle game?

PART SIX

Financing the
Government

The roots of inflation often lie in war. Traditionally, politicians tend to be reluctant to raise taxes to cover military expenditures. The German hyperinflation of 1922–1923 had its origin in World War I. Germany, like most of the other combatants, financed the cost of the war in the main by expanding the money supply. War expenditures by the German Reich during World War I totaled about 164 billion reichsmarks. Less than one-eighth of these war-related expenditures was financed by taxes. However, budget deficits were not the cause of inflation. If the public had purchased all of the increase in the government debt, very little inflation would have occurred. The German Reichsbank (the German central bank) caused the inflation by permitting the banking system to monetize much of that government debt. Even though the public was subject to strong political pressure to purchase war bonds, only about 60 percent of the war debt was purchased by the nonbank public. The rest was monetized by the banking system. The Reichsbank purposely set the discount rate so low that commercial banks found it highly profitable to borrow reserves to finance the purchase of treasury bills. This expansionary Reichsbank policy produced a more than ninefold increase in the money supply before the end of the war.

This incredible expansion in the money supply made inflation inevitable, although during the war much of the inflationary pressure was suppressed by wartime price controls and rationing. The price level rose only about 135 percent during the war years. After the war,

From Jens O. Parsson, *The Dying of Money* (Boston: Wellspring Press, 1974); and Thomas M. Humphrey, "Eliminating Runaway Inflation: Lessons from the German Hyperinflation," *Federal Reserve Bank of Richmond Economic Review*, 66(4), July/August 1980, pp. 3–7.

pent-up inflationary pressures were released during 1919 and Germany experienced an explosion of inflation. Although the money supply continued to increase rapidly, prices rose even faster. By the spring of 1920 the price level had increased by a factor roughly comparable to that of the money supply, creating a temporary equilibrium between the supply of and demand for money. The price level was now about 17 times the price level of 1914.

For a brief period during 1920 and early 1921 inflation came to a halt. This temporary cessation of inflation was due to the fiscal reforms of Matthias Erzberger, the minister of finance during the first postwar government formed under the Weimar Constitution. Faced with a huge war debt, Erzberger decided to make good on it by introducing tax legislation which would drastically increase the taxation of capital and property. At the same time, the Reichsbank was induced to follow a fairly restrictive monetary policy during the second half of 1919. As a result of this monetary and fiscal restraint, prices stopped increasing. Wholesale prices did not surpass their March 1920 level until August 1921.

Despite his success in stopping inflation, Erzberger was bitterly opposed by the political right. Erzberger had been a leader of the peace movement during the war and had signed the Treaty of Versailles, actions which the reactionary right found unforgivable. After the war, his attempts to tax property and capital were fiercely resisted by the propertied interests of the right. Erzberger's chief enemy was Karl Helfferich, the minister of finance during the war and the man most responsible for Germany's wartime inflation. Helfferich was a leader of the reactionary Nationalist Party and a determined opponent of the Weimar Republic. Helfferich and the Nationalist Party led a campaign of slander and vilification against Erzberger, accusing him of improprieties and conflicts of interest while in office. Erzberger finally brought a libel suit against Helfferich, which he technically won. However, the testimony at the trial did not remove all the doubts about his innocence of the alleged improprieties. His credibility was destroyed. Politically ruined, Erzberger resigned from the government. One year later he was assassinated by members of a right-wing terrorist group.

With Erzberger gone, the Reichstag reduced taxes; budget deficits soared again. The Reichsbank abandoned its restrictive policies and allowed the money supply to double between February 1920 and August 1921. The stage was set for another explosion of inflation. However, as so often happens, this rapid acceleration in the rate of monetary growth did not cause inflation immediately. Its first effect was to generate an economic boom. By September 1921, however, rapid inflation had started again.

The reichsmark received another shock on April 27, 1921, when the Allies presented the Weimar government with a staggering bill for reparations payments of 132 billion gold marks. This was about four times Germany's gross national product. Of course, the Germans never paid anything close to these absurd demands. During the entire period from the end of the war to the end of inflation the Germans paid only 2.4 billion gold marks—about 5 percent of one year's gross national product. However, the French army did occupy the German Ruhr in January 1923, attempting to enforce the demands. The mere threat of enforcing the reparation demands was enough to cause an extreme drop in the foreign exchange price of the mark. Throughout the rest of the inflation the foreign exchange value of the mark fell more rapidly than internal prices rose, making German exports extremely cheap. World markets were flooded with German products. Tourists flocked to Berlin, which was the cheapest capital to visit in Europe.

The final convulsion of the reichsmark began in 1922. During the eleven-month period beginning in July 1922 the price level rose 200 times. By November 1923 the price level was 1300 billion times its pre-World War I level. All the reichsmarks that existed in the summer of 1922 (190 billion of them) were not enough to buy a single newspaper by the end of 1923. Once the public learned to anticipate future inflation, people cut down on their purchasing power held in the form of money balances. Workers were paid several times a day and were given time off from work so that they could spend their money immediately. Had they held money for even a short period of time, their cash holdings would have become valueless. Individuals had an enormous incentive to buy goods the minute they received their money. This "flight from money" caused prices to rise even faster than the money supply. Despite the fact that the money supply was increasing at a rate of 1300 percent per month during the height of the inflation and 30 paper mills were working overtime to supply the Reichsbank with paper for its bank notes, the real or price-deflated money stock fell drastically. By October 1923 the real money stock was less than 6 percent of its March 1921 level.

Of course, all property denominated in reichsmarks, such as government bonds, mortgages, and bank deposits, became worthless. Investors in these monetary assets lost everything. Debtors, on the other hand, gained immensely. The heaviest losses were suffered by the middle class and pensioners. In the end, this inflation-induced redistribution of wealth from creditors to debtors destroyed the savings of the middle class and played no small role in the subsequent rise of Hitler and the National Socialist Movement.

The return to a stable currency was extraordinarily simple. On October 15, 1923, Dr. Hjalmar Schacht, the newly appointed commissioner for the national currency, issued a new currency called the *rentenmark* to circulate alongside the old reichsmark. The government decreed that a maximum of 2.4 billion rentenmarks could be issued.

Because of this upper limit on the amount of rentenmarks that could be issued, the new currency was in great demand. Simultaneously, the German finance minister balanced the budget and the Reichsbank was ordered to stop discounting treasury bills. The reform was an instant success. The new rentenmark circulated at a value equal to one trillion reichsmarks. Within weeks the rate of inflation, which had been raging at an annual rate of over 300,000 percent, dropped to virtually zero.

Behavior of Nominal and Real Money Stock
in the German Hyperinflation (1913 = 1)

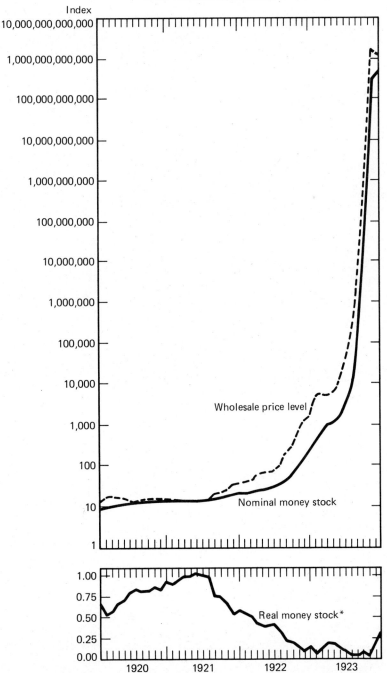

*Index of the German Money Stock (1913 = 1) divided by the index of Wholesale Prices (1913 = 1).

Source: Frank D. Graham, *Exchange, Prices, and Production in Hyperinflation: Germany, 1920–1923* (Princeton, N.J.: Princeton University Press, 1930), pp. 105–106.

Government in the Circular Flow of Income and Expenditure

The German hyperinflation of 1922–1923 is an extreme example of how a weak government can survive for some time through inflationary finance. Governments can cause inflation by creating money and that expansion in the money supply enables the government to finance some of its expenditures. This is one of the reasons why inflation has been associated historically with weak governments lacking the political will or power to collect enough taxes to pay for government expenditures. Unable to finance their expenditures through taxation, these politically weak governments resort to money creation to pay their bills.

Governments can also finance their budget deficits by borrowing instead of creating money. This method of financing budget deficits is far less inflationary than creating money, but such debt finance can only postpone the plight of a fiscally irresponsible government. A government that finds it politically impossible to limit its expenditures to tax revenue currently available will probably find it just as difficult to raise future tax revenue to pay the interest on government bonds.

Government in the Macroeconomic Model

Flow Equilibrium In order to analyze the macroeconomic aspects of government finance, it is extremely useful to start again with the concept of flow equilibrium. Flow equilibrium between income and desired expenditures for an economy with no government sector was discussed in Chapter 11. When government enters the circular flow, some of the output produced in the economy is purchased by the government instead of the private sector. Hence, the condition for flow equilibrium in an economy with a government sector becomes

$$
\begin{aligned}
\text{Gross national product} =\ & \text{Desired expenditures on goods and} \\
& \text{services by the private sector} \\[6pt]
+\ & \text{Government purchases of goods and} \\
& \text{services} \hspace{2cm} (13.1)
\end{aligned}
$$

This condition for flow equilibrium can be restated as

$$
\begin{aligned}
\text{Government purchases} =\ & \text{Gross national product} \\
\text{of goods and services} & \\[6pt]
-\ & \text{Desired expenditures on goods and} \\
& \text{services by the private sector} \hspace{1cm} (13.2)
\end{aligned}
$$

The condition for flow equilibrium provides an illuminating framework for analyzing the macroeconomic aspects of government finance. If the government is to succeed in purchasing some of national production, private expenditures on output must be less than the total income generated from the sale of gross national product. How such a gap between this total income and private expenditures on gross national product is created depends on the method used to finance government expenditures.

Government Budget Constraint The government budget constraint relates total government expenditures for all purposes to their sources of finance. To analyze the government budget constraint, the central bank (the Fed in the case of the United States) is here consolidated with the Treasury to simplify the analysis of the government budget constraint. This is done because the macroeconomic effects of their separate financial activities depend only on net transactions with the private sector. Total government expenditures consist of expenditures on goods and services, interest payments on the government debt held by the private sector, and transfer payments other than interest. These expenditures can be financed in three different ways: imposing taxes, borrowing from the private sector, or creating high-powered money. Thus, the consolidated government sector budget constraint can be represented as

$$
\begin{aligned}
\text{Government purchases} &= \text{Tax revenue} \\
\text{of goods and services} & \qquad\qquad + \\
+ & \quad \text{Net borrowing from the private} \\
\text{Interest payments on} & \quad \text{sector by both the Treasury and} \\
\text{the government debt} & \quad \text{the Fed} \\
+ & \qquad\qquad + \\
\text{Transfer payments} & \quad \text{Increase in high-powered money} \quad (13.3)
\end{aligned}
$$

Net Taxes Taxes take purchasing power out of the private sector, but some of that purchasing power is returned immediately in the form of transfer payments and interest payments on the government debt. From the standpoint of the circular flow of income and expenditures, it is the net reduction in private purchasing power which is important. Thus, the government budget constraint can be simplified by introducing the concept of *net taxes*—total tax revenue minus transfer payments and interest payments:

> Government purchases = Net taxes
> of goods and services
> +
> Net borrowing from the private
> sector by both the Treasury and
> the Fed
> +
> Increase in high-powered money   (13.4)

Budget Deficit The budget deficit is the difference between government purchases of goods and services and net taxes. Consequently, the government budget constraint implies that there are only two ways to finance a government deficit—net borrowing from the private sector or increases in high-powered money:

> Budget = Government purchases = Net borrowing from
> deficit   of goods and services   the private sector by
> −   both the Treasury and
> Net taxes   the Fed
> +
> Increase in high-
> powered money   (13.5)

The method used to finance the deficit depends ultimately on the Fed's monetary policy.

Financing a Budget Deficit

In order to illustrate how the separate actions of the Treasury and the Federal Reserve fit into the government budget constraint, it is assumed that the federal budget deficit is $1 billion. The Treasure has two ways of financing the deficit: (1) drawing down its deposits at the Fed banks or (2) selling financial securities.

Drawing down Treasury Deposits at the Fed If the Treasury writes checks on its deposits at Fed banks, the individuals who receive those checks will deposit them at depository institutions. When the checks are cleared, the Fed debits the deposits of the Treasury and credits the depository institutions' deposits. Since depository institution deposits are part of high-powered money while treasury deposits are not, this transfer increases the stock of high-powered money. It can be illustrated by the following T-accounts:

Depository Institutions

Assets		Liabilities	
Reserves	+ 1	Private demand deposits	+ 1

Federal Reserve

Assets		Liabilities	
		Depository institution deposits	+ 1
		U.S. Treasury account	− 1

In terms of the government budget constraint, drawing down its deposits at the Fed allows the Treasury to avoid borrowing, but it produces an increase in high-powered money.

The Treasury could also finance the deficit by drawing down its tax and loan accounts at commercial banks. Treasury deposits at commercial banks would be transferred to private accounts at depository institutions. Since treasury deposits at commercial banks are not included in the money supply while private bank deposits are, this transfer would also increase the money supply. However, high-powered money would not be affected. Consequently, no multiple expansion in the money supply would occur in this case.

In reality, drawing down deposits at the Fed banks is a rather unimportant method of financing budget deficits. Treasury deposits at the Fed are usually quite small, making it impossible to finance large deficits by this method. Moreover, the Treasury usually keeps those balances at a fairly constant level. Ultimately, the Treasury has to finance most of any large budget deficits by selling financial securities.

Open Market Purchases   The degree to which treasury borrowing affects high-powered money depends critically on the response of the Fed. If the Fed chooses, it can purchase treasury securities in open market operations to "make room" for the newly issued treasury securities. In this case the Fed would write a check on itself to pay for the purchase of treasury securities. The individual who sold the securities to the Fed would then deposit the check at a depository institution. When the check cleared, depository institution deposits at the Fed would increase, adding to the stock of high-powered money. These transactions are illustrated in the following T-accounts:

Depository Institutions

Assets		Liabilities	
Reserves	+ 1	Private demand deposits	+ 1

Federal Reserve

Assets		Liabilities	
Treasury securities	+ 1	Depository institution deposits	+ 1

The Treasury is selling $1 billion of securities to the private sector, but the Fed is simultaneously purchasing $1 billion of securities in open market operations. In terms of the government budget constraint, there is *no* net borrowing from the private sector. Again, the deficit is financed by increasing the stock of high-powered money.

Increased Advances and Discounts from the Fed

The Fed could choose to provide funds to depository institutions through advances and discounts, which would allow them to purchase the new securities issued by the Treasury. (As was discussed earlier, this was the practice of the Reichsbank during the German hyperinflation.) The transactions involved in this method of financing the deficit are shown in the following T-accounts. When the depository institutions purchase treasury securities with funds borrowed from the Fed (advances and discounts), the transaction involves the following changes:

Depository Institutions

Assets		Liabilities	
Treasury securities	+ 1	Borrowings from the Federal Reserve (advances and discounts)	+ 1

Federal Reserve

Assets		Liabilities	
Advances and discounts	+ 1	Treasury deposits	+ 1

However, after the Treasury spends the proceeds from the sale of securities, the public deposits the funds in depository institutions, and high-powered money increases:

Depository Institutions

Assets		Liabilities	
Reserves	+ 1	Private demand deposits	+ 1

Federal Reserve

Assets		Liabilities	
		Depository institution deposits	+ 1
		Treasury deposits	− 1

The Treasury is borrowing from the private sector through the sale of securities, but advances and discounts constitute a loan to the private sector by the Fed. Again, there is no net borrowing from the private sector. The deficit is financed by increasing the stock of high-powered money.

Debt Monetization

When the Federal Reserve buys government securities in open market operations or extends loans to depository institutions, enabling them to acquire newly issued treasury securities, high-powered money increases. These Federal Reserve actions are often referred to as *monetizing the debt*. However, the Fed can force the Treasury to borrow in private capital markets by refusing to monetize the debt. This option leaves the stock of high-powered money unchanged.

Treasury Borrowing from the Nonbank Private Sector

To illustrate the details of treasury sales of securities to the private sector, assume that the Treasury sells its securities to the public. The individuals who purchase the newly issued treasury securities pay for them by writing checks on their accounts at depository institutions. When the checks clear, funds are transferred from depository institution deposits to the Treasury's account at the Fed:

Depository Institutions

Assets		Liabilities	
Reserves	− 1	Private demand deposits	− 1

Federal Reserve

Assets		Liabilities	
		Depository institution deposits	− 1
		Treasury deposits	+ 1

Then, when the Treasury spends the proceeds to finance the deficit, the above changes are reversed, and the money supply returns to its initial level:

Depository Institutions

Assets		Liabilities	
Reserves	+ 1	Private demand deposits	+ 1

Federal Reserve

Assets		Liabilities	
		Depository institution deposits	+ 1
		Treasury deposits	− 1

Although the net effect of these transactions is to leave high-powered money and the money supply unchanged, there is an increase in the non-bank private sector's holdings of government securities. This implies that the public has used some of its purchasing power that could have been spent on goods and services to purchase newly issued treasury securities. Thus, government borrowing from the nonbank private sector directly reduces the income available for private expenditures on goods and services.

Treasury Borrowing from Depository Institutions

Of course, the depository institutions could also purchase newly issued treasury securities. However, if the Fed does not increase total reserves through open market purchases of securities or an increase in advances and discounts, the depository institutions can buy treasury securities only by selling some of their other investments in private capital markets or by reducing their outstanding loans to the public. The details of the transactions involved in this method of financing the deficit are as follows. First, the depository institutions sell some of their investments or reduce outstanding loans. The individuals who purchase the investments or repay their loans must write checks on their demand deposits:

Depository Institutions

Assets		Liabilities	
Loans and other investments	− 1	Private demand deposits	− 1

Then, when the depository institutions purchase newly issued treasury securities, funds are transferred from depository institution deposits to treasury deposits at the Federal Reserve:

Depository Institutions

Assets		Liabilities
Reserves	− 1	
Treasury securities	+ 1	

Federal Reserve

Assets	Liabilities	
	Depository institution deposits	− 1
	Treasury deposits	+ 1

Finally, after the Treasury spends the proceeds from the sale of securities to finance the deficit, the public deposits the funds in depository institutions, returning the money supply and high-powered money to their original levels:

Depository Institutions

Assets		Liabilities	
Reserves	+ 1	Private demand deposits	+ 1

Federal Reserve

Assets	Liabilities	
	Depository institution deposits	+ 1
	Treasury deposits	− 1

The net effect of these transactions is to leave the money supply and high-powered money unchanged. However, the nonbank private sector must purchase the investments sold by the depository institutions or repay loans, thus reducing its purchasing power available for spending on goods and services.

Government Finance and the
Circular Flow of Income and Expenditure

Reducing Private Expenditures
An important macroeconomic principle lies behind the choice of method used to finance government expenditures. If the government is to succeed in purchasing some of national production, private expenditures on gross national product must be less than total income. In order to understand

how the method of government finance creates such a gap between total income and private expenditures on gross national product, it is extremely useful to examine the connection between the government budget constraint and the budget constraint of the nonbank private sector.

Budget Constraint of the Nonbank Private Sector

Consider the budget constraint of an individual. The individual's income may be used: (1) to pay taxes, (2) to purchase financial securities (including loans to other individuals), (3) to purchase goods and services, or (4) to build up money balances. Consequently, the individual's budget constraint may be written as

$$\text{Income} = \text{Taxes (net of government transfers)}$$
$$+$$
$$\text{Net lending (net purchase of financial assets)}$$
$$+$$
$$\text{Expenditures on gross national product}$$
$$+$$
$$\text{Increases in money balances} \qquad (13.6)$$

Some individuals may be borrowing to spend more than after-tax income, while other individuals are lending. After aggregating all these budget constraints, borrowing and lending between individuals in the private sector cancel out. Only the credit flows between the nonbank private sector and the government sector (including the Fed) or between the nonbank private sector and depository institutions remain. Thus, the aggregate budget constraint for the nonbank private sector can be represented as follows:

Total income derived from the sale of gross national product	= Changes in money balances
	+
	Net taxes
+	+
Net loans to the nonbank private sector from depository institutions	Net purchases of government securities
	+
	Nonbank private sector expenditures on gross national product (13.7)

Treasury Borrowing from the Nonbank Private Sector

The connection between the government budget constraint and the nonbank private sector's budget constraint is clear-cut in the case where government expenditures are financed by taxes or borrowing from the nonbank private sector. In this case, there is no change in high-powered money. If the money supply multiplier is constant, the money supply will also remain constant. Net taxes and the purchase of financial securities issued by the Treasury directly reduce the purchasing power available for spending on gross national product. If individuals remain satisfied with their current money balances, taxes and government borrowing from the nonbank private sector must create a gap between total income and desired private expenditures on gross national product exactly equal to government spending on goods and services. This is readily demonstrated in the following equations:

Government Budget Constraint

Increases in high-powered money	= 0 =	Government spending on goods and services
		−
		Net taxes
		−
		Net borrowing from the nonbank private sector by the Treasury or Fed (13.8)

Therefore,

Government spending on goods and services	=	Net taxes
		+
		Net borrowing from the nonbank private sector by the Treasury or Fed (13.9)

And, by rearranging equation (13.7):

Nonbank Private Sector's Budget Constraint

Desired increases in money balances	= 0 =	Total income
		−
		Net taxes
		−
		Net purchases of government securities
		−
		Desired private expenditures on gross national product (13.10)

Or

Total income	=	Net taxes
−		+
Desired private expenditures on gross national product		Net purchases of government securities
	=	Government spending on goods and services (13.11)

Treasury Borrowing from Depository Institutions   In the case where the Treasury sells financial securities to depository institutions, the details are slightly different but the net result is the same. If high-powered money and the money supply multiplier remain unchanged, depository institutions can purchase government securities only by selling some other investments or reducing loans outstanding. This implies that the nonbank private sector is purchasing the investments sold by depository institutions or repaying loans to depository institutions, both of which reduce the purchasing power available for spending on gross national product. This is demonstrated in the following equations:

Government Budget Constraint

Government spending on goods and services	=	Net taxes
		+
		Treasury sales of securities to depository institutions (13.12)

Depository Institutions

Purchase of newly issued treasury securities	=	Sale of other investments
		+
		Reduction in outstanding loans (13.13)

Nonbank Private Sector

Desired increases in money balances	= 0 =	Total income
		−
		Net taxes
		−
		Purchase of investments sold by depository institutions
		−
		Repayment of loans extended by depository institutions
		−
		Desired private expenditures on gross national product (13.14)

Therefore,

Total income	=	Net taxes
−		+
Desired private expenditures on gross national product		Purchase of investments sold by depository institutions
		+
		Repayment of loans extended by depository institutions
= Net taxes	=	Government expenditures on goods and services
+		
Treasury securities sold to depository institutions		

(13.15

Increasing High-Powered Money

Financing government expenditures by increasing the stock of high powered money does not directly reduce the purchasing power of the private sector, as does taxation or borrowing. Instead, the resulting in crease in the money supply causes inflation, which indirectly reduces the real output purchased by the private sector. As prices rise, each individual' initial money balances purchase fewer goods and services. When indi viduals are faced with a reduction in the purchasing power of their mone balances, they typically desire to replace at least part of that purchasing power by using some of their income to increase the number of dollars the are holding. This diversion of income to build up the number of dollars in each individual's money balances reduces the funds available for spending on goods and services, allowing the government to acquire some of the available output. Inflation does indirectly what taxes do directly. For thi reason, economists sometimes refer to inflation as a *tax on money balances.*

More High-Powered Money Increases Money Supply

In order to illustrate the macroeconomic effects of financing governmen expenditures through increasing the stock of high-powered money, as sume that $10 billion of government expenditures are financed entirely by increasing high-powered money:

Government expenditures = $10b = Increase in the stock
    on goods and services   of high-powered money   (13.16

Under a fractional reserve banking system, this increase in high-powered money results in a multiple expansion in the money supply. If the money supply multiplier were $2\frac{1}{2}$, for example, the $10 billion increase in high powered money would cause a $25 billion increase in the money supply

This increase in the money supply can be divided into two different components: (1) the initial increase in high-powered money ($10 billion) which finances government expenditures and (2) the increase in depository institution loans or investments ($15 billion) made possible by the increase in reserves.

Increased Money Supply Raises Aggregate Demand

Instead of reducing private funds available for purchasing output, financing government expenditures through increases in high-powered money actually adds to the nominal purchasing power of the private sector because the increase in reserves enables depository institutions to make additional loans to the private sector or to purchase more financial securities in private capital markets. Since government spending financed by increasing the stock of high-powered money adds to the purchasing power of the private sector, total spending on goods and services increases by much more than the initial increase in government spending. Gross national product increases until the demand for money equals the supply of money. If the Cambridge k (the ratio of desired money balances to gross national product) is 1/4, then gross national product would rise by $100 billion:

Cambridge Equation

$$\Delta(\text{Money supply}) = k \cdot \Delta(\text{Gross national product})$$
$$(+25) \quad = \quad (1/4) \cdot (+100) \quad\quad (13.17)$$

Increased GNP Raises Money Demand

It is this $25 billion increase in the demand for money that creates the gap between total income and private expenditures, which enables the government to acquire some of gross national product.[1] Although gross national product rises by $100 billion, private expenditures on goods and services rise by only $90 billion because some of the private sector's available purchasing power must be used to increase its money balances. This is shown in the following identities:

Nonbank Private Sector's Budget Constraint

Desired increases in money balances (+25)	= Total income (+100)	+ Net borrowing from depository institutions (+15)	− Desired private expenditures on gross national product (+90)	(13.18)

[1]Milton Friedman, "Discussion of the Inflationary Gap" in *Essays in Positive Economics* by Milton Friedman (Chicago: University of Chicago Press, 1963), pp. 251–262.

$$\begin{array}{llll}
\text{Total} & - \text{ Desired private} & = \text{Desired} & - \text{ Net borrowing} \\
\text{income} & \text{ expenditures on} & \text{increases in} & \text{ from depository} \\
(+100) & \text{ gross national} & \text{money balances} & \text{ institutions} \\
 & \text{ product} & (+25) & (+15) \\
 & (+90) & & \\
\end{array}$$

$$\begin{array}{lll}
 & = \text{Change in} & = \text{Increase in} \\
 & \text{ high-powered} & \text{government} \\
 & \text{ money} & \text{expenditures} \\
 & (+10) & (+10) \hspace{3cm} (13.19)\\
\end{array}$$

Summary

1. Government expenditure on gross national product requires the private sector to spend less than its total income. Government expenditure can be financed through imposing taxes, borrowing from the private sector, or creating high-powered money.

2. The budget deficit equals government purchases of goods and services minus net tax revenue. It also equals the government's net borrowing from the private sector plus any increase in high-powered money.

3. The division between borrowing and high-powered money creation is determined by the Fed's actions. Fed open market purchases increase high-powered money and, at the same time, reduce private sector holdings of treasury bonds. Therefore, open market purchases reduce the government's net borrowing from the private sector and increase the supply of high-powered money.

4. Taxes and borrowing from the private sector reduce directly the private sector's purchases of goods and services. Increasing high-powered money reduces private sector spending indirectly through inflation.

5. An increase in high-powered money creates a multiple expansion in the money supply. This increases private funds available for purchasing output. Total spending increases and nominal gross national product rises. The rise in GNP increases money demand, hence absorbing some of the increased nominal income. In the new equilibrium situation, the desired increase in the private sector's nominal expenditure will fall short of the nominal increase in gross national product by an amount exactly equal to the increase in high-powered money.

Questions

1. What is the flow equilibrium condition when the government purchases some of gross national product?

2. What are net taxes?

3. Define the government's budget constraint in terms of its three sources of revenue.

4. What is a government budget deficit and how is it financed?

5. How do open market purchases by the Fed affect government deficit financing?

6. How does government borrowing from the private sector reduce private aggregate demand?

7. How does increasing high-powered money to finance a government deficit eventually reduce private sector expenditure in relation to GNP?

8. With $m = 4$, $k = 1/5$, and $\Delta H = \$5$ billion, calculate the change in nominal gross national product needed to raise money demand sufficiently to equilibrate money supply and demand.

14 Inflationary Finance

The Inflation Tax

When the government finances expenditures by increasing the stock of high-powered money, total spending and nominal gross national product increase. The increase in nominal gross national product then produces an increase in the demand for nominal money balances. Individuals must use some of their purchasing power to build up their nominal money balances. The amount of real gross national product the government can acquire by increasing the stock of high-powered money is exactly equal to the amount of real private purchasing power that is absorbed in the process of building up nominal money balances.

Change in Real Money Balances The real purchasing power absorbed by adding to money balances is the increase in nominal money balances divided by the price level (ΔM)/P. This term can be broken down into the rate of monetary growth times the quantity of real money balances demanded by the public:

$$\frac{\Delta M}{P} = \frac{\Delta M}{M} \cdot \frac{M}{P} \tag{14.1}$$

Some of the purchasing power absorbed by increasing money balances is offset by depository institutions' lending to the public, thus increasing the purchasing power of the private sector again.

Net Reduction in Real Purchasing Power The increase in money balances can be broken down into two different sources: (1) an increase in high-powered money ΔH and (2) the secondary expansion of the money supply that occurs when depository institutions extend additional credit to the private sector ΔB:

$$\Delta M = \Delta H + \Delta B \qquad (14.2)$$

Since this increase in bank credit to the private sector adds to the purchasing power available for spending on goods and services, the net reduction in the *real* purchasing power of the private sector is only $\Delta H/P$:

Net reduction in the purchasing power of the private sector $= \dfrac{\Delta M - \Delta B}{P} = \dfrac{\Delta H}{P}$ (14.3)

Decomposition of Change in High-Powered Money   The amount of real gross national product the government can acquire by increasing the stock of high-powered money is G/P. It can also be expressed as the product of three different variables: (1) the rate of increase in high-powered money, (2) the inverse of the money supply multiplier, and (3) the amount of real purchasing power the public wants to hold in money balances:

$$G/P = \frac{\Delta H}{P} = \frac{\Delta H}{H} \cdot \frac{H}{M} \cdot \frac{M}{P} \qquad (14.4)$$

Money Demand and Government Revenue from High-Powered Money Creation   Substituting the Cambridge equation's specification of the demand for money into this expression, one can restate the relationship in terms of the fraction of gross national product the government can acquire by increasing high-powered money:

$$\frac{G}{P} = \frac{\Delta H}{H} \cdot \frac{H}{M} \cdot \frac{M}{P} = \frac{\Delta H}{H} \cdot \frac{H}{M} \cdot k \cdot y \qquad (14.5)$$

or

$$\frac{G}{Py} = \frac{\Delta H}{H} \cdot \frac{H}{M} \cdot k \qquad (14.6)$$

Cambridge k Falls as Inflation Rises   Were k (desired money balances expressed as a fraction of gross national product) a constant, there would be no limit to the fraction of real gross national product the government could acquire through increasing high-powered money. With a constant k, the government could acquire all of gross national product with a sufficiently high rate of expansion in high-powered money. But k is not a constant. It is a function of the cost of holding money. The real purchasing power of money balances depreciates at the rate of inflation. Thus, inflation is one of the costs of holding money balances. An increase in the expected rate of inflation creates an incentive for individuals to economize on their holdings of money balances. During the German hyperinflation of 1922–1923, for example, the enormous cost of holding money balances led to a shortening of the payments period. Workers were paid two or three times a day and then were given time off after each payment so that they could spend their money immediately.

Although the shortening of the payments period may be inconvenient (and inefficient from a social point of view), it does reduce the amount of money balances people hold as a fraction of gross national product.

Money Growth and Inflation

Once the effect of the expected rate of inflation on the demand for purchasing power held in money balances is taken into account, the relationship between the rate of monetary growth and inflation becomes a little more complex. To illustrate the effect of an acceleration in the rate of monetary growth on the rate of inflation, consider the following hypothetical economy:

1. The demand for money is specified by the Cambridge equation.
2. The money supply multiplier is constant so that high-powered money and the money supply grow at the same rate.
3. The money supply and real output are increasing at a 4 percent rate and this rate is expected to remain constant.

These initial conditions imply that both the demand for and the supply of money will grow at an annual rate of 4 percent:

$$\Delta\ln(M) = \Delta\ln(k) + \Delta\ln(y) + \pi$$
$$(+4\%) \quad\;\; (0\%) \quad\;\; (+4\%) \quad (0\%) \tag{14.7}$$

Acceleration in the Rate of Money Growth

Now suppose the rate of monetary growth accelerates to an annual rate of 104 percent. To maintain the previous 4 percent rate of growth in real money balances, inflation would have to accelerate to 100 percent:

$$\Delta\ln(M) = \Delta\ln(k) + \Delta\ln(y) + \pi$$
$$(+104\%) \quad (0\%) \quad\;\; (+4\%) \quad (+100\%) \tag{14.8}$$

However, when the public begins to expect that prices will rise at 100 percent per year, they will have an incentive to reduce their money balances relative to income; that is, k will fall. The Cambridge k is negatively related to the expected rate of inflation π^e. Because of this reduction in the ratio of money balances to gross national product, the rate of inflation must overshoot the long-run equilibrium level of 100 percent during the time that individuals are reducing k to a new level consistent with the higher cost of holding money, as shown in Figure 14.1.

Falling Real Money Demand Limits Inflation Tax Revenue

The tendency of the public to economize on their holdings of money balances when faced with a high rate of inflation limits the extent to which a government can finance its expenditures by increasing high-powered money. In this hypothetical economy, the long-run equilibrium rate of inflation will rise percentage point for percentage point with the rate of growth in

Figure 14.1 The Overshoot of Inflation during Adjustment to a Higher Rate of Monetary Growth

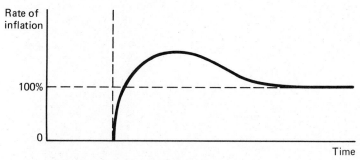

Assume the following initial conditions:

1. The demand for money function is $M^d = k \cdot y \cdot P$; $k = f(\pi^e)$.
2. Real output grows at a constant rate of 4 percent per annum.
3. The money supply is initially growing at 4 percent per annum.
4. The price level is constant and is expected to remain constant.

Now suppose the money supply accelerates to a 104 percent per annum rate of growth. To maintain a 4 percent annual growth of real money balances, inflation would accelerate to a new rate of 100 percent per year. However, when the equilibrium inflation of 100 percent per year is fully anticipated, the increased cost of holding money will induce individuals to desire smaller money balances relative to nominal income. Thus, the rate of inflation must overshoot its equilibrium rate of 100 percent per year during the time that individuals are adjusting their holdings of money balances to a level consistent with the higher cost of holding money.

high-powered money. However, as individuals learn to expect higher rates of inflation, k will fall. At some point, higher rates of growth in high-powered money actually yield fewer resources for the government because k will fall more than proportionately to an increase in $\Delta H/H$ (Appendix).

Inflation and the Tax System

Bracket Creep   Not only does an expansion of high-powered money finance directly some of the government's expenditures, but the resulting inflation also increases the yield from a progressive income tax system. An income tax system is affected by inflation with respect to both the real value of nominal tax allowances and the structure of tax brackets. Real tax liabilities increase as prices rise because inflation reduces the real value of tax exemptions and deductions fixed in nominal terms and pushes individuals into higher tax brackets. This phenomenon is known as *bracket creep*. For example, consider the hypothetical income tax schedule depicted in Figure 14.2. The solid line represents the legal tax structure stated in nominal terms for some

Figure 14.2   Effects of a 100 Percent Price Increase on a Hypothetical Income Tax Schedule

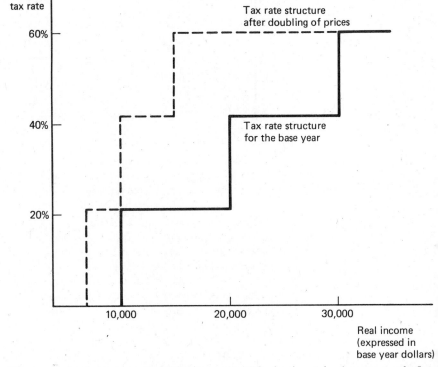

The vertical axis measures marginal tax rates. The horizontal axis measures before tax real income expressed in terms of base year dollars. The solid line represents the tax rate structure for some base year, and the broken line shows the same tax rate schedule after prices double.

base year. If prices increase by 100 percent, the real value of any given nominal income falls by half. Each tax bracket now corresponds to a lower value of real income. The broken line represents the tax brackets as a function of real income after prices have doubled.

Inflation and Historical Cost Depreciation

Other ways in which inflation increases real taxation involve the treatment of (1) depreciation, (2) inventory profits, and (3) changes in asset value. Under the current U.S. tax law, the depreciation allowances that corporations can deduct from their taxable income are based upon the original cost of capital equipment. With inflation, the real value of depreciation allowances is reduced. Depreciation allowances based on historical costs are not adequate to replace buildings and equipment at the inflated prices that will prevail when the need for replacement comes. The reduced real value of these depreciation allowances effectively amounts to an increased tax on the return to capital.

Inflation and Illusory Inventory Profits

A similar problem occurs in the treatment of inventory profits. The most widely used method of accounting for inventories is FIFO (first-in-first-out). Under the FIFO method of inventory accounting the costs of production used in calculating profits on sales out of inventories are based on the costs of producing the oldest units in the inventory. Costs are assigned to units sold in the same order as they entered inventory. During periods of rising prices, older and thus lower costs are subtracted in calculating reported earnings. Because historical costs rather than inventory replacement costs are used in calculating profits, the apparent income of a corporation using this method of accounting would be artificially inflated by the "paper profits" on the inventories produced by inflation. However, paper profits on the sale of inventories produced in the past are not available for capital investment or distribution as dividends, because those inventories must be replaced at the new higher price level.

LIFO Accounting and Replacement Cost

Since corporations must pay taxes on these illusory inventory profits, many corporations have recently switched to a last-in-first-out (LIFO) basis of accounting because of inflation. This method treats inventory costs as though units of inventory were accumulated in a pile, with the newest units removed from the top and assigned to units sold. Unless older units are liquidated by depleting inventories, they can remain at the bottom of the pile indefinitely. Thus, this method uses the cost of producing the last units added to the inventory in calculating the profit on sales out of inventories. This cost will usually be much closer to the actual cost of replacing depleted inventories during periods of inflation.

Inflation and Nominal Capital Gains

Similar effects are produced by the taxation of nominal capital gains. Suppose an investor purchased United Airlines stock at $20. If the price of the stock rises to $40 over the next 10 years and the price level doubles, the investment has just maintained its real value. However, if the investor sells, he or she must pay taxes on the realized nominal gain of $20 per share. Consequently, nominal capital gains taxation reduces net real stock values in the face of inflation. The higher is the inflation rate, the greater is the incentive to evade capital gains taxation by investing in unrecorded assets, such as gold, art work, and antiques.

Inflation and the National Debt

Inflation allows the government to make its interest payments to bondholders in dollars that are worth less than the dollars initially lent. Since the cost of servicing the government debt is a future tax liability of the public, unanticipated inflation transfers wealth from the owners of government bonds to the taxpaying public in general. Of course, bondholders suffer real losses only if inflation is unanticipated. If bondholders anticipated correctly future changes in prices, nominal interest rates would reflect the change in the purchasing power of the dollar. A higher nominal interest rate would compensate for the declining real value of the bond. The relationship between expected inflation and interest rates is discussed in Chapter 16.

Indexing the Tax System

As the previous discussion makes clear, the current U.S. tax system was designed for a world of little or no inflation. The persistence of inflation during the last two decades has generated proposals for indexing the tax system. Under a fully indexed tax system, tax brackets, personal exemptions, depreciation allowances, and the cost basis for calculating capital gains would all be adjusted by some price index for inflation. With such indexation, an increase in nominal income just sufficient to compensate for a higher cost of living would not push an individual into a higher tax bracket. Similarly, the base for calculating capital gains and inventory profits would be adjusted to eliminate paper profits arising from general inflation. To eliminate the transfer of wealth from bondholders to taxpayers resulting from unanticipated inflation, the government would issue only purchasing power bonds. Government bonds would be issued with an interest coupon of, say, 3 percent. On each interest date the par value of the bond would be adjusted to take account of the inflation, or deflation, which had taken place since the bond was issued. Were the rate of inflation 10 percent during the first year, then the par value of the bond would be adjusted upwards from $1000 to $1100. The interest paid that year would be 3 percent of $1100 or $33. At maturity, the accumulated change in the purchasing power of the dollar would determine the final settlement. If the price level had tripled, then the bondholder would be paid $3000.

The Inflation Tax and Democracy

In a democracy, a strong case can be made that all forms of taxation should be approved explicitly by the legislature. It may be argued that money creation and use of inflation to raise real tax rates without specific legislation is basically incompatible with democratic government. However, politicians have incentives both to spend taxpayers' money in order to win the support of those who receive the benefits and to avoid voting for explicit tax increases. These incentives may bias a government towards inflationary finance.

Appendix

For those who are mathematically inclined, the rate of growth in high-powered money which maximizes the resources acquired by the government can be found by differentiating G/Py with respect to $\Delta H/H$ and setting the term equal to zero:

$$\frac{G}{Py} = \frac{\Delta H}{H} \cdot \frac{H}{M} \cdot k \qquad \text{(A.1)}$$

Therefore,

$$0 = \frac{\partial(G/Py)}{\partial(\Delta H/H)} = \frac{H}{M} \cdot k + \frac{\Delta H}{H} \cdot \frac{H}{M} \cdot \frac{\partial k}{\partial(\Delta H/H)}$$

$$= k \cdot \frac{H}{M}\left(1 + \frac{\Delta H/H}{k} \cdot \frac{\partial k}{\partial(\Delta H/H)}\right) \qquad (A.2)$$

or

$$\frac{\Delta H/H}{k} \cdot \frac{\partial k}{\partial(\Delta H/H)} = -1 \qquad (A.3)$$

Once k has adjusted to an equilibrium level consistent with the cost of holding money, the rate of growth in high-powered money will be equal to the rate of inflation plus the rate of growth of real output:

$$\frac{\Delta H}{H} = \pi + \frac{\Delta y}{y} \qquad (A.4)$$

Consequently, the government revenue-maximizing condition may be rewritten as follows:

$$\frac{\Delta H/H}{k} \cdot \frac{\partial k}{\partial(\Delta H/H)} = \frac{\pi + (\Delta y/y)}{\pi} \cdot \frac{\pi}{k} \cdot \frac{\partial k}{\partial \pi} = -1 \qquad (A.5)$$

or

$$\frac{\pi}{k} \cdot \frac{\partial k}{\partial \pi} = \frac{\text{elasticity of } k \text{ with respect to}}{\text{the rate of inflation}} = -\frac{\pi}{\pi + (\Delta y/y)} \qquad (A.6)$$

Summary

1. The amount of real GNP that the government can acquire by increasing high-powered money equals the amount of real private sector purchasing power absorbed in accumulating higher nominal money balances.

2. Real private sector purchasing power absorbed in building up money balances equals $\Delta M/P$. However, some of this change in money balances is recycled to the private sector in the form of additional credit ΔB. Since $\Delta M = \Delta H + \Delta B$, the net absorption of real private sector purchasing power equals $\Delta H/P$.

3. As inflation accelerates, money demand as a proportion of gross national product falls; the Cambridge k declines. This fall in k produces an overshoot in the inflation rate above its higher long-run equilibrium

level until k stabilizes at its new smaller value, since the inflation rate can be expressed $\pi = \Delta\ln(M) - \Delta\ln(k) - \Delta\ln(y)$.

4. The inflation tax can be decomposed into the real tax base H/P and the tax rate $\Delta H/H$. With a constant money supply multiplier, H/P is proportional to M/P and $\Delta H/H$ equals $\Delta M/M$. As inflation rises, M/P and hence H/P decline due to the fall in k. Hence, the tax base moves inversely to the tax rate. The real tax proceeds are maximized when a 1 percent increase in the tax rate is exactly offset by a 1 percent decrease in the tax base.

5. The present tax system produces bracket creep in times of inflation. Real income may remain constant but higher nominal income pushes individuals into higher tax brackets.

6. Inflation also affects taxation because of the treatment of depreciation, inventory profits, and capital gains. Deductions of historical cost depreciation against income are not adequate to finance replacements in the presence of inflation. Illusory profits on inventory appreciation and nominal capital gains are taxed, despite the fact that asset values may not have increased at all in real terms.

7. Tax indexation implies neutralizing the effects of inflation on the real value of tax liabilities. Complete indexation would not only eliminate bracket creep but also prevent taxation of nominal as opposed to real capital gains.

8. The inflation tax is not a form of taxation approved by the legislature.

Questions

1. How does the inflation tax transfer resources from the private sector to the government?

2. If inflation accelerated, what would happen to k and why?

3. Why does inflation overshoot before settling down to a new higher equilibrium rate?

4. How can the inflation-induced change in k limit the real revenue that can be obtained from the inflation tax?

5. During the 1922–1923 German hyperinflation, prices rose faster than the money supply. By October 1923 the real money stock was less than 6 percent of its March 1921 level. German central bankers used this fact to argue that "easy money" was not to blame for the inflation because money was a smaller fraction of national income in 1923 than it was in 1921. What is wrong with their argument?

6. What is bracket creep?

7. How does inflation have a real effect on the tax treatment of depreciation?

8. How does inflation have a real effect on the taxation of inventory profits?

9. How does inflation have a real effect on the taxation of capital gains?

10. What is tax indexation?

PART SEVEN

Interest

The political unrest of the 1890s grew out of frustration over falling prices. During the period from 1892 to 1897 the money supply did not increase at all and prices fell at an average rate of 3 percent a year. This period of falling prices was particularly agonizing for western farmers. During the 1880s there had been a feverish boom in the west. Railroads made it possible to develop the rich soils of the trans-Mississippi states; as a result, there was a nearly 50 percent increase in the number of farms in the United States during the last two decades of the nineteenth century. Eastern banks loaned tremendous sums on western farm mortgages to finance that expansion. The falling prices of the 1890s meant that those long-term debts were appreciating in real value, imposing an intolerable burden on debt-ridden western farmers.

The Free Silver Movement prescribed the free and unlimited coinage of silver at a ratio of 16 grams of silver to 1 of gold as the cure for falling prices. Free coinage of silver would inflate the money supply and produce rising prices. In effect, the Free Silver Movement proposed that the United States return to the bimetallic gold and silver standard of the 1837 Coinage Act. That act had also provided for free and unlimited coinage of silver at a mint ratio of 16 to 1, but shortly after its passage, increased production of gold caused gold prices to decline relative to silver. As a result, the market price of silver rose above the mint price, and no silver was delivered to government mints for coinage. In 1873

From Milton Friedman and Anna J. Schwartz, *A Monetary History of the United States, 1867–1960* (Princeton, N.J.: Princeton University Press for the National Bureau of Economic Research, 1963); and Stanley L. Jones, *The Presidential Election of 1896* (Madison: University of Wisconsin Press, 1964).

Congress passed a new coinage law which made no provision for the coinage of silver. At the time, little publicity was given to the demonetization of silver because no silver was being minted anyway. However, soon after the act of 1873 was passed, rich new silver mines opened in the American west, and the increased production of silver brought prices down. By 1875 silver producers discovered that it would be profitable to bring silver to the mints for coinage at the old 16 to 1 ratio but the act of 1873 prevented them from doing so. From that time on, orators of the Silver Movement portrayed the "crime of 1873" as a conspiracy of Wall Street bankers and British capitalists to raise the value of U.S. government bonds by insuring payment in gold only. Although the Silver Movement was originally dominated by silver-mining interests, their arguments quickly caught hold with western and southern farmers. Falling prices were bad enough for debt-ridden farmers, but when they became convinced that their condition was the result of a conspiracy of Wall Street and British financiers, political unrest reached a boiling point.

The political campaign of 1896 was essentially a struggle between debtors and creditors over the future purchasing power of the dollar. Class and sectional conflicts over the "money" issue divided both major political parties. The Democratic convention in Chicago was the scene of a bitter struggle between silver Democrats from the west and south and the gold Democrats of the east. After a brief battle over the seating of contested delegates, it became obvious that the free-silver delegates would control the convention. The silver Democrats urged the adoption of a free-silver plank, declaring "that the act of 1873 demonetizing silver . . . has resulted in the appreciation of gold and a corresponding fall in the prices of commodities produced by the people; a heavy increase in the burdens of taxation and of all debts, public and private; the enrichment of the moneylending class at home and abroad; the prostration of industry and the impoverishment of the people."

The final speech in favor of adoption was given by the editor of the Omaha (Nebraska) *World Herald,* William Jennings Bryan. As Bryan approached the speaker's stand, the delegates were beside themselves with excitement. The gold Democrats had made persuasive arguments against adoption of the silver plank and the outcome of the final vote was uncertain. Once Bryan began to speak, however, the convention was under his control. In the climactic final passage, he answered the argument that the United States should wait for England to agree to establish international bimetallism before remonetizing silver with the stirring phrases which were to become the battle cry of the campaign: "You shall not press down upon the brow of labor this crown of thorns, you shall not crucify mankind upon a cross of gold."

The silver Democrats had found their voice. After Bryan's speech there was no more doubt about the outcome of the free-silver plank. Six hundred and twenty eight delegates voted for free silver, while three hundred and one voted against it. Bryan, whose dark horse candidacy had been merely amusing before his speech, won the Democratic nomination on the fifth ballot. He was 34 years of age, the youngest man ever nominated by a major political party.

In the weeks that followed, Bryan also received the nominations of the Populists and the National Silver party at separate conventions in St. Louis. Eastern Democrats, who found the free-silver plank of the Democratic platform distasteful, formed the National Democratic Party. At their convention in Indianapolis, Indiana, they nominated John Palmer to run on a platform that declared support for the gold standard, but denounced the protective tariff.

The Republican party was also divided over the money issue. When their convention in St. Louis passed a monetary plank supporting the existing gold standard, many silver supporters left the convention and the Republican party. The Republicans nominated William McKinley on the first ballot to run on a campaign platform of sound money and a protective tariff.

While McKinley stayed at home in Canton, Ohio, receiving thousands of people who traveled from all sections of the country to visit him, Bryan decided to take the money issue to the people in an extensive cross-country tour. Throughout a barnstorming campaign that took him 18,000 miles, Bryan answered Republican accusations that he was supporting the creation of a dishonest dollar with the reply: "A dollar approaches honesty as its purchasing power approaches stability."

Ironically, the agitation over silver caused by Bryan's campaign had made money even scarcer. The closer the Free Silver Movement came to victory, the less confidence investors had in the convertibility of their financial securities into gold. This uncertainty about the maintenance of the gold standard caused a flight from the dollar. Investors sold dollar-denominated securities in order to buy securities denominated in currencies rigidly pegged to gold. In order to finance these adverse capital flows, gold flowed out of the country, reducing the money supply and creating an economic downturn and more deflation. The Republicans were quick to warn that a victory for Bryan would mean that even more gold would leave the country, causing the money supply to be even smaller than it had been under the gold standard.

The election brought forth the greatest outpouring of voters the country had ever seen. Bryan received 6,500,000 votes (more than had ever before voted for a president), but he lost the election to McKinley, who received 7,000,000. The defeat of Bryan allayed much of the uncertainty about the monetary standard, and speculation against the dollar was reduced. In the twelve months ending June 30, 1896, the United States exported some $79 million in gold. In the succeeding three years it imported $201 million of gold. These gold inflows, together with domestic gold production, raised the monetary gold stock from $502 million on June 30, 1896, to $859 million by June 30, 1899. This increase in the gold stock caused a 35 percent increase in the money supply.

As it turned out, 1896 was the last year of the long price decline. Beginning in 1897, prices started to rise. By September 1902, wholesale prices were 32 percent higher than they had been in June 1897. As better extraction methods and new gold discoveries in South Africa, Alaska, and Colorado increased gold output substantially, "cheap" gold became the monetary standard of the United States, and the cries of the silverites were silenced.

15 Interest, Saving, and Investment

Nominal and Real Rates of Interest

Nominal Debts and Inflation

Unanticipated inflation or deflation can cause enormous transfers of wealth between creditors and debtors. Those individuals who owe a lot of money tend to benefit from inflation because the money they pay back to creditors is worth less than the money they borrowed. However, a windfall transfer of wealth from creditor to debtor occurs only if the inflation is unanticipated. If creditors and debtors correctly anticipate future changes in prices, financial contracts will make provisions to offset the effects of inflation.

Indexation of Loan Principal

One way to correct loan contracts for the effect of inflation is to index the principal to be repaid. For example, consider a loan of $1000 for a year at 3 percent interest. If the rate of inflation were 10 percent, at the end of the year the lender would receive $30 of interest plus the indexed principal of $1100, making a total of $1130.

Inflation Premium in Nominal Interest Rates

However, loan contracts are not usually indexed; the principal is usually contracted in nominal dollars. In this type of contract, the nominal interest paid would have to offset the expected depreciation in the real purchasing power of the principal. Were the rate of inflation expected to be 10 percent, the nominal interest rate on a loan with a fixed, nominal principal would have to include an inflation premium of 10 percentage points to compensate creditors for the effects of inflation. To be equivalent to the 3 percent indexed loan, the rate of interest on a loan with a fixed nominal principal would have to be 13 percent. At the end of the year the lender of $1000 would receive $130 in interest and $1000 for the repayment of the principal, making $1130. In real terms, the inflation premium is not a true interest expense, but rather a capital transfer involving the repayment of the principal.

Complete Indexation   The two loan contracts discussed above have the same present value. However, neither of these contracts is completely indexed with respect to inflation. The indexed contract calls for the payment of $30 interest plus the indexed principal at the end of the year. Although the principal is indexed, the purchasing power of the $30 in interest certainly depends on the rate of inflation which has occurred since the beginning of the contract. A completely indexed contract would have to pay $0.03 \cdot (\$1000) \cdot (1 + \pi)$ in real interest plus the repayment of the indexed principal $\$1000(1 + \pi)$, where π is the rate of inflation.

Nominal versus Real Interest Rates   Irving Fisher first described the relationship between interest rates and the expected rate of inflation in 1896 (coincidentally, the same year William Jennings Bryan first ran for president). Fisher made a crucial distinction between nominal or money interest and real interest. Nominal interest rates measure the rate of exchange between current and future dollars and are thus relevant to loan contracts with a fixed nominal principal. Real rates of interest measure the rate of exchange between current and future purchasing power. If an individual loans $1 for one year at a nominal rate of interest of i, he or she will receive $(1 + i)$ dollars in one year. However, if prices are rising, the $(1 + i)$ dollars that he or she receives will have only the purchasing power of $(1 + i)/(1 + \pi)$ dollars measured in terms of the purchasing power of beginning-period dollars. Consequently, in a world of certainty the real rate of interest r which measures the rate of exchange between current and future purchasing power can be derived as follows:

$$1 + r = (1 + i)/(1 + \pi) \tag{15.1}$$

or

$$r = (i - \pi)/(1 + \pi) \tag{15.2}$$

where i, r, and π are all expressed as proportions rather than percentages. Equation (15.1) may be rewritten

$$i = r(1 + \pi) + \pi = r + \pi + r \cdot \pi \tag{15.3}$$

The shorter the compounding period, the less significant is the cross product term $r \cdot \pi$. With continuous compounding, the cross product term vanishes and the nominal rate of interest is exactly equal to the real rate of interest plus the rate of inflation. The continuously compounded inflation rate is $\Delta \ln P$, where P is the price level.

| Real Interest and Expected Inflation | Fisher pointed out that individuals make their saving and investment decisions on the basis of the *ex ante* or expected real rate of interest rather than the *ex post* rate observed afterwards. Since the future inflation rate is unknown in an uncertain world, the relevant variable in equations (15.1) to (15.3) is not π but rather π^e, the expected rate of inflation. |

Interest and Consumption

| Motives for Saving | One of the most important topics in macroeconomics is the division of aggregate income between consumption and saving. Fisher treated consumption as the sole end of economic activity. Saving does not generate any utility in and of itself but rather consists of deferred consumption. There are basically two motives for saving. One is to smooth out the stream of consumption expenditures. By appropriate timing of borrowing and lending, an individual can stabilize his or her consumption expenditures in the face of fluctuating receipts. The other motive for saving is to receive interest. |

| Timing of Consumption | Consumers allocate their wealth between current consumption and future consumption to achieve an optimal time pattern of consumption. Irving Fisher's time preference diagram (Figure 15.1) analyzes this problem of intertemporal choice by examining the tradeoff between consumption in two time periods.[1] The consumer's time preference function is represented by the indifference curves U', U'', U'''. Each indifference curve depicts the combinations of current and future consumption which provide a given amount of lifetime utility. The consumer attempts to achieve the highest level of lifetime utility, given the market value of the individual's endowment. The line *MM* represents the opportunity set of consumption pairs of an individual who faces the choice of using his or her endowment to consume in two discrete time periods, t and $t + x$. The optimal time pattern of consumption is given by the point of tangency between the highest attainable indifference curve and the opportunity or budget line, also known as the *wealth constraint, MM,* point A. |

| Wealth Constraint | The opportunity line *MM* has a horizontal intercept of w_0 (the market value of his or her endowment), because the maximum amount the individual can consume in time period t is his or her entire wealth. The slope of the opportunity line $\Delta c_{t+x}/\Delta c_t$ is $-(1 + r)^x$, where r is the real rate of interest. This implies that for every unit of consumption the individual sacrifices in time period t, he or she can invest the funds in an asset yielding a real rate of return r and thus provide for an additional $(1 + r)^x$ units of consumption in time period $t + x$. |

[1]Irving Fisher, *The Theory of Interest* (New York: Macmillan, 1930), Chapters 10–12.

Figure 15.1   Irving Fisher's Time Preference Diagram

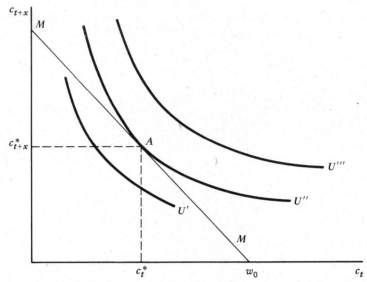

The indifference curves U', U'', U''' represent the individual's time preference func-tion. Each indifference curve depicts the combinations of current and future con-sumption which provide a given amount of lifetime utility. The opportunity line MM is the set of consumption pairs attainable by an individual who faces the choice of using his or her endowment to consume in two discrete time periods, t and $t + x$. The opportunity line intercepts the horizontal axis at w_0, the individual's current wealth, and has a slope $-(1 + r)^x$, where r is the real rate of interest. The optimal time pattern of consumption would be the point of tangency between the highest attainable indifference curve and the opportunity line MM, point A. Here, the individual consumes c_t^* this year and c_{t+x}^* in time period $t + x$.

Income Effect   Given the individual's time preference function, all changes in consump-tion can be separated into two components: an income effect and a sub-stitution effect. The income effect consists of the change in consumption resulting from a change in income received in any year, holding the real rate of interest constant. Because individuals tend to smooth out their stream of consumption, an increase in the receipt of income in any given year immediately affects both current and future consumption. Wealth is the present value of the income stream y_{t+x} produced by the individual's endowment of assets:

$$w_t = \sum_{x=0}^{\infty} \left[\frac{y_{t+x}}{(1 + r)^x} \right]$$

(15.4)

Consequently, if the income to be received in time period $t + x$ increases by 1, the horizontal intercept of the opportunity line representing current

Figure 15.2   Income Effect of a $1 Increase in Income in Time Period $t + x$

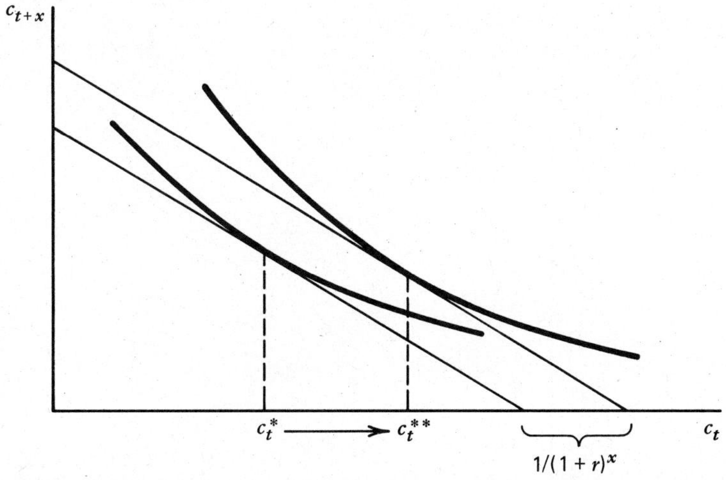

An increase in the income to be received in time period $t + x$ of $1 will shift the horizontal intercept of the opportunity line out by $$1/(1 + r)^x$. That shift represents the increase in current wealth. The optimum level of current consumption increases form c_t^* to c_t^{**}.

wealth will shift out by $$1/(1 + r)^x$. The income effect resulting from this shift in the opportunity line will cause present consumption to increase, as is shown in Figure 15.2.

Substitution Effect   The substitution effect represents the change in consumption which results from a change in the real rate of interest, holding the stream of income yielded by the individual's endowment of assets constant. Since wealth is the present value of that income stream, an increase in the real rate of interest will cause current wealth to fall because the income stream is being discounted by a higher real rate of interest:

$$w_t = \sum_{x=0}^{\infty} \left\{ \frac{y_{t+x}}{(1 + r)^x} \right\}$$

$$\downarrow \qquad\qquad \uparrow \qquad\qquad\qquad (15.5)$$

The slope of the opportunity line $-(1 + r)^x$ will also become more negative or steeper. An increase in the interest rate would pivot the opportunity line around some interior point, causing a reduction in current consumption, as shown in Figure 15.3. A rise in the real rate of interest implies a reduction in the relative price of future consumption, since the cost of one unit of future consumption in terms of current consumption is $1/(1 + r)^x$. The individual must sacrifice $1/(1 + r)^x$ units of current consumption to acquire one unit of future consumption. A rise in the real rate of interest, holding

Figure 15.3   Substitution Effect Resulting from an Increase in the Real Rate of Interest

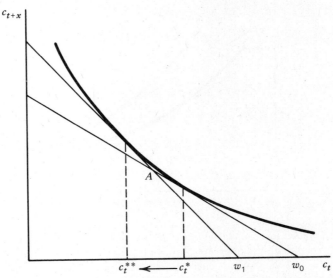

An increase in the real rate of interest pivots the opportunity line around some interior point A. Wealth falls from w_0 to w_1 because the individual's endowed income stream is discounted by a higher real rate of interest, and the slope of the budget line $-(1 + r)^x$ becomes steeper. This fall in the relative price of future consumption induces the individual to substitute future consumption for current consumption.

real income constant, will induce individuals to take advantage of the drop in the relative price of future consumption by substituting future consumption for current consumption.

Determinants of Current Consumption

Current consumption c_t can thus be expressed as a function of the stream of income yielded by the individual's endowment of assets and the real rate of interest:

$$c_t = c(\overset{+}{y_t}, \overset{+}{y_{t+1}}, \overset{+}{y_{t+x}}, \overset{+}{y_{t+\infty}}, \overset{-}{r}) \qquad (15.6)$$

Interest and Investment

Investment Creates Future Income Streams

The theory of investment also concerns the allocation of resources over time. Investment expenditures increase the current stock of capital and thus increase future production possibilities. Business firms must decide how many of these investment opportunities should be undertaken. Basically, each business enterprise desires to maximize its current net worth.

Consequently, it will find investment expenditures profitable only if the discounted value of the stream of revenue produced by the increased stock of capital is greater than the cost of the investment. In essence, business firms are creating future income streams through investment expenditures. Claims to those income streams are sold to savers in the household sector. Business firms can undertake profitably only those investments whose market values to savers in terms of future income streams exceed their cost.

Marginal Product of Capital and Investment In competitive markets the revenue produced by the capital stock in any time period is the marginal product of capital MPK (the incremental output generated by a marginal addition to the capital stock) times the price P at which output is sold. For example, consider a marginal addition to the capital stock *which starts to produce output in the next time period*. Each year the additional capital generates revenue of price times the marginal product of capital. Now assume, however, that the price at which output is sold is increasing at the rate of inflation π and the capital stock depreciates physically through time, thereby evaporating at a rate d per year. The market value of this nominal income stream can be found by discounting it to the present using the nominal rate of interest. If the cost of a unit of capital P_K at present is less than the discounted value of the income stream it produces, the investment can be profitably undertaken because it will increase the business firm's net worth. Thus, the investment rule calls for an increase in investment expenditures so long as

$$P_K < \sum_{t=1}^{\infty} \frac{P(1 + \pi)^t \cdot MPK(1 - d)^{t-1}}{(1 + i)^t}$$

(15.7)

Investment and Real Interest Rates Given the relationship in equation (15.1) between the real and the nominal interest rate, equation (15.7) can be rewritten in constant price terms:

$$P_K < \sum_{t=1}^{\infty} \frac{P \cdot MPK(1 - d)^{t-1}}{(1 + r)^t}$$

(15.8)

The summation of the infinite geometrically declining series in equation (15.8) can be simplified to

$$P_K < \frac{P \cdot MPK}{r + d}$$

(15.9)

User Cost of Capital Another way of expressing the investment rule is

$$P_K \cdot (r + d) < P \cdot MPK$$

(15.10)

In this form the investment rule calls for increasing the capital stock through new investment if the cost of *using* capital is less than the revenue it produces. The expression $P_K \cdot (r + d)$ corresponds to the cost of using one unit of capital for a year in real terms. For example, if a business firm uses borrowed funds to purchase one unit of capital at a price P_K, the firm would owe the lender $P_K \cdot (1 + r)$ in terms of constant purchasing power dollars at the end of the year. However, the resale value of that unit of capital at the end of the year (in constant purchasing power dollars) would be $P_K \cdot (1 - d)$, since the used capital has depreciated. The difference between the amount the firm owes the lender and this resale value is the cost of using capital for one year:

$$P_K \cdot (1 + r) - P_K \cdot (1 - d) = P_K \cdot (r + d) \qquad (15.11)$$

So long as this cost is less than the revenue the capital produces during the year $P \cdot MPK$, the use of additional capital by the firm is profitable.

Rate of Return on Investment

Alternatively, the investment decision rule can be expressed as

$$r < \frac{P \cdot MPK - P_K \cdot d}{P_K} = \frac{P \cdot MPK}{P_K} - d \qquad (15.12)$$

In this form the rule requires the rate of return on investment (net of depreciation) to be greater than the real interest expense of financing the investment.

Marginal Efficiency of Investment

This criterion for profitable investment can be used to derive a *marginal efficiency of investment* schedule. The net rate of return on the marginal investment is negatively related to the real quantity of investment for several reasons. For a given quantity of labor, new investment, which increases the capital stock, raises the ratio of capital to labor. This increase in the capital/labor ratio will reduce the marginal product of capital. Moreover, new capital is produced under conditions of increasing costs in any given time period. As additional resources are used in the production of capital goods, the relative price of capital goods P_K/P increases. For both of these reasons, the marginal efficiency of investment schedule is negatively related to the real quantity of investment, as shown in Figure 15.4. Were all profitable investment opportunities undertaken by business firms, the marginal efficiency of investment schedule would show the relationship between aggregate investment and the real rate of interest. If the real rate of interest were r_0, for example, the aggregate amount of investment undertaken by business firms would be represented by I_0/P in Figure 15.4.

Figure 15.4   The Marginal Efficiency of Investment Schedule

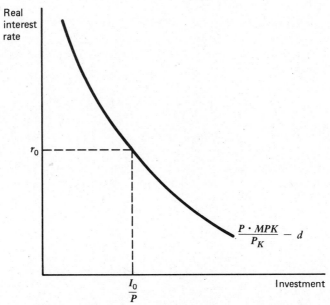

This diagram depicts the rate of return (net of depreciation) on marginal additions to the capital stock as a function of aggregate investment. The net rate of return on the marginal investment $P \cdot MPK/P_K - d$ is negatively related to the real quantity of investment for two reasons. First, investment increases the stock of capital and thus lowers the marginal product of capital MPK. Second, investment goods are produced under conditions of increasing cost in any given time period. As demand for the production of capital goods increases, the relative price of capital goods P_K/P increases. Investment is profitable so long as $r < P \cdot MPK/P_K - d$. Consequently, if business firms undertake all profitable investments, an aggregate investment of I_0/P will be undertaken at a real interest rate of r_0.

Saving, Investment, and the Circular Flow of Income and Expenditure

Saving and Investment in Equilibrium   In equilibrium, the circular flow of income and expenditure requires that desired expenditures in the aggregate be equal to total income. Private expenditures on goods and services can be divided into two categories: consumption and investment. Consumption expenditures create immediate utility. Investment expenditures do not create immediate utility but rather embody the supply of future consumption. Hence, the circular flow of income and expenditure in equilibrium requires total income Y to be equal to aggregate consumption C plus investment I plus government expenditures on goods and services G:

$$Y = C + I + G \tag{15.13}$$

If consumption C and taxes T are subtracted from both sides, this equality can be expressed as the equality between aggregate desired saving out of after-tax income S and the sum of investment I and the government deficit $G - T$:

$$Y - T - C = S = I + G - T \tag{15.14}$$

Saving and Investment Brought into Equilibrium by Real Interest Rate

Since both saving and investment are functions of the real rate of interest, there is a unique real rate of interest associated with flow equilibrium. To simplify matters, assume that all investment expenditures as well as the government deficit are financed by selling bonds. These bonds are purchased by individuals who save part of their after-tax income. In flow equilibrium, desired saving out of after-tax income generates a demand for bonds that is just equal to the supply of bonds necessary to finance desired investment expenditures and the government debt, as shown in Figure 15.5.

Figure 15.5　Saving, Investment, and the Equilibrium Real Rate of Interest

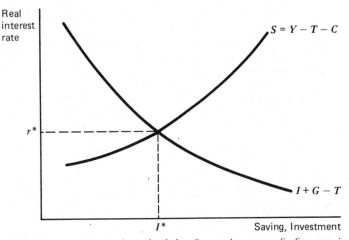

This diagram shows the schedules for saving out of after-tax income and investment plus the government deficit. Saving out of after-tax income rises as the real rate of interest increases, because consumers substitute against current consumption in favor of the relatively cheaper future consumption. However, investment falls as the real rate of interest rises because the higher interest expense makes fewer investment opportunities profitable to undertake. The flow equilibrium between income and expenditures requires saving out of after-tax income to be equal to investment plus the government deficit. The equilibrium real rate of interest r^* ensures that the economy's saving is absorbed by investment and deficit spending by the government.

Money Market Disequilibrium

However, the economy is not always in flow equilibrium. As was discussed in Chapter 11, stock disequilibrium between the supply of and demand for money creates flow disequilibrium between income and desired expenditures. For example, consider a situation of excess supply of money $M^s > M^d$. Because money and financial assets are such good substitutes as a form of holding wealth, individuals usually turn first to financial markets in their attempts to reduce their money balances. The excess supply of money then increases the demand for bonds as individuals try to reduce their money balances by purchasing bonds.[2]

Excess Money Supply Increases Demand for Bonds

The demand for bonds now has two sources: saving out of after-tax income to *add* to wealth and the transfer from money into bonds to *change the form* in which wealth is held:

$$\text{Demand for bonds} = S + (M^s - M^d) \qquad (15.15)$$

Consequently, the increased demand for bonds arising from the discrepancy between the supply of and demand for money raises bond prices, thus causing the real rate of interest to fall below the flow equilibrium level r^*. As the real interest rate falls, the increase in desired investment expenditures increases the supply of bonds, and the decline in saving reduces the demand for bonds. At the real rate of interest r'' in Figure 15.6, total demand and supply of bonds are equal:

$$\text{Demand for bonds} = S + (M^s - M^d) = \text{Supply of bonds} = I + G - T \qquad (15.16)$$

At this point the bond market is in equilibrium and the excess supply of money just equals the excess demand for goods and services:

$$M^s - M^d = (I + G - T) - S = (C + I + G - Y) \qquad (15.17)$$

Excess Money Demand Increases Supply of Bonds

Just the opposite occurs if there is excess demand for money $M^s < M^d$. The attempts by individuals to increase their money balances cause an increase in the supply of bonds as individuals try to adjust their portfolios. The increased supply of bonds lowers bond prices, thus raising the real rate of interest above its flow equilibrium level. At the interest rate r', the supply of and demand for bonds are equal:

$$\text{Demand for bonds} = S = \text{Supply of bonds} = I + G - T + (M^d - M^s) \qquad (15.18)$$

[2]Phillip Cagan, *The Channels of Monetary Effects on Interest Rates* (New York: Columbia University Press, 1972), Chapter 6.

Figure 15.6   Real Rates of Interest and Disequilibrium

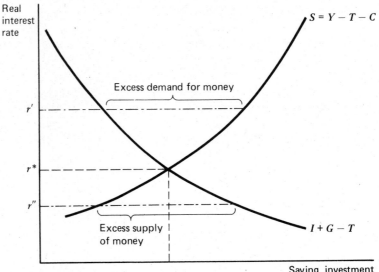

This diagram shows saving out of after-tax income and investment plus the government deficit. Flow equilibrium requires $S = I + G - T$. The equilibrium real rate of interest r^* ensures this equality. If there is excess supply of money, individuals will attempt to reduce their money balances and desired expenditures will exceed total income, $Y < C + I + G$. However, this implies that $S < I + G - T$ and the real interest rate will lie below r^* at r''. On the other hand, if there is excess demand for money, individuals will attempt to add to their money balances, causing desired expenditures to fall short of total income, $Y > C + I + G$. This implies that $S > I + G - T$ so the real rate of interest will lie above r^* at r'.

The bond market is in equilibrium when the excess demand for money just equals the excess supply of goods and services:

$$M^d - M^s = S - (I + G - T) = Y - (C + I + G) \qquad (15.19)$$

Nominal Interest Rates and Monetary Growth

Nominal and Real Interest Rates   The nominal or market rate of interest measures the rate of exchange between current and future dollars. One dollar exchanges for $(1 + i)$ dollars one year hence. Saving and investment decisions, however, depend on the real rate of interest. The real rate of interest measures the rate of exchange between current and future real goods and services. Of course, individuals do not know what the future rate of inflation will be, but their saving and investment decisions depend upon the expected or *ex ante* real rate of interest. As shown above, the real rate of interest *r* under conditions of uncertainty equals $(i - \pi^e)/(1 + \pi^e)$.

The Liquidity Effect   Consider a situation where the nominal money supply is increasing at a rate equal to the increase in the demand for real money balances. In this case the price level would be constant and the nominal interest rate would be equal to the real rate of interest *r** in Figure 15.7 of, say, 5 percent. Now assume that the rate of monetary growth suddenly accelerates by 10 percentage points. At the current rate of growth in nominal income, actual

Figure 15.7   Interest Rate Response to an Acceleration in Monetary Growth of 10 Percentage Points at Time t_0

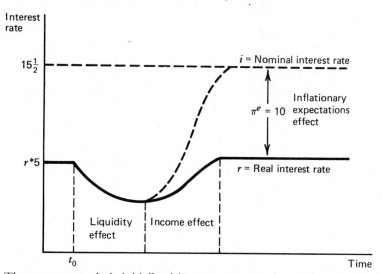

The money supply is initially rising at a rate equal to the increase in real money demand and inflation is zero. Hence, the nominal rate of interest is equal to the real rate of interest *r**. At time t_0 there is an unanticipated acceleration in the rate of monetary growth by 10 percentage points. Individuals soon find that they are holding undesired money balances and will attempt to reduce their money balances by purchasing bonds, lowering the real rate of interest. The real rate of interest falls to a level which creates sufficient excess demand for goods and services to offset the excess supply of money. This phenomenon is referred to as the *liquidity effect*. Then gross national product increases in response to the excess demand for goods and services. Eventually, the increase in income raises the demand for money sufficiently to eliminate the excess supply of money, and the real rate of interest returns to *r**. This phenomenon is referred to as the *income effect*. The nominal rate of interest will have risen to a rate higher than its previous level, reflecting expectations of inflation. The rate of inflation associated with this new moving equilibrium is now 10 percent. Consequently, once individuals fully anticipate this rate of inflation, the nominal rate of interest will be $r^* \cdot (1 + \pi^e) + \pi^e$ or $15\frac{1}{2}$ percent.

money balances start growing faster than desired money balances. Individuals soon find that they are holding excess money balances. Since the public's attempts to get rid of its excess money balances increase the demand for bonds, the real rate of interest falls below the flow equilibrium level to a level where the excess supply of money is offset by an excess demand for goods and services. This phenomenon is often referred to as the *liquidity effect* of monetary policy on interest rates.

The Income Effect

However, excess demand for goods and services implies that inventories are falling. Sooner or later business firms react to this drop in inventories and raise prices or increase output. Gross national product then rises, increasing the demand for money. Once gross national product rises sufficiently to make the demand for money equal to the supply of money, the circular flow of income and expenditures will again be in equilibrium and the real rate of interest will return to r^*, assuming the real rate of interest associated with flow equilibrium has not changed. The increase in income which returns the real rate of interest to its flow equilibrium level is referred to as the *income effect* on interest rates.

Higher Nominal Interest Rate in New Equilibrium

If real output and real money demand continue to rise at their former rates in the new long-run equilibrium, nominal money balances must now be increasing 10 percentage points faster than the rate of growth in real money balances. This implies that, in the new moving equilibrium, prices are rising by 10 percent a year. Once this inflation is fully anticipated, the nominal rate of interest must be $15\frac{1}{2}$ percent:

$$i = r \cdot (1 + \pi^e) + \pi^e$$
$$0.155 = 0.05 \cdot (1 + 0.10) + 0.10 \qquad (15.20)$$

Nominal Interest Rate Falls and then Rises

To summarize, an unanticipated acceleration in the rate of monetary growth produces divergent pressures on the nominal rate of interest. In the 1950s and 1960s the initial excess supply of money tended to reduce market rates of interest for about six months (the liquidity effect). Gross national product then started to respond to the increase in the rate of monetary growth. Eventually, the increase in income raised the demand for money balances sufficiently to eliminate the excess supply of money, and the real rate of interest returned to its flow equilibrium level (the income effect). Nominal rates of interest continued to rise, however, reflecting expectations of increased inflation. After about two years, nominal rates of interest were at the new equilibrium level, as seen in Figure 15.7. Since 1973, however, the liquidity effect has virtually disappeared and nominal interest rate movements have become dominated increasingly by changes in expected inflation.[3]

[3]Michael Melvin, "The Vanishing Liquidity Effect of Money on Interest: Analysis and Implications for Policy," *Economic Inquiry*, 21(2), April 1983, pp. 188–202.

Interest Rates and Government Deficits

Switch from Tax to Debt Finance

Because the government deficit has to be financed out of the private sector's saving, economists have often objected to the use of deficit finance on the grounds that it reduces investment expenditures and hence economic growth. The current controversy centers on the economic effects of a switch from tax to debt finance. Since a reduction in taxes offset by sales of government bonds has no effect on the supply of money, aggregate nominal gross national product remains constant, given the Cambridge equation specification of the demand for money. Although private after-tax income increases as a result of the tax cut, all of that increased purchasing power is absorbed by the purchase of newly issued government bonds. Even though private spending does not change, the composition of that spending may be affected by the tax cut. The increased government borrowing necessary to finance the tax cut might increase interest rates and thus reduce investment expenditures.

Wealth Effect Raises Real Interest Rate

To illustrate this possibility, consider the effects of a $1 billion tax cut shown in Figure 15.8. The deficit increases by $1 billion, increasing the supply for bonds (represented by the shift in the $I + G - T$ schedule). However, the saving schedule will also shift. The tax cut has increased after-tax income by $1 billion. If consumption remains constant, all of the increase in after-tax income will be saved, so there will be no change in interest rates. This is shown by schedule $S'S'$. However, individuals may feel wealthier as a result of the tax cut and choose to consume part of the increase in their after-tax income. As a result, the saving schedule would not shift out by the full $1 billion increase in after-tax income. This would cause a shortage of saving at the real interest rate r_0, as shown by schedule $S''S''$. In order to close the gap (representing excess supply of bonds), the real interest rate must rise to r_1. As the real rate of interest rises, saving increases and investment expenditures fall, eliminating the excess supply of bonds. The final result is that deficit finance reduces private investment expenditures from I_0 to I_1. Since private expenditures remain unchanged, this reduction in investment expenditures is exactly offset by an increase in consumption.

Crowding Out

Thus, even though a switch from tax to debt finance does not affect total spending, it can affect real interest rates and the division of gross national product between consumption and investment. So long as individuals feel wealthier as a result of the tax cut, private capital formation is lower when government expenditures are financed by debt rather than taxes. This phenomenon is known as *crowding out*. For this reason, deficit finance may impose a burden on future generations because they would inherit a smaller capital stock.

Figure 15.8 Effects of a Switch from Tax to Debt Finance Holding Real Income Constant

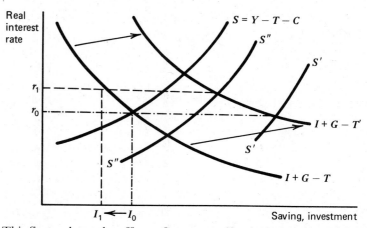

This figure shows the effects of a tax cut offset by borrowing. The deficit increases the supply of bonds, shifting the $I + G - T$ schedule to the right. If consumption remains constant, all of the increase in after-tax income will be saved, shifting the saving schedule out by an amount equal to the tax cut (shown by schedule $S'S'$). This leaves the interest rate unchanged at r_0. However, if individuals feel wealthier as a result of the tax cut, consumption will increase. As a result, only part of the increase in after-tax income will be saved and the shift in the saving schedule will not be as large (shown by schedule $S''S''$) as the shift in the investment schedule. In order to eliminate the shortage of saving, the real rate of interest will rise to r_1. Investment expenditures will fall from I_0 to I_1.

Zero Net Wealth Effect

However, the basis for this objection to deficit finance is the presumption that tax cuts have *wealth effects* on consumption. The preceding analysis of this wealth effect assumed that consumers treat the increase in after-tax income resulting from the tax cut like any other increase in income. In terms of the Fisherian time preference diagram, a tax cut is assumed to increase the individual's wealth as shown in Figure 15.9. This increase in the wealth constraint causes the individual to increase his or her consumption at the given real rate of interest. However, a switch from tax to debt finance does *not* affect the wealth position of the private sector as a whole. The presumed wealth effects of a tax cut occur only if taxpayers fail to foresee the future tax liabilities implicit in the government debt. If taxpayers recognized that the issue of $1 billion of government debt at an interest rate of 10 percent obliges them to pay $100 million a year in taxes to finance the interest payments to bondholders, they would not feel wealthier as a result of the tax cut. The present value of the increased tax liabilities of $100 million a year forever is exactly equal to the current increase in after-tax income:

Figure 15.9 The Presumed Wealth Effect of a Tax Cut

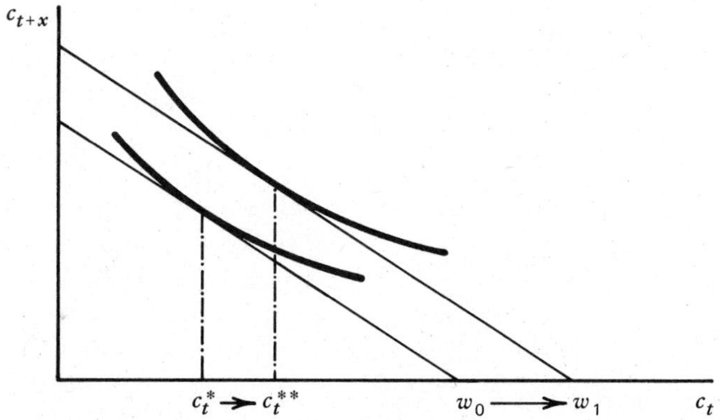

If taxpayers interpret the current increase in after-tax income as an increase in their wealth, the wealth constraint shifts out (from w_0 to w_1) and desired consumption for a given real rate of interest increases from c_t^* to c_t^{**}.

$$w_0 = (Y - T)_1 + \frac{(Y - T)_2}{(1 + i)} + \frac{(Y - T)_3}{(1 + i)^2} + \cdots + \cdots \quad (15.21)$$

$$\begin{array}{ccc} + \$1 & - \$100 & - \$100 \\ \text{billion} & \text{million} & \text{million} \end{array}$$

Perfect Foresight and Rational Behavior

If taxpayers had perfect foresight with respect to the future liabilities implicit in the government debt and behaved rationally, a switch from tax to debt finance would have no effect on private consumption.[4] Taxpayers would have to save all of the increase in after-tax incomes resulting from a tax cut in order to maintain their optimal stream of lifetime consumption in the face of these increased future tax liabilities. Consequently, the increase in government borrowing is completely offset by an increase in saving forthcoming at the existing real rate of interest. The real rate of interest does not rise, so investment expenditures are not crowded out by government borrowing. Government expenditures have the same effect on private consumption whether they are financed by taxes or borrowing.

Measuring Government Deficits

Whether or not such crowding out occurs, it is important to measure the government deficit in an economically meaningful way. For purposes of economic analysis, a deficit (expenditure minus income) must produce an increase in *real* indebtedness of the same magnitude. Present accounting practices treat all nominal interest payments as current expenditure. In fact, however, the true cost of borrowing is only the real rate of interest, as

[4]Levis A. Kochin, "Are Future Taxes Anticipated by Consumers?" *Journal of Money, Credit and Banking*, 6(3), August 1974, pp. 385–394.

shown earlier. The inflation premium in the nominal interest rate simply compensates for the declining real value of the principal. Hence, government payments of inflation premia should not be counted as current expenditure. Rather, such payments should be included in the capital account, since they are equivalent to debt retirement.

Illusory Deficit in 1979

With the U.S. government debt to the public equal to $488 billion at the end of 1978, the 1979 inflation rate of 8.5 percent wiped out $41 billion in real terms. At the end of 1979 the government debt stood at $523 billion in nominal terms or $482 billion in 1978 prices. In real terms, therefore, the government debt fell by $6 billion in 1979, and this decrease implies that government income must have exceeded current expenditure measured at 1978 prices by $6 billion. Because the accounts included the inflation premium as a current expenditure, they show a government deficit of $35 billion in 1978 prices for 1979. In other words, the government deficit is overstated by the value of the debt multiplied by the inflation rate.

Summary

1. The real rate of interest is the nominal interest rate adjusted for inflation. The real interest rate r is approximately equal to the nominal interest rate i minus the expected rate of inflation π^e. To be precise, $r = (i - \pi^e)/(1 + \pi^e)$, where r and i are both expressed as proportions and not percentages.

2. If the real rate of interest remains constant, an increase in either present or future income will increase present consumption. This phenomenon is known as the income effect.

3. If real income remains constant, a rise in the real rate of interest will cause a reduction in current consumption. This phenomenon is known as the substitution effect.

4. In fact, a change in the real rate of interest generally produces a change in real income. Hence, a change in the real rate of interest is accompanied by both the income and substitution effects on current consumption.

5. Profit-maximizing behavior requires a firm to invest if the investment costs less than the present value of the future income stream yielded by it. The investment rule can also be stated in terms of income and expenditure flows, and in terms of the investment's rate of return.

6. In the aggregate, there are more profitable investment opportunities the lower is the real rate of interest. Hence, the aggregate investment function is a negative function of the real interest rate. With constant real income, saving is a positive function of the real interest rate. The equilibrium real interest rate equates saving to investment plus the government deficit.

7. An excess supply of money increases the demand for bonds and lowers the real interest rate. An excess demand for money increases the supply of bonds and raises the real interest rate.

8. Initially, accelerated monetary growth produces an excess supply of money. Hence, interest rates fall. This phenomenon is the liquidity effect.

9. Evenutally, the excess aggregate demand caused by accelerated monetary growth raises nominal GNP. Money demand rises to eliminate the excess money supply and the real interest rate returns to its original level. This phenomenon is the income effect. The nominal interest rate will rise above its old level to incorporate a higher inflation premium.

10. A switch from tax to bond finance of government expenditure raises the real interest rate and crowds out investment *if* the public perceives that its wealth has been increased by the tax cut. Crowding out does not occur, however, if the public perceives that it will face higher future taxes to pay for the interest on the newly issued government bonds.

Questions

1. What is the relationship between the nominal and the real rate of interest?

2. Illustrate the income effect using Fisher's indifference-curve diagram.

3. Illustrate the substitution effect using Fisher's indifference-curve diagram.

4. How might a change in the real interest rate cause both a substitution and an income effect on current consumption?

5. Explain one form of the investment rule for a profit-maximizing firm.

6. Derive the aggregate investment function.

7. How does the equilibrium real interest rate equate saving with investment plus the government deficit?

8. How does an excess supply of money affect the real interest rate in the short run?

9. How is an excess supply of money eliminated in the long run and what happens to the real interest rate in the process?

10. What is the liquidity effect?

11. What happens in the short and long run to the nominal interest rate when the rate of monetary growth is increased?

12. What is crowding out and under what conditions would it exist?

16

The Effects of Taxation on Saving and Investment Decisions

Taxes and Investment Decisions

The Fisher Effect   During the 1960s and early 1970s the economics profession and the financial community became increasingly aware of the relationship between inflation and nominal rates of interest. The *Fisher effect* derived in the previous chapter shows that a one percentage point increase in anticipated inflation raises the nominal rate of interest by approximately one percentage point, leaving the real rate of interest unchanged. Since saving and investment decisions are assumed to depend on real rates of interest, an increase in the anticipated rate of inflation would have virtually no effect on equilibrium levels of saving and investment. However, Fisher's analysis ignores the taxation of income from capital. Once personal and corporate income taxes are taken into consideration, Irving Fisher's conclusions no longer hold.

Investment Rule without Taxes   In order to analyze the effects of taxes on investment decisions, first reconsider the investment rule for a world of no taxes. The discounted value of the income stream generated by the investment must be greater than its cost if the investment is to be profitable:

$$P_K < \frac{P \cdot MPK}{r + d} \tag{16.1}$$

One can express this investment rule in terms of income flows: the income produced in each time period must exceed the user cost of capital:

$$P_K(r + d) < P \cdot MPK \tag{16.2}$$

The user cost of capital (the term on the left) can be divided into two components: the real interest expense $P_K \cdot r$ and replacement cost depreciation $P_K \cdot d$.

Investment Rule with Corporate Tax

The current U.S. tax system was designed for a world of no inflation. Corporate income is taxed at the corporate income tax rate tc, but nominal interest expenses and depreciation based upon historical costs are deductible. In a world of taxes, the investment rule requires after-tax income to exceed after-tax expenses (before-tax expenses minus their value as a tax deduction). In a world of no inflation, the investment rule is the same as that for a world of no taxes because the nominal interest rate is the same as the real rate of interest:

$$P_K \cdot r(1 - tc) + P_K \cdot d(1 - tc) < (1 - tc)P \cdot MPK \qquad (16.3)$$

or

$$r + d < \frac{P \cdot MPK}{P_K} \qquad (16.4)$$

which can be obtained by dividing both sides of equation (16.3) by P_K and $(1 - tc)$. Any investment that is profitable in a world of no taxes would also be profitable under the current corporate income tax system.

Investment with Taxation and Inflation

In a world of inflation, however, the tax system is no longer neutral with respect to investment decisions.[1] Inflation affects investment decisions because there are two basic flaws in the tax system. The first flaw is the way interest is treated. Nominal interest expenses can be separated into two very different components: the real interest expense and an inflation premium. Only the real component is an expense to the borrower. The inflation premium is essentially a capital transfer to compensate the lender for the declining purchasing power of the principal. However, the tax system does not make any distinction between the real interest expense and the inflation premium. Borrowers can deduct all their nominal interest payments as an expense. The second flaw is the use of historical costs in computing depreciation allowances for tax purposes. Under existing tax law a firm is not allowed to deduct the full cost of replacing the worn-out portion of the asset in an inflationary world, because total depreciation allowances cannot exceed the original cost of the asset. If inflation increases the cost of replacing capital, depreciation allowances based on historical costs convert some of the cost of using up capital into taxable income.

[1]Michael R. Darby, "The Financial and Tax Effects of Monetary Policy on Interest Rates," *Economic Inquiry*, 13(2), June 1975, pp. 266–276; and Martin Feldstein, "Inflation, Income Taxes, and the Rate of Interest: A Theoretical Analysis," *American Economic Review*, 66(5), December 1976, pp. 809–820.

Investment Decisions and the Deductibility of Nominal Interest Payments

Investment Rule for Nondepreciating Assets

In order to illustrate the effects of deducting nominal interest payments as an expense, consider a nondepreciating asset ($d = 0$). Since the asset does not depreciate, there is no overtaxation from the use of historical cost depreciation, but the subsidy resulting from the deductibility of the inflation premium in nominal interest rates remains. Thus, the investment rule is

$$P_K \cdot r \; - \; \frac{tc \cdot P_K \cdot i}{(1 + \pi)} \; < \; (1 - tc) \cdot P \cdot MPK \qquad (16.5)$$

Real   Tax savings   After-tax income
interest   from deductibility
expense   of nominal
         interest rate

All three terms in equation (16.5) are expressed in base year prices. The first term is the original capital cost multiplied by the real interest rate to give the real annual user cost of capital. The second term is the nominal interest expense ($P_K \cdot i$) multiplied by the corporate tax rate tc to give the value of the nominal tax savings accruing at the end of the year. These nominal tax savings must be deflated to obtain their value in base year prices. The third term is the nominal revenue produced at the end of the year $P \cdot (1 + \pi) \cdot MPK$ multiplied by $(1 - tc)$ to provide after-tax revenue. This nominal value also has to be divided by $(1 + \pi)$ to yield the real value at base year prices.

Nominal Interest Deduction and Inflation

Since r equals $(i - \pi)/(1 + \pi)$, equation (16.5) can be rewritten

$$P_K \cdot \frac{(i - \pi - tc \cdot i)}{(1 + \pi)} < (1 - tc) \cdot P \cdot MPK \qquad (16.6)$$

or, rearranging terms:

$$\frac{i - \pi/(1 - tc)}{(1 + \pi)} < \frac{P \cdot MPK}{P_K} \qquad (16.7)$$

Before-tax rate of return
on investment

Assuming that tc equals 0.5, this last form of the investment rule shows that the nominal rate of interest at which an investment project would just be profitable rises slightly more than two percentage points for every one percentage point of inflation.

Zero Inflation and Interest Deduction In order to illustrate how the deductibility of the inflation premium produces this amazing result, consider a $100,000 investment project with a before-tax rate of return of 5 percent. In a world of no inflation a business firm could profitably undertake the investment if nominal interest rates were 5 percent or less. At a 5 percent interest rate the income produced by the investment would just offset the interest expense and taxable income would be zero:

$$\begin{array}{ll} \$\ \ 5000 \text{ (income)} & [5 \text{ percent of } 100,000] \\ -\underline{5000} \text{ (interest)} & [5 \text{ percent of } 100,000] \\ \ \ \ \ 0 \text{ (taxable income)} & \end{array}$$

Ten Percent Inflation and Interest Deduction In a world of 10 percent inflation this same investment could profitably be undertaken at a 25½ percent nominal rate of interest (assuming tc equals 0.5). To see this, set $P \cdot MPK/P_K$ in equation (16.7) equal to 5 percent. Rearrange to express i in terms of π, tc and $P \cdot MPK/P_K$:

$$i < \frac{P \cdot MPK}{P_K}(1 + \pi) + \frac{\pi}{1 - tc} \tag{16.8}$$

$$0.255 = 0.05 \cdot (1.10) + 0.10/0.5$$

At the end of the year the business firm would owe $25,500 in interest. Since the investment produces only $5500 in income at the end of the year $[P \cdot (1 + \pi) \cdot MPK]$, the investment shows a loss of $20,000 for tax purposes:

$$\begin{array}{l} \$\ \ \ \ 5,500 \text{ (income)} \\ -\underline{25,500} \text{ (interest payments)} \\ -20,000 \text{ (taxable income)} \end{array}$$

This tax loss can be used to shelter other income of the corporation from taxation, so the net after-tax loss of income is only $10,000:

$$\begin{array}{l} \$-20,000 \text{ (taxable income)} \\ +10,000 \text{ (tax savings from using these losses to reduce taxable} \\ \ \ \ \ \ \ \ \ \ \ \ \ \text{income produced by other investments)} \\ -10,000 \text{ (net after-tax loss of income)} \end{array}$$

Inflation Increases Net Worth Offsetting this $10,000 after-tax loss in income is the increase in equity generated by inflation. At the beginning of the investment period, the business firm's equity in the investment project was zero. One year later, however, the value of the investment in a nondepreciating asset has increased to \$110,000 because of inflation. Since the outstanding liability is still \$100,000, inflation has increased the corporation's net worth by \$10,000:

	Asset		Liability	
Base Year	Investment	\$100,000	Debt	\$100,000
			Net worth	0

	Asset		Liability	
Year 1	Investment	\$110,000	Debt	\$100,000
			Net worth	10,000

Hence, this additional \$100,000 investment project would raise the corporation's present value, provided it could be financed at a nominal interest rate of under $25\frac{1}{2}$ percent.

Historical Cost Depreciation and Investment in Depreciating Assets

Overtaxation of Capital under Inflation

The current historical cost method of calculating depreciation reduces the real value of future depreciation deductions under inflationary conditions. Some of the real cost of replacing worn-out capital is thus converted into taxable income. This overtaxation of capital resulting from the understatement of depreciation expenses tends to offset the tax subsidy resulting from the deductibility of the inflation premium in nominal rates of interest.

Depreciation Allowance

Consider an investment in an asset whose real value depreciates geometrically at a rate of d percent a year. Using this rate of physical depreciation for tax purposes, the present value of tax savings from the depreciation allowance based on historical cost is

$$PV_d = \sum_{t=1}^{\infty} \frac{tc \cdot d \cdot P_K \cdot (1 - d)^{t-1}}{(1 + i)^t} = \frac{tc \cdot d \cdot P_K}{i + d} \qquad (16.9)$$

The higher the inflation rate and hence the nominal rate of interest i, the smaller is the present value of these tax savings.

Nominal Interest Expenses

Since this investment is assumed to be financed entirely by debt, the outstanding loan principal is exactly equal to the current dollar value of the asset at the beginning of each time period. This current dollar value equals

$P_K(1 + \pi)^{t-1} \cdot (1 - d)^{t-1}$. Evidently, the nominal asset value could rise or fall, depending on whether inflation is greater or less than the depreciation rate. Hence, this firm might be increasing or decreasing its liabilities expressed in nominal terms. Under these conditions, the present value of tax savings from nominal interest expenses is

$$PV_i = \sum_{t=1}^{\infty} \frac{tc \cdot i \cdot (1 - d)^{t-1} \cdot P_K \cdot (1 + \pi)^{t-1}}{(1 + i)^t}$$

$$= \sum_{t=1}^{\infty} \frac{tc \cdot i \cdot (1 - d)^{t-1} \cdot P_K/(1 + \pi)}{(1 + i)^t/(1 + \pi)^t}$$

$$= \sum_{t=1}^{\infty} \frac{tc \cdot i \cdot (1 - d)^{t-1} \cdot P_K/(1 + \pi)}{(1 + r)^t}$$

$$= \frac{tc \cdot i \cdot P_K/(1 + \pi)}{r + d} \tag{16.10}$$

Clearly, the present value of these tax savings is positively related to the nominal interest rate and thus to the inflation rate.

Investment Rule for Depreciating Assets

In present value form, the investment decision for a depreciating asset becomes

$$P_K < \sum_{t=1}^{\infty} \frac{(1 - tc) \cdot P \cdot (1 + \pi)^t \cdot MPK \cdot (1 - d)^{t-1}}{(1 + i)^t} + PV_i + PV_d \tag{16.11}$$

or

$$P_K < \frac{(1 - tc) \cdot P \cdot MPK}{r + d} + \frac{tc \cdot i \cdot P_K/(1 + \pi)}{r + d} + \frac{tc \cdot d \cdot P_K}{i + d} \tag{16.12}$$

Asset Life of One Period

For an asset with a life of one period ($d = 1$), the investment rule is

$$P_K < \frac{(1 - tc) \cdot P \cdot MPK}{r + 1} + \frac{tc \cdot i \cdot P_K/(1 + \pi)}{r + 1} + \frac{tc \cdot P_K}{i + 1} \tag{16.13}$$

Since $(1 + r)$ equals $(1 + i)/(1 + \pi)$,

$$\frac{tc \cdot P_K}{i + 1} = \frac{tc \cdot P_K/(1 + \pi)}{r + 1} \tag{16.14}$$

Consequently, equation (16.13) can be rewritten

$$P_K \cdot (r + 1) < (1 - tc) \cdot P \cdot MPK + tc \cdot i \cdot P_K/(1 + \pi) + tc \cdot P_K/(1 + \pi) \tag{16.15}$$

or

$$P_K \cdot [r + 1 - tc \cdot i/(1 + \pi) - tc/(1 + \pi)] < (1 - tc) \cdot P \cdot MPK \tag{16.16}$$

or

$$\frac{[r + 1 - tc \cdot (1 + i)/(1 + \pi)]}{(1 - tc)} < \frac{P \cdot MPK}{P_K} \tag{16.17}$$

or

$$\frac{[(r + 1)(1 - tc)]}{(1 - tc)} < \frac{P \cdot MPK}{P_K} \tag{16.18}$$

or

$$r + 1 < \frac{P \cdot MPK}{P_K} \tag{16.19}$$

or

$$r < \frac{P \cdot MPK}{P_K} - 1 \tag{16.20}$$

Rate of return net of replacement
cost depreciation

In this case the overtaxation resulting from historical cost depreciation just cancels the subsidy resulting from the deductibility of the inflation premium in nominal interest payments.

Zero Inflation and Depreciation Allowance Consider, for example, an investment project with a life of one period ($d = 1$) and a before-tax rate of return of 5 percent. In a world of no inflation a business firm would just be willing to undertake the investment if the nominal rate of interest were 5 percent. Suppose the investment project costs $100,000. At the end of the year the investment would have to generate $105,000 of income to earn a before-tax net return of 5 percent:

$$P \cdot \frac{MPK}{P_K} - 1 = 0.05 \tag{16.21}$$

Before-tax rate of
return net of
replacement cost
depreciation

or

$$P \cdot MPK = 0.05P_K + P_K$$
$$105{,}000 = 5000 + 100{,}000 \qquad (16.22)$$

After the interest payments of $5000 and historical cost depreciation allowances of $100,000 were deducted, the investment project would have a taxable income of zero:

$$
\begin{array}{rl}
\$ \ \ 105{,}000 & \text{(income)} \\
-5{,}000 & \text{(interest expenses)} \\
-\underline{100{,}000} & \text{(historical cost depreciation)} \\
0 & \text{(taxable income)}
\end{array}
$$

Consequently, the business firm would pay no taxes and the income produced by the investment would just cover interest expenses plus the cost of recovering the depreciated capital.

Ten Percent Inflation and Depreciation Allowance

Now consider the same investment project in a world of 10 percent inflation. The investment rule now implies that a business firm would undertake the investment at a nominal rate of interest of $15\frac{1}{2}$ percent:

$$r = \frac{i - \pi}{1 + \pi} < \frac{P \cdot MPK}{P_K} - 1 = 0.05 \qquad (16.23)$$

or

$$i = r \cdot (1 + \pi) + \pi = 0.155 \qquad (16.24)$$

At the end of the year this investment would produce output worth $P \cdot (1 + \pi) \cdot MPK$. Since the before-tax rate of return $(P \cdot MPK/P_K - 1)$ equals 5 percent, the investment would now yield $115,500 in a world of 10 percent inflation. After the interest payments of $15,500 and historical cost depreciation of $100,000 were deducted, the investment project would have a taxable income of zero:

$$
\begin{array}{rl}
\$ \ \ 115{,}500 & \text{(income)} \\
-15{,}500 & \text{(interest expenses)} \\
-\underline{100{,}000} & \text{(historical cost depreciation)} \\
0 & \text{(taxable income)}
\end{array}
$$

Again, the business firm would pay no taxes, and the income produced by the investment would cover total expenses.

In this special case, the overtaxation from the use of historical cost depreciation just offsets the subsidy from the deductibility of the inflation premium in nominal rates of interest. For tax purposes, the business firm can deduct $15,500 as interest expenses although the real interest expense is only $5500. The $10,000 overstatement of real interest expenses is offset by the $10,000 understatement of replacement cost depreciation. The cost of replacing the depreciated capital is $110,000, not the $100,000 paid for the investment the previous year.

Tax and Saving Decisions

Personal Income Tax and After-Tax Return
Under the current U.S. tax system, the nominal interest earned by savers is taxed at the personal income tax rate tp. The after-tax real rate of return to the lender is the after-tax nominal interest return minus the rate of inflation deflated to the base-year price level:

$$r_{at} = [i \cdot (1 - tp) - \pi]/(1 + \pi) \tag{16.25}$$

The nominal interest rate can be expressed

$$i = \frac{r_{at} \cdot (1 + \pi) + \pi}{(1 - tp)} \tag{16.26}$$

These equations imply that the nominal interest rate must rise by more than one percentage point for every percentage point of inflation to leave the after-tax real rate of return on saving unchanged. Assuming a marginal tax rate of 50 percent, for example, the nominal rate of interest would have to rise by slightly more than two percentage points for every one percentage point of inflation to keep the real after-tax rate of return constant. With r_{at} equal to $2\frac{1}{2}$ percent and no inflation, i equals 5 percent. With inflation equal to 10 percent, equation (16.26) shows that the nominal interest rate required to hold r_{at} at $2\frac{1}{2}$ percent is $25\frac{1}{2}$ percent.

Overtaxing Saving under Inflation
Inflation overtaxes the returns to saving because the inflation premium in nominal interest rates is taxed as income. The inflation premium in nominal interest rates is not really income; it is simply compensation for the declining purchasing power of the principal that was lent. Because this capital transaction is treated as income to the lender, the nominal interest rate must exceed the real rate of interest by enough to compensate the lenders for the decline in the real value of the nominal principal and for the taxes they must pay on such capital transactions.

Inflation and Interest Rates

Inflation and the Investment Function
These microeconomic decision rules have important macroeconomic implications for the division of gross national product between consumption and investment. Most reproducible capital depreciates and is overtaxed

Figure 16.1   The Effects of Inflation on Investment in Depreciating Capital

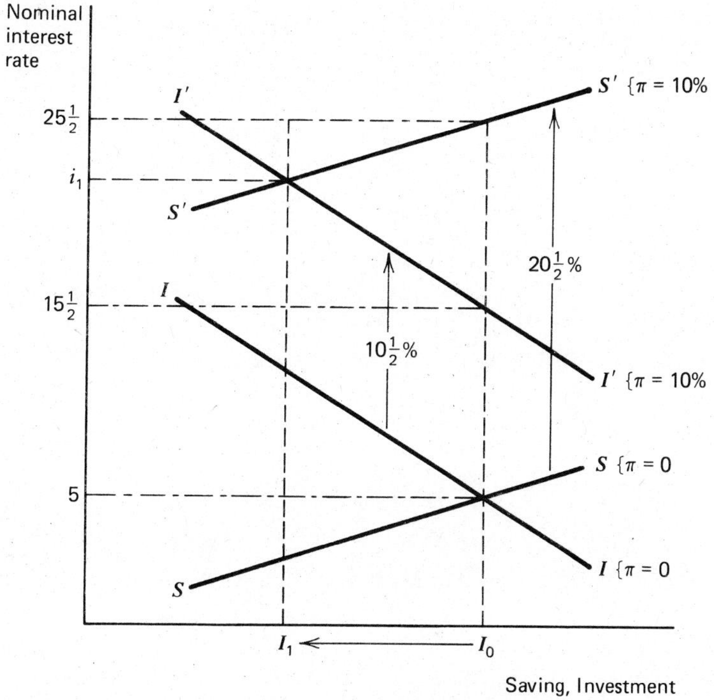

This diagram shows saving and investment schedules as a function of the nominal rate of interest. Since historical cost depreciation is used to calculate depreciation allowances for tax purposes, the investment schedule shifts up $10\frac{1}{2}$ percentage points with a 10 percent rate of inflation. Assuming a marginal personal income tax rate ot 50 percent, the saving schedule must shift up by $20\frac{1}{2}$ percentage points for a 10 percent inflation to keep the real after-tax return on savings constant. In the absence of inflation, aggregate saving and investment are equal at a nominal rate of interest of 5 percent. A rise in the rate of inflation of 10 percentage points will cause the nominal rate of interest to rise by more than $10\frac{1}{2}$ but less than $20\frac{1}{2}$ percentage points. Total investment falls because the decline in the real after-tax return reduces aggregate saving.

because of the historical cost method for calculating depreciation expenses. To simplify the analysis of the interaction of these saving and investment decisions, assume that reproducible capital has a life of one year ($d = 1$) and that the marginal corporate income tax rate is 50 percent. Figure 16.1 illustrates the aggregate effect of a 10 percentage point rise in inflation on the marginal efficiency of investment schedule for reproducible capital. In contrast to Figure 15.4, the vertical axis in Figure 16.1 is now calibrated in nominal rather than real interest rates. With no inflation, the quantity of profitable investment at a nominal interest rate of 5 percent would be I_0. In a world of 10 percent inflation, the same quantity of investment would be profitable at a nominal interest rate of $15\frac{1}{2}$ percent.

Inflation and the Saving Function	The saving schedule in Figure 16.1 is constructed under the assumption that the marginal personal income tax rate is also 50 percent. In the absence of inflation, savers will supply a quantity of saving equal to I_0 at a gross nominal return of 5 percent ($2\frac{1}{2}$ percent after tax). With 10 percent inflation, however, the same quantity of saving would be forthcoming only if the gross nominal interest rate rose to $25\frac{1}{2}$ percent. This increase in the gross nominal interest rate of $20\frac{1}{2}$ percentage points is required to hold the net real return constant at $2\frac{1}{2}$ percent.
Equilibrium Interest Rate under Inflation	The nominal market rate of interest cannot equal $15\frac{1}{2}$ and $25\frac{1}{2}$ percent at the same time. The asymmetry of the inflation effects on saving and investment produces a reduction in the quantity of investment in reproducible capital. This is because in the new equilibrium equating saving and investment the nominal rate of interest i_1 is greater than $15\frac{1}{2}$ percent. At the same time, the net real return to saving falls because the gross nominal interest rate i_1 is less than $25\frac{1}{2}$ percent. It is this decline in the net real return that reduces the quantity of saving.

Owner-Occupied Housing

Imputed Rent Avoids Tax	The current U.S. tax system provides very special treatment for one specific depreciating asset, namely owner-occupied housing. First, its net yield in the form of imputed rent less depreciation is not subject to tax. Since no taxable income is produced by this investment, owner-occupied housing is not affected by historical cost depreciation. Second, capital gains on owner-occupied housing escape taxation to a large extent because of rollover provisions, deferral, and the $100,000 one-time exemption for those over 55 years of age. Hence, inflation does not penalize investment in owner-occupied housing as it does investment in other depreciating assets.
Investment Rule	Investing in owner-occupied housing becomes relatively more attractive than investing in other depreciating assets as the rate of inflation increases. This fact is illustrated in Figure 16.2. Panel a shows the effect of a 10 percent inflation rate on investment in owner-occupied housing. If one still assumes that all investment is financed with borrowed funds and that owner-occupiers have a marginal income tax rate of 50 percent, the investment schedule for owner-occupied housing would shift up by $20\frac{1}{2}$ percentage points when inflation rises from zero to 10 percent. However, the investment schedule for other depreciating assets ($d = 1$) shown in panel b would shift up by only $10\frac{1}{2}$ percentage points, as explained above.
Market Equilibrium under Inflation	Panel c in Figure 16.2 superimposes the saving schedule from Figure 16.1 on the aggregate investment schedule, which comprises investment in both owner-occupied housing and other depreciating assets. A rise in inflation

Figure 16.2 The Effects of Inflation on Saving and Investment in a World with Two Depreciating Capital Assets: (a) Owner-Occupied Housing, (b) Other Depreciating Assets, (c) Total Saving and Investment

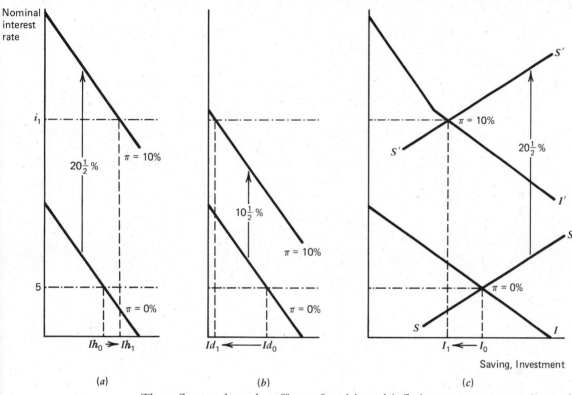

These figures show the effects of anticipated inflation on aggregate saving and investment with personal and corporate tax rates of 50 percent. Figure 16.2a shows the effects of inflation on the marginal efficiency of investment schedule for owner-occupied housing. Figure 16.2b shows the effects of inflation on the marginal efficiency of investment schedule for other depreciating capital assets. The interaction between the aggregate saving schedule and these two marginal efficiency of investment schedules is shown in Figure 16.2c. A rise in the rate of inflation of 10 percentage points will increase interest rates by more than $10\frac{1}{2}$ but less than $20\frac{1}{2}$ percentage points to i_1. Total saving and investment fall, but investment in owner-occupied housing increases.

from zero to 10 percent cuts back aggregate investment from I_0 to I_1. Since, however, the new market equilibrium nominal interest rate i_1 does not increase to $25\frac{1}{2}$ percent, investment in owner-occupied housing actually rises. This increase in investment in owner-occupied housing absorbs some aggregate saving, thus crowding out investment in other depreciating assets even more. Available empirical evidence suggests that the effects of this differential tax treatment of investment in owner-occupied housing has been substantial.

The Wealth Effect of Appreciating Inflation Hedges

Nondepreciating Assets in Fixed Supply

Owner-occupied housing and nondepreciating assets like land or gold are known as *inflation hedges* because they escape the tax penalties associated with historical cost depreciation. Most nondepreciating assets are also non-reproducible and hence have a fixed supply. As inflation increases, investment in these assets becomes more attractive relative to investment in depreciating assets. If the supply of the nondepreciating asset is fixed, purchases of this asset cannot constitute aggregate net investment. The increased attractiveness of the nondepreciating asset resulting from inflation merely bids up its real as well as its nominal value. For example, consider investment financed by debt in a plot of land that yields a real rental income stream of Ro dollars of constant purchasing power. The market value of this land P_L would be

$$P_L = \sum_{t=1}^{\infty} \frac{(1 - tp) \cdot Ro(1 + \pi)^t}{(1 + i)^t} + \sum_{t=1}^{\infty} \frac{tp \cdot i \cdot P_L \cdot (1 + \pi)^{t-1}}{(1 + i)^t} \quad (16.27)$$

            Present value of the   Present value of the tax
            after-tax rental income   savings resulting from
            stream   the deductibility of
                                    nominal interest
                                      expenses

or

$$P_L = \frac{(1 - tp) \cdot Ro}{r} + \frac{tp \cdot i \cdot P_L \cdot (1 + \pi)}{r} \quad (16.28)$$

or

$$P_L = \frac{(1 - tp) \cdot Ro \cdot (1 + \pi)}{i(1 - tp) - \pi} \quad (16.29)$$

Were the nominal rate of interest to increase by less than $1/(1 - tp)$ percentage points for every percentage point of inflation, the real value of the land would appreciate. This appreciation in the real value of land increases the wealth of home-owners and other landowners, encouraging them to consume more and therefore to save less.

Land Prices and Saving Decisions

To illustrate the effects of the real appreciation of land prices on saving decisions, consider the hypothetical economy represented in Figure 16.3. The only reproducible capital good is assumed to have a life of one year (d

Figure 16.3   Effects of Inflation on Saving and Investment with a Nondepreciating Asset in Fixed Supply

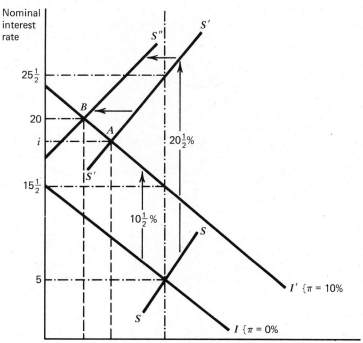

This figure shows the effects of anticipated inflation on aggregate saving and investment with personal and corporate tax rates of 50 percent. The only reproducible capital good has a life of one year ($d = 1$). Consequently, the marginal efficiency of investment schedule shifts up $10\frac{1}{2}$ percentage points with a 10 percent rate of inflation. In the absence of any nondepreciating assets, the nominal rate of interest could be less than twice the inflation rate at A. However, given the existence of a nondepreciating asset in fixed supply, such as land, point A cannot represent equilibrium because this asset would have an infinite price. As the price of the nondepreciating asset rises, the wealth-to-income ratio increases, reducing saving out of after-tax income. The saving schedule thus shifts to the left until it intersects the marginal efficiency of investment schedule at a point such as B, where the nominal interest rate is at least twice the inflation rate.

$= 1$). Let both corporate and personal tax rates be 50 percent. In the absence of any nondepreciating assets, the nominal rate of interest could be less than twice the inflation rate, as shown by the intersection of the saving and investment schedules at point A. However, this cannot be the equilibrium interest rate, given the existence of a nondepreciating asset like land. A nondepreciating asset in fixed supply would have an infinite price if the nominal rate of interest were less than twice the rate of inflation because the after-tax nominal interest expense $i \cdot (1 - tp)$ would be less than the rate of inflation. As the price of the nondepreciating asset rises, the wealth-to-income ratio increases and thus reduces saving out of after-tax income. This causes the aggregate saving schedule to shift to the left until it intersects the marginal efficiency of investment schedule at *B,* where the interest rate is at least twice the inflation rate.

Accelerated Depreciation and the Investment Tax Credit

Although the use of historical cost methods for calculating depreciation allowances reduces the real value of future depreciation deductions in inflationary periods and thus reduces the after-tax return on investment, there are other provisions in the corporate income tax law which increase the after-tax rate of return on investment. The two most important of these tax provisions to encourage capital investment are accelerated depreciation and the investment tax credit.

Accelerated Depreciation

Accelerated depreciation allows business firms to write off their investments at an artificially high rate for tax purposes. Although the total depreciation allowances are the same, the tax savings are realized at an earlier date and thus have a higher present value. For example, consider equation (16.9), which gives the present value of the tax savings from historical cost depreciation allowances. If the corporate tax rate were 50 percent and the nominal rate of interest were 10 percent, the present value of the tax savings resulting from depreciating a $100,000 investment with a depreciation rate of 10 percent would be ${100,000 [0.5][0.1/(0.1 + 0.1)]}$ or $25,000. If the tax law allows the corporation to depreciate the investment at an artificially higher rate of 40 percent, the present value of the tax savings from depreciation allowances would increase to ${100,000[0.5][0.4/(0.4 + 0.1)]}$ or $40,000.

Investment Tax Credit

The investment tax credit is in many ways similar to accelerated depreciation but it provides a permanent saving in taxes rather than a shift forward in time. The investment tax credit allows businesses to deduct some portion of current investment from their current tax liabilities. For example, if the investment tax credit were 10 percent, a corporation making an investment of $100,000 could immediately deduct $10,000 from the taxes it owes the government. This tax break essentially lowers the cost of investment by 10 percent.

Effects on the Composition of Investment

Of course, by reducing the present value of the tax liabilities associated with new investment projects, accelerated depreciation and the investment tax credit encourage additional investment. However, not all investment benefits from these tax provisions. Nondepreciating assets and owner-oc-

Figure 16.4   Effects of Accelerated Depreciation on Saving and Investment (a) Nondepreciating Asset, (b) Depreciating Asset, (c) Aggregate Saving and Investment

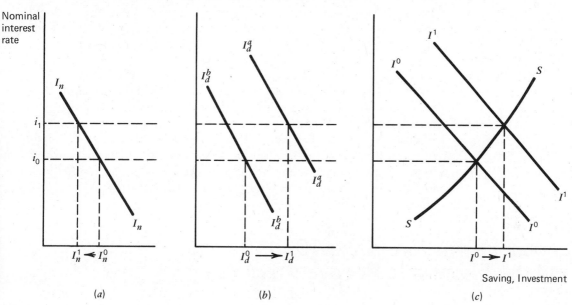

The acceleration of depreciation allowances shifts the investment demand schedule for depreciating assets to the right, from $I^b_d I^b_d$ to $I^a_d I^a_d$, causing the aggregate demand for investment to shift outward from $I^0 I^0$ to $I^1 I^1$. As a result, interest rates rise from i_0 to i_1, causing investment in the nondepreciating asset to fall from I^0_n to I^1_n. The combined effects of rising interest rates and accelerated depreciation increase investment in depreciating assets by $(I^1_d - I^0_d)$.

cupied housing do not receive any tax relief from accelerated depreciation. Moreover, the investment tax credit can be applied only to certain types of investment. As a result, one of the main effects of these investment incentives is to change the composition of investment. Accelerated depreciation tends to increase investment in depreciating investment goods at the expense of nondepreciating assets and owner-occupied housing.[2]

Illustration of Accelerated Depreciation   In order to illustrate the effects of accelerated depreciation on investment and interest rates, consider Figure 16.4. Panel a shows investment in nondepreciating assets and owner-occupied housing as a function of the interest rate. Panel b shows investment in depreciating assets as a function of the interest rate before and after the introduction of accelerated depreciation. Panel c depicts the aggregate saving and investment schedules. As a consequence of accelerated depreciation, the investment schedule for depreciating assets shifts outwards from $I^b_d I^b_d$ to $I^a_d I^a_d$, and the aggregate invest-

[2]Arnold C. Harberger, "Discussion," in Gary Fromm, ed., *Tax Incentives and Capital Spending* (Washington, D.C.: Brookings Institution, 1971), pp. 256–269.

ment schedule shifts outwards from I^0I^0 to I^1I^1. The result is a rise in the interest rate from i_0 to i_1 and an increase in aggregate saving from S^0 to S^1. The increase in interest rates reduces investment in nondepreciating assets from I_n^0 to I_n^1. The combined effects of a higher interest rate and accelerated depreciation produce a net increase in depreciating assets of $I_d^1 - I_d^0$.

Tax Revenue Effect
This analysis neglects the effect of accelerated depreciation on tax revenue. To the extent that accelerated depreciation reduced tax revenue, the budget deficit and after-tax income would increase. As was discussed in Chapter 15, the effect of a tax cut on interest rates and investment depends on whether individuals feel wealthier as a result of the tax cut. If individuals discount the future tax liabilities resulting from the increased government debt, the loss of tax revenue will have no effect. However, if individuals feel wealthier, increased consumption will cause interest rates to rise above i_1, crowding out some investment.

Capital Formation in the 1970s and the Economic Recovery Tax Act of 1981

Slowdown in Productivity Growth
Associated with the acceleration in the rate of inflation that began in 1968 has been a significant slowdown in productivity growth as measured by output per hour. From 1960 to 1968, output per hour increased at an annual rate of 3.4 percent. However, once inflation reared its head in 1968, output per work hour growth started to slow. From 1969 to 1977, output per hour growth slowed to an annual rate of 1.8 percent. During the Carter years of 1977 to 1980, output per hour actually declined at an annual rate of 0.3 percent. Paralleling this slowdown in growth of output per hour has been a similar decline in the growth of real wage rates.

Inflation, Taxation, and Productivity Growth
Of course, there are many factors contributing to this slowdown in productivity growth, including the decline in average labor force skills as the postwar baby boom entered the labor market, the rise in energy prices, and environmental legislation increasing the costs of production. At least part of the slowdown in economic growth, however, has been caused by the effect of double-digit inflation on the tax system. In the presence of double-digit inflation, the whole tax system becomes distorted, diminishing incentives both to save and to invest. At the corporate level, taxable profits are overstated because of historical cost depreciation. At the individual level, the taxation of nominal capital gains means that savers must pay capital gains on the illusory paper profits produced by inflation as well as on the real appreciation in the price of their assets. For example, investors who purchased a diversified portfolio of common stocks in 1957 would

have more than doubled their investment by 1977. However, prices also rose by an equivalent amount, leaving these investors no better off than when they started. If the securities are sold, however, the tax laws do not allow inflation to be taken into account, so taxes on the full increase in the nominal value of the stocks must be paid.

Tax Burden on Corporate Capital

These inflation-induced distortions in our tax system have imposed a very heavy tax burden on corporate capital. The total taxes paid by corporations, stockholders, and creditors in 1965 amounted to only 55 percent of the real income of the corporate nonfinancial sector. Once inflation began to accelerate in 1965, the effective tax on corporate capital rose dramatically. Despite the liberalization of depreciation allowances, the increases in the investment tax credits, and a reduction in the corporate income tax rate, inflation had increased the effective tax on corporate capital to 74.5 percent by 1979. Given this dramatic increase in the effective tax rate on corporate capital, it is not surprising that the share of net business fixed investment fell from 3.1 percent of GNP in the 1960s to only 2.4 percent of GNP in the 1970s.[3]

Household Portfolio Shift

The overtaxation of depreciating capital caused by historical cost depreciation induced individuals to substitute land, antiques, gold, housing, and other inflation hedges for corporate capital in their investment portfolios. This shift in the composition of wealth is dramatically illustrated if one compares the market value of corporate capital with that of owner-occupied housing. In 1965 the market value of corporate capital exceeded that of owner-occupied housing by nearly 30 percent. By the end of 1979, however, the value of owner-occupied housing was almost twice the value of corporate capital.

Impact on Productivity Growth

Investment in inflation hedges does not lead to any increase in productivity. For the most part, these assets are in relatively fixed supply. Although an individual may consider the purchase of land to be a valid alternative to investment in productive equipment, the purchase of land does not constitute net investment for the economy as a whole. The asset simply changes hands at higher and higher prices. The appreciation in the real value of these inflation hedges increases the wealth-to-income ratio and thus reduces the saving rate.

Wealth and Consumption

One of the most glaring manifestations of the effect of the appreciation of inflation hedges on the saving rate is the use of home equity to raise funds for consumption. As investors discovered that investment in housing provided a very good inflation hedge, demand for housing pushed up housing

[3]These figures are from Laurence Summers, "Inflation, the Stock Market, and Owner-Occupied Housing," *American Economic Review*, 71(2), May 1981, pp. 429–434.

prices considerably faster than the overall price level. From 1976 to 1980, home prices grew at an annual rate of 12 percent, versus 9.2 percent for the consumer price index. This real capital gain increased home-owner wealth and induced home-owners to consume more and save less out of current after-tax income.[4]

1981 Economic Recovery Act

The Economic Recovery Act of 1981, signed into law by President Reagan on August 13, 1981, was designed to offset the overtaxation of capital caused by historical cost depreciation. The accelerated cost recovery provisions in the act allow taxpayers to depreciate the cost of property used in business at an accelerated rate. Business property is divided into five different classes of assets for tax purposes. Automobiles, light trucks and machinery, and equipment used in research and development can be depreciated over three years. In addition, the investor also receives a 6 percent investment tax credit. For all other machinery and equipment, including public utility property, the asset can be depreciated over five years and the investor receives a 10 percent investment tax credit. Factories, stores, and warehouses can be depreciated in 10 years, but other nonresidential buildings, such as office buildings and leased stores, are depreciated over 15 years.

These provisions for accelerated depreciation go a long way towards correcting the overtaxation of corporate capital arising from the use of historical cost depreciation. By raising the after-tax rate of return on new plant and equipment, business firms will be able to pay higher real rates of interest for borrowed funds. As a result, corporations and other businesses will be able to bid capital away from housing (and other inflation hedges) and provide additional incentive for individuals to save rather than consume.

Summary

1. With no inflation, corporate tax has no effect on the investment rule because all costs are deductible against income before profits are taxed.

2. With inflation, the interest deduction is too high because part of the nominal interest rate is really repayment of principal in real terms.

3. With inflation, the historical cost depreciation allowance is too low because it does not enable capital to be replaced at higher prices.

4. Income from savings is overtaxed under inflationary conditions because all nominal interest is treated as income rather than part income and part repayment of principal in real terms.

[4]See, for example, Joe Peek, "Capital Gains and Personal Saving Behavior," *Journal of Money, Credit, and Banking*, 15(1), February 1983, pp. 1–23.

5. Inflation shifts the investment function for reproducible capital with a one-year life up percentage point for percentage point on a nominal interest rate axis. However, inflation shifts the saving function up by more than the inflation rate increase on the interest rate axis. Hence, both investment and saving decline as inflation rises.

6. Inflation hedges are nondepreciating assets like land that benefit under inflation from the interest deduction but are unaffected by historical cost depreciation (because they do not depreciate). Inflation makes inflation hedges relatively more attractive than depreciating capital and hence produces a portfolio shift.

7. Accelerated depreciation offsets in part the negative impact of historical cost depreciation on investment in productive capital, as does the investment tax credit.

8. Productivity growth in the United States slowed down substantially after 1968, when inflation accelerated. This slowdown can be explained in part by the inflation-induced increase in the effective rate of tax on income from capital from 55 percent in 1965 to 75 percent in 1979.

9. The increase in real house prices between 1976 and 1980 lowered the saving rate as households borrowed against the higher values of their homes in order to consume more.

Questions

1. Why does corporate tax have no effect on the investment rule in the absence of inflation?

2. How can corporate taxation affect investment decisions when inflation accelerates?

3. How does historical cost depreciation affect investment decisions under inflation?

4. What is the tax-adjusted Fisher equation for an economy with a proportional income tax system?

5. How does inflation affect the investment rule for a depreciating asset that lasts only one year?

6. What happens to the composition of the household sector's asset portfolio when inflation increases?

7. How have land prices affected the saving rate?

8. What is accelerated depreciation and what does it influence?

9. What is an investment tax credit and what is its effect on investment?

10. How has inflation affected productivity growth in the United States since 1969?

PART EIGHT

Foreign Money

With the outbreak of World War I in 1914, most countries (with the exception of the United States) abandoned the gold standard. The decade following the war witnessed its restoration. Despite strong opposition led by John Maynard Keynes, Chancellor of the Exchequer Winston Churchill restored the British pound to its prewar gold parity of $4.86 in April 1925. At $4.86, the pound was clearly overvalued, causing economic distress for British industry and labor already suffering extensive unemployment. With the subsequent stabilization of the French franc at an undervalued rate of 3.92 cents in 1926 and France's official return to the gold standard at this rate in June 1928, the burden of maintaining the pound exchange rate was made even greater. The advantage given to French exports by the undervalued franc, together with capital inflows stimulated by the prospect of a future increase in the gold value of the franc, generated a substantial balance of payments surplus, with gold pouring into France. The accompanying gold drain from other gold-bloc countries made it difficult for many of them to remain on the gold standard without adopting extremely deflationary monetary policies to protect their gold reserves.

With the international monetary system already under severe strain as a result of the undervalued franc, the Federal Reserve switched to a restrictive monetary policy in 1929. This was followed by widespread

From Gustav Cassel, *The Downfall of the Gold Standard* (London: Oxford University Press, 1936); Lester Chandler, *American Monetary Policy, 1928–1941* (New York: Harper and Row, 1971); Milton Friedman and Anna J. Schwartz, *A Monetary History of the United States, 1867–1960* (Princeton, N.J.: Princeton University Press, 1963); John Kenneth Galbraith, *Money—Whence It Came, Where It Went* (Boston: Houghton Mifflin, 1975); Arthur Schlesinger, *The Coming of the New Deal* (Boston: Houghton Mifflin, 1959).

bank failures in 1930 and 1931. The decline in the U.S. money supply and the associated fall in nominal income reduced the amount Americans spent on foreign goods and services. By 1931 American payments for imports of goods and services had fallen some 47 percent from their level of 1929. American foreign lending had fallen even more sharply.

With this drop in the amount of dollars spent or lent abroad, countries in the rest of the gold bloc were confronted with the choice of deflating their money supplies along with the United States or losing gold reserves. France chose to deflate even faster than the United States so that it not only protected its gold stock but actually added over a billion dollars to its gold reserves from December 1928 to August 1931. Britain, where unemployment was an extremely sensitive political issue, chose to resist deflation by increasing central bank credit and consequently lost gold.

The crisis that was to sweep most countries off the gold standard started when the Credit Anstalt, the largest bank in Austria, failed in May 1931. The run on banks quickly spread to Hungary and Germany. This banking crisis also shook confidence in London money-center banks because they held large amounts of deposits in German and Austrian banks.

This loss of confidence in pound assets could not have come at a more difficult time. Britain was already in the midst of a budgetary crisis. The British had gone further than any other people in providing unemployment compensation for their workers. Unfortunately, this made the British budget extremely sensitive to deflation. As deflation reduced employment and incomes, tax revenue fell but dole payments to the unemployed soared. The large budget deficits which resulted served to weaken confidence in the pound even more.

In a last-minute attempt to save the pound, Prime Minister MacDonald proposed a new budget with higher taxation and reduced expenditure. When the prime minister's own Labor Party refused to support him, he resigned and formed a new National Government, whose sole objective was to keep Britain on the gold standard. Even these heroic efforts were not enough, however. Gold reserves had fallen to such a low level by September 18, 1931, that it was impossible for Britain to remain on the gold standard. The British government decided over the weekend that it should act while it still held some £130 million in gold reserves. Gold payments were suspended on Monday, September 21, and the pound immediately depreciated from $4.86 to about $3.50. Within weeks, the rest of the British Empire and the Scandinavian countries also left the gold standard.

With the abandonment of the gold standard in 1931, the destructive process of deflation came to an end in Britain and the other paper-standard countries. The depreciation of their currencies against the gold-bloc countries provided considerable stimulus to their exports. Even more important was the monetary freedom they gained by severing the link with gold. The Bank of England adopted a vigorous policy of monetary expansion which quickly brought economic revival. While England recovered, the gold-bloc countries continued to be ravaged by deflation and deeper depression.

Until the devaluation of the pound, gold inflows into the United States helped to cushion the deflationary impact of the currency drain from U.S. banks. The sudden depreciation of the pound, together with continuing deflation in France, reversed the American balance-of-payments position and the United States began to lose gold. From mid-September to the end of October 1931 the U.S. gold stock fell 15 percent, triggering one of the most violent deflations in U.S. history. While prices remained approximately constant in Britain, U.S. prices fell 17 percent from August 1931 to February 1933. Industrial production dropped over 20 percent. By the time Franklin Roosevelt was inaugurated, over 25 percent of the labor force was unemployed.

The day after Roosevelt assumed office, he invoked the 1917 Trading with the Enemy Act to close the banks and prohibit the export of gold. By March 15, 1933, the banks had reopened, but the prohibition of dealings in gold and foreign exchange remained in force. On April 5 Roosevelt took another unprecedented step by nationalizing all gold outside Federal Reserve banks. Owners of gold were required to deliver all their gold coin, bullion, or gold certificates to Federal Reserve banks before May 1 and to exchange the gold for currency or deposits at a rate of $20.67 an ounce. Roosevelt's calling in all the gold stock ended the domestic convertibility of the dollar into gold and thus put the government in a position to secure all the profits from any increase in the price of gold. These actions effectively severed all links between the dollar and gold, but it was still widely believed that the United States would soon return to the gold standard.

With the gold standard in a state of limbo, delegates from 66 countries gathered in London to attend the Economic and Monetary Conference. The London conference had been planned in 1932 to discuss currency stabilization and the elimination of beggar-my-neighbor tariffs and other trade barriers. At the time, the United States was still on the gold standard and wanted the immediate return of the paper-standard countries to the gold standard. However, when the conference convened in June 1933, the United States had left the gold standard and its position on currency stabilization was still unclear. This confusion was reflected in an American delegation composed of men of all persuasions on the issue of stabilization. The chairman was Cordell Hull, the secretary of state. The vice-chairman was James Cox, the Democratic candidate for president in 1920, when Roosevelt had been his running mate.

Hull, Cox, and Representative Samuel McReynolds of Tennessee were generally in favor of stabilizing exchange rates. At the other extreme, Senator Key Pittman of Nevada was a fanatical supporter of the remonetization of silver. Representative James Couzens of Michigan was also an outright inflationist. Ralph Morrison, a businessman from Texas who had made substantial contributions to the Democratic Party, had no position at all on the currency question. The disunity of the American delegation became apparent immediately when Cordell Hull's proposal to reduce tariffs by 10 percent was opposed vehemently by Senator Key Pittman, who succeeded in having the proposal withdrawn.

Pittman, clearly the most colorful of the American delegates, regarded the conference as a well-deserved respite from prohibition and remained drunk for the duration. Despite his constant state of inebriation, he was a forceful, and sometimes violent, spokesman for the silver interests. Indeed, he chased an American adviser through the halls of Claridge's Hotel with a bowie knife because the gentleman failed to show enough enthusiasm for silver. The man was so frightened by the incident that he bought a handgun for protection. On another occasion Pittman was found naked, sitting in the kitchen sink at Claridge's, convinced that he was a statue in a fountain.

With the withdrawal of Hull's proposal to reduce tariffs, attention shifted from trade barriers to monetary issues and the conference immediately reached an impasse. The gold-bloc countries, led by France and Italy, took the implacable position that no other issues could be discussed in the conference until the paper-standard countries returned to the gold standard. Although the paper-standard countries were willing to discuss some eventual return to the gold standard, they were unwilling to abandon expansionary policies that had succeeded in improving employment conditions. Stabilization of domestic prices at predepression levels was the most important economic objective for the paper-standrad countries, not the stabilization of exchange rates.

With the conference stalemated, delegates anxiously awaited the outcome of a parallel meeting of representatives of the treasuries and central banks of the United States, Britain, and France being held at the Bank of England. The bankers' conference finally worked out a rather innocuous proposal calling for eventual stabilization of exchange rates and limits on exchange speculation. The American representatives cabled Roosevelt that approval of the bankers' agreement was absolutely essential to appease the French. Otherwise, the conference would be wrecked. Despite the fact that the declaration was so general that it committed no country to stabilize anything in the near future, President Roosevelt saw it as an attempt by France to force the United States back on the gold standard.

Roosevelt's reply to the stabilization proposal, received by the conference on July 3, 1933, was a bombshell:

I would regard it as a catastrophe amounting to a world tragedy if the greatest conference of nations, called to bring about a more real and permanent financial stability and a greater prosperity to the masses of all nations, should, in advance of any serious effort to consider these broader problems, allow itself to be diverted by the proposal of a purely artificial and temporary experiment affecting the monetary exchange of a few nations only. . . .

. . . old fetishes of so-called international bankers are being replaced by efforts to plan national currencies with the objective of giving those currencies a continuing purchasing power which does not vary greatly in terms of the commodities and need of modern civilization.

Let me be frank in saying that the United States seeks the kind of dollar which a generation hence will have the same purchasing power and debt-paying power as the dollar we hope to attain in the near future. That objective means more to the good of other nations than a fixed ratio for a month or two in terms of the pound or franc.

The conference was called to better and perhaps to cure fundamental economic ills. It must not be diverted from that effort.

Roosevelt's message made it appallingly clear that the United States would not be pressured by France into a premature return to the gold standard. Taking up the gauntlet, the gold-bloc delegates reacted immediately and violently. They announced that it was impossible for them to take part in any future discussions of monetary questions and threatened to return home at once. It took all of Cordell Hull's skills as a diplomat to keep the conference going another three weeks before it finally collapsed. In order to save face, the conference was never officially closed, only adjourned, and to this day it remains adjourned.

Ironically, the only acomplishment of the conference was an international agreement to raise silver prices negotiated by Senator Key Pittman. The agreement limited sales of silver by the governments of India, China, and Spain, and it provided for the absorption of newly mined silver through purchases by the governments of the five leading silver-producing countries. The United States was committed to purchase 24.4 million ounces a year. On December 21, 1933, Roosevelt ordered the mints to fulfill this obligation under the agreement by purchasing newly mined domestic silver at a price of almost 65¢ an ounce, about double the price prevailing in New York before the London conference. Despite his scandalous behavior, Pittman had come away from the conference with everything he wanted.

Now that it was apparent that the United States had no intention of returning to the gold standard at the former par value, the dollar fell sharply against the gold-bloc currencies. By late July 1933 the dollar price of the French franc had risen 40 percent. America's abandonment of the gold standard was, in one respect, a unique experience. Britain and the other paper-standard countries had been forced off gold by inadequate gold reserves. The United States was in no danger of exhausting its gold reserves; in January 1933 the United States held gold reserves of over $4 billion, more than one-third of the world's total. Rather, the break with gold was undertaken intentionally to raise commodity prices. The sudden depreciation of the dollar in June and July did succeed in producing a boom in commodity prices, but by August the dollar had started to rise against gold, and farm prices sagged. Roosevelt feared that he would face an agrarian revolt unless he took positive actions to depress the dollar.

On October 25, 1933, Roosevelt authorized the Reconstruction Finance Corporation (RFC) to purchase newly mined gold from domestic producers at steadily rising prices. Unfortunately, it was soon evident that these purchases had very little economic effect. Since the RFC paid for the gold by issuing interest-bearing debentures, the gold purchases had no effect on bank reserves. Moreover, the prohibition against private gold transactions effectively insulated the United States from the world gold market. So long as the purchases were confined to domestically produced gold, they had no effect on world gold prices or exchange rates. However, as soon as the administration authorized the purchase of gold in world markets, the dollar depreciated sharply against foreign currencies. To some extent, this arrested the decline in the price level.

The floating dollar era finally came to an end on January 31, 1934, when President Roosevelt fixed the price of gold at $35 an ounce, 69 percent above the old mint price. In essence, the United States returned to a sort of gold standard, but the restrictions on private ownership of gold continued. The dollar was convertible into gold abroad, but not at home. At $35 an ounce, the dollar was now clearly undervalued with respect to the gold-bloc countries. The competitive advantage of an undervalued dollar, together with the flight of capital from gold-bloc currencies which were in danger of being forced to devalue, generated huge balance-of-payments surpluses which were financed by gold inflows. Gold imports by the United States during the years 1934–1937 amounted to $5578 million. Unlike the gold-buying program of the RFC, these gold purchases directly added to high-powered money. Together with treasury purchases of silver, the gold purchases produced a 60 percent increase in high-powered money from March 1933 to May 1937 and the economy recovered. Net national product rose 76 percent in current prices and 59 percent in constant prices from 1933 to 1937.

While the United States and Britain, the two countries with depreciated currencies, reinflated and their economies recovered, the gold-bloc countries still defending the old par values of their currencies continued their deflationary plunge. Nowhere was depression more severe than in France, where economic conditions continued to worsen until France left the gold standard in 1936. By late 1936 no currency was freely convertible into gold at its 1929 gold parity value. Thus ended the international gold standard. No international system would take its place until 1946.

17

Foreign Exchange Rates, Balance of Payments, and Money

The Foreign Exchange Market and the Macroeconomics of an Open Economy

Markets for Foreign Currencies

Buyers of foreign products usually pay for those imports in their own money. However, the sellers of those products wish to receive payment in their own currency. Consequently, foreign trade usually involves the conversion of one currency into another. When Americans purchase Scotch whisky, they must convert dollars into pounds because Scotch distillers want to be paid in British currency. Similarly, when the British purchase American wheat or IBM computers, they must convert pounds into dollars. The *foreign exchange market* is a figure of speech for an interconnected network of commercial and central banks which provides for the convertibility of different national monies.

Foreign Exchange Rate

The rate at which one currency can be converted into another is called the *exchange rate*. Like any other price, exchange rates are determined by supply and demand. The supply of dollars to the foreign exchange market is provided by U.S. residents who wish to purchase foreign goods and services or foreign financial assets. The demand for dollars comes from foreign residents who wish to purchase American goods and services or American financial assets.

Demand and Supply under Fixed Exchange Rates

The exact process by which the supply and demand for dollars determines exchange rates depends upon whether or not central banks intervene in the purchases or sales of foreign exchange. Under a fixed exchange rate system, the supply of and demand for dollars on the foreign exchange market will balance at the official exchange rate because central banks, such as the Federal Reserve, the Bank of England, or the German Bundesbank, agree to buy or sell unlimited quantities of dollars at the official exchange rate.

The Price of a Dollar in Foreign Currency

Figure 17.1 shows the supply of and demand for dollars on the foreign exchange market in a world of two countries, the United States and Britain. As the pound price of the dollar rises, Americans supply more dollars to the foreign exchange market in order to purchase British goods, services, and financial securities. Conversely, the rise in the pound price of the dollar reduces the demand for dollars by the British, because they tend to

Figure 17.1   The Foreign Exchange Market and the Balance of Payments

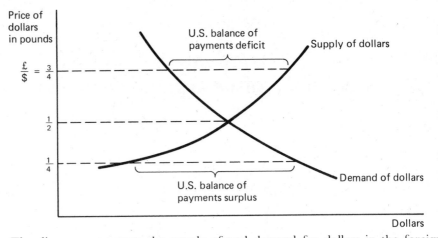

The diagram represents the supply of and demand for dollars in the foreign exchange market at various exchange rates. Only two countries, Britain and the United States, trade with each other. As the pound price of the dollar rises, U.S. residents supply more dollars to the foreign exchange market in order to purchase British goods, services, and financial securities. Conversely, a rise in the pound price of the dollar reduces the demand for dollars by British residents because they tend to buy fewer American goods, services, and financial securities. If central banks do not intervene, the market will clear at an exchange rate of $\frac{1}{2}$ of a pound per dollar. If the central banks peg the exchange rate above $\frac{1}{2}$, say at $\frac{3}{4}$, the supply of dollars will exceed the demand for dollars. This situation is called an official settlements balance-of-payments deficit for the United States. In order to prevent the foreign exchange price of the dollar from falling, the central banks must sell pounds and buy dollars. If the central banks peg the exchange rate below $\frac{1}{2}$, say at $\frac{1}{4}$, the demand for dollars will exceed the supply of dollars. The United States would then have a balance-of-payments surplus. In order to prevent the foreign exchange price of the dollar from rising, the central banks would have to buy pounds and sell dollars.

purchase fewer American goods, services, and financial securities. In the absence of any intervention by central banks, the market will clear at an exchange rate of one-half of a pound per dollar. On the other hand, if the governments of Britain and the United States had agreed to peg the exchange rate at three-quarters of a pound per dollar, the supply of dollars would exceed the demand for dollars. In order to prevent the foreign exchange price of the dollar from falling, central banks (the Federal Reserve and/or the Bank of England) must sell pounds to buy up the excess supply of dollars.

Official Settlements Balance The official settlements balance-of-payments deficit or surplus measures the extent to which central banks have intervened to clear the market at some pegged exchange rate. If central banks had to buy up unsold dollars at the official exchange rate, the United States would have a balance-of-payments deficit. A balance-of-payments surplus implies that there is excess demand for dollars at the official exchange rate, requiring central bank sales of dollars in the foreign exchange market.

The Balance-of-Payments Identity

The balance of payments records all economic transactions between residents of the home country and the rest of the world that give rise to a supply of or demand for that country's currency on the foreign exchange market. The balance of payments consists of a current account, a capital account, and the official settlements account.

Current Account The current account records imports and exports of goods and services as well as transfers such as workers' remittances and pensions. A current account shows a surplus when earnings from exports and net transfers exceed expenditures on imports. A current account surplus implies that the country is accumulating foreign financial assets, whereas a current account deficit means that the country is increasing its net international indebtedness.

Capital Account The capital account records international borrowing and lending. Capital inflows refer to the demand for dollars on the foreign exchange market created by the purchase of U.S. financial assets by foreigners and borrowing by Americans from foreigners. Capital outflows refer to the supply of dollars on the foreign exchange market created by the purchase of foreign assets by Americans and American loans to foreigners. Any imbalance between the supply of and demand for currency on the combined current and the capital accounts is offset by central bank intervention, which is recorded in the official settlements balance.

U.S. Balance of Payments

Table 17.1 shows the U.S. balance of payments for the years 1976 to 1982. Transactions that create a demand for dollars on the foreign exchange market are entered as positive items, and transactions that create a supply of dollars to the foreign exchange market are entered as negative items. The current account shows a surplus in 1976, 1980, and 1981, implying that the exports of goods and services were greater than imports, thus creating a demand for dollars on the foreign exchange market. In 1977, 1978, 1979, and 1982 there were current account deficits, implying that imports of goods and services exceeded exports. The capital account shows that there were net capital outflows in all years except 1979 and 1982, implying that U.S. lending to foreigners and purchases of foreign assets exceeded U.S. borrowing from foreigners and foreign purchases of U.S. assets. These capital outflows represent a supply of dollars to the foreign exchange market. In 1979 and 1982 the capital account indicates that there were net capital inflows. The sum of the current and capital accounts shows whether there is net excess supply of or demand for the currency on the foreign exchange market. Except in 1979 and 1982, the combined current and capital accounts were negative, indicating a balance-of-payments deficit. This deficit was financed by the intervention of central banks, shown in the official settlements balance. Balance-of-payments deficits become positive entries in the official settlements balance because they represent purchases of dollars by central banks to clear the market. In 1979 and 1982 the United States had overall (current plus capital account) balance-of-payments surpluses.

Balance-of-Payments Accounting

The balance-of-payments identity is simply another way of saying that the supply of a currency on the foreign exchange market must equal the demand for that currency. The supply of dollars on the foreign exchange market equals American imports of foreign goods and services IM. The demand for dollars is generated by American exports of goods and services X plus net capital inflows K. Consequently, the balance-of-payments identity requires that

$$\text{Official settlements balance-of-payments deficit} = \text{Net purchases of dollars by central banks} = IM - X - K \qquad (17.1)$$

Table 17.1   U.S. Balance of Payments, 1976–1982 (in billions of U.S. dollars)

	1976	1977	1978	1979	1980	1981	1982
Current account	4.4	−14.1	−14.8	−0.5	1.5	4.4	−8.0
Capital account	−14.9	−21.0	−18.7	10.4	−10.5	−5.2	9.9
Official settlements	10.5	35.1	33.5	−9.9	9.0	0.8	−1.9

Source: International Financial Statistics, 36(5), May 1983, p. 430.

National Income Accounts for Open Economies

Closed-Economy Equilibrium Accounting for transactions between residents and foreigners modifies the condition for equilibrium in the circular flow of income and expenditures. In a closed economy with no foreign trade or payments, equilibrium in the goods market requires desired expenditures on goods and services to be equal to gross national product:

$$Y = C + I + G \tag{17.2}$$

In an economy that engages in trade and payments with other countries, this is no longer the case. Some of the desired expenditures on goods and services by residents represent imports of foreign goods and services. Similarly, some of the demand for domestic output represents exports to foreigners.

Exports and Imports In order to account for the openness of the economy, total income and desired expenditures on goods and services must incorporate transactions in the current account balance of payments. Income derived from the sale of domestically produced output Y can be divided into output sold to residents O^h plus exports X:

$$Y = O^h + X \tag{17.3}$$

Similarly, desired expenditures on goods and services $C + I + G$ can be divided into expenditures on domestically produced output E^h plus imports IM:

$$C + I + G = E^h + IM \tag{17.4}$$

Open-Economy Equilibrium The circular flow of income and expenditures is in equilibrium when desired expenditures on domestically produced output is equal to the output available for sale to residents:

$$E^h = O^h \tag{17.5}$$

or, substituting into equations (17.3) and (17.4):

$$C + I + G - IM = Y - X \tag{17.6}$$

which can be rearranged to show that the net current account surplus equals the gap between total income and desired expenditures on goods and services:

$$Y - (C + I + G) = X - IM \tag{17.7}$$

Balance of Payments and High-Powered Money

Fed Sales of Foreign Exchange Reduce High-Powered Money

When the Federal Reserve (or any other central bank) intervenes in the foreign exchange market, these transactions directly affect the stock of high-powered money. Purchases (or sales) of foreign exchange have the same effect on high-powered money as open market purchases (or sales) of bonds. If the Fed sells foreign exchange (say pounds), the individual who purchases those pounds writes a check on his or her bank in payment. When the Fed receives the check, it will debit the reserves of the depository institution on which it is drawn, reducing high-powered money. This will result in a multiple contraction of the money supply.

Fed Purchases of Foreign Exchange Increase High-Powered Money

When the Fed buys pounds, it writes out a check on itself. When the seller of those pounds deposits the check at a depository institution, the Fed credits that institution with newly created reserves. High-powered money increases, causing a multiple expansion of the money supply.

Modified Government Budget Constraint

In order to account for these transactions, the government budget constraint developed in Chapter 13 must be modified to include sales of foreign exchange by the Fed:

$$\Delta H \quad = \quad G \quad - \quad T \quad - \quad \Delta D \quad - \quad F_{us} \tag{17.8}$$

| Increase in high-powered money | = | Government purchases of goods and services | − | Net taxes | − | Net borrowing from the private sector by both the Treasury and the Fed | − | Net sales of foreign exchange by the Fed |

Of course, the Fed can offset the effects of purchases or sales of foreign exchange on high-powered money through open market operations. If the Fed simultaneously buys government bonds when it sells foreign exchange, these offsetting transactions leave the stock of high-powered money unchanged. Hence, such a *sterilization policy* can insulate a country's money supply from the balance of payments.

Financial Flows and the Circular Flow of Income and Expenditure

Foreign Exchange Market Equilibrium

In equilibrium, a surplus on the current account implies that desired expenditures on goods and services by residents are less than total income. Conversely, a current account deficit implies that desired expenditures on goods and services by residents exceed total income. In order to see how financial flows produce this macroeconomic equilibrium, consider the balance-of-payments identity for the United States:

$$
\begin{array}{l}
\text{Balance-of-payments} \\
\text{surplus}
\end{array}
=
\begin{array}{l}
\text{Net sale of} \\
\text{dollars by} \\
\text{central banks}
\end{array}
=
\begin{array}{l}
\text{Current} \\
\text{account} \\
\text{surplus}
\end{array}
-
\begin{array}{l}
\text{Capital} \\
\text{outflows}
\end{array}
\quad (17.9)
$$

A current account surplus tends to create an excess demand for dollars on the foreign exchange market. Consequently, the market clears only when the current account surplus is offset by capital outflows or the sale of dollars by central banks. Both of these counterparts to the current account surplus have important effects on aggregate expenditures by the private sector.

Nonbank Private Sector's Budget Constraint
To analyze the impact of the current account on aggregate expenditures by the private sector, consider the budget constraint of the nonbank private sector for an open economy analogous to equation (13.7) for a closed economy:

$$
\begin{array}{l}
\text{Desired increases} \\
\text{in money balances}
\end{array}
=
\begin{array}{l}
\text{Total income} \\
\quad - \\
\text{Net taxes} \\
\quad - \\
\text{Net purchases of financial securities} \\
\text{sold by the Treasury, the Fed,} \\
\text{foreign central banks, or foreign} \\
\text{individuals} \\
\quad + \\
\text{Net loans to the nonbank private} \\
\text{sector from depository institutions} \\
\quad - \\
\text{Desired private expenditures on} \\
\text{gross national product}
\end{array}
\quad (17.10)
$$

When the current account surplus is financed by capital outflows, the purchase of foreign financial securities directly absorbs purchasing power which could otherwise have been used to purchase goods and services. Consequently, assuming that the demand for money is unaffected, private expenditures on goods and services must be reduced by the capital outflows. Thus, the absorption of private purchasing power by the net purchase of foreign financial assets produces the gap between total income and desired expenditures on goods and services necessary for macroeconomic equilibrium.

Central Bank Intervention   When the U.S. current account surplus is not offset by capital outflows, foreign central banks and/or the Fed must intervene to supply the dollars which are in excess demand. Foreign central banks hold most of their dollar reserves in the form of U.S. government securities. If they decide to sell dollars to prevent the foreign exchange price of the dollar from rising, they must first sell some of the U.S. government securities they are holding as reserves. However, the sale of those government securities absorbs purchasing power of the private sector which could otherwise have been used to purchase goods and services. Again, assuming the demand for money is unaffected, private expenditures on goods and services fall, thereby creating the necessary gap between total income and desired expenditures on goods and services.

Sterilization Policy   When the current account surplus is offset by the sale of dollars by the Fed (the purchase of foreign exchange), high-powered money in the United States will increase unless the purchase of foreign exchange is sterilized by an offsetting open market sale of bonds. If the Fed follows a policy of sterilization and insulates the money supply from the purchase of foreign exchange by simultaneously selling bonds, high-powered money will not increase. The sale of bonds in open market operations will absorb private purchasing power which could otherwise have been used to purchase goods and services. Consequently, assuming that the demand for money is unaffected, the gap between income and desired expenditures is created by open market sales of bonds to the public.

Fed Foreign Exchange Purchases without Sterilization   When the purchase of foreign exchange by the Fed is *not* sterilized, high-powered money will increase, causing a multiple expansion of the money supply. In this case the gap between total income and desired expenditures on goods and services is created by the increase in the demand for money resulting from a rise in nominal gross national product. For example assume that the Fed purchases foreign exchange worth $10 billion to finance the balance-of-payments surplus ($F_{us} = -10$). Equation (17.8) shows that high-powered money increases by $10 billion:

$$\Delta H = G - T - \Delta D - F_{us} \qquad (17.11)$$
$$(+10) \qquad\qquad\qquad (-10)$$

The money supply will increase by a multiple of that increase in high powered money because additional reserves will allow the commercial banks to extend additional credit to the private sector ΔB, causing a secondary increase in the money supply. With a money supply multiplier of 2.5, the money supply will increase by $25 billion:

$$\Delta M = \frac{M}{H} \cdot \Delta H = \Delta H + \Delta B \qquad (17.12)$$
$$(+25) \quad (2.5) \quad (+10) \quad (+10) \quad (+15)$$

This increase in the money supply will ultimately generate an increase in gross national product which will raise the nominal demand for money to equal the greater supply of money. Using the Cambridge specification of the demand for money function with a k of $\frac{1}{4}$, gross national product will rise by \$100 billion:

$$\Delta M \;=\; k \;\cdot\; \Delta(y \cdot P)$$
$$\text{(+25)} \quad \text{(1/4)} \quad \text{(+100)} \tag{17.13}$$

Current Account Surplus and Income-Expenditure Gap

Since the rise in nominal gross national product induces the private sector to use some of its purchasing power to increase its money balances, desired expenditures on goods and services will not rise as much as total income:

Budget Constraint of the Nonbank Private Sector

Desired increases in money balances (+25)	= Total income	(+100)
	+	
	Net loans to the nonbank private sector from depository institutions	(+15)
	Desired private expenditures on gross national product	(+90) (17.14)

Thus, the gap between income and desired expenditures is created when the private sector uses some of its purchasing power to increase money balances:

$$X - IM = \quad Y \quad - (C + I + G)$$
$$\text{(+10)} \quad \text{(+100)} \quad \text{(+90)} \tag{17.15}$$

Traded and Nontraded Goods

Prices of Traded and Nontraded Goods

Changes in relative prices have significant effects on the composition of domestic spending and production. In the context of an open economy, these relative price effects play an important role in determining the current account surplus or deficit. In order to analyze these relative price effects, it is useful to divide gross national product into two different categories: traded and nontraded goods. *Traded goods and services* (such as steel, automobiles, and textiles) are sold in world markets. In the absence of transportation costs or tariffs, these traded goods must sell for approximately the same price (in terms of a common currency) in all markets. *Nontraded goods and services* are insulated from world markets because of prohibitive transportation costs, tariffs, or quantitative restrictions such as quotas. Housing and personal services like haircuts are examples of non-traded goods and services. The price of a haircut in San Francisco does not depend on the price of a haircut in London because the two markets are insulated from one another. On the other hand, the price of American automobiles is limited by the availability of Japanese imports. If the price of American automobiles rises relative to the price of Japanese automobiles, American automobile companies will lose a substantial share of their market to Japanese automobile companies in the absence of quantitative restrictions.

Supply of Traded Goods

To develop the supply schedule of traded goods, assume that the two sectors have a fixed amount of capital. The total labor force is also fixed so that the composition of aggregate output depends on the allocation of labor between the two sectors. In each sector of the economy, firms employ labor up to the point where price times the marginal product of labor is equal to the wage rate:

$$\text{Traded goods sector: } W_T = P_T \cdot MPL_T \qquad (17.16)$$

$$\text{Nontraded goods sector: } W_{NT} = P_{NT} \cdot MPL_{NT} \qquad (17.17)$$

Since workers will move from the low-wage sector to the high-wage sector, eventually wage rates for a standard unit of labor in the two sectors will be equal. Now assume that there is a sudden increase in the relative price of traded goods P_T/P_{NT}. Since the price of traded goods has risen relative to the price of nontraded goods, the traded goods sector will bid labor away from the nontraded goods sector and increase its production.

Domestic Demand for Traded Goods

Similarly, domestic demand for traded goods also depends upon the relative price of traded goods. As the relative price of traded goods rises, domestic demand for traded goods will decrease as consumers substitute the cheaper nontraded goods for the relatively more expensive traded goods.

Net Exports of Traded Goods

Figure 17.2 shows domestic supply and demand schedules for traded goods. At the relative price $(P_T/P_{NT})_0$, the domestic supply of traded goods is exactly equal to the domestic demand for traded goods. If the relative price of traded goods rises to $(P_T/P_{NT})_1$, the domestic supply of traded goods will increase as labor is bid away from the nontraded goods sector and domestic demand for traded goods falls as consumers substitute the relatively cheaper nontraded goods for traded goods. The difference between domestic supply and domestic demand represents net exports of traded goods. Similarly, if the relative price of traded goods drops below $(P_T/P_{NT})_0$, domestic demand will exceed domestic supply. This gap is closed by net imports of traded goods.

Figure 17.2   Domestic Supply of and Demand for Traded Goods

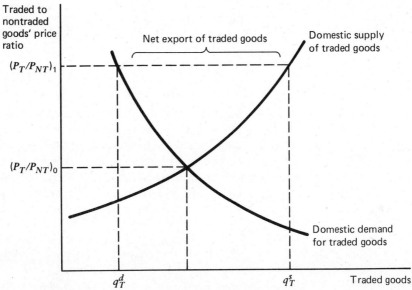

An increase in the relative price of traded goods enables the traded goods industries to bid resources away from the nontraded goods industries, thus increasing the domestic supply of traded goods. Domestic demand for traded goods falls as the relative price increases, because consumers substitute the relatively cheaper nontraded goods for traded goods. At a relative price above $(P_T/P_{NT})_0$, domestic supply will exceed domestic demand. This difference between domestic supply and domestic demand represents net exports of traded goods. At a relative price below $(P_T/P_{NT})_0$, domestic demand for traded goods exceeds domestic supply, implying net imports of traded goods.

Law of One Price   To simplify the analysis of traded goods prices, assume that the United States is a price taker in the world market for traded goods. This implies that the domestic supply of and demand for traded goods has virtually no effect on the world price of traded goods. If tariffs and transportation costs are ignored, the process of arbitrage will make the price of identical traded goods the same everywhere in terms of a common currency. This phenomenon is known as the *law of one price*. Consequently, the price of traded goods in terms of dollars $\$P_T$ must be equal to the world price of traded goods in terms of foreign exchange $£P_T$ divided by the foreign exchange price of the dollar $£/\$$:

$$\$P_T = £P_T / \frac{£}{\$}$$

(17.18)

Exchange Rate and Relative Price of Traded Goods

If the relative price of traded to nontraded goods is to remain constant, the foreign exchange price of the dollar must adjust to offset the difference between the U.S. inflation rate and the foreign inflation rate. The price level in the United States P_{us} is a weighted average of the prices of traded and nontraded goods:

$$P_{us} = \omega \$ P_T + (1 - \omega) \$ P_{NT} \tag{17.19}$$

Suppose, for example, that U.S. prices rise by a continuously compounded rate of 10 percent while the rest of the world has stable prices. To keep the relative price of traded goods constant, both traded and nontraded goods must rise at the same rate, 10 percent a year. Since foreign prices are constant, the foreign exchange price of the dollar must depreciate by a continuously compounded rate of 10 percent a year. This is shown by expressing equation (17.18) in first differences of natural logarithms:

$$\Delta\ln(\$ P_T) = \Delta\ln(\pounds P_T) - \Delta\ln(\pounds/\$)$$
$$(+10\%) \qquad (0\%) \qquad (-10\%) \tag{17.20}$$

If the foreign exchange price of the dollar depreciates by less than 10 percent a year, the relative price of traded goods will fall, thus reducing domestic supply of traded goods and increasing domestic demand for traded goods. On the other hand, if the foreign exchange price of the dollar depreciates by more than 10 percent a year, the relative price of traded goods will rise, increasing domestic supply of traded goods and reducing domestic demand for traded goods.

Purchasing Power Parity and Exchange Rates

Foreign Exchange Market Equilibrium without Capital Flows

The relationship between exchange rates and the relative price of traded goods provides an explanation of exchange rate movements in a world with no capital flows. Figure 17.3a shows the demand for and supply of dollars in the foreign exchange market for a two-country world consisting of Britain and the United States. With no capital flows, the demand for and supply of dollars are determined solely by current account transactions. Consequently, the foreign exchange market will clear only if the current account is in balance. This occurs initially at a pound price of the dollar of $(\pounds/\$)_0$.

Domestic Inflation Creates Current Account Deficit

Now assume that prices in the United States rise by 10 percent while prices in Britain remain constant. If the exchange rate remained constant, the price of traded goods would not increase. All of the increase in U.S. prices would be concentrated in the nontraded goods sector of the economy,

Figure 17.3   Illustration of Purchasing Power Parity: (a) Foreign Exchange Market, (b) Traded Goods Market

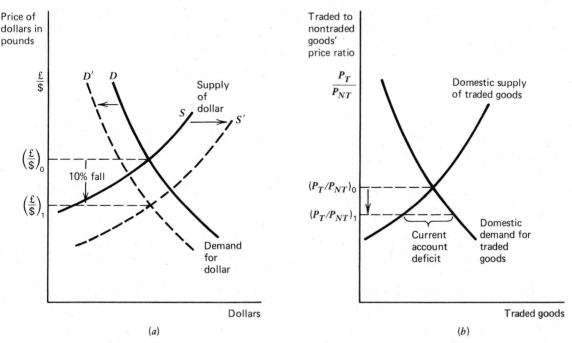

(a)   (b)

Figure 17.3a shows the demand for and supply of dollars in the foreign exchange market for a two-country world consisting of Britain and the United States. There are no capital flows so the demand for and supply of dollars result solely from current account transactions. The foreign exchange market is initially in equilibrium at an exchange rate $(£/\$)_0$. Now assume that prices in the United States rise by 10 percent while prices in Britain remain constant. If the exchange rate remained constant, the price of traded goods in the United States could not increase. All of the increase in U.S. prices would be concentrated in the nontraded goods sector of the economy. The fall in the relative price of traded goods would reduce domestic production of traded goods and increase domestic demand for traded goods, causing a current account deficit, as shown in Figure 17.3b. Of course, a current account deficit implies that there is excess supply of dollars in the foreign exchange market. This is shown in Figure 17.3a by a shift in the supply schedule to the right and a shift in the demand schedule to the left. If central banks do not intervene to purchase dollars, the excess supply of dollars will cause the pound price of the dollar to fall by 10 percent. This exchange rate depreciation raises the price of traded goods back to $(P_T/P_{NT})_0$ and restores balance in the current account.

causing the relative price of traded goods to fall from $(P_T/P_{NT})_0$ to $(P_T/P_{NT})_1$. This drop in the relative price of traded goods would reduce domestic production of traded goods and increase domestic demand for traded goods, causing the United States to become a net importer of traded goods, as shown in Figure 17.3b. This increase in net imports involves an increase in imports and/or a decrease in exports. The increase in imports is represented by a rightward shift in the dollar supply schedule in Figure 17.3a. The reduction in the supply of exports is shown as a leftward shift in the dollar demand schedule. If central banks do not intervene to purchase dollars, the excess supply of dollars on the foreign exchange market will cause the pound price of the dollar to fall and the relative price of traded goods to rise until the current account is again in balance.

Foreign Exchange Rate Changes to Restore Current Account Balance

In order to keep the current account in balance, the relative price of traded goods must return to its equilibrium level of $(P_T/P_{NT})_0$ in Figure 17.3b. In the present example, this implies that the pound price of the dollar must fall by 10 percent. As was shown in equation (17.20), a 10 percent depreciation in the pound price of the dollar would increase the dollar price of traded goods by 10 percent. Since traded goods prices would then rise proportionally with the overall price index, the relative price of traded goods would remain constant and keep the current account in balance.

Purchasing Power Parity Equation

The *purchasing power parity* equation gives the change in exchange rates necessary to keep the relative price of traded goods constant and the current account in balance. This relationship requires the foreign exchange price of the dollar to depreciate at a continuously compounded rate equal to the difference between the U.S. rate of inflation and foreign inflation:

$$\Delta\ln(\pounds/\$) = \Delta\ln(P_{uk}) - \Delta\ln(P_{us}) \tag{17.21}$$

Capital Flows and Exchange Rates

Capital Flows and Purchasing Power Parity

Although the purchasing power parity equation provides the condition for current account balance, it does not account for changes in exchange rates arising from capital flows. Capital flows can cause exchange rates to deviate significantly from purchasing power parity. Capital inflows cause the home currency to appreciate and hence reduce the relative price of traded goods. Conversely, capital outflows tend to depreciate the home currency and thus raise the relative price of traded goods.

Capital Inflows Appreciate the Dollar

To illustrate the effects of capital flows on exchange rates, consider Figure 17.4. In the absence of any capital flows, the foreign exchange market is in equilibrium at one-half of a pound per dollar. This is the exchange rate that produces current account balance. If foreigners suddenly decide to purchase $10 billion of American financial securities, these capital inflows will add to the demand for dollars on the foreign exchange market. Consequently, these capital inflows will shift the demand schedule for dollars rightwards by $10 billion. If central banks do not intervene, the dollar must appreciate to three-quarters of a pound per dollar.

Figure 17.4 Effect of Capital Inflows on the Exchange Rate

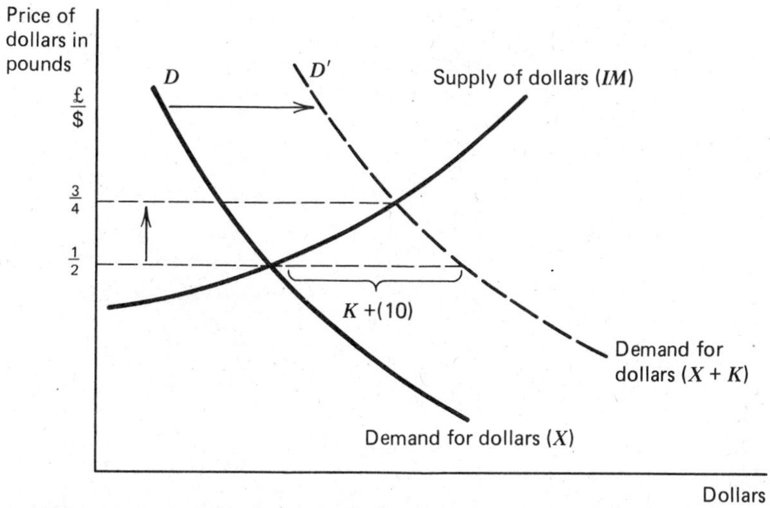

This figure shows the foreign exchange market in equilibrium at $\frac{1}{2}$ a pound per dollar in the absence of capital flows. Capital inflows of $10 billion add to the demand for dollars, shifting the demand schedule to the right. If central banks do not intervene, the dollar will appreciate to $\frac{3}{4}$ pound per dollar.

Capital Inflows Create Current Account Deficit
At the new exchange rate the supply of dollars is again equal to the demand for dollars on the foreign exchange market. However, this implies that the demand for dollars to finance the capital inflows must be offset by a net supply of dollars from a current account deficit. The process by which an appreciation of the dollar eliminates the initial excess demand involves changes in the domestic production and consumption of traded goods. The appreciation of the exchange rate represents a deviation from purchasing power parity which causes the relative price of traded goods to fall:

$$\$P_T = \text{\pounds}\bar{P}_T / \frac{\text{\pounds}}{\$}$$
$$\qquad \downarrow \qquad\qquad \uparrow \qquad\qquad (17.22)$$

As shown in Figure 17.5, this reduction in the relative price of traded goods will produce a current account deficit. Domestic demand for traded goods will increase as consumers substitute the relatively cheaper traded goods for nontraded goods. The reduced profitability of the traded goods industries will enable the nontraded goods sector to bid labor and other resources away from the traded goods industries, hence decreasing the supply of traded goods. The resulting excess of domestic demand over domestic supply represents net imports of traded goods and services which constitute the current account deficit.

Figure 17.5   Effect of Currency Appreciation on the Supply of and Demand for Traded Goods

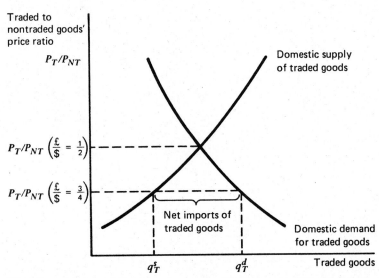

This figure shows the domestic demand and supply schedules for traded goods initially in equilibrium when the exchange rate is $\frac{1}{2}$ a pound per dollar. If the exchange rate appreciates to $\frac{3}{4}$ pound per dollar, the dollar price of traded goods falls. Consumers will substitute the relatively cheaper traded goods for nontraded goods, increasing the domestic demand for traded goods. The reduced profitability of the traded goods industries will cause them to lose resources to the nontraded goods industries, thus reducing supply. The resulting excess of domestic demand over domestic supply represents net imports of traded goods.

In the absence of intervention by central banks, the balance of payments identity requires capital inflows to be equal to the current account deficit:

$$K = IM - X \tag{17.23}$$

Deviations from purchasing power parity are the means by which the current account accommodates capital flows.

Macroeconomic Effects of Capital Flows   Capital flows produce important macroeconomic effects. For an open economy, flow equilibrium requires income to be equal to desired domestic expenditures plus net exports:

$$Y = C + I + G + (X - IM) \tag{17.24}$$

When taxes and consumption are subtracted from each side, the condition for flow equilibrium can be rewritten

$$Y - T - C = S = I + (G - T) + (X - IM) \qquad (17.25)$$

Saving out of after-tax income must equal investment plus the government deficit plus the current account surplus.

Effects of Capital Inflows on Saving and Investment

Figure 17.6 represents saving and investment schedules for an economy with a constant real gross national product. In the absence of capital flows or central bank intervention, the balance of payments identity requires the current account to be balanced. Consequently, the real rate of interest which produces flow equilibrium is r_0. If the economy now experiences capital inflows, the appreciation of the home currency will reduce the relative price of traded goods and produce a current account deficit. The

Figure 17.6   The Effects of Capital Inflows on Saving and Investment

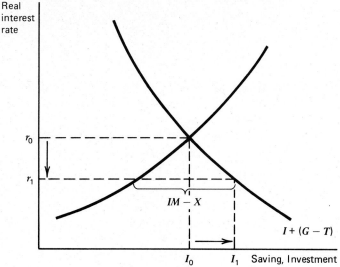

This figure shows saving and investment schedules with real income constant. In the absence of capital flows or central bank intervention in the foreign exchange market, the balance-of-payments identity requires the current account to be in balance. Consequently, $S = I + (G - T)$ and the real rate of interest which produces flow equilibrium is r_0. Capital inflows would produce an appreciation of the home currency and a current account deficit. Flow equilibrium now requires $IM - X = I + (G - T) - S$ because some of investment or government borrowing is now financed by capital inflows. This foreign source of finance increases the total supply of saving, lowering real interest rates and increasing investment from I_0 to I_1.

condition for flow equilibrium now requires investment plus the government deficit to exceed saving out of after-tax income by the current account deficit:

$$IM - X = I + (G - T) - S \qquad (17.26)$$

The real rate of interest that produced this flow equilibrium would be r_1. Some investment or government borrowing is now financed by the capital inflows which are a counterpart to the current account deficit. Because of this foreign source of finance, the total supply of saving increases, lowering real interest rates and increasing investment.

Summary

1. The demand for foreign exchange is derived from the demand for imports and the demand for foreign financial assets. The supply of foreign exchange comes from export proceeds and sales of foreign financial assets.

2. The foreign exchange rate can be expressed as the price of $1 in terms of a foreign currency. The foreign exchange rate is determined by the interaction of demand and supply. However, central banks may peg the exchange rate by offering to buy and sell unlimited quantities of their own currencies at a fixed price.

3. The official settlements balance-of-payments deficit or surplus measures the extent to which central banks have to intervene in order to clear the market at some pegged exchange rate. An overall balance-of-payments deficit implies central bank sales of foreign exchange.

4. An overall balance of payments deficit equals imports minus exports minus net capital inflows. If capital outflows exceed capital inflows, net capital inflows are negative.

5. In equilibrium, the net current account surplus (exports minus imports of goods and services) equals the gap between total income and desired expenditures on goods and services.

6. When a current account deficit is financed by net capital inflows, the sale of securities to foreigners generates purchasing power to buy more goods and services than can be financed solely from income.

7. Central bank intervention in the foreign exchange market can affect high-powered money. Subsequent changes in the money supply will affect nominal gross national product. If a balance-of-payments deficit on current account is financed by Fed sales of foreign exchange, high-powered money is reduced. The subsequent fall in GNP and reduction in money demand produces an excess of desired expenditures over income exactly equal to the current account deficit.

8. If the relative price of traded to nontraded goods falls, the domestic supply of traded goods decreases while domestic demand rises. The gap represents net imports of traded goods.

9. Arbitrage tends to equalize prices of traded goods all over the world. If the relative price of traded to nontraded goods is to remain constant, foreign exchange rates must adjust to offset different inflation rates. This is the basis of the purchasing power parity equation.

10. Capital flows produce deviations from purchasing power parity. They also affect investment and the level of national saving.

Questions

1. What factors determine demand for and supply of foreign exchange?

2. How can central banks peg exchange rates?

3. Explain balance-of-payments equilibrium in terms of demand for and supply of foreign exchange.

4. What is the balance-of-payments identity? How can there be balance-of-payments surpluses and deficits if the balance of payments always balances?

5. How do exports and imports enter the circular flow of income and expenditure?

6. What would happen if the Fed pursued a "sterilization" policy?

7. Why is the distinction between traded and nontraded goods useful for balance-of-payments analysis?

8. What is the purchasing power parity equation? Under what conditions might it hold?

9. How do capital flows affect exchange rates?

10. How can capital flows affect saving and investment?

18

Monetary Policy under Fixed and Flexible Exchange Rates

Monetary Policy under Flexible Exchange Rates

Long-Run Equilibrium

Monetary policy affects exchange rates in the long run primarily through changes in the domestic rate of inflation relative to inflation abroad. If the current account is to remain in balance, purchasing power parity requires the foreign exchange price of the dollar to change at a rate equal to the difference between the foreign inflation rate and the U.S. inflation rate, as shown in equation (17.21). This purchasing power parity explanation of exchange rates does very well in describing the long-run trend in the foreign exchange price of the dollar.

Purchasing Power Parity and the Capital Account

Purchasing power parity also keeps the capital account in balance. Capital flows are determined primarily by the relative yields on financial assets denominated in different currencies. American investors using dollars to buy a one-year pound-denominated bond yielding i_{uk} will receive a dollar return of $(1 + i_{uk}) \cdot (1 + [\Delta\$/£]/[\$/£]) - 1$ in simple interest. In continuously compounded rates, this return is $i_{uk} + \Delta\ln(\$/£)$. If this return is higher than the U.S. interest rate i_{us}, investors will sell dollars and buy pound-denominated financial assets. This produces capital outflows from the United States. On the other hand, if the U.S. interest rate is higher, investors will sell pounds and buy dollar-denominated assets. This produces capital inflows to the United States. For the capital account to remain in balance, the change in exchange rates must offset exactly the differences in interest rates between countries:

$$i_{uk} + \Delta\ln(\$/£) = i_{us} \tag{18.1}$$

If purchasing power parity holds, the change in exchange rates will reflect international differences in inflation rates:

$$\Delta\ln(\$/\pounds) = \Delta\ln(P_{us}) - \Delta\ln(P_{uk}) \qquad (18.2)$$

By substituting equation (18.2) into equation (18.1), the following relationships are obtained:

$$i_{uk} - \Delta\ln(P_{uk}) = i_{us} - \Delta\ln(P_{us}) \qquad (18.3)$$

or

$$r_{uk} = r_{us} \qquad (18.4)$$

Thus, so long as purchasing power parity holds, relative real rates of return on financial assets denominated in different currencies will be unaffected, provided the nominal interest rate rises by 1 percentage point for each percentage point increase in the inflation rate, as specified by the Fisher relationship in equation (15.1).

Inflation, Taxation, and the Capital Account   With inflation-induced tax distortions of the kind discussed in Chapter 16, the nominal interest rate can be expected to rise by more than 1 percentage point for each percentage point increase in the inflation rate. In an international context, this means that countries raising their relative inflation rates will tend to offer higher gross or before-tax real rates of return on their financial assets. This will induce capital inflows, since tax in foreign countries is unaffected by U.S. inflation. The value of the dollar will be bid up above its purchasing power parity level in this process until the expected future depreciation in the dollar is raised above the inflation differential by exactly the amount of the differential in real interest rates.

Effects of Monetary Disequilibrium   In the short run, the liquidity effect of monetary policy on real rates of interest must also be considered. When real rates of interest in the United States are higher than those abroad because of a restrictive monetary policy, capital will tend to flow into the United States. Conversely, the United States tends to experience capital outflows when the real rates of interest fall below foreign real rates of interest because of an expansionary monetary policy. These capital flows can cause the exchange rate to deviate substantially from purchasing power parity in the short run.

Zero Inflation and Exchange Rate Stability   To illustrate these monetary effects on exchange rates, consider the following hypothetical example. Suppose real output is growing at a continuously compounded rate of 4 percent a year and prices are initially stable. If the ratio of desired money balances to nominal income (the Cambridge k) remains constant, the money supply must be growing by 4 percent a year in order to accommodate the increase in money demand:

$$\Delta\ln(M) = \Delta\ln(k) + \Delta\ln(y) + \pi$$
$$(+4\%) \quad (0\%) \quad (+4\%) \quad (+0\%) \tag{18.5}$$

If foreign prices are also constant, purchasing power parity is maintained with no change in exchange rates.

Monetary Acceleration and Exchange Rate Depreciation

Now consider what happens if growth in the money supply suddenly accelerates (at time t_0) to 14 percent a year. Ultimately, growth in nominal gross national product must also rise to 14 percent a year to equate money demand with the increase in the money supply. If output continues to grow at 4 percent a year, the rate of inflation must rise to 10 percent a year:

$$\Delta\ln(M) = \Delta\ln(k) + \Delta\ln(y) + \pi$$
$$(+14\%) \quad (0\%) \quad (+4\%) \quad (+10\%) \tag{18.6}$$

If foreign prices remain constant, the 10 percent rate of inflation in the United States now requires the exchange rate to depreciate by 10 percent a year in order to keep the current account in balance:

$$\Delta\ln(\pounds/\$) = \Delta\ln(P_{uk}) - \Delta\ln(P_{us})$$
$$(-10\%) \quad (0\%) \quad (+10\%) \tag{18.7}$$

This purchasing power parity path of exchange rates is represented by the dotted line in Figure 18.1a. At time t_0, the 10 percentage point acceleration in the rate of monetary growth causes the exchange rate to depreciate at a rate of 10 percent per year.

Monetary Acceleration and the Liquidity Effect

However, the actual path of exchange rates must also account for the liquidity effect on real rates of interest. As was discussed in Chapter 15, an acceleration in the rate of monetary growth usually creates a temporary drop in the real rate of interest. Nominal gross national product does not immediately adjust to the higher rate of monetary growth and, for some time, the supply of money will exceed the demand for money. This excess supply of money tends to depress the real rate of interest below its equilibrium level, as shown in Figure 18.1b. Once nominal gross national product adjusts to the new rate of monetary growth, this temporary liquidity effect vanishes and the real rate of interest returns to its equilibrium level.

Liquidity Effect and Deviations from Purchasing Power Parity

Although this liquidity effect is temporary and thus has no permanent effect on exchange rates, it can produce substantial short-run deviations from purchasing power parity. If foreign central banks do not lower their real rates of interest through monetary expansion, the liquidity effect of the U.S. monetary expansion reduces the relative attractiveness of investing in U.S. financial securities, inducing investors to look elsewhere for foreign financial assets yielding a higher real rate of return. Some of the

Figure 18.1   The Effects of Monetary Expansion on Exchange Rates: (a) Exchange Rate, (b) Real Interest Rate

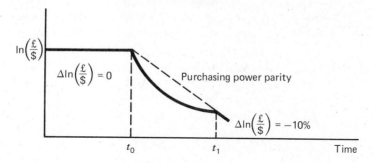

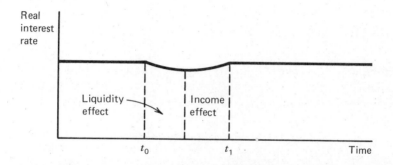

These figures show the typical responses of the exchange rate and the real rate of interest to an acceleration in the rate of monetary growth. Initially, the economy is in equilibrium with real output growth of 4 percent and price stability. If the Cambridge k is constant, the money supply must grow at 4 percent a year in order to accommodate the increase in money demand. Foreign prices are assumed to be stable as well, so purchasing power parity can be maintained with no change in exchange rates. At time t_0, the rate of growth in the money supply suddenly accelerates to 14 percent a year. If output continues to grow at 4 percent a year, inflation must ultimately accelerate to 10 percent a year to equate money demand with the increase in money supply. With stable foreign prices, purchasing power parity now requires a 10 percent per year depreciation of the dollar against foreign currencies to offset the 10 percent inflation. The path of exchange rates corresponding to purchasing power parity is shown by the dotted line in Figure 18.1a. However, an acceleration in the rate of monetary growth usually creates a temporary drop in real rates of interest until nominal income fully adjusts. This liquidity effect of an acceleration in the rate of monetary growth is shown in Figure 18.1b. The drop in real rates of interest reduces the incentive to invest in U.S. financial securities and thus creates capital outflows. As long as this temporary liquidity effect exists (from time t_0 to t_1), the exchange rate must lie below the purchasing power parity level, as illustrated by the solid line in Figure 18.1a. This deviation from purchasing power parity is needed to create a current account surplus to offset the capital outflows.

demand for bonds resulting from the excess supply of money spills over into foreign financial markets, creating capital outflows. In the absence of central bank intervention in the foreign exchange market, the foreign exchange price of the dollar must fall below the purchasing power parity level so that a current account surplus can offset the capital outflow.

The typical response of exchange rates to the acceleration in monetary growth is represented by the solid line in Figure 18.1a. While the temporary liquidity effect exists (from time t_0 to t_1), the exchange rate must lie below the purchasing power parity level. However, as nominal gross national product adjusts to the new rate of monetary growth, the liquidity effect of the excess supply of money is eliminated and the exchange rate returns to its purchasing power parity level.

Fixed Exchange Rates and Monetary Policy

Balance-of-Payments Deficit Drains Foreign Exchange Reserves

In the previous section the effects of monetary policy on exchange rates were analyzed in the context of flexible exchange rates. It was assumed that central banks pursued independent monetary policies but did not intervene in the foreign exchange market. Under this system the exchange rate serves as the adjustment mechanism for preventing payments imbalances. Once countries decide to maintain fixed exchange rates, however, payments imbalances must be financed by foreign exchange reserves. Therefore, the independence of national monetary policies is constrained by the availability of these reserves. When a country has a balance-of-payments deficit in a fixed exchange rate system, it must buy back its currency in order to prevent the exchange rate from depreciating. In practice, a country cannot run a deficit in its balance of payments for very long or its foreign exchange reserves will be exhausted. Governments can, of course, finance balance-of-payments deficits by borrowing abroad, but no country will lend to another indefinitely. If a fixed exchange rate system is to prevent recurring currency crises, there must be some adjustment mechanism to limit the loss of reserves by deficit countries.

Monetary Policy as Adjustment Mechanism

The essential feature of a stable fixed exchange rate system is that each country's monetary policy becomes the mechanism for international adjustment. Countries with surpluses inflate, while those with deficits deflate. In fact, fixed exchange rates tend automatically to produce such adjustments if central banks do not sterilize. The very act of purchasing or selling foreign exchange produces a change in the money supply in the direction needed to correct the imbalance. Suppose, for example, Britain has a balance-of-payments deficit at the pegged exchange rate as shown in Figure 18.2a. To prevent a devaluation of the pound, the Bank of England must be a residual buyer of pounds and a seller of foreign exchange. This intervention on the foreign exchange market would automatically decrease

Figure 18.2 The Monetary Mechanism of International Adjustment under Fixed Exchange Rates: (a) Foreign Exchange Market, (b) Market for Traded Goods

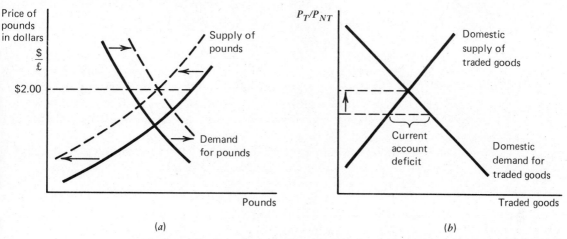

(a)   (b)

Figure 18.2a shows that, at the pegged exchange rate of $2 to £1, Britain has a balance-of-payments deficit (solid lines indicate initial supply and demand for pounds). Assume that this balance of payments deficit results from a deficit on the current account represented in Figure 18.2b. To prevent the pound from depreciating, the Bank of England must sell foreign exchange and buy the pounds that are in excess supply. This would reduce the stock of high-powered money, causing a contraction in the money supply. The reduction in the money supply temporarily raises real rates of interest, attracting capital inflows and thus shifting the demand curve to the right in Figure 18.2a. Hence, the capital account contributes to the elimination of the balance-of-payments deficit. Moreover, since the prices of traded goods are determined in world markets, the resulting deflation raises the relative price of traded goods as seen in Figure 18.2b. This increase in the relative price of traded goods operates to eliminate the current account deficit by shifting consumption away from traded goods and shifting resources into the production of traded goods. The impact of this improvement in the current account on the foreign exchange market is represented by shifts in the supply and demand schedules for pounds in Figure 18.2a, thus eliminating the excess supply of pounds on the foreign exchange market.

high-powered money in Britain, hence causing a multiple contraction of the money supply:

$$\overset{(-)}{\Delta H_{uk}} = G_{uk} - I_{uk} - \Delta D_{uk} - \overset{(+)}{F_{uk}} \tag{18.8}$$

Sale of foreign
exchange

$$\overset{(-)}{\Delta M_{uk}} = \frac{M}{H} \cdot \overset{(-)}{\Delta H_{uk}} \tag{18.9}$$

Money Supply Decline Closes Balance-of-Payments Deficit

This reduction in the money supply has two important effects tending to eliminate the balance-of-payments deficit. First, the liquidity effect of the money supply contraction increases real interest rates in the short run, thus attracting capital inflows. These inflows are represented by a rightward shift in the demand schedule in Figure 18.2a. Second, the reduction in the money supply will reduce aggregate nominal expenditures on goods and services, some of which will be imports. Hence, the supply of dollars on the foreign exchange market will be reduced. In the long run, the reduction in the money supply will lower the domestic price level. Since the prices of traded goods are determined in world markets, most of this deflationary pressure will be concentrated on the prices of nontraded goods. Thus, one result of deflation is an increase in the relative price of traded goods. This operates to improve the current account balance by shifting domestic consumption away from traded goods and shifting domestic resources into the production of traded goods, as illustrated in Figure 18.2b. The reduction in net imports takes place through a decrease in imports and/or an increase in exports. Figure 18.2a shows the corresponding shifts in demand for and supply of pounds on the foreign exchange market.

Sterilization and Balance-of-Payments Problems

For the adjustment mechanism discussed in the previous section to operate, countries must allow their money supplies to be determined by the balance of payments. If purchases or sales of foreign exchange are allowed to have their impact on the money supply, they produce adjustments which eliminate balance-of-payments surpluses or deficits. Chronic balance-of-payments problems arise because central banks interfere with this adjustment mechanism. Central banks can prevent a balance-of-payments deficit from reducing the quantity of money by offsetting sales of foreign exchange with open market purchases of bonds:

$$\Delta H = G - T - \overset{(-)}{\Delta D} - \overset{(+)}{F} \qquad (18.10)$$

$$\underset{\substack{\text{Purchases} \\ \text{of bonds}}}{} \quad \underset{\substack{\text{Sales of} \\ \text{foreign} \\ \text{exchange}}}{}$$

Conversely, countries with a balance-of-payments surplus can prevent their money supplies from increasing by offsetting purchases of foreign exchange with open market sales of bonds. These sterilization policies insulate the money supply from the balance of payments and thus prevent the adjustment mechanism from operating.

Independent Monetary Policy Incompatible with Fixed Exchange Rate

Truly fixed exchange rates can be maintained only when countries allow their monetary policy to be an instrument of international adjustment. Sterilization enables central banks to formulate monetary policy on the basis of domestic economic considerations rather than payments imbalances, thus preventing this adjustment mechanism from operating.

However, chronic payments deficits will eventually exhaust a country's foreign exchange reserves. At this point, adjustment must take place through exchange rate changes, if monetary policy continues to be directed towards domestic objectives.

Currency Crises under Fixed Exchange Rates

Although countries that are members of the International Monetary Fund agreed to peg exchange rates, the main international adjustment mechanism during the 1950s and 1960s took place through exchange rate changes. For example, Germany appreciated its currency because it refused to increase its money supply in response to chronic balance-of-payments surpluses. A number of other countries devalued their currencies to avoid decreasing their money supplies in response to chronic balance-of-payments deficits. However, most of these exchange rate changes occurred only after payments imbalances had been allowed to grow over time to major proportions, culminating in a currency crisis. A currency crisis invariably takes the form of a run on the country's international reserves in the same way that a banking crisis involves a run on the banks' reserves (Chapter 6).

Expected Returns and Expected Devaluation

Once chronic balance-of-payments deficits threaten to exhaust a country's foreign exchange reserves, investors begin to expect a devaluation of the domestic currency. These expectations of a devaluation affect the relative attractiveness of financial assets denominated in different currencies. Consider a British investor deciding whether to purchase an American bond denominated in dollars or a British bond denominated in pounds. If the pound is expected to depreciate, the British investor will receive a capital gain in terms of pounds on the funds invested in the American bond. In comparing the expected rates of return on these two bonds, the investor must adjust the interest received on the American bond for the expected rate at which the pound depreciates over the investment period to get its total return in pounds. In simple interest, the return on American bonds in pounds equals $(1 + i_{us})/(1 + \Delta[\$/£]^e/[\$/£])$, where $\Delta[\$/£]^e$ is the expected change in the exchange rate. Expectations of an imminent devaluation of the pound would typically swamp any interest rate differential and induce British investors to sell British financial assets and buy American securities.

Similarly, an expected devaluation of the pound adversely affects the relative attractiveness of British assets to foreign investors. A devaluation of the pound creates capital losses in terms of dollars on funds invested in British financial securities. The return in dollars on British assets is $(1 + i_{uk}) \cdot (1 + \Delta[\$/£]^e/[\$/£])$. Consequently, expectations of an imminent devaluation of the pound will induce American investors to sell British bonds and buy American bonds.

Speculation Worsens Balance-of-Payments Deficit

Capital flight induced by expectation of currency devaluation intensifies the deficit country's balance-of-payments problems. Capital outflows add to the balance-of-payments deficit, requiring the central bank to deplete its reserves even faster in order to maintain the current exchange rate. The flow of capital out of a country in anticipation of a devaluation intensifies the pressure on exchange rates and increases the probability that devaluation will occur. In a limited sense, expectations of devaluation tend to become self-fulfilling prophecies because the outflow of capital alone may force the country to devalue.

Devaluation as an Adjustment Mechanism

Devaluation and the Current Account

For a currency devaluation to serve as a mechanism for international adjustment, it must have the effect of improving the balance of payments. One way a devaluation can improve the balance of payments is by raising the relative price of traded goods. This will induce resources to shift into the production of traded goods and consumption to shift away from traded goods. However, in analyzing the effect of exchange rate depreciation on the current account, one must be careful to distinguish between exchange rate depreciation which simply reflects inflation differentials and a sudden devaluation designed to correct an already existing current account deficit. The purchasing power parity relationship between prices and exchange rates shows that a depreciation of the exchange rate equal to the difference between the domestic rate of inflation and the foreign rate of inflation would prevent the current account from deteriorating. On the other hand, if a country tries to maintain fixed exchange rates in a period when domestic inflation exceeds the foreign rate of inflation, the relative price of traded goods will fall, causing a current account deficit. A subsequent devaluation of the currency will tend to raise the relative price of traded goods, but once the current account deficit has become significant, it will take some time for production and consumption to respond to price changes. Because of these lags in adjustment to a change in relative prices, a current account that is already in deficit may actually deteriorate even further following a devaluation before it improves.

Devaluation and Short-Run Deterioration in the Current Account

To illustrate how a devaluation could worsen a current account deficit, assume that Britain initially has a current account deficit of $£P_T(q_T^d - q_T^s)$, as shown in Figures 18.3a and 18.3b. At time t_0 the pound is suddenly devalued. Assuming the world price of traded goods remains constant, the pound price must immediately rise:

$$\$P_T = £\overline{P}_T / \frac{£}{\$}$$
$$\uparrow \qquad\qquad \downarrow$$

$$(18.11)$$

This devaluation-induced increase in the relative price of traded goods shifts domestic consumption away from traded goods and shifts domestic

Figure 18.3 Devaluation and the J—Curve: (a) Traded Goods Market, (b) Current Account

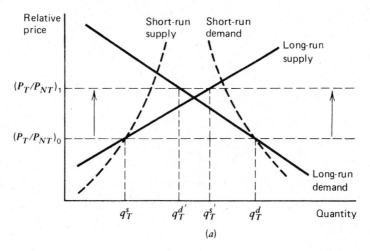

(a)

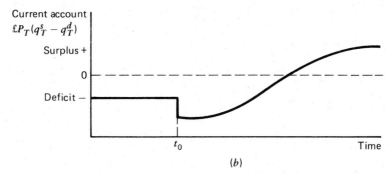

(b)

These figures illustrate the effects of a devaluation on the current account of a country with an initial deficit. Figure 18.3a shows that Britain has an initial current account deficit of $£P_T(q_T^d - q_T^s)$. Suddenly, at time t_0 the pound is devalued, raising the price of traded goods. However, it takes time for consumption and production to respond to those price changes because of adjustment costs. Consequently, the supply and demand schedules are less elastic in the short run than in the long run, as shown in Figure 18.3a. In the short run, net imports of traded goods are reduced but not eliminated. However, the pound price of traded goods rises immediately. Since the current account deficit is equal to the pound price of traded goods times the volume of net imports, a devaluation of the pound will worsen the current account if the percentage rise in the price of traded goods exceeds the percentage fall in the volume of imports. This worsening of the current account is shown in Figure 18.3b. In the long run, the rise in the relative price of traded goods will produce a current account surplus, as shown in Figure 18.3a. In the short run, however, the lag of adjustment in consumption and production of traded goods creates a J-curve depicting a worsening in the current account before improvement.

resources into the production of traded goods. However, it takes time for consumption and production to respond to those price changes because of adjustment costs. In other words, the supply and demand schedules for traded goods are less elastic (more vertical) in the short run than in the long run, as shown in Figure 18.3a. The devaluation-induced rise in the relative price of traded goods starts reducing the volume of net imports of traded goods, but it does not immediately eliminate net imports. However, the pound price of traded goods rises almost immediately. Consequently, the current account deficit expressed in terms of pounds may initially worsen even though the volume of net imports is decreasing. Since the current account deficit is equal to the pound price of traded goods ($£P_T$) times the volume of net imports ($q_T^d - q_T^s$), a devaluation of the pound will worsen the current account deficit if the percentage rise in the price of traded goods is greater than the percentage fall in the volume of net imports:

$$\text{Current account deficit (in pounds)} = £P_T(\underset{\uparrow}{q_T^d} - \underset{\downarrow}{q_T^s}) \qquad (18.12)$$

Devaluation and the J-Curve

It is quite common for an existing current account deficit to experience further deterioration immediately following a subsequent devaluation. After a year or so, however, changes in the volume of net imports are usually sufficient to improve the current account. This adjustment process produces a J-curve, which is economic jargon for the notion that the current account worsens before it improves.

The reader is justified in feeling uneasy with the prospect of a devaluation's causing a current account deficit to deteriorate. Clearly, devaluation cannot be a useful adjustment mechanism if it increases the excess supply of the home currency on the foreign exchange market. In fact, a devaluation does not have to rely solely on its current account effects to improve the balance of payments because it is likely to improve the capital account immediately.

Devaluation and the Capital Account

Devaluation affects the capital account primarily through its effect on expectations of future exchange rate changes. Normally, currency crises are associated with outflows of capital induced by expectations of an imminent devaluation. Once that devaluation has occurred, the expectation of future depreciation in the currency should diminish and thus the relative attractiveness of assets denominated in the domestic currency is increased. If the devaluation restores purchasing power parity, expectations of future long run exchange rate movements should reflect only the difference in inflation rates between the two countries. With such expectations, real interest rates would be equated across countries.

There is another reason why devaluation tends to improve the capital account. Investors tend to hold diversified portfolios of assets in order to minimize risk. Such diversification usually involves holding securities de nominated in different currencies. For example, investors may hold half of their assets in dollar-denominated securities and half in pound-denominated securities. If the pound is suddenly devalued, they now hold fewer pound assets relative to dollar assets than they had when their portfolios were in balance. If no future depreciation is expected, these investors would tend to sell some dollar assets and buy pound assets to rebalance their portfolios. This effect of devaluation stimulates capital inflows which tend to offset any short-run perverse effects devaluation may have on the current account.

Summary

1. Monetary acceleration reduces the real interest rate in the short run. This liquidity effect encourages capital outflows and hence causes the exchange rate to fall temporarily below its purchasing power parity rate.

2. Under a fixed exchange rate system a balance-of-payments deficit produces a loss of foreign exchange reserves. If the central bank does not sterilize the foreign exchange drain, high-powered money will decline. This decline in turn reduces aggregate desired expenditures and improves the balance of payments.

3. If the central bank sterilizes the loss of foreign exchange reserves and pursues an independent monetary policy for domestic objectives, there is no automatic mechanism to reestablish balance of payments equilibrium. In that case adjustment eventually requires an exchange rate change.

4. When severe current account deficits threaten to exhaust a country's foreign exchange reserves under a fixed exchange rate system, the expected return on foreign financial assets becomes increasingly attractive relative to the return on domestic assets. This is due to the positive probability of a devaluation. Hence, the capital account will tend to move into deficit too.

5. A devaluation may worsen the current account deficit measured in domestic currency in the short run. This occurs if the percentage increase in traded goods' prices exceeds the percentage decline in the quantity of net imports.

6. A devaluation tends to improve the capital account by reducing the probability of a further devaluation. Hence, relative returns on domestic assets are increased and capital flows back. If the devaluation is accompanied by tighter monetary policy, real interest rates will rise and even more capital will flow in.

Questions

1. How does the liquidity effect of monetary policy influence the balance of payments on capital account?

2. How can the liquidity effect cause a deviation in the exchange rate from its purchasing power parity level under a flexible exchange rate system?

3. How can an overall balance-of-payments surplus under a fixed exchange rate system affect high-powered money?

4. How does the effect of a reserve drain on high-powered money produce an automatic adjustment mechanism?

5. What is a sterilization policy and how does it eliminate the automatic adjustment mechanism under a fixed exchange rate system?

6. Why does the balance of payments on capital account tend to worsen when a chronic current account deficit is allowed to persist?

7. How can a devaluation cause an initial deterioration in the balance of payments on current account?

8. Why does the balance of payments on current account generally improve gradually after a devaluation?

9. Under what circumstances would one expect a discrete devaluation to have virtually no positive effect on the current account balance?

10. Explain how a devaluation can improve the balance of payments on capital account.

PART NINE

Demand for Money

T he amount of currency in circulation is really quite astounding. For example, there was $132.6 billion of currency in circulation at the end of 1982. That sum represents $571.58 for each person in America or $2460 per family. Another startling fact is that 40 percent of all currency in circulation consists of $100 bills. In other words, there are about ten $100 bills for every household in the United States.

The growth in the volume of $100 bills has also been dramatic. In 1960 there was $5.9 billion in $100 bills, or 1.2 percent of gross national product. By 1982 the value had increased tenfold to $59.4 billion or 1.9 percent of GNP. Some of that increase is explicable in terms of inflation. The 1960 dollar was worth only 33 cents in 1982. Another part of the $100 bill explosion can be attributed to the fact that the Federal Reserve banks have stopped issuing $500, $1000, and $10,000 bills. Even in combination, however, these two factors are nowhere near sufficient to explain this phenomenal growth in the demand for $100 bills.

Have American families been stashing away increasing amounts of money under their mattresses? This seems a reasonable answer at first blush, since $100 bills are so rarely used for everyday transactions. Furthermore, there has been increasing use of checks and credit cards, particularly for high-value purchases. In fact, however, this explanation doesn't wash. As a matter of fact, 30 percent of the $100 bills circulate back through the Federal Reserve banks once a year.

From C. Daniel Vencill, *The Multi-Billion Dollar Laundromat* (San Francisco: San Francisco State University, May 1973); *Cocaine and Marihuana Trafficking in Southeastern United States: Hearings before the Select Committee on Narcotics Abuse and Control, House of Representatives, June 9–10, 1978* (Washington, D.C.: U.S. Government Printing Office, SCNAC-95-2-6, 1978); and *Financial Investigation of Drug Trafficking: Hearing before the Select Committee on Narcotics Abuse and Control, House of Representatives, October 9, 1981* (Washington, D.C.: U.S. Government Printing Office, SCNAC-97-1-7, 1981).

Are business firms responsible for the amazing demand for $100 bills? Since the currency does circulate, as evinced by the statistics on note flows through the Fed banks, this might appear to be the only answer left. Nevertheless, the revolution in cash management techniques over the past two decades suggests that most business firms hold less rather than more money in relation to the value of their output than they did in 1960.

There is, however, one industry—among the five largest industries in the United States and the largest growth sector of the economy since 1970—that conducts virtually all of its transactions in cash. The illegal narcotics business is now estimated at over $100 billion a year. Transactions are invariably conducted in currency because currency leaves no trace. Or, to be more accurate, currency leaves less of a trace than a check or credit card transaction.

In the aggregate, however, currency does provide a sufficient trace to link the $100 bill mystery to the illegal drug trade. The first link can be derived by examining regional disparities in currency flows through the Fed. Clearly, since currency in circulation has increased in every year since 1949, the Fed banks as a whole issue more currency than they take in from depository institutions. However, the Florida branches of the Federal Reserve Bank of Atlanta located in Jacksonville and Miami receive more currency than they issue.

The second link is established by the fact that these two Fed branches receive a proportion of large-denomination notes that is twice the average for the Fed as a whole. Over the period 1975–1982 the volume of large-denomination notes received by the Fed as a whole increased by 20 percent a year. The figure for the Jacksonville and Miami branches is 40 percent a year.

The disproportionate amount of and growth in $100 bills received by the Florida branches of the Fed can be tied to the narcotics trade by two additional factors. First, convictions for "laundering" money are high in southern Florida, a part of the country designated a crime disaster area. Currency acquired from drug sales is laundered by siphoning it through legitimate businesses, such as laundromats and video game halls, that produce large cash flows. Extra currency from narcotics profits is combined with the legal cash take of these businesses and then deposited in a depository institution. Excess currency holdings of depository institutions are in turn deposited in the Fed branches.

Second, the central bank of Colombia—a country with marijuana fields as large as some of the states of the United States—arranged to make regular deposits of U.S. currency directly with the Miami branch of the Atlanta Fed in 1975. Previously, it had used the New York Fed. Apparently, the volume of currency involved had grown so large by 1975 that a move became necessary for logistical and security reasons. Colombia is awash with $100 bills. It is the only country in the world where the black market exchange rate is below the official rate!

19 Theories of the Demand for Money

Keynes's Liquidity Preference Function

Cambridge Equation and the Opportunity Cost of Holding Money

The money demand function used in the preceding chapters has been the Cambridge equation:

$$M^d = k \cdot y \cdot P \qquad (19.1)$$

where M^d is the demand for money, k is the public's desired ratio of money balances to income, y is real income, and P is the price level. Unfortunately, this specification of the demand for money does not consider explicitly factors that affect the Cambridge k. One such factor is the interest rate. As was explained in Chapter 1, there are two sorts of costs associated with money balances. The opportunity cost of *accumulating* or adding to money balances is the foregone consumption of goods and services. On the other hand, the opportunity cost of *holding* money balances is the foregone earnings from alternative assets. Since the money demand function describes the demand to *hold* a stock of money balances, yields on assets competing with money should have a significant effect on money demand.

Motives for Holding Money

John Maynard Keynes criticized the Cambridge equation precisely because, in its simple form used here, it neglects the role of interest rates in determining the demand for money. In *The General Theory of Employment Interest and Money* (1936) Keynes offered an alternative formulation of the demand for money which he called *liquidity preference*. According to Keynes, people hold money balances for three basic reasons. They hold *transactions* balances in order to bridge the gap between planned receipts and expenditures. They hold *precautionary* balances to meet unexpected bills.

Finally, they may hold *speculative* balances if they expect the market value of alternative assets to fall.

**Transactions and
Precautionary
Balances**

Although Keynes recognized that the demand for transactions and precautionary balances might be affected by the interest rate, he did not stress its importance at this point. Basically, Keynes followed the Cambridge equation tradition and made the demand for transactions and precautionary money balances some fraction of income. Keynes felt that the primary importance of the interest rate lay in its influence on the demand for speculative money balances.

**Keynes's Portfolio
Choice Theory**

Keynes viewed the speculative demand for money as arising from decisions about the allocation of wealth. Instead of considering all forms of wealth, Keynes assumed for simplicity that the choice was between holding *consols*—government bonds that pay a fixed coupon or dividend each year forever—and holding money. Consols always yield the market interest rate i. Since the coupon or dividend DIV remains constant, the market price of the consol P_C fluctuates inversely with changes in the market interest rate:

$$P_C = DIV/i \qquad\qquad (19.2)$$

This relationship was developed in Chapter 3 (equations 3.6 and 3.7). If DIV is \$10 and i is 0.1 or 10 percent, P_C is \$100. If i rises to 0.12, P_C must fall to \$83.33.

**Speculative
Demand for Money**

The speculative motive for holding money arises from the desire to maximize wealth. So long as expected capital losses are not sufficient to offset the coupon income from the consol, the individual will continue to keep all of his or her investment portfolio in consols. However, if capital losses are expected to be large enough to more than wipe out the coupon income, money is clearly more attractive than consols as a form in which to hold one's wealth. This means that the demand for speculative money balances is produced by an expectation that the percentage fall in the market price of consols will exceed the current market rate of interest. When the interest rate is low, a relatively small percentage drop in the market price of consols will wipe out interest earnings. With higher interest rates, the percentage fall in the market price of consols has to be more substantial for interest earnings to be completely offset. Thus, the incentive for individuals to hold speculative money balances as opposed to consols is greater the lower is the interest rate.

**The Normal Level
of Interest Rates**

Keynes argued that at every moment in time there is some value of the interest rate which individuals consider to be "normal." When interest rates rise above this normal level, there is a tendency for people to expect interest rates to fall. On the other hand, when the interest rate lies below this

Figure 19.1   Speculative Demand for Money

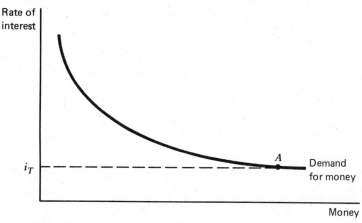

The higher the interest rate, the lower is the market price of bonds. As the interest rate rises higher and higher above its "normal" level, more people expect it to fall in the future. Hence, they expect bond prices to rise. The higher the current yield and the greater the expectations of capital appreciation, the greater the demand for bonds and the *lower* the demand for money. Hence, speculative demand for money is related inversely to the interest rate. At i_T the demand for money becomes perfectly interest elastic. Demand for money is insatiable at this interest rate.

normal level, it is expected to rise. The lower the interest rate relative to the normal level, the greater will be the expected capital loss from an expected rise in the interest rate if wealth is held in consols.

Aggregate Speculative Demand for Money

Since individuals have *different* expectations about future changes in bond prices, the switch from money to bonds in the aggregate will be gradual. However, the lower the current interest rate relative to the level generally considered to be normal, the larger is the number of people who expect a future fall in the market price of consols sufficient to wipe out interest earnings, and so prefer to hold their wealth in the form of money balances. Summing everyone's speculative demand for money produces the relationship between interest rates and the aggregate demand for speculative money balances shown in Figure 19.1.

The Liquidity Trap

Figure 19.1 shows a demand curve that becomes perfectly interest elastic at a low rate of interest i_T. At point A the interest rate has fallen so far below its normal level that virtually everyone has the *same* expectation that the interest rate will rise sufficiently to wipe out interest earnings on bonds.[1] At this point, therefore, a very small change in the interest rate elicits a huge

[1]John Maynard Keynes, *The General Theory of Employment Interest and Money* (London: Macmillan, 1936), p. 172.

switch in desired portfolio composition. The massive dumping of bonds when the interest rate falls as low as i_T ensures that bond prices rise no further and hence that the market interest rate can no longer fall. This phenomenon is now known as the *liquidity trap*. If it exists, then monetary policy could become impotent—a change in the money supply would have no effect on the market rate of interest. Equilibrium in the money market would persist at the same interest rate i_T no matter how much the money supply was increased. In terms of the Cambridge equation, the liquidity trap implies that any given increase in M would produce a proportional change in k. Hence, $y \cdot P$ would remain unaffected.

Current Interest Rate Incorporates Expected Future Interest Rates

One problem with Keynes's demand for speculative money balances is that it fails to take into account the fact that the buying and selling of bonds for speculative purposes has an immediate impact on the market price of bonds. If everyone expected the interest rate to rise, they would try to sell their bonds and hold money. This creates an excess supply of bonds at the existing interest rate. However, there must be a buyer for each seller of bonds. In order to clear the market, the price of bonds must fall, raising the yield on bonds, until the public no longer expects capital losses to exceed interest income. At every moment in time, the market price of bonds already reflects expectations about future interest rates.

Opportunity Cost of Holding Money

Nevertheless, Keynes emphasized for the first time that *holding* money balances involves an opportunity cost in the form of yields on alternative assets. This insight led to a series of studies in the postwar period which considered explicitly the opportunity cost of holding money as an argument in money demand functions. Keynes also stressed the fact that money is an asset and therefore must be analyzed within a framework of portfolio choice and the theory of capital.

Liquidity Preference and Loanable Funds Theories of the Interest Rate

Interest Rate Determined by Demand for and Supply of Money

The liquidity preference function played a crucial role in Keynes's theory of interest. Keynes treated the interest rate as a purely monetary phenomenon: it is determined by the supply of and demand for money. Figure 19.2 shows the Keynesian liquidity preference function for a given level of income. The demand for money increases as interest rates fall because the opportunity cost of holding money falls. The interest rate is determined by the equilibrium between money demand and money supply. If the money supply were to increase, say from M_0 to M_1, the interest rate would have to fall to the level at which the public will willingly hold the additional money balances.

Figure 19.2 Liquidity Preference and the Interest Rate

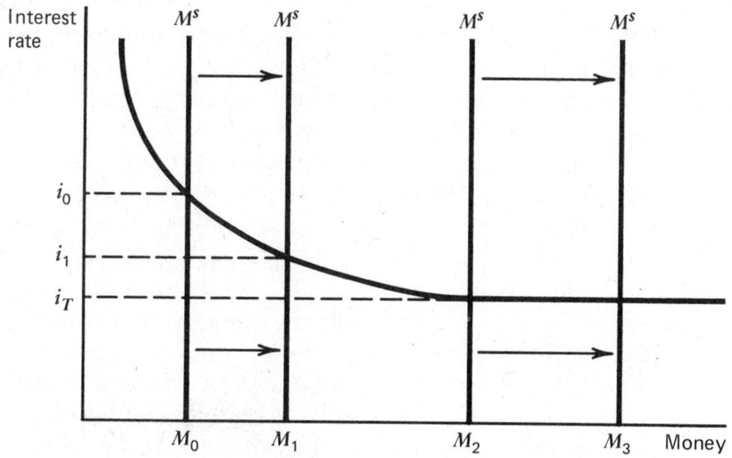

The interest rate is determined by money demand M^d and money supply M^s. An increase in the money supply from M_0 to M_1 reduces the equilibrium interest rate from i_0 to i_1. However, when the liquidity trap is encountered, an increase in the money supply from M_2 to M_3 has no effect on the equilibrium interest rate i_T.

Interest Rate Determined by Demand for and Supply of Bonds

There is, however, an alternative way of looking at the determination of interest rates which does not revolve around liquidity preference. The discussion of interest rates in Chapter 15 presented this *loanable funds* theory of interest. The loanable funds theory assumes that the interest rate is determined by equating the supply of and demand for bonds, not the supply of and demand for money. Indeed, in the loanable funds model it is quite possible to have considerable disequilibrium between the supply of and demand for money. This disequilibrium between money supply and demand plays a role in determining the supply and demand for bonds. The demand for bonds is derived from two sources: from saving part of current income to add to wealth (S), and from the desire to convert excess money balances into bonds ($M^s - M^d$). The supply of bonds also has two components: the sale of bonds to finance investment and the government deficit ($I + G - T$), and borrowing to increase money balances ($M^d - M^s$). In flow equilibrium when money demand and supply are equal, the interest rate is determined by equilibrium between saving and investment plus the government deficit ($S = I + G - T$), as was shown in Figure 15.6. However, disequilibrium between the supply of and demand for money also exerts an additional effect on the interest rate. Excess supply of money ($M^s > M^d$) generates an additional demand for bonds and pushes the interest rate below the level associated with flow equilibrium. Conversely, excess demand for money ($M^d > M^s$) generates an additional supply of bonds and pushes the interest rate above the level associated with flow equilibrium.

Liquidity Preference Theory Has No Direct Role for Saving and Investment

Both of these models conclude that the initial impact of an increase in the money supply will be to lower interest rates. However, the Keynesian model assumes that the demand for money is always equal to the supply of money. As a result, Keynes's analysis revolves around the proposition that the demand for money is negatively related to the interest rate. Since the interest rate is treated as a purely monetary phenomenon, changes in the marginal efficiency of investment and the propensity to save have no direct effect on the interest rate. Their effects on the interest rate must operate indirectly through their possible effects on income.

Compatibility of Liquidity Preference and Loanable Funds Theories

The loanable funds model, on the other hand, does not treat the interest rate as a purely monetary phenomenon. Although the interest rate is affected by monetary shocks, these effects result from monetary disequilibrium and are temporary. In flow equilibrium, where the demand for money equals the supply of money, the interest rate is determined in the goods market and is thus directly affected by the marginal efficiency of investment and the propensity to save. While the Keynesian liquidity preference function is compatible with the loanable funds model as a description of equilibrium between the supply of and demand for money, it is not crucial for the determination of interest rates. The loanable funds theory provides an adequate explanation of interest-rate determination even with an interest-inelastic demand for money function such as the Cambridge equation.

Interest Rates and the Demand for Transactions Balances

Lump Sum Incomes and Continuous Expenditures

Although Keynes argued that the transactions demand for money should be negatively related to interest rates, he did not emphasize the role of interest at that point in his analysis of the demand for money. In fact economists did not analyze the effect of the interest rate on the demand for transactions balances rigorously until 1952, when William Baumol developed a formal model of the demand for transactions balances.[2] Baumol analyzed the demand for transactions balances in terms of an economy consisting of households receiving income payments at the beginning of each time period and spending this income at a constant rate until it is exhausted at the end of the period. Business firms in this economy receive a constant flow of income from sales followed by a lump sum payment of wages at the end of the period.

[2]William J. Baumol, "The Transactions Demand for Cash: An Inventory Theoretic Approach," *Quarterly Journal of Economics*, 66(4), November 1952, pp. 545–556.

Figure 19.3   A Household's Transactions Demand for Money

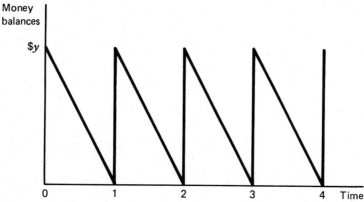

The household receives $y income at time $t = 0$ and spends it smoothly and continuously until the next payday at time $t = 1$. Hence, its transactions money balances decline from $y to zero and, on average, the household holds $y/2 in transactions money balances.

Average Transactions Balance over Income Payment Period

For example, consider the case where there are no assets other than money. At time 0, the representative household receives $y income which is spent at a constant rate until it is exhausted at time 1, as shown in Figure 19.3. Since the initial income of $y is spent at a constant rate, the average money balance held by the household during the time period is $y/2. On the other hand, business firms must accumulate cash throughout the month so that they can make the income payments to households at the beginning of the next time period. The representative business firm begins each time period with zero money balances and ends the time period with $E just before households are paid again, as shown in Figure 19.4. Therefore, the typical firm holds average money balances during the time period of $E/2. Since the sum of all disbursements by business firms $\left(\sum_{i=1}^{m} \$ E_i \right)$ must be equal to the sum of household incomes $\left(\sum_{j=1}^{n} \$y_j \right)$, the total demand for transactions balances is one period's income.

Transactions Balances in Relation to Annual Income

So far, the demand for transactions balances has been expressed in terms of the income earned during some arbitrary income payment period. In order to specify the demand for transactions balances as a fraction of annual income (as the Cambridge equation does), one must divide by the number of income payment periods in a year. For example, an income

Figure 19.4 A Business Firm's Transactions Demand for Money

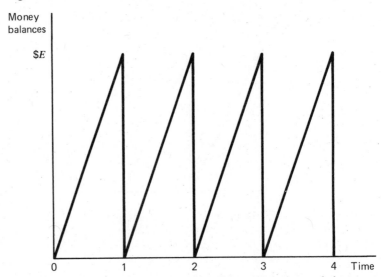

The business firm receives income smoothly and continuously but pays wages at the beginning of each time period. Hence, its transactions money balance rises from zero to $E and, on average, the business firm holds $E/2 in transactions money balances.

payment period of one month would create a demand for transactions balances (M_T^d) equal to one-twelfth of a year's income:

$$M_T^d = y/12 \tag{19.3}$$

If the income payment period were reduced to two weeks, the demand for money balances would fall by one-half to $y/24. The shorter the payment period, the lower will be the demand for transactions balances.

Bond Holding and Bond Transaction Costs

Now consider the case where households and business firms can hold bonds as well as money. Bonds yield i percent interest each time period but involve a fixed transaction cost of $b each time they are bought or sold regardless of the amount. This assumption of a fixed brokerage fee for buying and selling bonds is not as unrealistic as it may seem. The time and paper work involved in transferring the ownership of $1000 in bonds is approximately the same as that in transferring $1,000,000.

A household making two bond transactions (one purchase and one sale of bonds) during the time period can maximize interest earnings by putting exactly one-half of its income in bonds at the beginning of the period and selling them when its money balances run out at time $t = \frac{1}{2}$, as shown in Figure 19.5 (see Appendix for the mathematical proof). The

Figure 19.5   A Household's Transactions Demand for Money with Two Bond Transactions: (a) Money Balances, (b) Bond Holdings

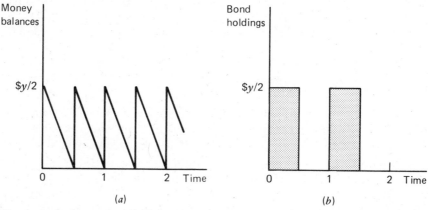

(a)   (b)

The household receives $y income at time $t = 0$ and buys $y/2 bonds. Hence, it starts the period with $y/2 transactions money balances as shown in panel (a) and $y/2 bonds as shown in panel (b). At time $t = \frac{1}{2}$ the household runs out of transactions money balances and sells its bond holdings. This sequence is repeated at time $t = 1$. On average, this household holds $y/4 in transactions money balances and $y/4 in bonds.

Figure 19.6   A Household's Transactions Demand for Money with Three Bond Transactions: (a) Money Balances, (b) Bond Holdings

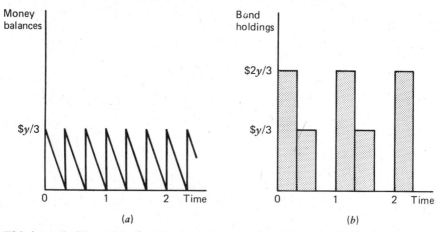

(a)   (b)

This household receives $y income at time $t = 0$ and buys $2y/3 bonds. Hence, it starts the period with $y/3 transactions money balances as shown in panel (a) and $2y/3 bonds as shown in panel (b). At time $t = \frac{1}{3}$ the household runs out of transactions money balances and sells $y/3 bonds. At time $t = \frac{2}{3}$ the household again runs out of transactions money balances and sells $y/3 bonds. This sequence is repeated at time $t = 1$. On average, this household holds $y/6 in transactions money balances and $y/3 in bonds.

average value of bond holdings during the period would be $y/4, produc-
ing interest income net of transactions costs of $(i · y/4 − 2b).

A household making three transactions during the period can maximize interest earnings by purchasing $2y/3 bonds at the beginning of the
period and then selling one-half of its bond holdings at time $t = \frac{1}{3}$ and the
remainder at time $t = \frac{2}{3}$, as shown in Figure 19.6. The average bond holdings during the period would be $y/3, producing interest income net of
transactions costs of $(i · y/3 − 3b).

Variable Number *n* of Bond Market Transactions

In general, a household making *n* transactions during the period will maximize interest earnings with an initial purchase of bonds equal to $y · (n −
1)/n. Since the individual begins the period with bond holdings of $y · (n −
1)/n and ends with zero holdings, the average value of bond holdings must
be $y · (n − 1)/2n, producing interest income net of transactions costs of

$$\frac{\text{Interest earnings net}}{\text{of transactions costs}} = i \cdot y \cdot (n - 1)/2n - n \cdot b \qquad (19.4$$

The individual's average money holdings is $y/2n (for all values of *n* great-
er than one).

Maximizing Net Income for Bond Holdings

The problem faced by the household is to choose the number of transactions *n* that maximizes net interest income. Equation (19.4) shows that a
higher value for *n* raises gross interest income but also increases transaction
costs. The profit-maximizing household increases *n* until the higher interest income no longer exceeds the extra transaction costs. For one more
transaction, the extra transaction cost remains constant at $b. On the other
hand, the additional interest income gets smaller and smaller as *n* rises.
Provided the additional interest income exceeds the extra transaction cost
at some small value of *n*, there must be a higher value of *n* at which the
additional interest income falls below the extra transaction cost, as shown in
Figure 19.7.

Numerical Example of Maximizing Net Income

Consider the following numerical example: $y equals $2000, *i* is 0.01 (or
percent) a month, and *b* is $2. If no bonds are held, interest income is zero.
With one purchase and one sale of bonds (n = 2), interest income is $5
since $1000 is held in bonds until halfway through the month. Transaction
costs, however, rise from zero to $4. With three bond transactions (n = 3)
two-thirds of the income is invested in bonds for one-third of the month
and one-third of the income is invested for another third of the month
giving an interest income of $6.67: $(⅔) · (2000) · 0.01/3 + $(⅓) · (2000) ·
0.01/3. Marginal revenue, therefore, is $1.67, but marginal cost (the cost of
one more bond transaction) is $2. Hence, net income falls from $1 to 67¢.
Clearly, two rather than three bond transactions are optimal in this case
and average money balances will be $500: ($y/2n).

Figure 19.7 Marginal Cost and Revenue from Increasing Transactions in Bonds

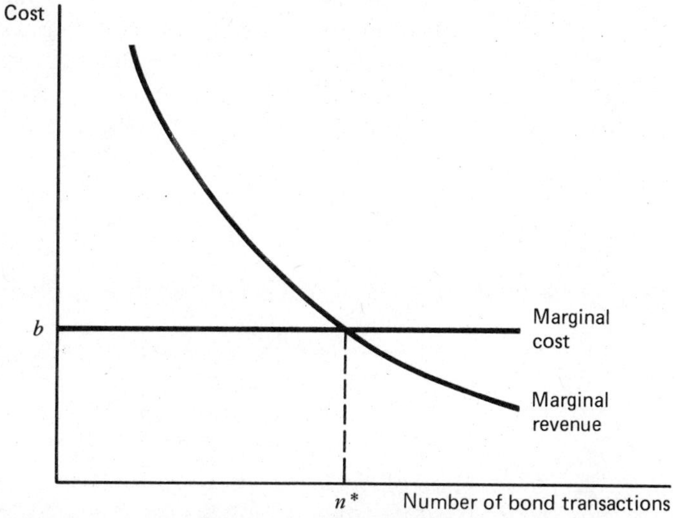

With a very small number of bond transactions, raising n from n to $n + 1$ produces a relatively large increase in average bond holdings and, hence, in interest income or marginal revenue. At this point, marginal revenue exceeds marginal cost b from one additional bond transaction. As n gets bigger and bigger, the *increase* in average bond holdings made possible by increasing n gets smaller and smaller. At n^* bond transactions, marginal revenue equals marginal cost and a higher value for n would yield a marginal revenue less than the marginal cost of one more bond transaction.

Higher Interest Rate Reduces Transactions Balances

Now consider what happens when the interest rate goes up to 0.02 (2 percent) a month. Total interest revenue for $n = 2$ is $10, for $n = 3$ $13.33, and for $n = 4$ $15. Marginal revenue, therefore, is $10 for $n = 2$, $3.33 for $n = 3$, and $1.67 for $n = 4$. Since marginal cost is always $2, the optimal number of bond transactions in this case is 3 and average money balances will be $333.33.

Optimal Level of Transactions Balances

Using calculus, the optimal number of transactions can be found by differentiating equation (19.4) with respect to n and setting the result equal to zero:

$$i \cdot y/2n^2 - b = 0 \tag{19.5}$$

or

$$i \cdot y/2n^2 = b \tag{19.6}$$

or

$$n = \sqrt{i \cdot y/2b} \tag{19.7}$$

This value of n maximizing net income from bond holding can be denoted n^*. On the left-hand side of equation (19.6) is the additional interest income from increasing n by one. On the right-hand side is the extra transaction cost. Equation (19.6) shows that additional interest income declines as n gets larger. The average transactions balance associated with n^* is $\$y/2n^*$. Consequently, equation (19.7) can be used to show that the optimal average level of transactions balances is

$$M_T^d = (\tfrac{1}{2})\sqrt{2b \cdot y/i} \tag{19.8}$$

Implications of Baumol's Transactions Demand for Money

This model yields several interesting insights into the transactions demand for money:

1. The household must make at least two transactions if it is to hold any bonds at all. Consequently, if $i \cdot y/4$ is less than $2b$, the household will hold no bonds and average transactions balances will be $\$y/2$.

2. A doubling of income and transaction costs will cause the demand for transactions balances to double.

3. A 1 percent rise in the interest rate reduces the demand for transactions balances by $\tfrac{1}{2}$ percent. (The *interest elasticity* of the demand for transactions balances is $-\tfrac{1}{2}$).

4. A 1 percent rise in income (holding the transaction cost constant) will raise the demand for transactions balances by $\tfrac{1}{2}$ percent. (The *income elasticity* of the demand for transactions balances is $\tfrac{1}{2}$).

Transactions Balances Held by Firms

Of course, the analysis so far has considered only the holdings of transactions balances by households. Whereas households receive income at the beginning of the period and spend it continuously, business firms accumulate a constant flow of receipts and make a lump sum payment at the end of the period. Business firms may find it profitable to purchase bonds with some of the receipts they are accumulating and then sell all their bond holdings at the end of the period. This produces a demand for transactions balances by business firms very similar to the households' transactions demand function. In fact, business firm money demand is essentially a mirror image of household money demand. Using the same analytical techniques, business firm money demand can be derived:

$$M_T^d = (\tfrac{1}{2})\sqrt{2b \cdot E/i} \tag{19.9}$$

The Precautionary Demand for Money

Uncertain Receipts and Expenditures

The transactions demand for money discussed above springs from the desire to bridge the gap between planned receipts and expenditures when there are transaction costs associated with buying and selling bonds. The precautionary demand for money, on the other hand, arises from the uncertainty about cash inflows and outflows. Households and business firms rarely know their future receipts and expenditures with any certainty. They must be prepared to meet sudden emergencies that require unexpected expenditures. If bonds have to be sold to meet these expenditures, a transaction cost will be incurred. Consequently, households and firms may find it advantageous to hold precautionary money balances in order to avoid incurring those transaction costs.

Probability of Net Receipt Shortfalls   Consider the cumulative probability distribution of possible shortfalls (expenditures minus receipts) of a representative household, shown in Figure 19.8. On average, during the payments period ahead receipts will equal expenditures, hence producing a zero shortfall. It is possible, however, to have a positive or a negative shortfall. The larger such discrepancy between expenditures and receipts, the less frequently it occurs. If the household holds M_P in precautionary money balances, it can meet all net receipt shortfalls of M_P or less without having to sell bonds. When shortfalls exceed M_P, however, the household must sell some of its bond holdings and incur the transaction cost b. Consequently, the expected cost of meeting net receipt shortfalls is the probability that the shortfall will exceed M_P, $p(SF > M_P)$, where p is probability, times b, the transaction cost. In this case, $p(SF > M_P)$ is .2 and b is $2. Hence, the expected cost is 40¢.

Figure 19.8   Cumulative Distribution Function of Net Receipt Shortfalls

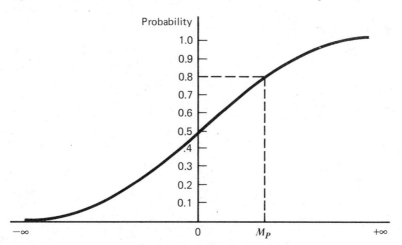

This figure shows the probability of a net receipt shortfall (expenditures minus receipts) over a given time interval falling in the range $-\infty$ to x. If $x = M_p$, the probability of net receipt shortfalls lying in the range $-\infty$ to M_P is .8. Hence, the probability of net receipt shortfalls exceeding M_P (the level of precautionary money balances) is .2.

Marginal Cost and Benefit of Precautionary Balances

If the household adds one dollar to its precautionary money balances, the expected cost of meeting shortfalls is reduced to $b \cdot p(SF > M_P + 1)$. The savings in expected costs of meeting shortfalls that results from adding one dollar to precautionary money balances is $[b \cdot p(SF > M_P)] - [b \cdot p(SF > M_P + 1)]$ or $b \cdot p(M_P < SF < M_P + 1)$. If $p(SF > M_P)$ is .2 and $p(SF > M_P + 1)$ is .19, then the expected marginal savings or benefit from holding an extra dollar is 2¢. However, this saving does not come free. If the household increases its precautionary money balances, it loses the interest it could have earned had the dollar been held in bonds. Consequently, the household will add to its precautionary money balances only if the savings in the expected cost of meeting shortfalls offset the interest lost.

Optimal Level of Precautionary Balances

Figure 19.9 shows the savings generated by an additional dollar of precautionary balances, $b \cdot p(M_P < SF < M_P + 1)$ as a function of the amount of precautionary balances held. The cost-minimizing strategy is to hold precautionary balances of M^*_P. If larger precautionary balances are held, the savings generated by the additional money balances will not offset the interest lost. Once again, the demand for money depends critically on the interest rate. As the interest rate rises, households and business firms hold smaller money balances.

Figure 19.9   Precautionary Demand for Money

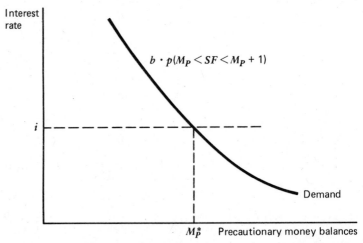

The demand for precautionary money balances is determined by the expected saving from not having to sell bonds to meet unanticipated expenditures. The marginal benefit of holding $1 more in precautionary balances equals the cost of a bond sale b times the reduced probability of such a sale's being needed $p(M_P < SF < M_P + 1)$. This is equated with the marginal cost i of holding $1 more at M^*_P.

The Speculative Demand for Money

Money as an Asset   As was discussed earlier, the real novelty in Keynes's liquidity preference function lay in his treatment of the speculative demand for money. Unlike the demand for transactions and precautionary balances, Keynes's demand for speculative balances arises, not from transaction costs, but from the expectation of a future fall in the price of long-term bonds. This approach stressed two crucial points. First, money is an asset. Second, the cost of holding money is the net income foregone from not holding income-earning assets such as bonds.

Certain Expectations in Keynes's Model   James Tobin extended the approach that Keynes used to analyze the speculative demand for money by introducing the role played by risk in the demand for money function.[3] As in Keynes's model, Tobin analyzes the choice between holding bonds or money. Tobin's analysis is very different, however. Keynes assumed that individuals hold *certain* expectations about what will happen to interest rates. If the capital losses associated with the individual's expectation exceeded interest earnings, the individual would hold nothing but money. Otherwise, he or she would hold nothing but bonds. There is an aggregate demand for bonds *and* speculative money balances only because Keynes assumed that individuals had different expectations about the future. At every moment in time, some individuals hold nothing but money while others hold nothing but bonds.

Uncertainty about Future Bond Yields in Tobin's Model   Tobin, on the other hand, assumes that individuals have *uncertain* expectations about the future. As a result of this uncertainty, they usually hold a diversified portfolio of bonds and money. In Tobin's model, individuals can hold money and/or bonds. Money earns no interest but is riskless in the sense that it has a guaranteed nominal value at the end of the period. Tobin does not analyze the risk of price level changes. Bonds, on the other hand, provide interest income. However, the total return or yield on the bond is the interest income accruing to the bondholder, an amount that is certain, plus uncertain capital gains or losses. Since the individual's expectations about capital gains and losses are uncertain, expectations about the total return from holding bonds must be described by a subjective cumulative distribution of possible returns, such as that shown in Figure 19.10. The mean of this distribution is the expected bond yield i_b^e, in this case 2 percent. The dispersion of the distribution measures the uncertainty associated with the forecast. This dispersion is commonly measured by the *standard deviation* σ_i of the distribution—the square root of the average of the squared deviations from the expected return i_b^e. Figure 19.11 shows two

[3]James Tobin, "Liquidity Preference as Behavior towards Risk," *Review of Economic Studies*, 25(2), February 1958, pp. 65–86.

Figure 19.10　Cumulative Distribution Function of Bond Yields

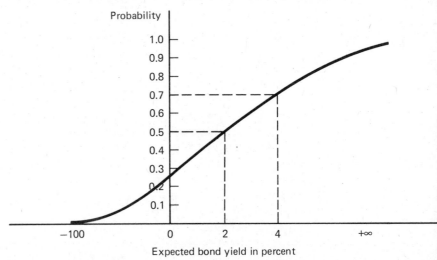

This diagram shows that there is a probability of .5 that the bond yield will be less than 2 percent. The probability that the bond yield will fall in the range 0–4 percent is .44.

Figure 19.11　Two Cumulative Distribution Functions of Bond Yields

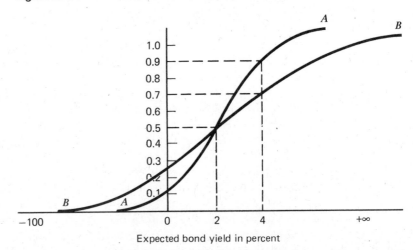

Distribution *A* has a smaller standard deviation and hence less uncertainty than does distribution *B*. For example, the probability of the bond yield falling in the range 0–4 percent is .88 for *A* but only .44 for *B*.

cumulative distribution functions—A has a smaller standard deviation and hence less uncertainty than B.

Risk and Return Given the subjective probability distribution of possible bonds yields, individuals must choose between holding money and bonds. Bonds earn interest, but they are risky because of the uncertainty about future bond prices. Holding money is riskless but offers zero yield. If individuals hold all of their portfolio in bonds, they will receive an expected return of i_b^e, but that return is accompanied by risk measured by σ_i. At the other extreme, people could hold all of their portfolios in money earning an expected return of zero with an associated risk of zero. In general, individuals holding a proportion a of their portfolios in bonds and $(1 - a)$ in money will have an expected return on the whole portfolio R of

$$R = a \cdot i_b^e \qquad (19.10)$$

with associated risk σ_R of

$$\sigma_R = a \cdot \sigma_i \qquad (19.11)$$

Portfolio Composition Figure 19.12 shows the possible combinations of portfolio risk and return facing certain individuals. If they hold nothing but money, both their expected return and risk are zero. Alternatively, if they hold nothing but

Figure 19.12   Risk and Return from a Diversified Portfolio

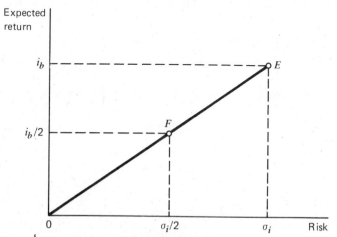

A portfolio consisting of nothing but bonds is represented by point E. A portfolio with half bonds and half money is represented by point F, where the expected yield is $i_b/2$ and the risk is $\sigma_i/2$. An all-money portfolio lies at the origin with zero return and zero risk. Any combination of money and bonds gives a portfolio with expected return and risk lying at some point on the straight line between zero and E.

bonds, their portfolio will yield an expected return of i_b and possess risk of σ_i. This is illustrated by point E in Figure 19.12. A diversified portfolio of one-half money and one-half bonds is represented by point F, yielding $i_b/2$ return with $\sigma_i/2$ risk. All other possible portfolio combinations are represented by the straight line running from the origin, where a equals zero, to E, where a equals one. If i_b or σ_i is known, the proportion of bonds a in the portfolio can be readily calculated from the portfolio's expected yield $a \cdot i_b$ or risk $a \cdot \sigma_i$.

Yield Rises but Risk Remains Constant   Suppose i_b rises but σ_i remains constant. In this case, point E', representing an all-bond portfolio with the new higher yield i_b', must lie exactly above E, as shown in Figure 19.13a. In this case the horizontal axis still exhibits the same relationship between portfolio risk and portfolio composition as it did before. What has changed, however, is the relationship between portfolio return and portfolio composition.

Yield Remains Constant but Risk Rises   Conversely, if i_b remains unchanged but σ_i rises (a shift from A to B in Figure 19.11), point E'', representing an all-bond portfolio with the new higher risk σ_i', must lie exactly to the right of E, as shown in Figure 19.13b.

Figure 19.13   A Change in Bond Yield and Bond Risk: (a) Change in Bond Yield, (b) Change in Bond Risk

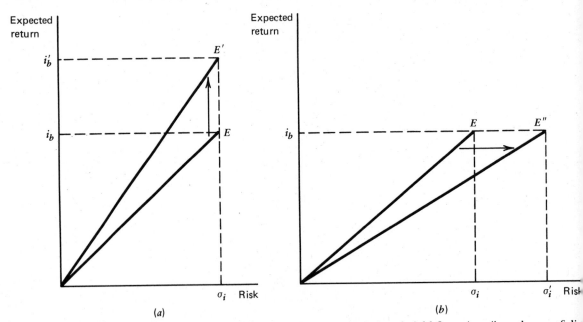

Panel (a) shows the effect of an increase in bond yield from i_b to i_b' on the portfolio return and risk represented by the straight line. Similarly, panel (b) illustrates the effect of an increase in risk from σ_i to σ_i' on the portfolio line.

Here, the vertical axis provides the same relationship between portfolio return and portfolio composition but the horizontal axis has been altered.

Risk Lovers and Risk Averters

Tobin characterizes individuals as either risk lovers or risk averters. Risk lovers are those who willingly give up return in order to increase risk. Risk averters will assume more risk only if it is accompanied by a larger expected return. Tobin further separates risk averters into *plungers* and *diversifiers*. A plunger requires a fixed compensation in the form of higher expected return for each unit of risk he or she accepts. A diversifier requires increasing compensation for each additional unit of risk he or she accepts.

Diversifiers and Demand for Money

The key to Tobin's analysis of the demand for money lies in the behavior of diversifiers. The preference function of diversifiers is shown in Figure 19.14. Each indifference curve, I_1, I_2, and I_3, gives the combinations of portfolio risk and expected return that leave these individuals equally well off. Since diversifiers require increasing compensation for each extra unit of risk, these indifference curves are concave upwards. Utilities are maximized at the tangency of the highest indifference curve with the portfolio line. Although diversifiers might find themselves with a corner solution (holding all bonds or all money), they will usually hold both money and bonds, as shown at F in Figure 19.14.

Figure 19.14   Diversifiers

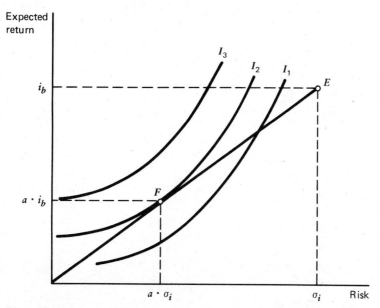

Diversifiers have indifference curves that are concave upwards. Hence, their optimal portfolio is at F on the highest attainable indifference curve I_2.

Figure 19.15   Portfolio Shift from an Increase in the Expected Bond Yield: (a) Reduced Money Demand, (b) Increased Money Demand

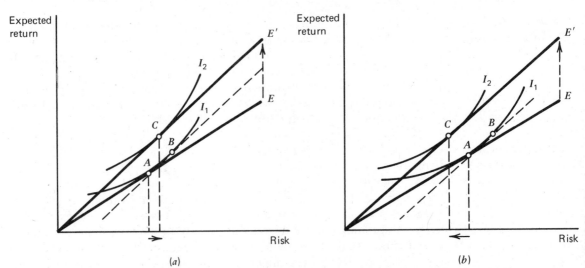

An increase in the expected bond yield produces both an income and a substitution effect. Using the risk axis, the substitution effect from A to B shows that more bonds are held as their yield rises, provided there is no change in income. If money is a normal good, an increase in income increases money demand as shown by the leftward movement from B to C. In panel (a) the substitution effect dominates and money demand falls with an increase in the bond yield. In panel (b) the income effect dominates and more money is held when the interest rate rises.

Change in Money Demand when Yield Rises but Risk Remains Constant

Now consider what happens when the expected yield on bonds increases, enabling the individual to obtain a higher expected return for the same risk. This is shown by the counterclockwise rotation of the portfolio line about the origin in Figure 19.15. In this case the horizontal axis continues to provide a fixed relationship between portfolio risk and portfolio composition. Hence, any change in portfolio risk involves a proportional change in portfolio composition. A 10 percent decline in portfolio risk means that the proportion of bonds in the portfolio a has declined by 10 percent. The rightward move along the horizontal axis shown in Figure 19.15a implies a decrease in money demand, while the leftward move in Figure 19.15b is an increase in money demand, provided the portfolio's value and bond risk are held constant.

Income and Substitution Effects

As shown in Figure 19.15, the effect of a rise in the expected rate of return on bonds has an ambiguous effect on the demand for money in Tobin's model. The change in the expected bond yield produces both a substitution and an income effect. The substitution effect is clear. An increase in the expected bond yield with no income effect causes substitution into bonds from money, as shown by the shift from A to B along I_1 in Figure 19.15. However, the rise in the expected return on bonds also moves the individual to a higher indifference curve I_2, creating an income effect. If money is a normal good, an increase in real income will tend to increase the demand for money, as shown by the leftward shift from B to C in Figure 19.15. Were money an inferior good, a rise in real income would of course reduce the demand for money.

Ambiguous Effect of Interest on Money Demand

The total effect of a rise in the expected return on bonds depends on whether or not the substitution effect outweighs the income effect. In Figure 19.15a the substitution effect outweighs the income effect. Consequently, individuals increase their risk by reducing their money balances. In Figure 19.15b on the other hand, the income effect outweighs the substitution effect, and these individuals choose to reduce their portfolio risk by increasing their money balances.

Yield Rises but Wealth Falls

The counterclockwise rotation of the opportunity line about the origin in Figure 19.15 is applicable when wealth remains constant. However, a rise in the market interest rate reduces the market value of bonds. When these capital losses are considered, there is no basis for supposing that the income effect could be important. As a result, one would generally expect the substitution effect to dominate.

Change in Money Demand When Yield Remains Constant but Risk Increases

Tobin's model also produces ambiguous results for the effects of an increase in risk on the demand for money. An increase in bond risk involves a shift in σ_i to the right, so that the opportunity line becomes flatter, as shown in Figure 19.16. This means that individuals can now get less return for every unit of risk they accept, producing a substitution (A to B) away from bonds into money. However, an increase in risk moves individuals to lower indifference curves, thus creating a negative income effect. If money is a normal good, the reduction in real income tends to reduce the demand for money (B to C).

Ambiguous Effect of Risk on Money Demand

Again the total effect on the demand for money depends on whether or not the income effect offsets the substitution effect. In Figure 19.16a the substitution effect (A to B) dominates the income effect (B to C). As a result, the new portfolio yields a return below the original yield. Hence, money demand has increased. In Figure 19.16b the income effect (B to C) dominates the substitution effect (A to B), causing the new expected return to lie above its original level.

Risk and Portfolio Diversification

Tobin's model provides a much more sophisticated rationale for holding speculative money balances than does Keynes's model. Moreover, people generally do hold diversified portfolios of money and bonds and rarely switch all their wealth from money to bonds and back again, as implied by

Figure 19.16   Portfolio Shift from an Increase in the Bond Yield Risk: (a) Increased Money Demand, (b) Reduced Money Demand

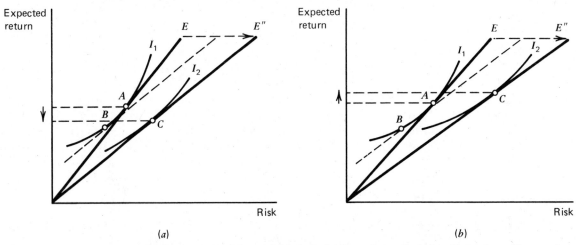

(a)   (b)

An increase in risk on the bond yield produces both a substitution effect and an income effect. Using the expected return axis, the substitution effect from A to B shows that fewer bonds are held as risk rises. A reduction in income—the income effect—reduces money demand, as is shown by the increased risk from B to C. In panel (a) the substitution effect dominates and more risk increases money demand. In panel (b) the income effect dominates and more risk reduces money demand.

Keynes's theory. Tobin's model constitutes an important building block not only for money demand theory but for the theory of portfolio choice in which decisions about diversification among many income-earning assets are analyzed. In general, portfolio diversification can reduce risk without lowering expected return.

The Generalized Demand for Money Function

Money Services   Although the money demand models described above provide many insights into both the nature of money and the determinants of the demand for money, they are based on extremely restrictive assumptions. Because of the influence of Milton Friedman, who published his major theoretical paper on the demand for money in 1956,[4] the standard approach today is to treat money as a durable asset yielding a stream of services to money-holders. The derived demand for money can be analyzed in exactly the

---

[4]Milton Friedman, "The Quantity Theory of Money—A Restatement" in *Studies in the Quantity Theory of Money*, ed. Milton Friedman (Chicago: University of Chicago Press, 1956), pp. 1–21.

same way as the demand for anything else. Other things equal, the quantity demanded will vary inversely with its price or cost. The demand to hold money, therefore, will be related inversely to the opportunity cost of holding money. As with other applications of demand theory, consumption of money services is limited by a budget constraint.

Opportunity Costs   Friedman's generalized theory of the demand for money recognizes that there are many assets besides money and bonds. Friedman considers five specific forms in which wealth can be held: money, bonds, shares, physical goods (machinery, equipment, and inflation hedges), and human capital (a combination of brute strength, intelligence, and embodied knowledge over a lifetime, discounted to present value). All forms of wealth yield a return of one kind or another; otherwise, present value would be zero. The return on money is taken by Friedman to be "solely in kind, in the usual form of convenience, security, etc." The return on bonds is the nominal yield i_b, as is the return i_e on shares. The return on physical goods is the expected rate of inflation π^e, because, on average, prices of goods rise at the rate of inflation.

Budget Constraint   Although it may be a convenient simplification to model consumption as dependent upon relative prices and income, discussion of the consumption function in Chapter 15 made it clear that current income is not the relevant variable. Future income also has a direct effect on current consumption of goods and services. For this reason, Friedman developed the concept of *permanent income* y_p—the perpetual income stream that can be produced by the current stock of wealth—as the relevant income concept in both consumption and demand for money functions.[5]

Friedman's Money   Friedman's demand for money function takes the form
Demand Function

$$M^d = f(i_b, i_e, \pi^e; w; y_p; u)P \qquad (19.12)$$

where w is the ratio of nonhuman to human wealth or the ratio of income from nonhuman to human wealth, and u is a "tastes and preferences" variable. Tastes and preferences with respect to holding money change, for example, when people start moving more and/or face more uncertainty than usual. This is precisely what happens in wartime and may well explain the fact that the ratio of money to income k usually increases during a war.

Three important concepts in Friedman's theory, which he called a restatement of the quantity theory of money although it borrows several important ideas from Keynes, are: (1) money demand is a function of

---

[5]Milton Friedman, *A Theory of the Consumption Function* (Princeton, N.J.: Princeton University Press for the National Bureau of Economic Research, 1957), and "The Demand for Money: Some Theoretical and Empirical Results," *Journal of Political Economy*, 67(4), August 1959, pp. 327–351.

wealth or permanent income rather than the actual level of income; (2) substitution can take place between money and goods as well as between money and bonds; and (3) the perceived return from holding goods is expected rather than actual inflation.

Competitive Interest Payments on Deposits and the Demand for Money

Explicit and Implicit Interest on Deposit Money

One problem with all the demand for money functions discussed so far is that they are based on the assumption that money earns no interest. Hence, the opportunity cost of holding money is simply the foregone interest on alternative assets. While the Banking Act of 1933 prohibited the payment of interest on checking account balances, all depository institutions are now permitted to pay explicit interest on NOW and Super NOW accounts, both transactions-type deposits. Since transactions-type deposits constitute over 70 percent of M1, deposit interest should be taken into account in calculating the opportunity cost of holding money. With interest paid on deposits, the opportunity cost of holding this kind of money is the difference only between the interest rate on alternative assets and the interest paid on deposits. Moreover, as Benjamin Klein points out, the earlier prohibition against payment of *explicit* interest on deposits did not prevent banks from paying *implicit* interest on deposits in the form of services provided to depositors at below cost.[6] Any implicit interest payments on deposits must also be deducted from yields on alternative assets in order to derive the opportunity cost of holding money.

Compensating Balances

Depositors hold their accounts at those depository institutions offering the highest return in the form of explicit plus implicit interest. Implicit interest consists of the below-cost banking services that depository institutions provide their depositors. These implicit interest payments take many forms. One of the major vehicles for such payments is reduced-rate loans to depositors. Depository institutions commonly tie reduced-rate loans to deposits through *compensating balance requirements*. These requirements force the borrower to hold some minimum level of average deposit during the period of the loan. Depository institutions also typically provide free check-clearing services to depositors. Another indirect way these institutions can attract deposits is by providing greater convenience in the form of additional branches and longer business hours.

Competitive Equilibrium

The reason why depository institutions provide below-cost services to depositors was discussed in Chapter 7. Deposit liabilities have two costs—an explicit payment to depositors, i_D, and an implicit, noncash payment to

---

[6]Benjamin Klein, "Competitive Interest Payments on Bank Deposits and the Long-Run Demand for Money," *American Economic Review*, 64(6), December 1974, pp. 931–949.

depositors, i_D^*. The depository institution uses the funds provided by depositors to acquire additional assets. Since they must hold part of their deposit funds in the form of non-income-earning required reserves, the income from assets acquired with \$1 of additional deposits is $\$i_L \cdot (1 - rrd)$, where i_L is the yield on earning assets and rrd is the required reserve ratio. As long as the marginal cost of acquiring additional deposits is less than the return on the income and non-income-earning assets acquired with these funds, depository institutions can increase their profits by attracting more deposits. To attract these deposits from competing institutions, however, each depository institution has to increase explicit or implicit interest payments to depositors. Under conditions of pure competition, depository institutions would bid up the return to depositors until deposits were no longer a low-cost source of funds. Thus, in competitive equilibrium,

$$i_D + i_D^* = (1 - rrd) \cdot i_L - ic \qquad (19.13)$$

where ic is the marginal cost of financial intermediation per unit of deposits. Equation (19.13) is closely related to equation (7.1).

Implications for Money Demand Analysis

The relationship between the competitive return on deposits and the market rate of interest sheds new light on the interest elasticity of the demand for money. Under competitive conditions, depository institutions would pay explicit and/or implicit interest of $(1 - rrd) \cdot i_L - ic$ on their deposits. The opportunity cost of holding money would then be the difference between the market rate of interest and the return on money, or $rrd \cdot i_L - ic$:

$$i_L - (1 - rrd) \cdot i_L - ic = rrd \cdot i_L - ic \qquad (19.14)$$

When the yield on income-earning assets increases, depository institutions spend more to attract deposits. Clearly, this reduces considerably the effect of interest rates on the demand for money. If rrd were 0.15, for example, a one percentage point rise in the market rate of interest would raise the opportunity cost of holding money by only 0.15 of a percentage point. Hence, when the return on money is not included in the demand for money function, the interest elasticity of demand for money will appear to be greater, the higher is the required reserve ratio.

Appendix

The optimality of putting exactly half of an individual's income into bonds can be proved mathematically in the following way. The household which invests some portion x of its income at the beginning of the period will earn interest income of $x \cdot y \cdot (1 - x) \cdot i$ or $(x - x^2) \cdot y \cdot i$. The term $(1 - x)$ is the fraction of the period that income can remain invested in bonds if consumption expenditure occurs smoothly over the period. To maximize income earned with respect to x, take the partial derivative of interest earnings with respect to x and set it equal to zero: $(1 - 2x) \cdot y \cdot i = 0$. This expression is satisfied only when x equals $\frac{1}{2}$. More generally, it can be shown that, for more than two transactions, the value of each bond sale will be identical if income is to be maximized.

Summary

1. Keynes's liquidity preference formulation of the demand for money suggests that money holdings can be analyzed in terms of transactions balances, precautionary balances, and speculative balances.

2. The Keynesian speculative motive makes money demand interest elastic. Individuals hold speculative money balances if they expect a fall in bond prices to offset interest earnings. The lower the interest rate, the larger the number of individuals holding such expectations and hence the higher is the demand for money.

3. Keynes used his liquidity preference theory to explain the determination of the interest rate by the supply of and demand for money. It is compatible with the loanable funds theory for equilibrium conditions. However, the loanable funds theory recognizes explicitly that money market disequilibrium can have an important short-run effect on the interest rate.

4. The transactions demand for money may also be influenced by the interest rate. Baumol's model shows that the higher the interest rate, the more incentive there is to hold bonds, even for a relatively short period of time. Optimal transactions balances occur when marginal interest earnings from an additional bond transaction just equal the cost of that extra transaction.

5. The precautionary demand for money is also interest elastic. Precautionary balances are held against the possibility of a shortfall in receipts over expenditures. The greater is the level of precautionary balances, the smaller the probability of a net receipt shortfall that would necessitate a bond transaction (bond sales). Optimal precautionary balances are reached when the marginal expected cost of a net receipt shortfall equals the opportunity cost of holding an extra $1 in money.

6. Tobin analyzes demand for money as behavior towards risk. Money has zero yield and zero interest risk. Bonds earn interest but suffer from interest risk. Diversifiers require increasing compensation for accepting more and more risk. Hence, diversifiers may well maximize utility by holding some bonds and some money in their portfolios. A change in expected return and/or risk, however, will change that optimal portfolio. The effects of interest-rate changes trace out the demand for money within the portfolio.

7. Friedman generalized the theory of demand for money by considering five alternative forms in which wealth can be held and suggesting that wealth rather than income was the appropriate budget constraint.

8. The true opportunity cost of holding money is the difference between market rates of interest and the return on deposits. Depository institutions pay interest or provide below-cost services to depositors in order to attract deposits from competing institutions.

Questions

1. Outline the three motives for holding money in Keynes's liquidity preference theory.

2. What is Keynes's speculative demand for money and how would one test this theory of speculative demand for money?

3. What happens to the market interest rate and why, when people expect it to fall?

4. How can Keynes's liquidity preference theory be used as a theory of interest-rate determination?

5. How can the loanable funds theory of interest be used to analyze the effects of money market disequilibrium on the interest rate?

6. How is the optimal level of transactions balances determined in Baumol's model?

7. What happens, and why, to the optimal level of transactions balances if all wages, incomes, and prices (including the price of bond transactions) double?

8. How can the cumulative distribution function be used to determine the optimum level of precautionary money balances?

9. What role does interest or market risk play in Tobin's money demand theory?

10. What are "diversifiers" and why would one expect them to hold some money and some bonds in their portfolios?

11. In what way did Friedman generalize the theory of demand for money?

12. Explain the role of permanent income (as opposed to current income) in Friedman's theory of demand for money.

13. How do competitive interest payments on deposits affect the demand for money?

20 Evidence on the Demand for Money

Demand for Money and Monetary Policy

Demand Stability and Effective Monetary Targeting

The stability and predictability of demand for money are crucial for the successful deployment of monetary aggregates as monetary policy targets. Control over the supply of money can be used to pursue such goals as price stability only if money demand is stable. Indeed, as explained in Chapter 10, the Fed's switch to the supply of money as the main target of monetary policy took place only after an overwhelming body of empirical evidence had been generated showing that the demand for money was in fact stable.

Cambridge Money Demand Function with k and y Constant

Figure 20.1 shows the demand for money function implied by the Cambridge equation $M^d = k\, y \cdot P$. The price or value of a dollar is the inverse of the general price level, or $1/P$. Here, a 1 percent decline in the price of a dollar elicits a 1 percent increase in the quantity of money demanded. This is the same as saying that a 1 percent increase in P produces a 1 percent increase in M^d, as expressed directly in the Cambridge equation. With k and y constant at k_0 and y_0, money demand is given by the curve M_0^d in Figure 20.1. If the Fed fixes the money supply at M_0^s, the value of money will be $1/P_0$ and the price level P_0. Provided that the Fed can indeed fix the money supply, it can maintain price stability simply by holding the money supply constant.

Cambridge Money Demand Function with k Constant

In fact, of course, real income y does vary. Hence, the demand for money function shown in Figure 20.1 shifts too. Figure 20.2 shows the effect of a rise in real income from y_0 to y_1. The demand for money shifts from M_0^d to M_1^d and money supply must be increased by exactly the same amount to maintain price stability. The Cambridge equation has a 1 percent increase

Figure 20.1 Cambridge Money Demand Function

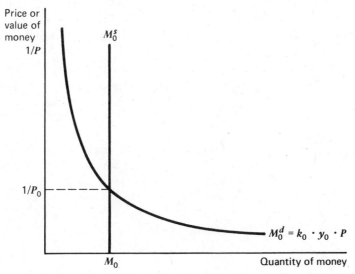

This figure shows the Cambridge equation formulation of the demand for money at income level y_0 and the Cambridge k equal to k_0. With the money supply fixed at M_0, the equilibrium price level is P_0.

Figure 20.2 Shift in the Cambridge Money Demand Function

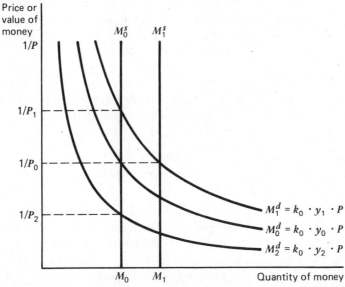

A rise in income from y_0 to y_1 raises money demand, shifting the money demand function rightwards from M_0^d to M_1^d. Price stability can be maintained by increasing the money supply from M_0^s to M_1^s. If the money supply is held constant at M_0^s, the price level will fall from P_0 to P_1 with a rise in income from y_0 to y_1. The price level will rise from P_0 to P_2 if real income falls from y_0 to y_2.

in y producing a 1 percent increase in M^d. In this case, a 1 percent increase in M^s is required to maintain price stability. Since y can be estimated with a relatively short lag and predicted fairly accurately for the immediate future, this source of demand disturbance does not produce any serious obstacles for monetary policy. The money supply can be changed proportionally with changes in income to keep prices stable.

Stabilizing Nominal GNP
An anticyclical monetary policy might have the ultimate goal of stabilizing nominal GNP. If M^s were held constant, P would rise automatically, hence stimulating production, when y fell. With M and k constant, an increase in y from y_0 to y_1 would shift the money demand curve to the right from M_0^d to M_1^d in Figure 20.2 and so increase the value of money, thus lowering P from P_0 to P_1. Conversely, a fall in y from y_0 to y_2 would shift the curve to the left from M_0^d to M_2^d in Figure 20.2 and the price level would rise from P_0 to P_2.

Cambridge Equation with Unpredictable Fluctuations in k
A very different situation occurs if the money demand curve shifts because of random and unpredictable changes in k. If the demand curve shifts without warning because of a random change in k, the Fed may be unable to respond fast enough in changing the money supply to prevent price *or* nominal GNP fluctuations. In this case, control over the money supply cannot ensure the achievement of the ultimate goals of monetary policy. If the demand for money is unstable, the Fed has to find an alternative way of stabilizing the price level or nominal GNP. For price stability, the Fed needs to make the money supply perfectly elastic or horizontal at some chosen value of money. Then random fluctuations in the demand curve will change only the quantity of money but not its value. In a sense, this is what the gold standard attempted to do. In practice, however, money demand in the United States has been fairly stable and predictable. This is why the Fed attempts to achieve its ultimate goals through control over the quantity of money supplied.

Stability of the Money Demand Function

Statistical Stability
If control of the money supply is to enable the Fed to produce a predictable effect on the economy, the demand for money must be stable. In this context, stability involves three key elements.[1] First, stability implies that the demand for money is highly predictable. For example, suppose the demand for money function takes the form

$$M^d = b_0 + b_1 i + b_2 Y \qquad (20.1)$$

---

[1]John P. Judd and John L. Scadding, "The Search for a Stable Money Demand Function: A Survey of the Post-1973 Literature," *Journal of Economic Literature,* 20(3), September 1982, pp. 993–1023.

If one had estimated values for the coefficients or constants b_0, b_1, and b_2, then for any pair of observations on the interest rate i and nominal GNP Y the calculated or predicted value of M^d from the right-hand side of equation (20.1) would be very close to the actual value of M^d.[2] A stable demand for money function would also imply that the coefficients b_0, b_1, and b_2 estimated from data over a period such as 1950–1983 would not change in 1984. Hence, the relationship could be used to forecast money demand in 1984 from predicted values of i and Y. Suppose, for example, that the coefficients were estimated to be $b_0 = -90$, $b_1 = -1000$, and $b_2 = 0.2$, and i and Y are predicted to be 0.1 and \$3700 billion, respectively, in 1984. In this case, predicted money demand is \$550 billion. If the demand for money function is indeed stable, then the money supply must be set at \$550 billion in 1984 for the interest rate of 10 percent and nominal GNP of \$3700 billion to materialize. If less than \$550 billion is supplied, the interest rate will be above 10 percent, or GNP will be below \$3700 billion, or both. Were nominal GNP the ultimate goal of monetary policy and the interest rate were predicted to be 10 percent under all circumstances, then the money supply could be used to achieve the desired level of GNP. Had the GNP goal been \$3500 billion rather than \$3700, the money supply should have been fixed at \$510 billion rather than \$550 billion.

Relatively Few Explanatory Variables

Stability of the money demand function also implies that money demand can be predicted from a relatively small number of explanatory variables. If it takes hundreds of variables to predict money demand, then money demand is in effect unpredictable. In practice, monetary control becomes worthless if money demand can be brought back into equilibrium after a change in money supply through changes in any number of explanatory variables in the demand function. Even in the case of equation (20.1), one more equation is required to explain i before a unique relationship between M and Y can be pinned down. Each additional variable in the demand for money function has to be predicted before the key relationship between P and M or Y and M can be isolated. In some cases, as in the case of the interest rate, explanatory variables may themselves be affected by the money supply. The difficulties of modeling the relationship between M and Y or M and P escalate to unmanageable proportions if it takes more than five or six variables to predict the demand for money.

Links to Economic Activity

The final stability requirement is that the few variables used to predict money demand must represent important links to aggregate spending and the real level of economic activity. Were money demand explained perfectly by nothing but sun-spot activity, demand for money would be irrelevant as far as monetary policy was concerned. It is precisely because money demand is determined by economic variables such as the interest rate and

[2]For a clear explanation of estimation techniques used in econometrics, see Jack Johnston, *Econometric Methods,* 3rd ed. (New York: McGraw-Hill, 1984).

GNP, wealth, or permanent income that money is linked to and can thereby influence economic activity.

Empirical Support for the Cambridge Equation

Observed Money Stock Is Money Demand in Equilibrium

The Cambridge equation has been used throughout this book as the basic formulation of the demand for money function. It was chosen for two reasons: first, it is a simple and easy-to-use equation; second, it provides a good first approximation to the long-run relationship between money and income in the United States over the past 100 years. The Cambridge equation is expressed

$$M^d = k \cdot y \cdot P = k \cdot Y \tag{20.2}$$

If the money market is in equilibrium, then demand equals supply: $M^d = M^s$. Hence, the observed money stock is both the quantity supplied and the quantity demanded.

Long Run versus Short Run

Even if the Cambridge equation provides reasonable predictions of money demand over the long run, there are at least three reasons to doubt its ability to predict short-run changes in the money stock. First, the money market may well be in disequilibrium in the short run, as was discussed in Chapter 15. In this case, money supply does not equal money demand and money demand is unobservable. Second, there may be a lag as people adjust their money holdings after a change in income. Even if individuals generally hold money balances equal to 25 percent of their income, they would be most unlikely to double their money holdings immediately their salaries were doubled, even if they could. With an initial income of $12,000 a year, money balances would be $3000. Now income is doubled to $24,000–$2000 a month instead of $1000 a month. Even if all the extra income was used to increase money holdings, it would take three months to build up money balances to the desired level of $6000—and most people would feel that there was more to life than keeping their money balances in strict proportion to their income. Indeed, this is really the third reason why the Cambridge equation is unlikely to hold in the short run. Money acts as a shock absorber—the precautionary motive. Money is held precisely because it can be used in emergencies. It is also the asset held initially after an unanticipated receipt of income.[3] In sum, the Cambridge k can be expected to fluctuate in the short run, even if it returns to some constant value in the long run.

[3]Michael R. Darby, "The Allocation of Transitory Income Among Consumers' Assets," *American Economic Review*, 62(5), December 1972, pp. 928–941.

Long-Run Constancy of k

To test the Cambridge equation specification of the demand for money over the long run, Milton Friedman and Anna Schwartz converted data on money, income, and prices into averages for phases of the business cycle—the expansion phase running from trough to peak, and the contraction phase running from peak to trough.[4] On average, these phases are of two years' duration. Friedman and Schwartz then expressed equation (20.2) in logarithms:

$$\ln(M) = \ln(k) + \ln(Y) \tag{20.3}$$

where M is the M2 definition of money and Y is nominal *net* rather than gross national product. Using the average or mean value of $\ln(k)$ over the period 1873–1975, they predicted the logarithm of the money stock from the observed values of Y. The predicted values are denoted $\ln(\hat{M})$. The error in predicting the left-hand side variable in equation (20.3) is $\ln(M) - \ln(\hat{M})$. The predicted values $\ln(\hat{M})$ explain or account for 96 percent of the variations (technically, the variance) in the actual values of $\ln(M)$ from its average or mean level.

As a first approximation, a constant Cambridge k or its inverse velocity of circulation V (since $V = 1/k$), gives the Cambridge equation remarkably high powers of prediction. Since this conclusion runs in the face of the conventional wisdom that k or V is fairly volatile, it is worth quoting Friedman and Schwartz's summary comments on their test:[5]

> Table 6.1 makes it clear that a numerically constant velocity does not deserve the sneering condescension that has become the conventional stance of economists. It is an impressive first approximation that by almost any measure accounts for a good deal more than half of the phase-to-phase movements in money or income. Almost certainly, measurement errors aside, it accounts for a far larger part of such movements than the other extreme hypothesis—that velocity is a will-o'-the-wisp reflecting independent changes in money and income. Yet, for most of the period since the mid-1930s, the will-o'-the-wisp extreme has been nearly the orthodox view among economists!

Early Empirical Estimates

Estimating Keynes's Liquidity Preference Function

In the liquidity trap, money demand is insatiable. Any additional supply will be absorbed without accompanying changes in income or interest rates. In such case, there is no stable relationship between money M and nominal income Y and hence the Cambridge k or its inverse velocity V is a volatile,

[4]Milton Friedman and Anna J. Schwartz, *Monetary Trends in the United States and the United Kingdom: Their Relation to Income, Prices, and Interest Rates, 1867–1975* (Chicago: University of Chicago Press for the National Bureau of Economic Research, 1982), pp. 73–74.

[5]*Ibid.*, p. 215.

unpredictable will-o'-the-wisp. This is therefore an appropriate point to examine some of the early modern empirical studies that tested Keynes's demand for money function.

Separating Money Held for Different Motives

Some of the first demand for money estimates based on modern econometric techniques attempted to separate money held for transactions purposes M_T^d from money held for speculative and precautionary motives M_S^d. One way of doing this was to calculate the Cambridge k for each year of the observation period: $k = M/Y$. For the year with the lowest k, it was assumed that speculative demand for money was zero. Then, using this minimum value k_{min} and the actual values of Y, transactions demand for money in all other years could be calculated:

$$\hat{M}_T^d = k_{min} \cdot Y \tag{20.4}$$

Speculative money demand equals $M - \hat{M}_T^d$. This variable M_S^d was then estimated as a function of the interest rate.

Testing for the Liquidity Trap

Whether one uses M^d or M_S^d as the dependent or left-hand side variable, the choice of functional form is crucial for a test of the liquidity trap hypothesis. The straightforward linear equation

$$M_S^d = b_0 + b_1 i \tag{20.5}$$

Figure 20.3   Speculative Demand for Money from $M_S^d = b_0 + b_1 i$

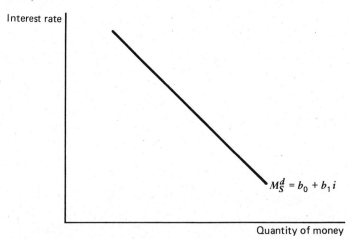

This money demand function shows that the quantity of money demanded is related negatively to the interest rate. This functional form is incompatible with the liquidity trap hypothesis, which holds that money demand becomes infinitely interest elastic at some interest rate.

Figure 20.4   Speculative Demand for Money from $M_S^d = b_0 + b_1[1/(i - i_T)]$

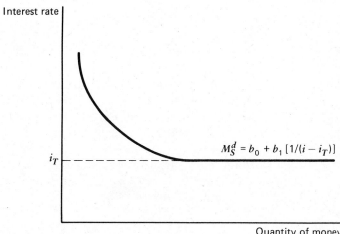

This money demand function has a liquidity trap at an interest rate i_T. Here, $1/(i - i_T)$ becomes infinite. Hence, with a positive value for b_1, money demand also becomes infinitely large.

produces a demand curve of the form shown in Figure 20.3, provided b_0 is positive and b_1 is negative. Clearly, this functional form is inconsistent with a liquidity trap hypothesis. However, one functional form that is consistent with the liquidity trap takes the form

$$M_s^d = b_0 + b_1 \frac{1}{(i - i_T)} \qquad (20.6)$$

where i_T is the interest rate at which the liquidity trap exists. Equation (20.6) is illustrated in Figure 20.4, where both b_0 and b_1 are positive. In this case, the speculative demand for money become infinitely large at i_T.

Liquidity Trap in the Cambridge Equation   Attempts to separate transactions from speculative demands for money had been abandoned by the 1950s because of the arbitrariness of the split. Instead, aggregate money demand could be represented as being determined by both i and Y. In such case, k is a function of i. The liquidity trap can be incorporated in the Cambridge equation as follows:

$$k = b_0 + b_1 \left(\frac{1}{i - i_T} \right) \qquad (20.7)$$

$$M^d = k \cdot Y \qquad (20.8)$$

$$M^d = \left[b_0 + b_1 \left(\frac{1}{i - i_T} \right) \right] \cdot Y \qquad (20.9)$$

Finally, both sides of equation (20.9) can be divided by Y to produce the linear equation

$$\frac{M^d}{Y} = b_0 + b_1\left(\frac{1}{i - i_T}\right) \tag{20.10}$$

Two direct tests of a demand for money function similar to equation (20.10) have been run on U.S. data. Howard Pifer tried a range of alternative values for i_T.[6] He found that the explanatory power of the equation was just as good when i_T was set at zero as it was for any positive value of i_T. Hence, Pifer concluded that there was no liquidity trap at any positive interest rate. Pifer's results were challenged by Robert Eisner on the basis of incorrect statistical methodology.[7] Eisner concluded that there was a liquidity trap at an interest rate of 2 percent.

Liquidity Trap during the Great Depression

If a liquidity trap has ever existed in the United States, it would surely have appeared during the Great Depression, 1929–1933. The demand for money over this period has been studied in detail by Arthur Gandolfi.[8] Gandolfi finds that the demand for money function was stable in these years, with no tendency for the interest elasticity of demand to rise as nominal interest rates fell. Nor have other tests found any evidence that the interest elasticity of demand for money is higher at low interest rates than at high interest rates. Hence, there is no convincing empirical support for the existence of a liquidity trap in the United States.

Interest Elasticity of the Demand for Money

In the early 1950s Henry Latané estimated an equation rather similar to equation (20.10):

$$\frac{M^d}{Y} = b_0 + b_1\frac{1}{i_L} \tag{20.11}$$

where i_L is the interest rate on long-term bonds. The estimate predicted 76 percent of the variations in the actual values of M/Y or k from its mean.[9] However, although virtually all money demand studies for the United States conducted since 1959 have found an important role for an interest-rate variable, estimated interest elasticities are usually much less than 1 in absolute magnitude.

[6]Howard W. Pifer, "A Nonlinear, Maximum Likelihood Estimate of the Liquidity Trap," *Econometrica*, 37(2), April 1969, pp. 324–332.

[7]Robert Eisner, "Non-Linear Estimates of the Liquidity Trap," *Econometrica*, 39(5), September 1971, pp. 861–864.

[8]Arthur E. Gandolfi, "Stability of the Demand for Money during the Great Contraction—1929–1933," *Journal of Political Economy*, 82(5), September/October 1974, pp. 969–983.

[9]Henry A. Latané, "Cash Balances and the Interest Rate: A Pragmatic Approach," *Review of Economics and Statistics*, 36(4), November 1954, pp. 456–460.

Income Elasticity of Demand for Money

Aggregate Nominal Income The Cambridge equation postulates that a 1 percent rise in income will generate an increase in money demand for 1 percent. In other words, it assumes that the income elasticity of demand for money is one. However, money, like any other commodity, might be a luxury good with an income elasticity greater than 1 or an inferior good with an income elasticity less than 1.

One way of allowing income elasticity to take any value is to modify the Cambridge equation as follows:

$$M^d = k \cdot Y^\alpha \tag{20.12}$$

Here, α is the elasticity of aggregate money demand with respect to aggregate nominal income. Were α 1.2, for example, then a 10 percent increase in Y would produce a 12 percent increase in M^d.

Aggregate Real Income An increase in nominal income can be produced by either a rise in the price level or a rise in real income. However, the effect on money demand will not be the same in both cases, at least not according to Baumol's transactions demand model. This problem can be handled by rewriting the Cambridge equation

$$M^d = k \cdot y^\alpha \cdot P^\beta \tag{20.13}$$

According to Baumol's model, $\alpha = 0.5$ and $\beta = 1$.

Per Capita Real Income An increase in aggregate real income can in turn be produced by either a rise in population N or a rise in per capita real income z. Again, the effects on money demand need not be the same. Hence, the Cambridge equation can be modified one more time:

$$M^d = k \cdot z^\alpha \cdot P^\beta \cdot N^\gamma \tag{20.14}$$

Per Capita Real Money Stock Equation (20.14) is difficult to estimate as it stands because it is not a linear equation. However, by taking logarithms of both sides, equation (20.14) becomes

$$\ln(M^d) = \ln(k) + \alpha\ln(z) + \beta\ln(P) + \gamma\ln(N) \tag{20.15}$$

which can be estimated in the form

$$\ln(M) = b_0 + b_1\ln(z) + b_2\ln(P) + b_3\ln(N) \tag{20.16}$$

There is now a substantial volume of empirical evidence derived from estimates of equations similar to equation (20.16) indicating that the values of b_2 and b_3 are both 1. This, in turn, implies $\beta = \gamma = 1$ in equation (20.14). Dividing both sides of equation (20.14) by $P \cdot N$ when $\beta = \gamma = 1$ gives

$$\frac{M^d}{P \cdot N} = k \cdot z^\alpha \qquad (20.17)$$

or

$$m^d = k \cdot z^\alpha \qquad (20.18)$$

where m^d is per capita real money demand. Equation (20.18) can be expressed in logarithmic form and the coefficient of $\ln(z)$ will be the income elasticity of demand. Using M1 as the dependent variable, the elasticity with respect to income, permanent income, or wealth is usually found to lie between 0.5 and 1. With M2 as the left-hand side variable, however, α or the elasticity with respect to income, permanent income, or wealth generally lies above 1 in the range 1.2 to 1.8. In other words, M2 appears to be a luxury good.

Direction of Causality and Estimation

An important feature of equations (20.17) and (20.18) from the viewpoint of econometric estimation is that causality runs predominantly, if not exclusively, from per capita real income to per capita real money holdings and not vice versa, at least in the long run. In all other demand functions described previously in this chapter, causality runs predominantly from the nominal money stock on the left-hand side to prices, interest rates, and/or nominal income on the right-hand side. For the standard ordinary least squares estimation technique to yield unbiased results, it is important that causality should run from the right-hand side variables to the left-hand side variable. If causality runs the other way or if there is two-way causality, more elaborate estimation techniques must be used to eliminate the possibility of biased results.[10]

Short-Run Demand for Money Functions

Stock Adjustment Lags

The empirical estimates of money demand functions discussed so far have been based on annual or phase observations. It is not unreasonable to assume that over these time periods market disequilibria are resolved and adjustments to money holdings resulting from changes in real income and interest rates are completed. Such assumptions, however, are much less plausible when the estimates are run on quarterly or monthly data. As was already pointed out, adjustments to money holdings take time to complete.

[10]See Johnston, *op. cit.*, Chapter 11.

Hence, the money demand function estimated on a quarterly or monthly basis must be modified to incorporate lags in this adjustment process. The standard way of modeling stock adjustment lags is to specify first the long-run, equilibrium, or desired real money demand M^*/P in, say, logarithmic form:

$$\ln\left(\frac{M^*}{P}\right) = \beta_0 + \beta_1\ln(i) + \beta_2\ln(y)$$

(20.19)

Then the short-run or actual real demand for money M^d/P is adjusted each time period by some fraction θ of the gap between long-run or desired real money balances and the actual level of real money balances in the previous time period:

$$\ln\left(\frac{M^d}{P}\right) = \ln\left(\frac{M_{t-1}}{P_{t-1}}\right) + \theta\left[\ln\left(\frac{M^*}{P}\right) - \ln\left(\frac{M_{t-1}}{P_{t-1}}\right)\right]$$

$$= \theta\ln\left(\frac{M^*}{P}\right) + (1 - \theta)\ln\left(\frac{M_{t-1}}{P_{t-1}}\right)$$

(20.20)

Finally, equation (20.19) can be substituted into equation (20.20) to obtain short-run or actual real money demand in terms of observable variables (M^*/P cannot be observed):

$$\ln\left(\frac{M^d}{P}\right) = \theta b_0 + \theta b_1\ln(i) + \theta b_2\ln(y) + (1 - \theta)\ln\left(\frac{M_{t-1}}{P_{t-1}}\right)$$

(20.21)

Quarterly Estimates of Money Demand

In 1973 Stephen Goldfeld published an influential study on the demand for money in the United States over the period 1952(II)–1972(IV)—the Roman numerals indicate quarters of the year in question.[11] One of Goldfeld's major contributions was that he tested systematically alternative variables—money, interest rates, and income or wealth variables. His comparative tests indicated that the demand for money function was most stable when: (1) M1 rather than M2 or broader monetary aggregates was used as the definition of money; (2) a short-term interest rate such as the commercial paper rate i_{CP} rather than a long-term bond rate was included; (3) current real GNP y rather than a permanent income or wealth variable was employed; and (4) the lagged real money stock was introduced to allow for a stock adjustment lag. Goldfeld also included the return on time deposits i_{TD} as a second opportunity cost variable. His estimated money demand function is:

[11]Stephen M. Goldfeld, "The Demand for Money Revisited," *Brookings Papers on Economic Activity*, (3), 1973, pp. 577–638.

$$\ln\!\left(\frac{M1}{P}\right) = 0.271 - 0.019 \ln(i_{CP}) - 0.045 \ln(i_{TD})$$

$$+ \; 0.193 \ln(y) + 0.717 \ln\!\left(\frac{M1_{t-1}}{P_{t-1}}\right) \tag{20.22}$$

This equation explained 99.5 percent of the variations in $\ln(M1/P)$ around its mean.

Long- and Short-Run Elasticities　　The short-run interest and income elasticities of demand for money are simply the coefficients of $\ln(i_{CP})$, $\ln(i_{TD})$, and $\ln(y)$, respectively, in equation (20.22). In all three cases the short-run elasticities are very small. In equation (20.21) the short-run elasticities are $\theta\beta_1$ and $\theta\beta_2$. The long-run elasticities, however, are β_1 and β_2, as shown by the long-run money demand function of equation (20.19). Equation (20.22) provides an estimate of 0.717 for $(1 - \theta)$. Hence, θ is 0.283. Therefore, since $\theta\beta_2$ equals 0.193 and θ equals 0.283, the long-run income elasticity β_2 equals $\theta\beta_2/\theta$, or 0.193/0.283, or 0.682. In this case the income elasticity of demand for money, even in the long run, is significantly less than 1. The long-run interest-rate elasticities can be calculated in the same way: -0.067 for i_{CP} and -0.159 for i_{TD}.

Transactions versus Asset Theories　　Goldfeld's results came out conclusively in favor of transactions theories of money demand such as Baumol's model and against asset theories such as Tobin's and Friedman's models. Prior to Goldfeld's study, most published work on the demand for money had reported empirical tests of only one model. With different functional forms, different time periods, different data sets, and different estimating procedures, it had been impossible previously to conclude that one theory was superior to another. Both classes of demand for money theories had apparently impressive empirical support behind them. In 1973 the issue seemed to be resolved by Goldfeld's exhaustive and systematic comparative tests. The debate was over.

Post-1973 Demand for Money Estimates

Doubts about Goldfeld's Specification　　It is now evident that Goldfeld's study, although an extremely impressive piece of research work, had not provided conclusive evidence on the correct specification of the demand for money function. On the one hand, Thomas Cooley and Stephen LeRoy suggest that Goldfeld overinterpreted his results, despite the extensive specification search.[12] Indeed, they conclude that all empirical estimates of demand for money functions have been so heavily biased by the investigators' expectations that even "the

[12]Thomas F. Cooley and Stephen F. LeRoy, "Identification and Estimation of Money Demand," *American Economic Review*, 71(5) December 1981, pp. 825–844.

negative interest elasticity of money demand reported in the literature represents prior beliefs much more than sample information."[13] On the other hand, no sooner had Goldfeld provided an apparently definitive study than the demand for money in the United States seemed to become unstable.

Missing Money   Starting in 1974 Goldfeld's money demand equation, which had explained fluctuations in demand so precisely over the period 1952–1973, began to overpredict. Between 1974 (I) and 1976 (II), the money demand figures predicted by equation (20.22) drifted off course by nearly 9 percent. At the time, it was presumed that the actual demand for money function had shifted down or leftwards. Since money demand was more difficult to predict, the demand for money had by definition become unstable.

Reestimating the   Another serious problem also arose from the fact that when equation
Goldfeld Equation   (20.22) was reestimated to include post-1973 data, the new coefficients acquired peculiar values. In the first place, the coefficient of $\ln(M1_{t-1}/P_{t-1})$ increased in value to 1 or more. As $(1 - \theta)$ approaches 1, θ falls to zero, implying that the adjustment process grinds to a halt. When $(1 - \theta)$ is greater than 1, θ is negative, implying an unstable adjustment process that moves actual real money balances away from their long-run desired levels. In the second place, the coefficient of $\ln(y)$ became so small that it was not significantly different from zero. Finally, the long-run interest-rate and income elasticities became implausibly large because of the fall in the value of θ.[14]

Post-1973   The demand for money in the United States became unstable just as a
Regulatory   number of institutional changes were taking place within the financial sys-
Changes   tem. In one way or another, all these changes sprang from the accelerating rate of inflation. One set of changes occurring in the mid-1970s were regulatory changes. In 1974, for example, banks were authorized to offer interest-earning savings deposits to local governments. In 1975 this authorization was extended to business accounts. At the same time, NOW accounts were permitted on an experimental basis in New England. The existence of these new close substitutes for M1 did indeed reduce money demand. However, by themselves these regulatory changes can account for only one-quarter of the downward shift in the money demand function.[15]

Post-1973   From the viewpoint of explaining the money demand shift, the develop-
Financial   ment of repurchase agreements (RPs) is perhaps the most significant finan-
Innovation   cial innovation that has occurred since 1973. As was explained in Chapter

[13]*Ibid.*, p. 843.

[14]Judd and Scadding, *op. cit.*, p. 996.

[15]*Ibid.*, p. 998.

6, the lender of funds buys a government security from the borrower, and the borrower agrees to repurchase the security at a fixed price on a predetermined date. The risk in the RP market is very low because the security is provided as collateral. Of greatest importance here is the fact that transaction costs in the RP market are substantially lower than transaction costs in, for example, the treasury bill market. Baumol's demand for money model shows that this transaction cost is a key determinant of the quantity of money held.

**Interest Rate
Ratchet Effect**

In fact, there are no direct measures of transaction costs in financial markets. However, one might argue that all innovations in cash management techniques such as the use of RPs involve high fixed setup costs. Hence, such innovations will occur only when interest rates reach new peak levels. Once the setup costs are incurred, the new technique will be used even if interest rates subsequently fall. This suggests that the previous peak interest rate could be used as an indicator or proxy for a reduction in transaction costs produced by financial innovation. Including the previous peak interest rate as a variable in the money demand function does improve its ability to predict. Nevertheless, the improvement is not so dramatic as to suggest that transaction cost reductions explain all the misbehavior of the Goldfeld money demand equation since 1973.

Alternative Adjustment Mechanisms

**Lagged Stock-
Adjustment Models**

All the empirical work on the post-1973 period discussed to this point used the same stock-adjustment mechanism as Goldfeld. In other words, the estimated equation contained the lagged real money stock as an explanatory variable to allow for partial adjustment to changes in interest rates and income in any given time period. It turns out, however, that patching up the Goldfeld equation with this stock-adjustment process has proved much less successful than has respecifying completely the process of dynamic adjustment in the money market.

**Direction of
Causality**

Since nominal GNP is affected by changes in the money supply only after a lag of about six months (Chapter 11), the lagged stock-adjustment process incorporated in the Goldfeld equation makes economic sense only if the direction of causality runs from interest rates and income to changes in the nominal stock of money. In fact, this was how many economists believed monetary policy worked, at least until 1979 but possibly right up to February 1984 (when contemporaneous reserve accounting was readopted—Chapter 10). The Fed pursued interest rate targets and made the money supply perfectly elastic at the desired rate of interest. Hence, the stock of money would shift gradually as demand for money adjusted with a lag to any change in the interest-rate target. In this case, causality runs from the interest rate to the money stock, and the money supply is endogenous. An *endogenous variable* is determined by other variables in the model. An *exogenous variable*, on the other hand, is determined independently or outside the system or model under analysis.

Credit Is Endogenous but Money Is Exogenous

The belief that the money supply is endogenous when monetary policy is conducted through interest rate targets rests on a failure to distinguish between money and credit.[16] If interest rates are pegged, the supply of credit is perfectly elastic at the target interest rate. When investment prospects look better, businesses increase their demands for credit. In the process of meeting the increased demand for credit, depository institutions, accommodated by open market purchases by the Fed, increase the supply of money through the lending-depositing-lending sequence described in Chapter 8. Initially, however, neither the interest rate nor nominal GNP changes. Hence, demand for money stays unchanged, but money supply rises. The money stock is not therefore determined by the variables on the right-hand side of the demand for money function. Hence, the money stock is an exogenous variable in the money demand model. That is, the money stock is determined by conditions in the credit market that are outside the demand for money model.

Exogenous Money and Interest Rate Behavior

If the nominal money stock is exogenous and nominal GNP takes six months to react to changes in the money supply, the only variable left to equate the demand for and the supply of money in the Goldfeld model is the interest rate. Hence the interest rate is the endogenous variable in the short run. Suppose, therefore, that equations (20.19) and (20.21) are rearranged so that the interest-rate variable appears on the left-hand side:

$$\ln(i) = \frac{1}{\beta_1}\ln\left(\frac{M}{P}\right) - \frac{\beta_0}{\beta_1} - \frac{\beta_2}{\beta_1}\ln(y) \tag{20.23}$$

$$\ln(i) = \frac{1}{\theta\beta_1}\ln\left(\frac{M}{P}\right) - \frac{\beta_0}{\beta_1} - \frac{\beta_2}{\beta_1}\ln(y) - \frac{(1-\theta)}{\theta\beta_1}\ln\left(\frac{M_{t-1}}{P_{t-1}}\right) \tag{20.24}$$

Equation (20.23) shows the equilibrium effect of money on the interest rate, while equation (20.24) shows the short-run or impact effect. Now, if θ is less than 1, the impact effect of a change in the money stock is greater than its equilibrium or long-run effect, since $1/\theta\beta_1$ is larger than $1/\beta_1$. This indicates that interest rates will overshoot their long-run levels when the supply of money is changed because of the lagged stock-adjustment process.

[16]Karl Brunner and Allan H. Meltzer, "An Aggregate Theory for a Closed Economy" in *Monetarism*, ed. Jerome Stein (Amsterdam: North-Holland, 1976), pp. 69–103.

Rationale for Partial Stock Adjustment

John Judd and John Scadding point out that this result seems inconsistent with the whole rationale for partial short-run adjustment.[17] The basis for a partial response lies in the fact that the costs of adjusting one's portfolio make it suboptimal to adjust fully to external shocks each time period. If this is so, then individuals will not attempt to get rid of unanticipated increases in money balances immediately. The costs of portfolio adjustment will result in a gradual disposal of the excess cash over time.

Partial Adjustment to Excess Money Balances and Interest-Rate Behavior

If people initially hold these unanticipated increases in money balances without attempting any immediate disposal of the excess, the impact on interest rates in the short run will actually be smaller than the long-run effects that are felt when all portfolio adjustments have been completed. With this alternative adjustment process, interest rates do not overshoot, as implied by the Goldfeld equation. Rather they approach their long-run levels smoothly as the public attempts to dispose of excess money balances by buying bonds gradually over time. The actual behavior of interest rates is indeed consistent with this alternative stock-adjustment process and is inconsistent with that implied by the Goldfeld equation.

The Judd-Scadding Model

A number of economists, including Jack Carr and Michael Darby, Warren Coats, and David Laidler, have developed and tested money models incorporating the alternative adjustment mechanism discussed above.[18] For illustrative purposes, however, the monthly money demand equation developed by Judd and Scadding is discussed here.[19] The Judd-Scadding equation allows the money stock to adjust with a lag both to changes in demand factors (income, interest rates, and prices) like the Goldfeld equation and to changes in a supply factor. Recognizing the fact that the supply of money is changed exogenously in the lending-depositing-lending sequence resulting from a change in the supply of bank loans, their equation includes the volume of bank loans BL as an explanatory variable:

$$\Delta\ln(M_t) = \delta\Delta\ln(BL_t) + \theta[\ln(M_t^d) - \delta\Delta\ln(BL_t) - \ln(M_{t-1})] \quad (20.25)$$

[17]John P. Judd and John L. Scadding, "Dynamic Adjustment in the Demand for Money: Tests of Alternative Hypotheses," *Federal Reserve Bank of San Francisco Economic Review*, Fall 1982, pp. 19–30.

[18]Jack Carr and Michael R. Darby, "The Role of Money Supply Shocks in the Short-Run Demand for Money," *Journal of Monetary Economics*, 8(2), September 1981, pp. 183–200; Warren L. Coats, "Modeling the Short-Run Demand for Money with Exogenous Supply," *Economic Inquiry*, 20(2), April 1982, pp. 222–239; and David E. W. Laidler, "The Demand for Money in the United States—Yet Again," *Journal of Monetary Economics*, Supplement 12, Spring 1980, pp. 219–271.

[19]John P. Judd and John L. Scadding, "*Comment on* What Do Money Market Models Tell Us About How to Implement Monetary Policy?" *Journal of Money, Credit and Banking*, 14(4,ii), November 1982, pp. 868–877.

The rate of change in the nominal M1 money stock is affected positively by the rate of change in bank loans and by factors increasing desired money balances above the previous period's money balances $\theta[\ln(M_t^d) - \ln(M_{t-1})]$. The coefficient θ indicates that a standard Goldfeld stock adjustment process is included. Finally, the term $-\theta\delta\Delta\ln(BL_t)$ shows the proportion of excess money supply created by $\delta\Delta\ln(BL_t)$ that is eliminated through portfolio adjustments in the current month.

The Judd-Scadding Model and the 1982–1983 Monetary Explosion

Between mid-June 1982 and mid-June 1983 the M1 money stock in the United States grew by 13 percent, the highest growth rate over a full 12-month period in the postwar period up to that time. The Fed explained away this dramatic monetary acceleration by first pointing out that All Savers Certificates maturing towards the end of 1982 would be held initially in the form of M1 money balances and then suggesting that the Super NOW accounts introduced at the beginning of 1983 could be raising the *demand* for money.

If money demand had indeed been raised by either of these phenomena or any other financial innovation or reform, then money demand equations that ignored these demand-stimulating effects would have underpredicted the money stock by mid-1983. Although the Judd-Scadding money equation was underpredicting the money stock by mid-1983, the error was far too small to be significant. Hence, its ability to predict the rate of change in the nominal money stock relatively accurately without taking account of possible sources of demand shifts suggests that demand for money remained stable over this period. This conclusion is supported by recent work by the staff of the Fed Board indicating that the extra funds attracted into M1 money balances in the form of Super NOW accounts had been completely counteracted by the outflow of funds from M1 money balances into the equally new money market deposit accounts (Chapter 1).[20]

In fact, the Judd-Scadding equation points to the sharp decline in nominal interest rates from the summer of 1982 to the first quarter of 1983, and to the increase in bank loans from April to July 1983 as the primary causes of the monetary explosion over this 12-month period. By August 1983 there was an excess supply of money caused by the rapid growth in bank loans. Unless monetary growth slows substantially, long-run equilibrium will be restored by accelerated growth in nominal GNP in the second half of 1983 and early 1984. The conditional prediction that inflation will have accelerated by the end of 1983 unless monetary growth slows considerably in the second half of 1983 will have been put to the test by the time this book is published. The reader will therefore be in a better position to judge the efficacy of the Judd-Scadding model than were the authors in the summer of 1983!

[20]Frederick T. Furlong, "New Deposit Instruments," *Federal Reserve Bulletin*, 69(5), May 1983, pp. 319–326.

Summary

1. The stability of money demand is a prerequisite for effective monetary policy that uses money supply targets.

2. Stability involves three elements: (1) predictability; (2) relatively few explanatory variables; (3) these explanatory variables' representing important links to aggregate spending and the real level of economic activity.

3. Using 2-year phase averages, changes in nominal net national product explain 96 percent of the variations in the money stock in the United States 1873–1975 from its average with the Cambridge k held constant.

4. The liquidity trap theory can be tested by estimating the following equation: $M/Y = b_0 + b_1[1/(i - i_T)]$, where i_T is the interest rate at which the trap occurs. Virtually all empirical tests suggest that money demand has a relatively low interest elasticity and that this elasticity does not increase as the interest rate falls. In other words, there is no convincing empirical support for the liquidity trap.

5. Empirical estimates generally find price and population elasticities equal to 1. The elasticity of money demand with respect to per capita real income appears to lie between 0.5 and 1 for M1 and between 1.2 and 1.8 for M2.

6. In monthly and quarterly demand for money models, there is some indication that money demand adjusts with a lag to changes in current income and interest rates.

7. Since 1973 the standard stock adjustment model of short-run money demand has failed to predict the money stock accurately. In part, this failure may be due to regulatory changes and financial innovations. However, better results for the post-1973 period are produced by models using alternative dynamic adjustment mechanisms.

8. Money holdings adjust slowly not only to changes in income and interest rates but also to unanticipated changes in money receipts. If exogenous monetary shocks occur, individuals adjust slowly to excess or deficient money supply.

9. The Judd-Scadding model predicted the 1982–1983 monetary explosion relatively accurately. Its causes appeared to be a dramatic fall in interest rates and a rapid expansion of bank loans. By mid-1983 there was a considerable excess money supply.

10. The excess money supply existing in mid-1983 could be removed by a sharp tightening of monetary policy in the second half of 1983. Otherwise, it could be expected to produce an acceleration in inflation by early 1984.

Questions

1. Why is the stability of money demand crucial for effective monetary targeting?

2. If the goal of monetary policy is to stabilize nominal GNP, what is the implication for price level movements over the business cycle?

3. What is meant by a stable demand for money?

4. What is the empirical evidence on the Cambridge equation?

5. How can one test for the existence of a liquidity trap?

6. What is the empirical evidence on the liquidity trap?

7. How does Henry Latané's study of money demand estimate the interest elasticity within a Cambridge equation framework?

8. How can price, population, and income elasticity of demand for money be estimated?

9. What is the empirical evidence on price and population elasticity of money demand?

10. What is the empirical evidence on the per capita real income elasticity of demand for money?

11. What is the rationale for a stock-adjustment lag in the money demand function?

12. What were the main findings of Goldfeld's 1973 money demand study?

13. Explain the nature of two problems with the use of Goldfeld's equation after 1973.

14. How could regulatory changes and financial innovation explain at least part of the overprediction of money demand by the Goldfeld equation in the late 1970s?

15. Explain the interest rate ratchet effect.

16. What is the main idea behind the formulation of an alternative adjustment mechanism?

17. How does the Judd-Scadding model incorporate exogenous monetary shocks in the money demand equation?

18. What did the Judd-Scadding model predict about the behavior of nominal GNP in the second half of 1983?

PART TEN

Postwar U.S.
Monetary History

The devaluation of the dollar in 1934 brought an end to the Great Depression. At $35 an ounce, the dollar was now undervalued with respect to the gold-bloc countries. The new competitive advantage gained by an undervalued dollar and capital inflows, fleeing foreign currencies which were in danger of being devalued, generated huge payments surpluses that were financed by gold inflows. These gold inflows added billions of dollars to the stock of high-powered money. When the Treasury bought gold, either from abroad or from domestic sources, it paid with a check on its account at one of the Federal Reserve banks. When the check was cashed, member banks were credited with reserves, thus increasing the stock of high-powered money. The Treasury would then print gold certificates of a corresponding amount and redeposit them at Federal Reserve banks to replenish its accounts.

These gold purchases, supplemented by increases in Treasury currency resulting from Treasury purchases of silver for monetary purposes, accounted for almost all of the 60 percent increase in high-powered money from March 1933 to May 1937. Federal Reserve actions accounted for virtually none of the increase. Since discount rates were generally above market rates of interest during this period, banks retired virtually all of their borrowings from the Fed. Member bank borrowings never exceeded $25 million after July 1934. Moreover, the Fed's holdings of government securities remained virtually unchanged from November 1933 to the end of March 1937.

From Lester V. Chandler, *American Monetary Policy, 1928–1941* (New York: Harper and Row, 1971), Chapters 16, 19, and 20; and Milton Friedman and Anna J. Schwartz, *A Monetary History of the United States, 1867–1960* (Princeton, N.J.: Princeton University Press for the National Bureau of Economic Research, 1963), Chapter 9.

Gold inflows propelled a substantial recovery from the depressed levels of 1933. Real net national produce rose 59 percent from 1933 to a cyclical peak in 1937. However, given the depressed level from which it began, the recovery was still incomplete. Real income was still only 3 percent higher in 1937 than at the cyclical peak in 1929. Since the population had grown by 6 percent in the interim, per capita real income was actually about 3 percent lower than in 1929. The unemployment rate was still a substantial 14.3 percent in 1937.

After $2\frac{1}{2}$ years of relative inactivity, the Fed again became a significant destabilizing force in the economy. The Banking Act of 1935 gave the Federal Reserve Board a new tool to use in controlling the banking system: the authority to raise or lower the reserve requirements of member banks. The Board used this new power with tragic results in 1936 and 1937.

The trauma of the banking failures of the early 1930s, together with extremely low market rates of interest, led commercial banks to accumulate reserves far in excess of legal requirements as a source of liquidity to meet unanticipated withdrawals. By 1936 these excess reserves totaled some $3 billion. Federal Reserve officials felt that these excess reserves were serving no useful purpose and might later serve as a source of undesired bank credit expansion. In an attempt to immobilize some of these excess reserves, the Board increased legal reserve requirements by 50 percent on August 16, 1936. Unfortunately, the Fed did not understand that commercial banks desired their excess reserves as a source of liquidity. In the next five months the reserve/deposit ratio rose sharply as banks attempted to restore their excess reserve positions. The result was a decline in the money supply multiplier which held the growth rate of the money supply to less than half the growth rate of high-powered money.

In early 1937 the Treasury made the situation even worse, deciding to sterilize the effects of gold imports on high-powered money by financing its purchases of gold by issuing interest-bearing securities rather than drawing on its deposits at Federal Reserve banks. As a result of this sterilization policy, high-powered money did not grow at all during the first nine months of 1937. In the midst of this slowdown in the growth of high-powered money, the Fed again raised reserve requirements in two steps on March 1 and May 1, 1937. The combination of the slowdown in the growth of high-powered money and the decline in the money supply multiplier resulting from the banks' attempts to restore excess reserve positions caused the money supply to fall by 6 percent in 1937.

The decline in economic activity following this monetary contraction was extremely violent. Although the recession was relatively short, lasting only 13 months, it was the third worst cyclical decline in the twentieth century, being exceeded only in 1920–1921 and 1929–1933.

From May 1937 to June 1938 industrial production and factory employment fell 25 percent. The unemployment rate rose from 10.9 percent to almost 20 percent.

The recession was brought to a halt by a reversal of the Treasury's and Federal Reserve's earlier actions. In April 1938 the Fed reduced reserve requirements to a level that eliminated one-quarter of the combined earlier increases. More important, though, the Treasury abandoned its gold sterilization policy. The outbreak of war in Europe suddenly inundated the United States with gold inflows as European funds were transferred to the safety of the United States and the belligerent countries turned to the United States for war materials. Between July 1938 and the end of 1940 the monetary gold stock increased $8.9 billion. None of this increase was sterilized. As a result, the money supply increased 27 percent.

Economic recovery began in July 1938. By the time the United States entered the war, the unemployment rate had been reduced to well under 10 percent, the lowest rate since 1930.

U.S. Domestic Monetary Policy, 1945–1968

From the End of the War to the Treasury–Federal Reserve Accord

Pegging Government Security Prices

During World War II the Fed assumed the subordinate role of helping the U.S. Treasury sell government securities to finance the war effort. The Federal Open Market Committee announced that it would keep the rate on treasury bills fixed at the incredibly low annual yield of three-eighths of 1 percent. This meant that the Fed committed itself to buy or sell any quantity of treasury bills offered or demanded at that price. Although no such commitment was made with respect to other government securities, the Fed effectively pegged the rate on long-term government bonds at $2\frac{1}{2}$ percent, as shown in Figure 21.1. This policy of supporting the prices of government securities prevented the Fed from having any effective control over the money supply. Money supply growth had to be whatever was necessary to maintain the par value of government securities.

Fixed Interest Rates and Monetary Policy

If the level of interest rates implied by the pegged prices of government securities were below the interest rate consistent with flow equilibrium, monetary growth would have to be great enough to provide excess liquidity sufficient to depress market rates of interest below flow equilibrium. Conversely, to raise market rates of interest above flow equilibrium, monetary growth must be slow enough to produce a negative liquidity effect. Moreover, since the rate of monetary growth is itself a principal determinant of income growth and inflation, initially small discrepancies between the interest rate implied by the Fed's bond-pegging policy and that consistent with flow equilibrium can lead to runaway inflations or deflations.

Figure 21.1 Short-Term Interest Rates, 1940–1957

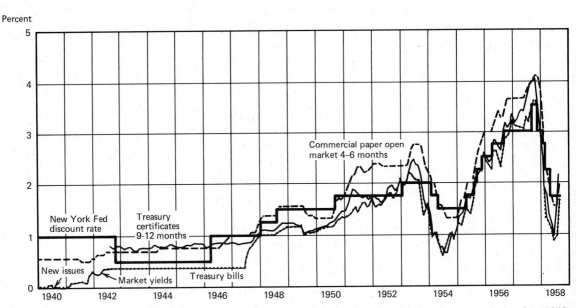

Source: Board of Governors of the Federal Reserve System, *Chart Book* (September 1958), p. 41.

Monetary Policy Instability

Consider the analytical example in Figure 21.2. The economy is assumed to be in flow equilibrium at an interest rate of i_0. If the Fed wants to keep the level of interest rates below i_0, say at $\bar{i}$, it must buy government securities in open market operations, thus increasing the money supply. The liquidity effect of an excess supply of money pushes interest rates below the level consistent with flow equilibrium, enabling the Fed to achieve its interest-rate target. However, the increase in the money supply will, after a lag, cause GNP to increase, and the demand for money will rise. In order for the interest-rate target of $\bar{i}$ to be maintained, the money supply must grow as fast as the demand for money increases so that the necessary excess supply of money is maintained. This acceleration in the rate of monetary growth will eventually lead to higher rates of inflation. When individuals come to expect higher inflation rates, saving and investment schedules will shift up (from S to S' and from I to I'), raising the interest rate consistent with flow equilibrium. Now the Fed must create an even larger gap between the supply of and demand for money to maintain its interest-rate target. This requires even larger open market purchases and a further acceleration in the rate of monetary growth, eventually leading to a further rise in the rate of inflation.

Figure 21.2   Interest Rates Pegged Below Flow Equilibrium

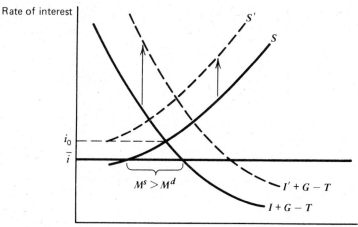

The economy is in flow equilibrium at an interest rate of i_0. The Fed attempts to hold the interest rate at $\bar{\imath}$ by producing an excess supply of money. Eventually, excess money supply will produce inflation. Higher expected inflation shifts the saving and investment functions up, raising the flow equilibrium interest rate. Now the Fed must create an even larger excess supply of money to keep the interest rate at $\bar{\imath}$.

Pegged Interest Rates and Inflationary Expectations

As long as the Fed follows a policy of pegging bond prices, inflationary expectations held by the public tend to be self-fulfilling prophecies. Inflationary expectations tend to raise the interest rate consistent with flow equilibrium. In order to maintain its interest-rate target, the Fed must accelerate the rate of monetary growth. Expectations of deflation, on the other hand, tend to reduce the interest rate consistent with flow equilibrium and thus force the Fed to reduce the rate of monetary growth.

Wartime Deficit Finance

In order to maintain interest rates below flow equilibrium during World War II, the Fed was forced to make open market purchases of government securities, thus financing some of the wartime expenditures by money creation. During the $4\frac{1}{2}$ years from January 1942 to June 1946 the money supply (the M1 definition is used throughout unless otherwise stated) rose 116 percent, an annual rate of growth of 17 percent. However, the inflationary pressure arising from this monetary expansion was largely repressed by wartime price controls and rationing. Wholesale prices rose only 15 percent from the imposition of price controls in May 1942 to the removal of controls in June 1946. Because of rationing and the shortage of automobiles and other consumer durables that were not produced during the war, consumers had few outlets for spending. The public was effective-

Figure 21.3 Gross National Product, M1 Money Stock, and the Cambridge *k*,
1916–1957

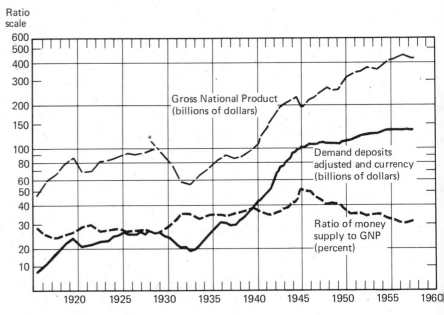

*Change in series.

Source: Board of Governors of the Federal Reserve System, *Chart Book* (September 1958), p. 11.

ly forced to accumulate money balances and government securities because their rising incomes could not be used to purchase consumer goods. By 1946 they held extraordinarily large money balances amounting to six months of gross national product, as shown in Figure 21.3.

Abolition of Price Controls   When price controls were suspended in mid-1946, prices soared. Wholesale prices rose 24 percent during the second half of 1946, more than they had during the preceding 4½ years. However, even with this sharp increase in the price level, the public still held money balances equal to five months of gross national product in 1948. This continued high ratio of money balances to income was probably due to widespread expectations of deflation. Individuals were still scarred by memories of the Great Depression. One survey taken in 1948 indicated that over 40 percent of the public thought that the nation was on the brink of a new depression that would be as bad as that of the 1930s. Because of these widespread expectations of deflation, money and government securities appeared to be an attractive form in which to hold wealth.

Postwar Interest-Rate Pegging and 1948–1949 Recession

Even after the war ended, the Fed continued to peg prices and yields of government securities. Early in 1947 the Fed was successful in persuading the Treasury to allow it to stop supporting the price of treasury bills, and the ⅜ percent interest-rate peg was terminated. However, the interest-rate peg for long-term government bonds remained at 2½ percent. Despite the continuing commitment to peg long-term government bond yields, the Fed made virtually no open market purchases in 1948. Indeed, with widespread expectations of deflation, the interest rate pegs maintained by the Fed were actually above the level of interest rates consistent with flow equilibrium, requiring a *reduction* in the money supply. After increasing at an annual rate of 5 percent since June 1946, the money supply fell 2 percent during 1948. This decline in the money supply precipitated a recession which began in November 1948. By July 1949 the unemployment rate had risen to 6.3 percent from 3 percent in late 1948. Almost twice as many Americans were out of work as had been a year earlier. However, the recession also brought a halt to the postwar inflation. By the end of 1949 the cost of living had fallen 5 percent and wholesale prices were down 11 percent from their peaks in August 1948.

The 1948–1949 recession turned out to be fairly mild. By early 1950, prices stopped declining and business activity started to recover. Then on June 24, 1950, North Korean forces crossed the thirty-eighth parallel in a full-scale invasion of South Korea. Three days later the United Nations Security Council adopted a U.S. resolution approving armed intervention on the side of the South Koreans. By July 1, U.S. troops had landed in Korea.

Korean War Boom

The outbreak of the Korean War drastically altered expectations. The public went on a buying spree. By mid-July department store sales were 50 percent higher than they had been the month before. Expectations of inflation pushed up the interest rate consistent with flow equilibrium to levels that again required the Fed to purchase government securities. The money supply started to grow at a rapid rate. The spending boom sparked off by the Korean War was also fueled by a rapid fall in the ratio of desired money holdings to gross national product (the Cambridge k); inflationary expectations made the holding of money balances less attractive. Between May 1950 and March 1951 the cost of living rose 8 percent and wholesale prices increased 19 percent.

The Fed versus the Treasury

The Fed felt that it had to abandon the pegging of government security yields to prevent runaway inflation. However, the Treasury insisted that the Fed continue to hold interest rates down to their pegged levels. The Fed under its chairman, Marriner S. Eccles, had proclaimed its independence from the Treasury with respect to pegging short-term government yields in 1947. Eccles's championship of an independent Fed produced continuous conflict between the Treasury and the Fed. When Eccles's term as chairman of the Federal Reserve Board expired on February 1, 1948, Truman did not reappoint him. Instead he appointed Thomas McCabe. However, Eccles did continue to serve out the last three years of his term as a governor of the Board. Eccles's reduction in rank combined with the outbreak of war served to bring the conflict between the Treasury and the Fed to a climax.

The 1951 Accord

The Fed-Treasury conflict finally became public in early 1951. In an address delivered at a luncheon meeting of the New York Board of Trade on January 18, the Secretary of the Treasury, John Snyder, stated: "In the firm belief that the 2½ percent long-term rate is fair and equitable to the investor and that market stability is essential, the Treasury Department has concluded, after joint conference with President Truman and Chairman McCabe of the Federal Reserve Board, that the refunding of new money issues will be financed within the pattern of that rate." The Fed quickly denied that it had made any such agreement. President Truman then summoned the Federal Open Market Committee to the White House on January 31. Following the meeting, he announced that the Fed had pledged to maintain yields on government securities at existing levels. Marriner Eccles immediately told the press that he was astonished at the president's version of what took place and that no agreement to support government bonds had been reached. The Federal Reserve Board then informed the Treasury that, as of February 19, it would no longer maintain existing prices in the government bond market. The president and the Treasury finally backed down on March 4, when the Treasury and the Fed issued a joint announcement which read:

> The Treasury and the Federal Reserve have reached a full accord with respect to debt management and monetary policies to be pursued in furthering their common purpose to assure the successful financing of the government's requirements and, at the same time, to minimize the monetization of the public debt.

Under the terms of the Accord, the Treasury exchanged new long-term bonds bearing a 2¾ percent yield for outstanding long-term bonds, and the Fed withdrew its active support from the government securities market.

By the end of March, Thomas McCabe had resigned as both chairman and member of the Board. Marriner Eccles retired in June. President Truman appointed as the new chairman of the Federal Reserve Board the Assistant Secretary of the Treasury, who had helped negotiate the Accord, William McChesney Martin.

Floating Interest Rates and Money Demand

The Treasury–Fed Accord marked the beginning of a revival of independent monetary policy in the United States. The abandonment of rigid support prices made government bonds far less liquid than they had been. Because their prices now fluctuated with market forces, long-term government bonds were no longer a close substitute for money balances. So long as the prices of government securities were pegged, the risk (measured by the standard deviation of the subjective probability distribution of possible bond yields) was close to zero. After the Accord, the public suddenly faced a much larger expected variance in the return on government bonds with little increase in expected yield. The effect of this shift in perceived bond price risk on the demand for money can be analyzed easily using Tobin's model of liquidity preference presented in Chapter 19.

Tobin's Model of Liquidity Preference

Consider the portfolio opportunity lines in Figure 21.4. The straight line OA represents the portfolio opportunity line during the period of bond price pegging. If people held all of their portfolios in long-term bonds, they could earn an expected return of $2\frac{1}{2}$ percent with very little risk.

Figure 21.4　The Accord's Effect on the Demand for Money

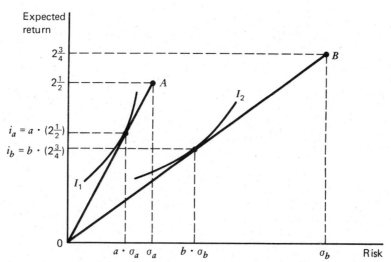

The straight line OA represents the opportunity line when bond prices are pegged at a yield of $2\frac{1}{2}$ percent. The risk of an all-bond portfolio is σ_a in this case. Individuals choose to hold a proportion a of their portfolios in bonds and the expected return on the portfolio is $a \cdot (2\frac{1}{2})$ percent. After the Fed stopped pegging rates, the government bond rate rose to $2\frac{3}{4}$ percent and the risk increased to σ_b. The new optimal portfolio where I_2 is tangential to OB consists of a proportion of only b in bonds. In this case, the portfolio's yield falls from i_a to i_b and demand for money increases.

Alternatively, they could hold money with a zero return and zero risk. Given the preference function represented by the indifference curves I_1 and I_2, these individuals would choose to hold a proportion a of their portfolios in bonds and $(1 - a)$ in money, yielding an expected return on the whole portfolio of $a \cdot (2\frac{1}{2})$ percent. After the Accord, the yield on government bonds rose to $2\frac{3}{4}$ percent, but the perceived risk increased substantially. As a result, the portfolio opportunity line rotated in a clockwise direction to OB. Given the individuals' preference function, they would now choose to hold a proportion b of their portfolios in bonds and $(1 - b)$ in money, yielding an expected overall return of i_b. Since $b \cdot (2\frac{3}{4})$ is less than $a \cdot (2\frac{1}{2})$, b must be smaller than a. That is, the net effect of the Treasury–Fed Accord was to decrease the portion of portfolios held in bonds. Thus, the immediate effect of the Accord was to increase the demand for money.

Decline in Cambridge *k* Reversed and Boom Ended

Despite a continuing increase in the stock of money, the Accord brought a halt to the fall in the Cambridge k and thus removed one source of inflationary pressure. In fact, the Cambridge k actually rose for about a year following the Accord. This rise in the demand for money brought an end to the spending boom, and the inflation which had begun with the outbreak of the Korean War was over.

The Eisenhower Years

Increased Discount Window Borrowing

Early in 1953 the Fed began to fear a resumption of inflation. Although prices had not actually begun to rise, the economy was operating close to capacity and the Fed detected some signs of inventory accumulation in anticipation of rising prices. The Fed was also very concerned about the rapid growth of bank loans. The elimination of consumer credit controls in 1952 allowed commercial banks to make lucrative consumer loans. The existence of these high-yielding loan opportunities made borrowing from the Fed's discount window highly attractive. From a level of $307 million in March 1952, member banks had increased their borrowings from the Fed to $1593 million in December.

Discount Rate Raised in 1953

On January 15, 1953, the Federal Reserve Board raised the discount rate from $1\frac{3}{4}$ to 2 percent. Commercial banks reacted to this increase by gradually reducing reserves borrowed from the Fed. Banks continued, however, to increase their loan portfolios. As a result, the entire burden of adjusting to the lower levels of reserves fell on the government securities market. Commercial banks sold $4.4 billion of government securities in the first four months of 1953.

Fed Abandons Government Security Price Support

In March 1953 the Federal Open Market Committee finally asserted its complete independence from the Treasury with respect to pegging the prices of government securities. The Federal Open Market Committee published the following changes in its operating procedures:

> It is not now the policy of the Committee to support any pattern of prices and yields in the Government securities market, and intervention in the Government securities market is solely to effectuate the objectives of monetary and credit policy. . . .

Interest Rates Soar

The new administration of President Dwight D. Eisenhower did not object to the Federal Open Market Committee's "hands-off" policy during periods of treasury financing. Eisenhower had campaigned for sound money and a lengthening of the maturity structure of the federal debt. Shortly after the Fed announced its new policy of not supporting prices of government securities, the Treasury announced in April that it would offer a 25 to 30-year bond with a $3\frac{1}{4}$ percent coupon rate. This news set off a drastic drop in bond prices. When the Treasury's new bonds were auctioned on April 13, only about $1 billion of the bids were accepted. These bonds sold at a $1\frac{1}{2}$ percent discount during the following week. Interest rates rose to their highest levels in 20 years. The financial community, accustomed to the artificial stability of bond prices during the era of Fed price support, was bewildered at the collapse of bond prices.

Fed Eases Monetary Policy under Criticism

Subject to a barrage of criticism by both Congress and the press, the Fed retreated in May. The Federal Open Market Committee purchased approximately $1 billion of government securities in May and June. The Board lowered reserve requirements in June and July, thus reducing required reserves by about $1.2 billion. Despite this easing of monetary policy, the Fed still kept a tight reign on the growth of the money supply. After increasing at a rate of $4\frac{1}{2}$ percent a year during 1950, 1951, and 1952, money supply growth slowed to 1 percent from May 1953 to January 1954.

Monetary Slowdown and the 1953–1954 Recession

This slowdown in the rate of monetary growth, together with the end of the Korean War in the third quarter of 1953, caused the 1953–1954 recession. Although many forecasters warned of an impending depression, the recession was extremely mild. The unemployment rate rose from the extraordinarily low level of 2 percent in early 1953 to 5 percent in 1954, well under the level reached in the 1948–1949 recession.

Monetary Stimulus in 1954

Early in 1954 the Fed took actions to relax its monetary restraint. The discount rate was reduced in February, April, and May 1954. Reserve requirements were lowered again in June and July. The rate of money supply growth accelerated to 4 percent a year from early 1954 to April

1955. This monetary stimulus brought the recession to an end in August 1954.

The 1953–1954 recession was followed by an economic boom. By mid-1955 the economy was approaching full employment, with the unemployment rate falling below 4 percent. Prices began to rise. The lag between the initial acceleration in the rate of monetary growth in early 1954 and the resulting acceleration in the rate of inflation was approximately $1\frac{1}{2}$ to 2 years, a lag which was to be typical in the postwar period.

Discount Rate Raised in 1955 and 1956

The Fed took action to restrain inflation by raising the discount rate from $1\frac{1}{2}$ to 3 percent in six increments of one-quarter percent each in April, August, September, and November 1955, and April and August 1956. Nevertheless, loan demand, fueled by an investment boom, pushed up short-term interest rates even faster. As a result, banks continued to borrow heavily at the discount window, causing the money supply to grow, albeit at a slower rate of 1.2 percent a year from April 1955 to January 1957.

Open Market Sales in 1957

In early 1957 the Fed increased its monetary restraint sharply by withdrawing unborrowed reserves from the banking system through open market sales. In August 1957 the discount rate was raised from 3 to $3\frac{1}{2}$ percent. These restrictive actions caused the money supply to fall at a rate of 0.8 percent a year during 1957. By August 1957 the economy had entered its third postwar recession.

1957–1958 Recession and Easier Monetary Policy

The recession of 1957–1958 was short, but fairly severe. The unemployment rate shot up from 4.2 percent in August 1957 to 7.4 percent in April 1958. The Fed reacted quickly to ease its monetary policy. In November 1957 the discount rate was reduced to 3 percent and further reductions brought it down to $1\frac{3}{4}$ percent by April 1958. The Federal Open Market Committee authorized modest purchases of government securities in March 1958 and the Board of Governors lowered member bank reserve requirements against demand deposits in February, March, and April. Market rates of interest fell sharply. The yield on treasury bills dropped from 3.6 percent in October 1957 to below 1 percent in May 1958. With this deliberate shift in monetary policy, the money supply grew at 4.1 percent a year from January 1958 to August 1959. The economy started to recover in April 1958 and by mid-1959 the unemployment rate had declined to 4.9 percent.

Discount Rate Raised in 1958 and 1959

The recovery, however, was to be short-lived. Fears of a resurgence of inflation and concern over gold outflows caused the Fed to raise the discount rate in five steps from $1\frac{3}{4}$ percent in April 1958 to 4 percent in September 1959. Despite these increases in the discount rate, sharply rising market rates of interest still made it attractive for banks to borrow from the discount window and the money supply continued to rise until the summer of 1959.

1959 Steel Strike and Shifts in the Investment Function

One factor that had a significant effect on monetary policy in 1959 was a steel strike which began on July 15. During the first half of 1959, inventories of steel were built up as a precaution against the possibility of strike-induced shortages. This inventory demand for steel shifted the investment schedule to the right and raised the level of interest rates consistent with flow equilibrium, as shown in Figure 21.5. Despite increases in the discount rate from $2\frac{1}{2}$ percent to 3 percent in March, and to $3\frac{1}{2}$ percent in June, the level of interest rates consistent with flow equilibrium rose just as fast, so the money supply continued to grow at about 4 percent a year.

When the strike actually began in July, however, the inventory accumulation of the first half of 1959 was reversed, and steel inventories were drawn down. As a result, the investment schedule shifted to the left and the interest rate consistent with flow equilibrium fell. This drop in the interest rate consistent with flow equilibrium, together with a further increase in the discount rate to 4 percent in September, brought the expansion in the money supply to a halt and the money supply fell at an annual rate of about 2 percent during the second half of 1959 and the first half of 1960. This decline in the money supply brought the recovery to an end and the country entered another recession before it had recovered completely from the previous one.

Figure 21.5   Effect of a Buildup in Steel Inventories on the Interest Rate Consistent with Flow Equilibrium

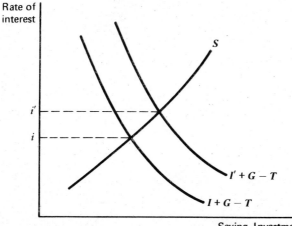

The buildup in steel inventories in anticipation of the 1959 steel strike shifted the investment schedule from I to I', raising the interest rate consistent with flow equilibrium from i to i'.

Monetary Policy and the 1960 Recession

Although the Eisenhower administration economists expressed little concern over the deteriorating economy, Vice-President Richard Nixon's economic adviser, Arthur Burns, warned Nixon that the Fed's monetary policy would produce a recession in 1960. This could seriously jeopardize Nixon's chances of being elected president. Besides teaching at Columbia University, Arthur Burns was the expert on business cycles at the National Bureau of Economic Research. His experience as chairman of the Council of Economic Advisors in the Eisenhower administration from 1953 to 1956 had convinced him of the potential importance of economic prosperity in election years. The prospects for 1960 did not look good for Richard Nixon. After all, the Fed under the leadership of William McChesney Martin (a Democrat) could not be expected to worry unduly about the political aspirations of a Republican candidate for president.

Recession and the 1960 Election

Although Nixon urged the administration to put pressure on the Fed to ease its monetary policy, Eisenhower refused to compromise the Fed's independence. Arthur Burn's prediction that the Fed's monetary policy would cost Nixon the election turned out to be accurate. Real output fell at an annual rate of $1\frac{1}{2}$ percent from the first to the fourth quarter of 1960. The unemployment rate rose from about 5 percent at the beginning of 1960 to over 6 percent by election day. Nixon's opponent, John F. Kennedy, concentrated his campaign on the economic issues of growth and employment. The Democratic campaign platform came out flatly for a 5 percent growth rate in real gross national product. In the final days of the campaign these economic issues became decisive as the apparent downturn in the economy created widespread fear of rising unemployment. "In October, usually a month of rising employment, the jobless rolls increased by 452,000," Nixon would write in his memoirs. "All the speeches, television broadcasts, and precinct work in the world could not counteract that one hard fact." On election day the country was in the midst of the fourth postwar recession and John Kennedy squeaked into the presidency by a margin of 0.2 percent of the popular vote—the narrowest in history.

Eisenhower and the Fed

During Eisenhower's two terms as president the economy had been through three recessions. Each of these recessions had been preceded by a deliberate slowdown in the rate of monetary growth engineered by the Fed to keep inflation in check. Eisenhower had found William McChesney Martin's views on monetary restraint congenial and had refrained from imposing White House pressure on Federal Reserve monetary policy, even when it cost the Republican party the 1960 election. As a result of the Fed's monetary restraint, the unemployment rate in December 1960 was 6.6 percent, more than twice the level it had been when Eisenhower came to office. Eisenhower later wrote in defense of his support for the Fed's policy: "Critics overlook the inflationary psychology during the mid-fifties and which I thought it necessary to defeat." This was to be the last time for more than a decade that the White House would seriously support the Fed's attempts to fight inflation for any length of time. Eisenhower's "defeat" of inflationary expectations left his successor with an extremely favorable short-run Phillips curve, thus making possible the long expansion that followed.

The Kennedy Era

Kennedy's Campaign Pledge

John F. Kennedy had based much of his campaign upon the need "to get the country moving again." Early in the campaign he said: "This costly tight money policy can—and must—be reversed." Later, while debating Senator Lyndon Johnson in front of the Texas delegation, he reiterated that it was "our great task as a party to demonstrate that we can make a free society work, that we can develop economic policies which will prevent a slide into recession which I think the high interest rate policies, hard money policies of this administration are going to bring about in the next twelve months unless there's a change in administration." Kennedy pledged to offer policies that would produce an annual growth in output of 5 percent, almost twice the average during the Eisenhower administration.

Easy Monetary Policy in 1960 and 1961

The independence of the Fed posed no problem for Kennedy's economic program. The Fed under the chairmanship of William McChesney Martin quickly embraced the White House's new philosophy of easy credit. Actually, the Fed had already begun to ease its restrictive monetary policy before Kennedy's election. Beginning in late March 1960 the Fed started supplying reserves to member banks through open market purchases. The discount rate was reduced from 4 to $3\frac{1}{2}$ percent in June and was reduced further to 3 percent in August. Reserve requirements were reduced in September and December 1960. These actions halted the decline in the money supply. From June 1960 to April 1962 the money supply increased at an annual rate of 2.35 percent. By the time John Kennedy was inaugurated on January 20, 1961, the economy had already begun to recover from the recession.

Recovery Slows in 1962

The first year of recovery saw real gross national product increase by over 7 percent. This recovery, however, started to lose steam during 1962. In early 1962 there was a definite slowdown in the rate of monetary growth; the money supply did not grow at all from April through October. This was followed by a slowdown in the rate of economic growth in the last part of 1962 and early 1963. After reaching a level of 7 percent in early 1961, the unemployment rate had fallen to $5\frac{1}{2}$ percent in early 1962. Now the slowdown in economic growth started to push it back up to 6 percent. The Fed shared the Kennedy administration's concern with the weakening economy but felt that interest rates should not be lowered further because of balance-of-payments considerations. The United States had a balance-of-payments deficit. Any reduction in interest rates relative to those abroad would cause capital outflows, making that deficit even worse.

Fiscal Policy in 1962

The Kennedy administration came up with a solution to this policy dilemma by proposing an extremely stimulative fiscal policy. By legislating tax incentives for new investment and increasing the federal budget deficit, Kennedy's fiscal policy substantially increased the demand for loanable funds. This fiscal policy enabled the money supply to resume its growth without interest rates falling. In 1962 Kennedy took two steps to stimulate private investment. He accelerated the rate at which businesses could depreciate their investments for tax purposes and instituted an investment tax credit permitting business firms to deduct from their tax bill an amount equal to 7 percent of newly purchased plant and equipment. These tax incentives to investment set off a surge in capital spending. After increasing only 4.5 percent in 1962, real gross nonresidential fixed investment rose 11 percent in 1963 and 12 percent in 1964. The increase in demand for loanable funds to finance this investment boom started to push up short-term interest rates in late 1962. The rise in loan rates made the Fed's 3 percent discount rate look very attractive. Member banks borrowed heavily from the Fed and the Federal Open Market Committee attempted to "lean against the wind" (of rising interest rates) by purchasing government securities. These actions accelerated the rate of growth in the money supply. After growing at an annual rate of 1.8 percent from June 1960 to September 1962, the money supply accelerated to 3.7 percent a year from September 1962 to March 1964, despite an increase in the discount rate from 3 to $3\frac{1}{2}$ percent in June 1963. Economic growth, which had begun to falter during late 1962 and early 1963, accelerated to a very rapid rate starting in the second quarter of 1963. From the second quarter of 1963 to the first quarter of 1964, real gross national product increased at a rate of almost 6 percent per year. Moreover, Kennedy's program of tax incentives for investment spending succeeded in stimulating economic growth without worsening the balance of payments; the acceleration in the rate of monetary growth occurred in the face of rising interest rates, as shown in Figures 21.6 and 21.7.

Tax Cut in 1964

In late 1962 President Kennedy proposed a sizable reduction in personal and corporate income tax rates as an additional fiscal stimulus. Kennedy never lived to see the passage of this legislation: on November 22, 1963, an assassin shot him down in Dallas. However, Congress did eventually pass a modified version of his proposed tax cut on February 26, 1964. Personal income tax rates were reduced by an average of 21 percent, two-thirds becoming effective in 1964 and the rest in 1965. The corporate income tax rate was reduced from 52 to 48 percent.

Figure 21.6   Money Supply and Interest Rates, 1958–1966

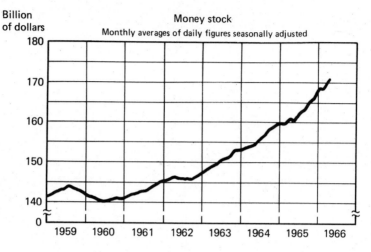

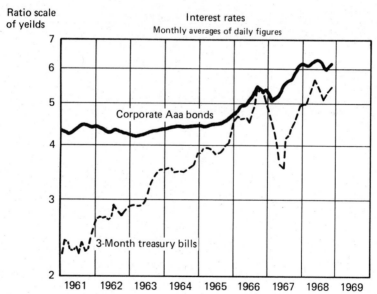

Source: *Federal Reserve Bank of St. Louis Review,* 48(5), May 1966, p. 2, and *Federal Reserve Bank of St. Louis Review,* 49(1), January 1967, p. 4.

By the time the 1964 tax cut took effect, the economy was already booming. The Fed did not attempt to maintain current levels of interest rates in the face of this additional fiscal stimulus. Indeed, the discount rate was raised from 3½ to 4 percent in November 1964. However, despite the increase in interest rates, the money supply continued to grow at about 4 percent a year.

Figure 21.7   Trends and Fluctuations of Money, Output, and Unemployment

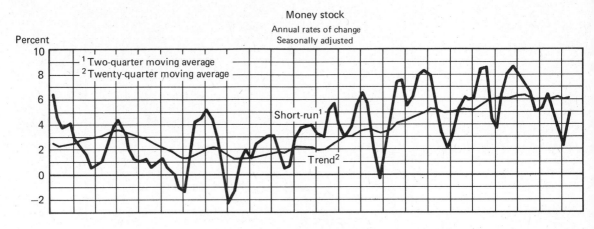

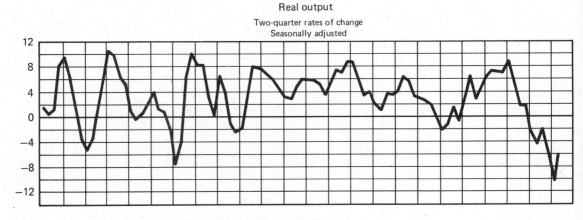

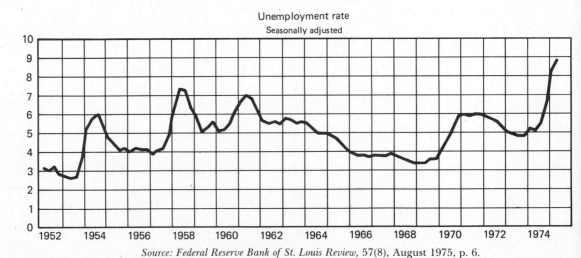

Source: Federal Reserve Bank of St. Louis Review, 57(8), August 1975, p. 6.

Lyndon Johnson and the Vietnam War

Economic Boom and the 1964 Election

By the election of November 1964, the economy was in the middle of the longest postwar expansion to date. The unemployment rate had fallen to 5 percent and prices were still rising by less than $1\frac{1}{2}$ percent a year. Lyndon Johnson was elected president in his own right by a landslide—winning by an all-time record 61.1 percent of the popular vote. Johnson had campaigned as the peace candidate and repeatedly promised "no wider war in Vietnam." In June 1965, however, 23,000 American "advisers" were committed to combat, and by the end of the year the United States would have 184,000 troops in the area. Government expenditures for defense and "Great Society" programs rose rapidly.

Budget Deficit Soars after 1965

The Johnson administration was reluctant to raise taxes to cover the increase in government spending. President Johnson feared that if he confronted Congress with a tax proposal to cover the increased expenditures for the war in Indochina, Congress would respond by slashing appropriations for his Great Society programs. As a result, the necessary tax increases were postponed and the unified budget deficit soared from $1.6 billion in 1965 to more than $25 billion in 1968. It was not until June 1968, three years after the rapid increase in military expenditures had started, that Congress finally passed legislation which imposed a 10 percent surtax on corporate and personal income taxes.

Monetary Acceleration in 1965 and 1966

Inflation was not the inevitable consequence of the growing government deficit. Inflation occurred because the Fed helped to finance the deficit through monetary expansion. After increasing at an annual rate of 3.9 percent from September 1962 to June 1965, the money supply accelerated to 6.9 percent from June 1965 to April 1966. This acceleration in the growth of the money supply took place at a time when the economy was operating very close to full capacity. Since the unemployment rate had fallen virtually to the "full employment" level of 4 percent by late 1965, very little further reduction in the unemployment rate was possible.

When the money supply increases rapidly but output cannot increase significantly because the economy is already producing at capacity, prices must rise. This is the classic case of demand-pull inflation. After increasing at a rate of about $1\frac{1}{2}$ percent per year from early 1961 to the summer of 1965, prices were rising at an annual rate of $3\frac{1}{2}$ percent by early 1966.

The Fed's Finest Hour and Monetary Restraint in 1966

In December 1965 the Federal Reserve Board, concerned about emerging inflation, signaled a shift to a more restrictive monetary policy by raising the discount rate from 4 to $4\frac{1}{2}$ percent, despite the objections of the Johnson administration. Lyndon Johnson, who had long opposed high interest rates, took the move by the Fed as a personal affront. He immediately called Chairman Martin to Texas, where both the president and Treasury

Secretary Fowler told Martin that they strongly opposed the increase in the discount rate.

This confrontation has been called "the Fed's finest hour" because Martin refused to heed President Johnson's request that the discount rate increase be rescinded. Nevertheless, partly because of White House criticism, the Fed continued to supply reserves through open market purchases of government securities until April 1966 and the money supply continued to grow at an extremely rapid rate. In May, however, the Fed switched sharply towards restraint. At its May meeting the Federal Open Market Committee inserted a "proviso clause" in its generally restrictive directive calling for even greater restraint if growth in reserves did not moderate substantially. Although the directive did not change the Fed's basic policy goal, that was the first time that the committee's instructions had focused directly on a monetary aggregate. Previously, the committee had stated its instructions only in terms of money market (interest-rate) conditions. The proviso clause focused attention on a desired reduction in reserve growth at a time when unanticipated increases in the demand for credit made money market conditions an increasingly unreliable guide for monetary policy. The extent to which the proviso clause helped the Fed to implement its policy of restraint is uncertain. What is clear is that monetary growth suddenly decelerated. From April to October 1966 the money supply actually fell at an annual rate of $1\frac{1}{2}$ percent. This monetary restraint brought on the 1966–1967 minirecession and a moderation of inflationary pressures.

Government Deficits and Interest Rates

The combination of large government deficits and a restrictive monetary policy also caused interest rates to rise to their highest levels since the 1920s. To illustrate the effects of government deficits on the level of interest rates, consider Figure 21.8. The economy is assumed to be in flow equilibrium at an interest rate of i_0. The increase in government expenditures associated with the war in Vietnam caused the government deficit to increase. As a result, the $I + G - T$ schedule shifted to the right, causing the level of interest rates consistent with flow equilibrium to rise from i_0 to i_1. Since government borrowing to pay for military expenditures competed with private borrowing for the funds available, interest rates had to rise in order to reduce private demands for funds. The restrictive monetary policy from April to October 1966 created excess demand for money, thus raising interest rates even further to i_2.

Higher Interest Rates and Thrift Institutions

As a result of the combination of large government deficits and a restrictive monetary policy, high-grade corporate bond rates rose from about $4\frac{1}{2}$ percent in 1965 to over 6 percent in the autumn of 1966. This sharp rise in interest rates caused severe problems for thrift institutions. With long-term, fixed-interest mortgages financed by short-term deposits, thrift institutions like savings and loan associations were now faced with the possibility of having to pay higher interest rates on their liabilities than they

Figure 21.8   The Credit Crunch of 1966

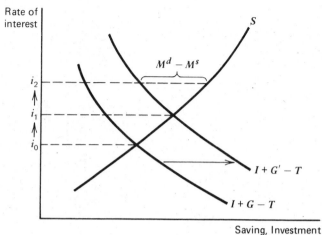

The economy begins in flow equilibrium at i_0. The Vietnam War increased government expenditure from G to G' with no corresponding change in revenue. Hence,
the $I + G - T$ curve shifted to the right, raising the flow equilibrium interest rate
from i_0 to i_1. The restrictive monetary policy from April to October 1966 produced
an excess demand for money that raised interest rates from i_1 to i_2.

were earning on their mortgage assets. In an attempt to insulate these thrift
institutions from rising interest costs, the Fed and the Federal Home Loan Bank
Board tried to keep deposit rates below market rates of interest by imposing interest-rate ceilings on deposits. The Fed had set maximum interest-
rate ceilings on time and savings deposits since 1935, but these ceilings
were usually above the yields on alternative assets. When market rates of
interest rose near or above ceiling rates on savings deposits, as in 1957 and
1962, the ceiling rates were raised. However, in 1966 the Fed maintained
the 4 percent ceiling rate on savings deposits even when other short-term
rates rose significantly above it. In fact, for some types of time deposits,
ceiling rates were actually lowered. The Fed felt that any increase in interest rates on bank savings deposits would force the thrift institutions to
raise their deposit rates to compete with banks for deposits. Moreover, the
Interest Rate Adjustment Act of 1966 extended the system of ceiling rates
to cover thrift institutions for the first time. These interest-rate ceilings on
the deposits of thrift institutions prevented the thrifts from competing with
each other for deposits. However, to give the thrift institutions an interest-
rate advantage over commercial banks, the 1966 Act set their ceiling rates
one percentage point higher than the ceiling on bank savings deposits.

Disintermediation   Although the interest-rate ceilings did lower the interest expenses of the
thrift institutions, it also led to disintermediation. This phenomenon is
depicted in Figure 21.9. In the absence of interest-rate ceilings, financial
intermediaries would pay an interest rate of i_d on deposits and supply

Figure 21.9   Disintermediation Caused by Interest Rate Ceiling

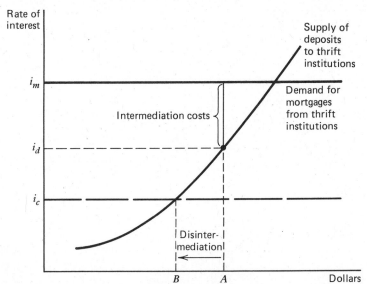

In the absence of a ceiling on deposit rates of interest, thrift institutions would offer a rate of i_d to depositors with the mortgage rate at i_m. An interest-rate ceiling of i_c cuts back deposits from A to B. As a result, thrift institutions will have fewer resources with which to extend new mortgage loans. The net deposit withdrawal caused by the ceiling is known as disintermediation.

mortgages to home buyers at the mortgage interest rate of i_m. The spread between the two interest rates reflects the costs of intermediation. With the imposition of an interest-rate ceiling i_c on deposits, depositors supply fewer funds to financial intermediaries. As a result, the financial intermediaries will have fewer funds to lend to home buyers.

Because of the interest-rate advantage given to thrift institutions, banks lost significant amounts of savings and time deposits in 1966. However, even the savings and loan associations experienced disintermediation. The net flow of funds into savings and loan associations fell to one-fourth of the previous year's level.

Interest Rates and Housing Starts   As a result of rising real interest rates produced by the growing government deficit combined with a restrictive monetary policy, housing starts fell to the lowest rate in 20 years. Houses are among the most durable assets in the economy. With higher real rates of interest, housing prices fall because their future services are discounted at a higher rate of interest. Thus, the home-building industry has always been extremely interest sensitive. The housing industry collapsed in 1966. After remaining at a relatively stable level of 1.5 million units a year during 1964–1965, housing starts fell to an annual rate of 960,000 by the fourth quarter of 1966. Purchases of other durable goods, such as automobiles, were also sharply curtailed. Fears of even higher real rates of interest with their devastating effect on the housing industry were partly responsible for the Fed's sharp turn to a highly expansionary monetary policy in early 1967.

Minirecession of 1967

As a result of the decline in the money supply from April to October 1966, the economy slowed down significantly during late 1966 and early 1967. Real gross national product actually fell during the first quarter of 1967. Although the National Bureau of Economic Research never designated it as an official recession because real gross national product rose the next quarter, it is often referred to as the minirecession of 1967. This economic slowdown, combined with a rapid increase in bank reserves created by open market purchases, caused interest rates to drop significantly in early 1967. The yield on three-month treasury bills declined from $5\frac{1}{2}$ percent in mid-September 1966 to only $3\frac{1}{2}$ percent in July 1967. The decline in market rates of interest relative to the legal maximum rates paid on time deposits brought large inflows of funds to financial intermediaries, especially savings and loan associations. These inflows, in turn, allowed nonbank depository institutions to provide new funds to the mortgage market, and residential construction recovered.

Monetary Acceleration in 1967

This decline in interest rates was short-lived. The Fed's expansionary open market purchases caused the money supply to soar at the extremely rapid rate of 7.4 percent from January 1967 to July 1968. Although this acceleration in the rate of monetary growth did have the short-run effect of bringing interest rates down, it also created a higher rate of inflation. By late 1969 the rate of inflation had reached 5.6 percent. By early 1970, expectations of continued inflation and a switch to a tighter monetary policy had pushed nominal interest rates up to $8\frac{1}{2}$ percent. Because of their inability to adapt quickly to these increases in interest rates, financial intermediaries again experienced a drastic drop in earnings in 1969–1970. The Fed's easy money policy had given them only a temporary reprieve.

Inflation and Tighter Fiscal Policy in 1968

By 1968 inflation had become an important political issue. Because the economy was already operating at capacity, output could not increase very much. As a result, the rapid growth of nominal gross national product associated with the expansionary monetary policy occurred primarily in the form of inflation. Prices rose 4.7 percent in 1968, more than three percentage points higher than they had been rising when Johnson took office in 1964. Instead of stimulating the economy in an election year, Johnson had to ask for a 10 percent surtax on personal and corporate income taxes and a reduction in federal expenditures of $6 billion to fight inflation in 1968. With the economy racked by inflation and the nation hopelessly mired in the Vietnam War, Johnson unexpectedly withdrew from the presidential race on March 31, 1968. In November Richard Nixon became president by narrowly defeating Johnson's vice-president, Hubert Humphrey.

Deficit Cut and Interest-Rate Decline in 1968

In June 1968 Congress finally passed Johnson's 10 percent surtax on personal and corporate income taxes. This tax increase, together with a cut in federal spending, reduced the federal deficit. Other demands for credit also moderated, perhaps reflecting a reduction in inflationary expectations. Monetary policy continued to be expansive, however. At the June meeting of the Federal Open Market Committee, the manager of the open market account was instructed that "if the proposed fiscal legislation is enacted, operations shall accommodate tendencies for short-term interest rates to decline in connection with such affirmative congressional action on the pending fiscal legislation as long as bank credit expansion does not exceed current projections." During the summer the treasury bill rate fell from $5\frac{3}{4}$ percent in May to about 5 percent in mid-August. Following the decline in market interest rates, the Fed lowered the discount rate from $5\frac{1}{2}$ to $5\frac{1}{4}$ percent in August. By the fall, however, it became apparent that the fiscal restraint was having less effect in slowing the growth of total spending than had been expected. Fears of continued inflation reemerged and market interest rates rose, retracing most of the earlier decline by early December.

Summary

1. From 1942 to 1951 the Fed pegged prices of government securities to hold interest costs of the government down. This strategy prevented the Fed from controlling the money supply.

2. The money supply under a paper standard is highly unstable if monetary policy is aimed solely at pegging interest rates. Once flow disequilibrium emerges, the monetary policy reaction will exacerbate the disequilibrium.

3. Under a pegged interest-rate policy, inflationary expectations tend to be self-fulfilling because upward pressure on interest rates resulting from higher expected inflation will be met by monetary acceleration.

4. The Cambridge k rose during World War II because of rationing and shortages. After price controls were lifted, prices exploded.

5. The Cambridge k fell rapidly during the Korean War boom as inflationary expectations rose. This added fuel to the inflationary fire caused by monetary acceleration aimed at keeping down interest rates.

6. The Fed stopped pegging government security prices after the 1951 Accord with the Treasury.

7. Floating interest rates after 1951 raised money demand by increasing the risk of holding bonds. The decline in the Cambridge k was reversed.

8. The threat of a steel strike in 1959 increased demand for inventories of steel. This raised the flow equilibrium interest rate and the money supply was increased to stabilize rates. After the strike began, inventories were drawn down, the flow equilibrium interest rate declined, and the money supply contracted. This episode illustrates the destabilizing effects of using interest rates or money market conditions as monetary policy targets. The monetary contraction heralded the 1960 recession.

9. An easy monetary policy was followed in the early 1960s. After economic growth slowed in 1962, the administration stimulated investment by introducing accelerated depreciation and investment tax credits. Interest rates rose, the money supply was expanded to counteract rising rates, and the economy boomed.

10. The government budget deficit expanded rapidly after 1965 with the increased Vietnam War expenditures. The monetization of a substantial part of this deficit ensured higher rates of inflation.

11. The higher interest rates produced by the government deficit and higher inflation caused solvency problems for thrift institutions. Deposit-rate ceilings imposed largely to keep the cost of liabilities below the return on long-term assets resulted in disintermediation—deposits were withdrawn from thrift institutions and invested in direct financial claims.

12. Rising interest rates reduced housing starts dramatically by the end of 1966. The economy entered a minirecession in 1967.

Questions

1. What was the effect of the policy of supporting government security prices on fluctuations in monetary growth?

2. Why do inflationary expectations tend to be self-fulfilling under a monetary policy of pegging interest rates?

3. Why did the Cambridge k rise during World War II but fall during the Korean War?

4. What was the Accord and how did it affect the conduct of monetary policy?

5. How did the Fed's abandonment of its government security price-support policy affect demand for money?

6. How does the 1959 steel strike illustrate the destabilizing monetary effects of using interest rates or money market conditions as monetary policy targets?

7. When interest rates are used as monetary policy targets, what is the relationship between monetary policy and fiscal policy?

8. Why was a substantial part of the government deficit after 1966 monetized?

9. How were the thrift institutions affected by rising nominal interest rates during 1966?

10. Why did housing starts decline in 1966?

22 U.S. Domestic Monetary Policy, 1969–1983

Monetary Policy During the Nixon-Ford Era

Tight Monetary Policy in 1969

It was not until after the election that, with the support of the new president-elect, Richard Nixon, Federal Reserve policy finally became restrictive. Discount rates were increased from $5\frac{1}{4}$ to $5\frac{3}{4}$ percent in December 1968 and to 6 percent in April 1969. Reserve requirements against demand deposits were increased $\frac{1}{2}$ percent in April. At the same time, the Federal Open Market Committee refused to provide unborrowed reserves through open market purchases. Market rates of interest soared. The three-month treasury bill yield, for example, rose from 5.45 percent in November 1968 to 7.87 percent in January 1970. Just as in 1966, the sharp increase in market rates of interest was accompanied by financial disintermediation and a sharp reduction in funds flowing into the mortgage market.

Monetary Slowdown and the 1969–1970 Recession

These restrictive measures by the Fed had a definite effect in slowing the rate of monetary growth. After increasing at an annual rate of 7.6 percent from January 1967 to January 1969, the rate of monetary growth slowed to 5.1 percent from January to June 1969. During the second half of 1969 the money stock showed almost no increase at all. This drastic slowdown in the rate of monetary growth in the face of an underlying inflation rate of over 5 percent produced a recession which started in the fourth quarter of 1969. The unemployment rate, which had averaged 3.3 percent in the first month of 1969, would climb to over 6 percent by late 1970.

Expansionary Policy in 1970

In early 1970 the Fed adopted a more expansionary monetary policy, partly in response to fears of financial panic associated with the bankruptcy of Penn Central Transportation Company. Not only did the Fed actively purchase government securities, it also encouraged banks to borrow from the Fed banks at a discount rate that was well below market rates of interest. In January the three-month treasury bill rate was 8 percent while the discount rate was only 6 percent. Moreover, as interest rates declined during the year in response to the recession and a reduction in inflationary expectations, the discount rate was reduced to $5\frac{1}{2}$ percent in November to keep it in line with market rates of interest. These actions caused money supply growth to accelerate to an annual rate of $5\frac{1}{2}$ percent during 1970.

President Richard Nixon also took steps to stimulate the economy. The 10 percent surtax on income taxes was terminated and federal expenditures increased sharply. Nixon also made sure that the Fed under the leadership of William McChesney Martin would not hurt his reelection chances. When Martin's term expired in March 1970, Nixon appointed his old friend Arthur Burns as chairman of the Federal Reserve Board of Governors.

Economic Recovery in 1971

Although the recovery from the 1969–1970 recession was postponed by a major automobile strike, the economy improved rapidly. Real output increased about 5 percent in 1971. Moreover, this recovery was accompanied by a gradual drop in the rate of inflation. Despite these improvements, however, inflation was still about $4\frac{1}{2}$ percent and the unemployment rate continued to hover at about 6 percent in the summer of 1971, as shown in Figures 22.1, 22.2, and 22.3.

Economic Stabilization Program

With an election just a little over a year ahead, Nixon decided to speed up progress towards lower inflation and unemployment rates. On Sunday, August 15, 1971, President Nixon announced a radically new Economic Stabilization Program in which wage and price controls played a dominant role. Using the authority granted to him by Congress in the Economic Stabilization Act of 1970, Nixon imposed a 90-day freeze on wages and prices. When the freeze ended in mid-November, it was followed by Phase II of the program which permitted wage increases of no more than $5\frac{1}{4}$ percent and price increases of no more than $2\frac{1}{2}$ percent a year.

Wage and Price Controls in 1971

Nixon's wage and price control program did appear to have a significant, albeit temporary, effect in reducing the rate of inflation. With the exception of farm prices, which were exempt from controls, the rate of price increase declined sharply. After rising at an annual rate of 4.3 percent from December 1970 to August 1971, nonfarm prices rose at an annual rate of only 1.2 percent during the freeze. Nonfarm prices did briefly accelerate to an annual rate of 3.6 percent immediately after the freeze, but then they decelerated again to an annual rate of only $1\frac{1}{2}$ percent from February to December 1972.

Figure 22.1 M1 Money Stock and Interest Rates, 1968–1976

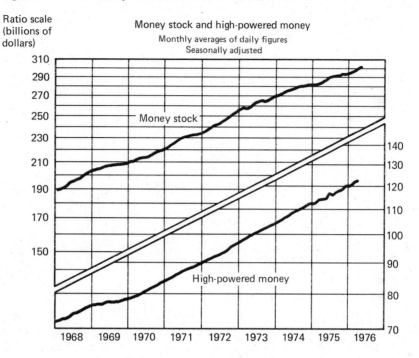

Ratio scale (billions of dollars)

Money stock and high-powered money
Monthly averages of daily figures
Seasonally adjusted

Money stock

High-powered money

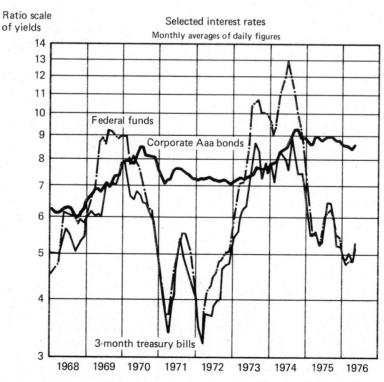

Ratio scale of yields

Selected interest rates
Monthly averages of daily figures

Federal funds

Corporate Aaa bonds

3-month treasury bills

Source: Federal Reserve Bank of St. Louis Review, 58(6), June 1976, p. 5.

Figure 22.2 GNP and Unemployment, 1967–1976

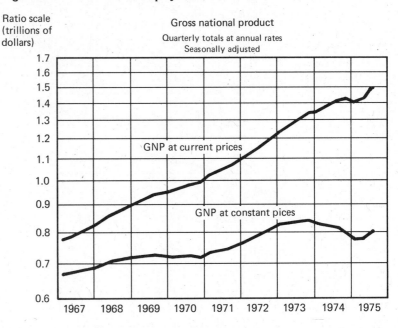

Ratio scale
(trillions of
dollars)

Gross national product

Quarterly totals at annual rates
Seasonally adjusted

GNP at current prices

GNP at constant pices

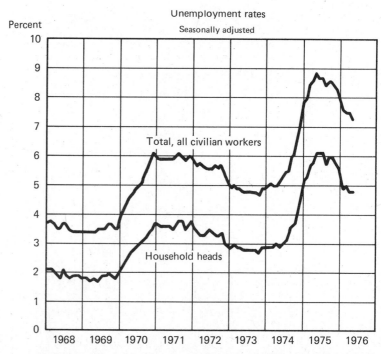

Unemployment rates

Percent

Seasonally adjusted

Total, all civilian workers

Household heads

Source: Federal Reserve Bank of St. Louis Review, 58(4), April 1976, p. 3, and *Federal Reserve Bank of St. Louis Review,* 58(6), June 1976, p. 7.

Figure 22.3   Inflation, 1948–1972

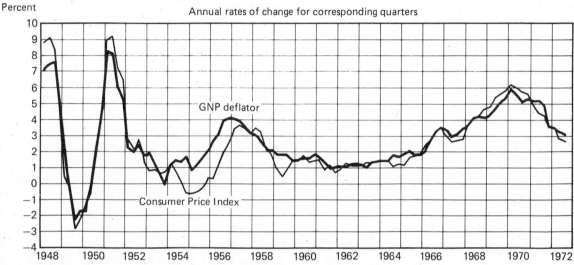

Source: *Federal Reserve Bank of St. Louis Review,* 54(12), December 1972, p. 8.

Fiscal Stimulus in 1972

With the wage and price controls in place, Nixon proceeded to stimulate the economy. The Revenue Act of 1971 increased personal tax exemptions, eliminated the excise tax on automobiles, and permitted a 7 percent tax credit on new, U.S.-built capital equipment. Moreover, despite the winding down of the Vietnam War, federal expenditures increased about 12 percent in 1972, compared with increases of 8 percent in 1970 and 9 percent in 1971.

Expansionary Monetary Policy in 1972

The Fed, now under Arthur Burns, accommodated Nixon's expansionary game plan. Although the money supply did experience a pause in its growth during the 90-day freeze, it exploded at an annual rate of 8.2 percent in 1972. As a result of this monetary and fiscal stimulus, the economy boomed. From the third quarter of 1971 to the end of 1972, real gross national product grew at an annual rate of 6¼ percent. By the 1972 election, the unemployment rate had fallen from 6 percent in late 1971 to only 5.2 percent. At the same time, the long-run effects of monetary restraint in 1969, combined with the wage and price controls, were holding down the rate of inflation. From February to December 1972, prices rose at an annual rate of only 3.2 percent, the lowest rate since 1965.

Nixon's Political Business Cycle

Economists and political scientists often point to Nixon's first term in office as a perfect example of the political business cycle. Just as this model of political behavior hypothesizes, Nixon pressured the Fed into reducing the rate of monetary growth early in his term. In the short run, this reduced

Figure 22.4   Nixon's Political Business Cycle

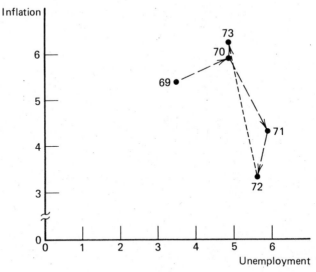

Source: Economic Report of the President, 1983, pp. 201 and 225.

rate of monetary growth caused the unemployment rate to rise, as shown in Figure 22.4. By late 1970 the unemployment rate had increased to over 6 percent. After a lag of about two years, however, reduced monetary growth reduces the rate of inflation. And, indeed, rates of inflation were much lower in 1971 and 1972 than they had been in 1969 and 1970. Nixon helped this process of disinflation along by introducing his wage and price control program in August 1971. In the last year of the incumbent's term, monetary growth was increased to produce rapid increases in output and a reduction in the unemployment rate. The combination of a low inflation rate and rapid economic growth helped reelect Richard Nixon by one of the biggest majorities in history. Nixon crushed his opponent, Senator George McGovern, by a margin of 61 to 38 percent. In retrospect, however, Nixon and the country paid dearly for that temporary economic boom. The economic cost of Nixon's game plan was the inflation of 1973–1974.

Accelerating Inflation in 1973

The rapid increase in the money supply during 1972 set the stage for an upsurge in inflation during 1973. Even wage and price controls could not contain the inflationary pressure without producing widespread shortages. If a price is held below its market clearing level, incentives to supply that product are reduced while at the same time demand is artificially stimulated, resulting in a shortage. For this reason, Nixon decided to modify the wage and price control programs to make them more flexible and move towards an end of the controls. Phase III, which began in January 1973, permitted companies to raise prices by more than 1½ percent only if their profit margins did not exceed the best two out of the three fiscal years preceding August 1971. Despite these controls, prices rose at an annual rate of over 6½ percent during the first half of 1973.

Agricultural Prices Soar in 1973

Nixon's Phase III controls were helpless in dealing with this inflation because most of the price increases were concentrated in agriculture, which was exempt from controls. The dramatic upsurge in food prices began in late 1972, when a change in ocean currents caused a drastic drop in the Peruvian anchovy catch to only one-tenth of normal. Anchovies are the main ingredient of high-protein fish meal which is used as feed for livestock. In addition, there were crop failures and droughts in Asia, Russia, and the Sahara. Russia had one of the severest droughts in recent history. Worldwide production of grains fell more than 3 percent from the previous year. These crop failures led to massive exports of U.S. food products. Russia alone contracted to buy 15 million tons of wheat and 6 million tons of feed grains. Moreover, the devaluation of the dollar in the spring of 1973 created an incentive to sell abroad. This unexpected increase in exports caused farm prices to rise drastically. Farm and food prices increased at an annual rate of 50 percent during the first half of 1973.

1973 Price Controls Produce Shortages

In June 1973 concern about this sharp increase in the rate of inflation prompted Nixon to substitute a 60-day price freeze that included agricultural prices for the more liberal Phase III controls. The freeze prevented increases in production costs from being passed on to consumers. Supply problems were especially serious in industries that used internationally traded raw materials as inputs. Price controls obviously could not hold the prices of these raw materials down because their prices are determined in world markets. When these raw material prices increased and the costs could not be passed along to customers, producers cut production. For example, when the cost of scrap steel, whose price is determined in world markets, went up sharply, many lines of steel products using scrap steel as an input were cut or discontinued. As a result, production bottlenecks occurred in many industries using steel. The price controls were also directly responsible for shortages of paper, beef, pork, fertilizer, gasoline, and dozens of other products.

After the 60-day freeze, Nixon imposed Phase IV controls, which were stricter than the Phase II controls; companies could "pass through" only the dollar amount of higher costs. Nevertheless, inflation continued to accelerate. By the fourth quarter of 1973, inflation had reached double digits.

1973 Oil Embargo Increases All Energy Prices

As food prices were beginning to level off in late 1973, the Arab-Israeli War prompted an embargo on Arab crude oil supplies to the United States. The embargo ended in March 1974, but the price of foreign crude oil quadrupled from a little more than $3 a barrel in early 1973 to almost $12.

Despite price controls on domestically produced crude oil, energy prices soared. Gasoline, which had cost 25¢ a gallon (excluding state and federal excise taxes) in January 1973, reached 43¢ a gallon by July 1974. These sudden increases in the price of petroleum products also bid up the prices of alternative sources of energy, such as coal and electricity.

Price Controls Removed in 1974

Realizing that controls were wrecking the economy, Nixon started to dismantle them in January 1974, with final abolition in April 1974. With the removal of controls and the sharp increase in oil prices, inflation exploded at an annual rate of 11 percent during the first three quarters of 1974.

Flow Equilibrium after a Change in Relative Prices

The explosive rise in food and energy prices made monetary policy decisions very difficult in 1973–1974. The equilibrium level of total income is that which makes the demand for money equal to the money supply. Without an increase in the money supply, a rise in food and energy prices would not affect the equilibrium level of nominal gross national product. Since demand for domestic food and energy products would increase as a result of foreign crop failures and higher foreign crude oil prices, total spending on these products would rise. If total spending on domestic output is to remain constant, an increase in expenditures on domestic food and energy products implies that expenditures on other goods decline.

Some Prices Could Fall

If the money supply and total spending remain constant in the face of rising food and energy prices, the prices or sales of other products will fall. In a world of flexible wages and prices, a rise in food and energy prices will have very little effect on the overall price level because the prices of other goods will fall. Money wage rates in those industries must also fall in proportion to prices if the labor force is to be kept profitably employed. However, if workers resist that reduction in money wage rates, employers will lay them off and production will be cut back.

Money Supply Could Be Increased

The Fed could, of course, accommodate a rise in food and energy prices by increasing the money supply. Nominal gross national product could be allowed to rise with expenditures on domestically produced food and energy products, leaving nominal expenditures on other products unchanged. Prices and wages in those industries would not have to fall for full employment to be maintained. However, since the overall price level would rise, the real wage rate of workers in those industries would actually fall.

Oil Price Rise Reduces Equilibrium Real Wages

Whether adjustment occurs by falling money wage rates or rising prices in the face of fixed money wages, a relative scarcity of food and energy products necessitates a fall in real wages of workers in other industries if full employment is to be maintained. An increase in the money supply can prevent unemployment by reducing real wage rates through inflation only if workers do not think in real terms. It is more likely that workers, discovering that the purchasing power of their money wages is being eroded by rising food and energy prices, would attempt to regain their lost purchasing power with demands for higher money wage rates. Moreover, many wage contracts are indexed to the consumer price index, so an increase in the overall price level would automatically raise money wage rates. In this sort of environment, even expansionary monetary policies cannot prevent unemployment. Full employment can exist only when workers accept the fact that crop failures and OPEC oil cartels have made them poorer. Any attempt to avoid that reduction in real wages will produce unemployment.

Inflation Explodes in 1974

Some of the acceleration in the 1973–1974 rate of inflation was certainly due to the excessive expansion in the money supply during 1972. However, one can hardly blame the Fed for the poor grain harvests, the shortages of fish meal, and the quadrupling of world oil prices. If it had not been for these special supply factors, the rate of inflation resulting from the earlier monetary growth would have been about 7 percent. Instead, prices increased at an incredible rate of 11.4 percent during 1974.

Monetary Restraint in 1974

The Fed refused to validate that double-digit inflation by allowing the money supply to grow fast enough to accommodate both inflation and real growth in output. The money supply increased by only 5.7 percent from the second quarter of 1973 to the second quarter of 1974, and prices increased by 9 percent during that period. With prices rising considerably faster than the rate of monetary growth, a recession was guaranteed.

During 1974 many economists urged the Fed to increase the money supply at a rate slightly faster than the rate of inflation in order to prevent the recession from becoming even deeper. Nevertheless, Arthur Burns adamantly refused to accommodate double-digit inflation. With allusions to the German hyperinflation of 1922–1923, Burns declared in May 1974: "Inflation at anything like the present rate would threaten the very foundations of our society. I do not believe I exaggerate in saying that the ultimate consequence of inflation could well be a significant decline in economic and political freedom for the American people."

Tight Monetary Policy and the 1974–1975 Recession

The Fed had already begun a move towards restraint on April 25, when it raised the discount rate from $7\frac{1}{2}$ to 8 percent. Following Burns's speech, open market operations also became very restrictive in their provision of unborrowed reserves. By late June the federal funds rate had reached a record level of $13\frac{1}{2}$ percent. The rate of monetary growth fell sharply. In the seven months from June 1974 to January 1975, the money supply grew at an annual rate of only 1.3 percent. Since prices rose at $10\frac{1}{2}$ percent during the third and fourth quarters, production fell at the fastest rate recorded since quarterly data were started in 1947. The economy plunged into the worst recession since the 1930s, with the unemployment rate climbing from 5 percent in the spring of 1974 to over 9 percent in May 1975.

Nixon Resigns in August 1974

In the midst of this economic disarray, with interest rates at record levels and the economy about to plunge into the worst recession of the postwar period, Richard Nixon announced that he would resign (because of Watergate), the first president ever to do so. On August 9, 1974, Vice-President Gerald Ford was sworn in as the thirty-eighth president of the United States.

Neutral Monetary Policy in 1975

In early 1975 Federal Reserve policy became more stimulative. Congress passed a resolution in March 1975 which called for the Board of Governors to set and disclose in Congressional hearings money supply targets for the four quarters immediately ahead. In May 1975 Arthur Burns initially announced long-term target ranges for growth in the money supply of 5 to $7\frac{1}{2}$ percent per year. The lower end of the range was reduced to $4\frac{1}{2}$ percent in the fourth quarter of 1975. The upper end of the range was reduced to 7 percent in the following quarter and reduced further to $6\frac{1}{2}$ percent in the third quarter of 1976.

Moderate Monetary Growth in 1975 and 1976

The Fed kept growth in the money supply near the bottom of the planned range. From the first quarter of 1975 through the third quarter of 1976 the money supply increased at an annual rate of only 5.3 percent, as shown in Figure 22.5. Although this represented a substantial acceleration from the extremely restrictive monetary policy pursued in late 1974, it was still a fairly modest growth rate for an economy with over 8 percent unemployment in an election year. Arthur Burns was determined that he would not be accused a second time of pumping up the money supply to reelect a Republican incumbent. In any case, President Gerald Ford and his Council of Economic Advisers under Alan Greenspan rejected the political expediency of pressuring the Fed into more rapid monetary growth.

Rapid Economic Growth in 1975 Followed by Moderate Growth in 1976

As a result of the switch to a moderately expansionary monetary policy in early 1975 and the fiscal stimulus from tax rebates that spring and summer, the economy started to recover in the second quarter of 1975. From the first quarter of 1975 to the first quarter of 1976 real output increased $7\frac{1}{2}$ percent and the unemployment rate, which had peaked at 9 percent in May 1975, fell to less than 8 percent. However, after the first quarter of 1976, growth in real gross national product slowed and further progress towards reducing the unemployment rate became more difficult. By the 1976 election, the unemployment rate was still 7.8 percent. However, the restrictive monetary policies in 1974 and 1975 did produce a dramatic slowdown in the rate of inflation. After rising at double-digit rates during

Figure 22.5   M1 Money Stock, 1975–1980

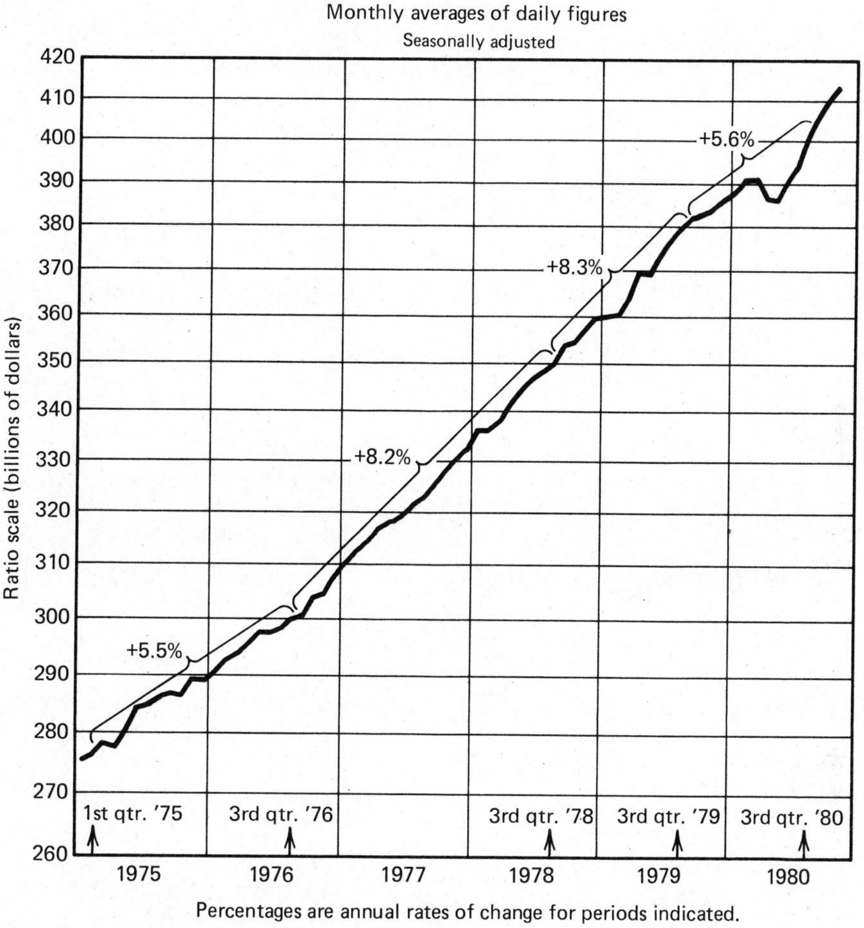

Monthly averages of daily figures
Seasonally adjusted

Percentages are annual rates of change for periods indicated.

Source: Federal Reserve Bank of St. Louis, *Monetary Trends,* December 26, 1980, p. 3.

1974, the rate of increase in the consumer price index fell to an annual rate of only 4.2 percent during the last quarter of 1976.

1976 Election   In many respects the 1976 election resembled the 1960 election. A Republican incumbent administration failed to produce rapid economic growth through monetary stimulus during an election year. Real output increased only 4½ percent during 1976, which was quite moderate considering that the unemployment rate averaged about 8 percent. The Democratic opposition argued for more stimulative policies to return the economy to full employment. As in the 1960 election, the Democratic candidate won by a very narrow margin.

Jimmy Carter and the Fed

Carter versus Burns

The relationship between President Jimmy Carter and the Republican chairman of the Federal Reserve Board, Arthur Burns, became extremely strained early in Carter's first year of office. Carter had campaigned on a platform that made a reduction in the unemployment rate the number one priority. Arthur Burns, on the other hand, preached monetary restraint, which would postpone any reduction in the unemployment rate. This dispute between Arthur Burns and President Carter over monetary policy eventually led to Burns's replacement. When Arthur Burns's term as chairman of the Federal Reserve Board ended on January 31, 1978, Jimmy Carter made it clear that he wanted a radically new direction for monetary policy by appointing G. William Miller, the president of Textron (a large conglomerate industrial corporation), as the new chairman. Miller acknowledged in his confirmation hearings before the Senate that he supported President Carter's plan for economic expansion through stimulative monetary policies.

Rapid Monetary Growth in 1977

Arthur Burns preached monetary restraint but, in practice, he had let Carter have an expansionary monetary policy. Although interest rates rose sharply, the money supply increased far more rapidly in 1977 than it had in 1976. From the third quarter of 1976 to the third quarter of 1978 the money supply accelerated to an annual rate of 8 percent. By the time G. William Miller was confirmed in April 1978, the inflationary consequences of this rapid monetary expansion were already apparent. The rate of inflation had accelerated to double-digit levels by the second quarter of 1978.

Inflation Accelerated in 1978

Carter's commitment to monetary expansion in 1977–1978 did have its intended effect of bringing the unemployment rate down. It fell from 7.8 percent in late 1976 to only 5.8 percent by October 1978. However, the price of this expansionary monetary policy was a 9 percent inflation rate during 1978, hardly a propitious development for the 1980 election. Carter's bias towards monetary expansion during 1977 and 1978 came back to haunt him. By the summer of 1978, public opinion polls showed that many Americans considered inflation to be the number one problem facing the United States.

Tighter Monetary Policy towards the End of 1978

In the autumn of 1978 Carter responded to these fears by shifting his economic priorities. The Fed under Carter's appointee, G. William Miller, responded to the administration's new commitment to bring inflation down by reducing the rate of monetary growth. On November 1, 1978, the Fed increased the discount rate by one percentage point and imposed a supplementary reserve requirement of two percentage points on large-denomination time deposits. Following these actions, growth of the money supply did slow. After growing at an annual rate of over 8 percent from the fourth quarter of 1976 to the fourth quarter of 1978, the money supply slowed to an annual growth rate of only 4.7 percent from September 1978 to February 1979. This slowdown in the rate of monetary growth almost guaranteed an economic downturn in the second quarter of 1979. Unfortunately, the downturn was made even worse by another oil crisis.

Oil Crisis of 1978–1979

In late 1978 an oil crisis would have seemed impossible. The OPEC cartel had exhibited considerable weakness since 1974. The OPEC price increases during the previous five years had been rather small; in fact, they had not even kept up with the rate of inflation. In real terms, the OPEC price of oil had fallen by about 20 percent since 1974. For most of 1978 there was a worldwide glut of oil that had induced many members of the OPEC cartel to give discounts in order to increase demand. However, the revolution in Iran, which led to the overthrow of the Shah, changed this oil glut into an acute shortage enabling OPEC oil prices to surge again.

As a result of the upheaval, Iranian oil production virtually stopped for 69 days, causing a severe drop in world production. Iranian exports, which had been running at about 5.5 million barrels a day prior to the revolution, fell to zero in late December 1978. Although other OPEC countries, principally Saudi Arabia, increased their production to offset partially the loss of Iran's exports, the net reduction in OPEC's exports was still about 2 million barrels a day. This is about the same reduction in world supply that occurred during the height of the Arab oil embargo in late 1973. Even when Iran resumed exporting oil on March 5, 1979, exports were only 55 percent of the amount exported under the Shah's regime. This loss of Iranian exports enabled OPEC to boost the price of Arabian light crude oil from $12.70 in December 1978 to $18 in July 1979, a jump of 42 percent.

Economic Downturn Followed by Monetary Expansion in 1979

The reduced rate of monetary growth combined with sharply rising energy prices plunged the economy into a downturn during the second quarter of 1979. Real gross national product fell at an annual rate of 2.3 percent. However, the Fed did not maintain its commitment to monetary restraint. As soon as the first signs of recession appeared, the Fed abandoned its monetary restraint and produced a virtual explosion in the rate of monetary growth. From February to September 1979 the money supply increased at an annual rate of approximately 11 percent. The monetary expansion aborted the recession and produced a recovery during the third quarter of 1979.

Speculation Against the Dollar

This capitulation in the face of relatively small increases in the unemployment rate convinced investors that the Fed under G. William Miller's leadership would be unable to withstand political pressures for strong monetary stimulus prior to the 1980 election. The loss of confidence in the Fed's resolve to fight inflation caused renewed speculation against the dollar on foreign exchange markets, and an international flight from the dollar into gold, silver, and other commodities took place.

Volcker Appointed Fed Chairman in August 1979

It was against this background of turmoil on the foreign exchange market that Carter moved G. William Miller to the Treasury and placed Paul Volcker as chairman of the Federal Reserve Board in August 1979. Perhaps the president would have preferred to appoint someone who would be more sensitive to political pressure from the White House. Volcker is said to have warned Carter before his nomination that he was not a team player. However the unstable condition of the dollar on the foreign exchange market and the fear of a continued flight from the dollar ruled out the choice of a more compliant chairman.

Discount Rate Raised in September 1979

Under Volcker's leadership, the Fed moved to restrain the rate of monetary growth. The discount rate was increased from $10\frac{1}{2}$ to 11 percent on September 18, 1979. However, instead of building confidence in the dollar, this move revealed how fragile Volcker's coalition really was. The Board was split 4–3 in favor of increasing the discount rate. Volcker's majority consisted of Frederick Schultz, Henry Wallich, Philip Coldwell, and himself. The three liberal members of the Board—Nancy Teeters, Charles Partee, and Emmett Rice—all voted against the increase. Because of this split, the increase in the discount rate did nothing to dispel speculation against the dollar. Despite rising interest rates, monetary growth continued at rapid rates.

The Fed's Operating Procedures

Interest Rate Targets and Nonborrowed Reserves

Much of the Fed's difficulty in controlling the rate of monetary growth sprang from the use of interest-rate targets to implement monetary policy. The Federal Open Market Committee issued directives to the Open Market Desk at the New York Fed to keep the federal funds rate within a narrow target range. These interest-rate targets could easily be realized by increasing or reducing the amount of nonborrowed reserves in the banking system through open market operations. For example, consider Figure 22.6 which shows the supply and demand for reserves as a function of the federal funds rate. The supply of reserves is of two types: nonborrowed reserves and borrowed reserves.

Nonpecuniary Costs of Borrowing at the Discount Window

As was discussed in Chapter 10, there are significant nonpecuniary costs associated with borrowing from the discount window. Although the discount window is always available to depository institutions, the Fed limits access to it by administrative surveillance. If it feels that a depository institution is borrowing too much from the discount window, the Fed reviews

Figure 22.6   Demand and Supply of Reserves

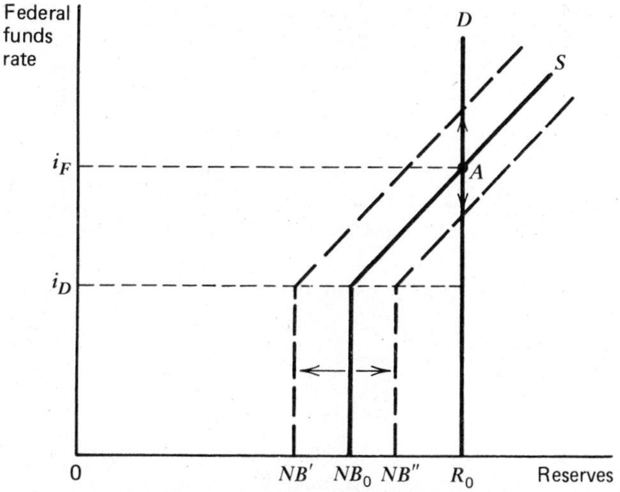

NB_0 represents the quantity of nonborrowed reserves in the banking system. As the federal funds rate rises above the discount rate, banks are induced to borrow additional reserves from the discount window. D is the demand schedule for total reserves based on bank deposits two weeks earlier. The federal funds rate is determined by the intersection of the supply and demand schedules, point A.

the situation with the institution's senior management. The possibility of such administrative discipline discouraged depository institutions from borrowing from the Fed.

Discount Rate and Federal Funds Rate

If the federal funds rate were equal to (or below) the discount rate, no depository institution would have any incentive to borrow from the Fed. It would be cheaper to obtain reserves in the federal funds market, and total reserves would be equal to nonborrowed reserves, represented by NB_0 in Figure 22.6. As the federal funds rate rises above the discount rate, however, banks will borrow some reserves from the discount window because the spread between the federal funds rate i_F and the discount rate i_D compensates for the nonpecuniary costs of borrowing from the Fed. Consequently, the total supply of reserves increases as the spread between the federal funds rate and the discount rate widens. The federal funds rate is thus determined by the intersection of the demand and supply schedules for total reserves, point A in Figure 22.6.

Aggregate Demand for Reserves before 1984

Prior to 1984 the demand for reserves was almost completed interest inelastic because required reserves were based on deposit levels two weeks earlier. As was explained in Chapter 10, this system of lagged reserve accounting was abandoned in February 1984.

Interest-Rate Targeting

Figure 22.6 illustrates how the Open Market Desk could realize the federal funds rate targets of the Open Market Committee. If the federal funds rate were below the target range, the Open Market Desk would sell government securities, reducing nonborrowed reserves from NB_0 to NB_1. With this reduction in nonborrowed reserves, borrowed reserves would have to increase in order to meet reserve requirements. Consequently, the federal funds rate would have to rise to provide the incentive necessary for depository institutions to increase their borrowings from the discount window. Conversely, if the federal funds rate exceeded the target range, the Open Market Desk would purchase government securities in open market operations. This would reduce the amount of borrowed reserves necessary to meet reserve requirements and allow the federal funds rate to drop.

Interest Rates and Monetary Targets

Through the use of open market operations, the Open Market Desk was able to hit the federal funds rate targets with a high degree of precision. Unfortunately, the federal funds rate targets were not the ultimate target of monetary policy. The federal funds rate targets were intermediate targets meant to generate some specific rate of monetary growth. The incentive that depository institutions have to acquire assets, and thus create deposits, is determined by the spread between the yield on income-earning assets i_L and the cost of funds represented by the federal funds rate i_F. By using its control over the federal funds rate, the Fed can manipulate the spread $i_L - i_F$ in the very short run and thus gain approximate, if not precise, control over the money supply. If the Fed wanted to slow the rate of monetary growth, it would raise its federal funds rate targets and thus reduce the spread $i_L - i_F$. This would discourage banks from acquiring assets and thus reduce deposit creation. To stimulate monetary growth, the Fed would lower its federal funds rate targets, increasing the spread $i_L - i_F$ temporarily, and thus encourage asset acquisition by banks.

Deposit Creation and Profitable Lending Opportunities

The main drawback to this method of controlling the money supply is the difficulty of estimating the appropriate federal funds rate needed to produce the desired money stock. Deposit creation is determined by $i_L - i_F$, not simply by i_F. In order to set the appropriate target for the federal funds rate, the Fed must accurately forecast the demand for bank loans during the target period. If demands for credit are greater than the Fed anticipates, the yield on earning assets will exceed its forecast value, and the Fed's target for the federal funds rate will be set too low. Consequently, the spread $i_L - i_F$ will be too large, and the rate of monetary growth will be greater than desired.

Difficulties with Federal Funds Targeting in 1979

Attempting to control the money supply by influencing the federal funds rate was especially troublesome during the fall of 1979. During August and September the Fed repeatedly raised the federal funds rate target in an attempt to slow the rate of monetary growth. However, despite record high federal funds rates, the money supply continued to expand rapidly because the yield on earning assets was rising even faster. Throughout August and September, credit demands fueled by rising expectations of inflation put upward pressure on market rates of interest. The Fed continued to underestimate the demand for credit and set the federal funds rate target too low. As a result, the rate of monetary growth continued to be excessive.

October 5 Change in Operating Procedures

Finally on October 5, 1979, the Federal Reserve Board placed a conference call to the presidents of Federal Reserve banks requesting an emergency meeting of the Federal Open Market Committee the next morning. At that meeting the Federal Open Market Committee approved a change in its operating procedures, giving reserve growth targets precedence over interest-rate targets. In a separate action the Federal Reserve Board raised the discount rate a full percentage point to 12 percent and raised reserve requirements on some categories of bank liabilities.

Control over Nonborrowed Reserves

Of course, the Fed could not control total reserves in the short run. Under the reserve requirement rules in effect from 1968 to 1984, required reserves were based on deposits existing two weeks earlier. The Fed had to supply enough reserves to satisfy those requirements or the banking system would be delinquent, but the Fed could control the mix of reserves between borrowed and nonborrowed reserves. What the Federal Open Market Committee really adopted at that historic meeting was a nonborrowed reserve target. Instead of issuing a directive to the Open Market Desk specifying a federal funds rate target, it specified a target growth rate in nonborrowed reserves. Unfortunately, the use of nonborrowed reserve targets to achieve some desired growth rate in the money supply involves many of the same difficulties that are associated with federal funds rate targets.[1] In order to calculate the appropriate nonborrowed reserve target, the Fed must first estimate the federal funds rate it believes will be consistent with the desired rate of monetary growth, just as it did with the previous federal funds rate targets. Instead of making this estimate of the appropriate federal funds rate the intermediate target for monetary policy, the Fed uses it to further derive an estimate of the appropriate nonborrowed reserve target.

Nonborrowed Reserve Target Procedure

To illustrate this nonborrowed reserve target procedure, consider Figure 22.7. Assume that the Fed estimates that a federal funds rate of 10 percent will provide the banking system with the appropriate incentive to acquire the necessary amount of assets to produce the desired growth in the money supply. With a discount rate of 6 percent, the spread between the federal funds rate and the discount rate would be 4 percentage points. If the Fed then estimates that banks will borrow $(R_0 - NR_0)$ from the discount window with this spread of 4 percentage points, one can easily estimate NB_0 as

---

[1]Robert D. Laurent, "A Critique of the Federal Reserve's New Operating Procedure" (Chicago: Federal Reserve Bank of Chicago, Staff Memoranda, January 1982).

Figure 22.7   Nonborrowed Reserve Targets

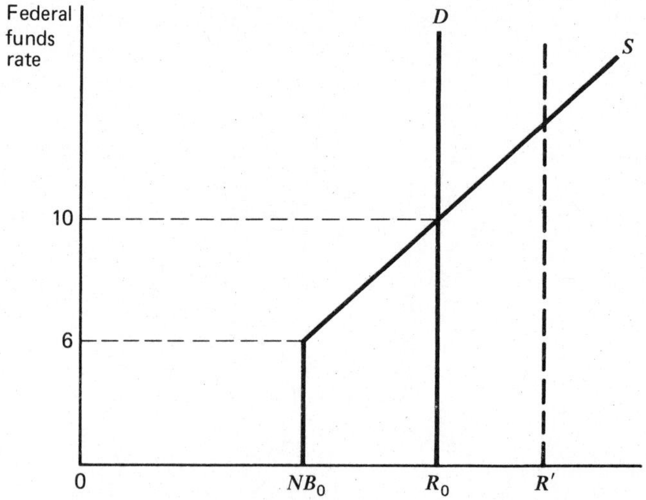

Let the Fed's estimate of the appropriate federal funds rate be 10 percent. The Fed then estimates the demand for borrowed reserves for a 4 percentage point spread between the federal funds rate and the discount rate (assumed to be $R_0 - NB_0$) and subtracts this estimate from the reserves necessary to support the desired money supply.

the appropriate nonborrowed reserve target by subtracting the estimate of the demand for borrowed reserves $(R_0 - NB_0)$ from the level of reserves necessary to support the desired money supply target R_0.

Forecast Errors

Unfortunately, if the Fed underestimates loan demand, the federal funds rate of 10 percent will provide too much of an incentive for banks to acquire assets, causing the money supply to rise above the desired level. In this sense, the nonborrowed reserve target suffers from the same defect that caused the Fed to abandon federal funds rate targets. However, the nonborrowed reserve target does have one important advantage over the federal funds rate target. After a two week lag the undesired expansion in the money supply will increase required reserves, shifting the demand for total reserves outwards to R', and thus automatically raise the federal funds rate above 10 percent, as shown in Figure 22.7. This increase in the federal funds rate will reduce the incentive for banks to acquire more assets, but the money supply will still remain above the desired level.

Estimating Demand for Nonborrowed Reserves

Although nonborrowed reserve targets have this one advantage over federal funds targets, they unfortunately introduce additional problems for the conduct of monetary policy. Even if the Fed estimates correctly the appropriate federal funds rate to achieve the desired rate of monetary growth, nonborrowed reserve targets require the additional estimation of the demand for borrowed reserves that may also be subject to error. The demand for borrowed reserves depends critically on depository institutions' perception of the nonpecuniary costs of borrowing from the discount window. Since these costs vary considerably through time and between Federal Reserve districts, it is not surprising that estimates of the demand for borrowed reserves are subject to considerable error. These errors introduce new difficulties in controlling the money supply. For example, consider Figure 22.8. Assume that the Fed estimates correctly that the appropriate federal funds rate is 10 percent. The Fed then estimates that the 4 percentage point spread between the 10 percent federal funds rate and the 6 percent discount rate will induce banks to borrow $R_0 - NB_0$ from the discount window. The Fed will consequently set the nonborrowed reserve target at NB_0. Suppose, however, that the Fed has overestimated depository institutions' perceived nonpecuniary costs of borrowing from the discount window. In fact, depository institutions can be induced to borrow $R_0 - NB_0$ from the discount window with a spread of only 2 percentage points. Hence, the actual supply schedule of total reserves is really S'. Because of the Fed's error, the nonborrowed reserve target NB_0 will actu-

Figure 22.8   The Effect of Errors in Estimating Nonpecuniary Costs of Borrowing from the Discount Window

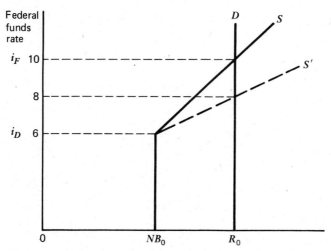

The Federal Reserve aims at producing a 10 percent federal funds rate with a nonborrowed reserve target. It estimates that the spread $(i_F - i_D)$ of 4 percentage points will induce depository institutions to borrow $R_0 - NB_0$ from the discount window, and consequently it sets the nonborrowed target at NB_0. If perceived nonpecuniary costs of borrowing from the discount window are less than the Fed estimated, the actual supply schedule of total reserves will be S', and the federal funds rate will lie below 10 percent.

Figure 22.9 M1 Money Stock and Interest Rates, 1978–1983

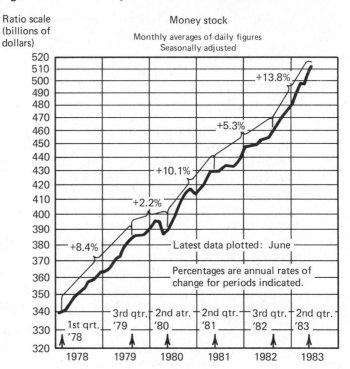

Ratio scale (billions of dollars)

Money stock

Monthly averages of daily figures
Seasonally adjusted

+13.8%

+5.3%

+10.1%

+2.2%

+8.4%

Latest data plotted: June

Percentages are annual rates of change for periods indicated.

| 1st qrt. '78 | 3rd qtr. '79 | 2nd atr. '80 | 2nd qtr. '81 | 3rd qtr. '82 | 2nd qtr. '83 |

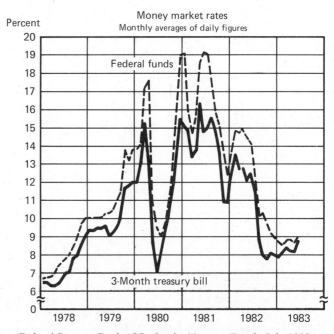

Percent

Money market rates

Monthly averages of daily figures

Federal funds

3-Month treasury bill

Source: Federal Reserve Bank of St. Louis, *Monetary Trends,* July 1983, pp. 3 and 12.

ally produce a federal funds rate below the appropriate level and the money supply will exceed its desired level. Conversely, if the Fed underestimates the nonpecuinary costs of borrowing from the discount window, its nonborrowed reserve target will produce a federal funds rate higher than the appropriate level, and the money supply will fall below the desired level.

Erratic Money Supply Behavior Whatever theoretical merits the nonborrowed reserve targets may have, the record of the behavior of the money supply following the change in operating procedures hardly indicates improvement in the conduct of monetary policy. Although the Fed did succeed in reducing the average rate of growth in the money supply from 7.6 percent a year in 1979 to only 5 percent a year in 1981, there is no reason to suppose that such a reduction could not have been achieved with federal funds rate targets. However, it is clear that the short-run behavior of the money supply has become far more erratic. It was evident from the beginning that the switch to nonborrowed reserve targets would increase the short-run volatility of interest rates, but it was assumed that this was simply the cost of achieving a more stable growth in the money supply. Unfortunately, the economy got the worst of both worlds. Not only did the volatility of interest rates increase following the change in operating procedures, the volatility of monetary growth increased as well, as shown in Figure 22.9.

Monetary Policy and the Roller Coaster Economy

Monetary Restraint and 1980 Recession Following the switch to nonborrowed reserve targets, the rate of monetary growth did slow. From September 1979 to January 1980 the money supply slowed to an annual rate of growth of less than 5 percent. In February 1980 the money supply started to grow at double-digit levels again. The Fed acted quickly to restrain monetary growth. In February the Fed again raised the discount rate to 13 percent, and in March a three percentage point surcharge was added to the 13 percent discount rate for large commercial banks that borrowed frequently from the Fed. As a result of these actions, the money supply fell at an annual rate of over 5 percent from February through May. This drastic monetary restraint caused output to drop at an annual rate of 9.6 percent during the second quarter of 1980 and pushed the unemployment rate up from 6 percent in early 1980 to 7.8 percent by the summer.

Expansionary Monetary Policy in 1980 The Fed again made a radical shift in monetary policy in late May. From the end of May 1980 until election day in November, the money supply rose at an annual rate of 16 percent—the fastest rise during any six-month period in the previous two decades. This monetary expansion brought the recession to a premature end and the economy recovered rapidly. One may be tempted to conclude that the Fed's actions were motivated by a desire to help Jimmy Carter get reelected. After all, by the spring of 1980 a majority of the Federal Reserve Board had been appointed by Carter. However, if that was their motivation, they started to play the political business cycle far too late. What is most surprising is the ingratitude of President Carter. Early in October, Carter tried to turn his campaign around by publicly attacking Federal Reserve monetary policy for being too restrictive—an incredible accusation to make when the money supply was increasing at 16 percent per year.

Monetary Policy under the Reagan Administration

Brief Economic Recovery in 1980–1981

The monetary explosion which began in May 1980 did have a dramatic effect in stimulating the economy, even though it came too late to salvage a victory for Jimmy Carter. After falling at an annual rate of 9.6 percent during the second quarter of 1980, real gross national product rose at an annual rate of 1.7 percent during the third quarter. The recovery became even more vigorous in the following two quarters. Real gross national product rose at an annual rate of 4.3 percent during the fourth quarter and an incredible 7.9 percent rate during the first quarter of 1981, after Reagan took office.

Reagan Supports Monetary Restraint

Ronald Reagan made monetary restraint one of the major components of his economic program. The Reagan administration's resolve to reduce the rate of monetary growth was enhanced by the appointment of Beryl Sprinkel as the Undersecretary of the Treasury for Monetary Affairs and Jerry Jordan as a member of the Council of Economic Advisers. Both of these men had been severe critics of the Fed's previous performance. By Reagan's inauguration, the Fed had already taken measures to slow the rate of monetary growth. In fact, the explosion of monetary growth which began in May 1980 ended just a few weeks after the election. From November 1980 through January 1981 the money supply slowed to an annual rate of growth of only 1.9 percent. This slowdown in the rate of monetary growth produced an economic downturn during the second quarter of 1981, with real gross national product falling during that quarter at an annual rate of $1\frac{1}{2}$ percent.

Expansionary Monetary Policy in 1981

Just as the economy started the downturn, however, monetary growth accelerated again. From the end of January to the end of April 1981 the money supply grew at an annual rate of 14 percent. This acceleration in the rate of monetary growth caused real gross national product to rise at an annual rate of 2.2 percent during the third quarter of 1981. Unfortunately, it also pushed the money supply over the top of the Fed's 1981 target range, and the Fed again took drastic steps to reduce the rate of monetary growth.

Restrictive Monetary Policy and 1981–1982 Recession

In early May the discount rate was raised from 13 to 14 percent and the surcharge imposed on depository institutions that borrowed too frequently at the discount window was raised from 2 to 4 percentage points. During the following six months (until late October) the money supply did not increase at all. This drastic slowdown in the rate of monetary growth precipitated another recession. Real gross national product fell at an annual rate of 5.3 percent during the fourth quarter of 1981 and by 5.1 percent during the first quarter of 1982. This made the recovery from the 1980 recession the second shortest in the more than 100 years of U.S. economic history for which economists have dated business cycles. Not since 1918–1920 had two recessions occurred in such a short period.

Monetary Policy Relaxed in Fall 1981

In late September 1981 the Fed again relaxed its monetary restraint. In a series of steps between the third week in September and early December the basic discount rate was lowered two percentage points to 12 percent, and the surcharge on frequent borrowing was eliminated. This reduction in the cost of funds to depository institutions caused a virtual explosion in the rate of monetary growth. From October 1981 to January 1982 the money supply grew at an annual rate of 15.3 percent, again pushing the money supply considerably above the Fed's targets. This monetary stimulus was sufficient to bring a halt to the economic decline, and real gross national product rose at an annual rate of 2.1 percent during the second quarter of 1982.

Restrictive Monetary Policy in Early 1982

This economic upturn was to be short-lived, however. In late January 1982 the Fed again shifted to restraint in an attempt to get the money supply back within its target range. Although the discount rate remained at 12 percent, the federal funds rate was raised from 12½ to 15 percent and the monetary expansion slowed considerably. From its peak in January to July 1982, the money supply increased at an annual rate of only 1.2 percent. This slowdown in monetary growth caused the economy to falter in the third quarter, with real gross national product rising at an annual rate of only 0.7 percent. In the fourth quarter of 1982 real gross national product fell at an annual rate of 1 percent.

Expansionary Monetary Policy Following Congressional Criticism in mid-1982

By the summer of 1982, with Congressional elections in the fall and the economy beginning to weaken after an upturn of only one quarter, Congress became extremely critical of Paul Volcker's restrictive policies. In fact, two leading Republicans, the House Republican Conference Chairman Jack Kemp and the House Minority Whip Trent Lott, introduced legislation that would force the Fed to reduce interest rates. This legislative assault on the Fed's independence, together with the fact that a sharp decline in the money supply during June had finally brought it within its target range for the first time in 1982, evidently convinced the Federal Open Market Committee that monetary restraint had gone far enough. Inflation had been beaten down from an annual rate of 10.2 percent in 1980 to only 4.4 percent during the first half of 1982 at the cost of two recessions. With the unemployment rate at 10 percent and rising, clearly the number one priority of the Fed was to bring a halt to the deterioration of the economy.

Monetary Acceleration in Second Half of 1982

The Federal Open Market Committee first started to ease its monetary restraint in early July. The federal funds rate fell from 14 percent in June to 11 percent in July. On July 20 the Federal Reserve Board approved a cut in the discount rate from 12 to $11\frac{1}{2}$ percent, the first of seven cuts in 1982 that would bring the discount rate down to $8\frac{1}{2}$ percent by December 14. Following this change in policy, the money supply grew at a very rapid rate. From early June to early October the money supply grew at an annual rate of 11.3 percent, again pushing the money supply above its target range.

Fed Abandons Monetary Targets in October 1982

By late September financial markets became extremely concerned that the Fed would again switch to a restrictive monetary policy in order to bring the money supply back within the target range. After all, the Fed had reacted sensitively to its money supply targets during the previous three years, producing a pattern of excessive expansion followed by excessive restraint. These fears were put to rest on October 9, when Paul Volcker announced that the Fed would temporarily abandon its strategy of targeting money supply growth. As additional proof that the Fed had decided to pay no attention to its 1982 money supply target growth range of $2\frac{1}{2}$ to $5\frac{1}{2}$ percent, the Board approved a reduction in the discount rate from 10 to $9\frac{1}{2}$ percent three days later, even though the money supply was growing twice as rapidly as the target range permitted.

Explosive Money Growth, June 1982–June 1983

The money supply continued to grow rapidly for the rest of 1982 and the first half of 1983, producing a one-year increase in the money supply of 13 percent for the period mid-June 1982 to mid-June 1983. This was the most rapid one-year growth rate in the postwar period. Some of that growth was explained away by the Fed as a shift of funds into the new Super NOW accounts that started on January 5, 1983. However, one study by a Fed Board economist has discounted this demand shift explanation.[2] Furthermore, the Judd-Scadding model discussed in Chapter 20 points to the increase in bank loans as a primary cause of this monetary explosion.[3]

[2]Furlong, *op. cit.*

[3]Judd and Scadding, *op. cit.*

1983 Economic Recovery

Propelled by this dramatic monetary expansion, the economy began a robust recovery in January 1983. Real gross national product grew at an annual rate of $2\frac{1}{2}$ percent during the first quarter and $9\frac{1}{2}$ percent during the second quarter. After peaking in December at 10.8 percent, the unemployment rate had fallen to 10 percent by June 1983, the sharpest decline since 1958. The strength of the recovery, together with an inflation rate which was less than one half the 1980 rate, suddenly turned the tide in Paul Volcker's favor. Forgotten were the facts that monetary policy in the postwar period had never been more erratic than during his tenure as chairman and that his policies had produced the highest unemployment rate in the postwar period. The same politicians who had characterized him as the villain behind the 1981–1982 recession and threatened to eliminate the Fed's independence now praised him for his courage in conquering inflation. So dramatic was his change in fortune that President Reagan announced two months in advance that he was reappointing Volcker as chairman when his term expired in August 1983.

Summary

1. Monetary policy was tightened after Nixon's election in 1968 and the 1969–1970 recession ensued.

2. Monetary and fiscal policies turned expansionary in 1970 to pull the economy out of the recession.

3. The economy recovered rapidly in 1971 with Arthur Burns now chairman of the Fed. Nixon introduced price controls in August 1971 and then further stimulated the economy.

4. With inflation kept low and economic growth rising rapidly under highly expansionary fiscal and monetary policy, Nixon was reelected by a landslide in 1972.

5. Inflation exploded in 1973–1974 as a result of the highly expansionary monetary policy in 1971–1972 as well as poor harvests worldwide and the oil embargo of 1973.

6. With higher relative food and energy prices due to falls in output, the equilibrium real wage rate in the United States fell. Since real wages did not fall sufficiently, the unemployment rate soared in 1974–1975.

7. Inflation hit 11.4 percent in 1974. Monetary policy was relatively tight in 1974 and neutral in 1975–1976. Inflation was reduced but economic growth was sluggish in 1976, despite the fact that the economy was emerging from the 1974–1975 recession. Ford lost the election to Carter.

8. The Carter administration stimulated the economy early in its term of office. Monetary policy was expansionary in 1977, and inflation accel-

erated in 1978. The 1978–1979 oil crisis compounded Carter's economic problems.

9. International speculation against the dollar obliged Carter to appoint Paul Volcker as Chairman of the Fed in August 1979. After further strong speculation against the dollar, the Fed announced its new operating procedures on October 5, 1979.

10. Monetary restraint in 1979–1980 produced a recession in 1980. Despite expansionary monetary policy in the second half of 1980, Carter lost the election to Reagan.

11. Reagan supported monetary restraint early in his term. This was followed by the 1981–1982 recession, but inflation was brought down rapidly.

12. An expansionary monetary policy started in July 1982. This was followed by a strong economic recovery in 1983.

Questions

1. Why did Nixon favor tighter monetary policy immediately after his 1968 election?

2. Why were monetary and fiscal policies both stimulative in 1970?

3. What was the purpose of the 1971 wage and price controls?

4. How could monetary policy have supported and complemented the 1971 price and wage controls?

5. How did monetary and fiscal policies in 1971–1972 work against the wage and price controls?

6. Why did Nixon pursue monetary and fiscal policies that conflicted with the wage and price controls?

7. What happened to inflation in 1973 and why?

8. If the money supply remains constant and food and energy prices rise, how can flow equilibrium be maintained?

9. How did the OPEC cartel reduce equilibrium real wages in the United States?

10. What was the effect of resisting a decline in real wages in the United States after the 1973–1974 oil crisis?

11. Analyze all the factors causing double-digit inflation in 1974.

12. How did Carter mismanage the political business cycle?

13. What were the main effects of tighter monetary policy in 1981–1982?

14. Why did the Fed allow the money supply to grow so fast from July 1982 to June 1983?

15. What were the main effects of the expansionary monetary policy of 1982–1983?

The Dollar in the Postwar International Monetary System

Keynes's International Clearing Union

Postwar Reconstruction

In 1944, representatives of the world's capitalist countries met in Bretton Woods, New Hampshire, to create a new international payments system to replace the gold standard that had collapsed during the 1930s. The main task was to create a monetary system that would provide for the relief and reconstruction of war-torn Western Europe. Europe had been devastated by the war and needed large amounts of imports in the immediate postwar years not only to feed and clothe the population but also to rebuild its productive capacity so that economic activity could be restored. Only the United States, which was undamaged by the war, had sufficient industrial capacity to supply those badly needed goods.

Sterilization by Surplus Countries

John Maynard Keynes, the foremost economist of his generation, was the head of the British delegation to that conference. Keynes was acutely concerned about what he called the "deflationary bias" in the gold standard. Keynes pointed out that under a managed gold standard, most of the pressure to restore equilibrium in the balance of payments would fall on the deficit countries. Under any fixed exchange rate regime, surplus country central banks have to purchase foreign exchange to keep their currencies from appreciating. If the purchase of foreign exchange were allowed to increase high-powered money, inflation would soon eliminate the surplus. However, surplus country central banks can insulate the money supply from the balance-of-payments surplus by offsetting purchases of foreign exchange with open market sales of government bonds. These sterilization policies enable surplus countries to avoid the costs of inflation. With such sterilization, the surplus will continue, but that fact is of little immediate concern to surplus countries because they can purchase virtually unlimited amounts of foreign exchange that can then be invested in foreign currency-denominated income-earning financial assets.

Deficit Countries Could Exhaust Reserves

Deficit country central banks, on the other hand, have to sell foreign exchange to prevent their currencies from depreciating. If the sales of foreign exchange were allowed to reduce high-powered money, the resulting deflation would eliminate the deficit. These deficit countries could, of course, offset the sales of foreign exchange with open market purchases of bonds and thus insulate their money supply from the balance-of-payments deficit. However, their ability to continue these sterilization policies is limited. If deficit countries do not deflate, balance-of-payments deficits will continue. However, unlike surplus countries, deficit countries cannot finance deficits forever, because they will eventually run out of foreign exchange reserves.

Deflationary Bias of Managed Gold Exchange Standard

Keynes argued that such a managed gold standard would put very little pressure on surplus countries to inflate, but the deficit countries, threatened with a loss of foreign exchange reserves, would be forced to deflate. Given the magnitude of the postwar needs for reconstruction and development, Keynes felt that a return to the gold standard would precipitate widespread deflation in Western Europe. To eliminate this deflationary bias of the gold standard, Keynes proposed his own plan for an International Clearing Union.

International Clearing Union

The International Clearing Union would provide an alternative means for deficit countries to finance their sales of gold or foreign exchange. Any member country would be entitled to settle its debts to any other member by making a *bancor* transfer from its own account to the account of the creditor country. Moreover, all member states would agree to accept such bancor transfers without limit. A deficit country threatened with a loss of foreign exchange reserves could use bancors to purchase additional gold or foreign exchange to continue the support of its currency on the foreign exchange market. When the deficit country ran out of bancors to sell, the International Clearing Union was then permitted to create new bancors to lend to the deficit country. The Union could not extend unlimited credits to the deficit country (debtors' overdrafts were to be limited to three-quarters of the sum of their exports and imports), but the plan would eliminate much of the pressure on deficit countries to deflate.

Adjustment Pressures on Surplus and Deficit Countries

In essence, Keynes's plan would require surplus nations to finance the deficits of other nations by lending them foreign exchange. Not only would the plan virtually eliminate the need for deficit countries to deflate, but it would also create pressures on surplus countries to inflate because the bancor balances being accumulated by the surplus countries would earn no interest. In fact, the plan gave the Union the right to place a penalty tax on those bancor balances if they exceeded one-quarter of the sum of the surplus country's exports and imports.

Keynes versus the United States

Keynes's plan was clever, but it was motivated by a preoccupation with Britain's huge deficits. Keynes knew that the United States would emerge as the surplus country in the immediate postwar period and feared that Britain and Europe would be forced to deflate. The American delegation headed by Harry Dexter White fought Keynes's proposal. The United States was a surplus nation which owned most of the world's gold stock. Keynes's plan would have forced the United States into lending unlimited foreign exchange reserves at a zero or negative interest rate to Europe.

Establishment of the International Monetary Fund

A compromise was finally adopted and President Truman signed the Bretton Woods Agreement Act on July 31, 1945. The articles of that agreement established a new permanent institution, the International Monetary Fund (IMF), to administer the Articles and to lend to those member countries in balance-of-payments deficit. Each Fund member, except the United States, would establish a par value for its currency in terms of the dollar.

Par Value System

Central banks were then obliged to intervene to prevent the value of their currency in foreign exchange markets from deviating by more than 1 percent from the declared par value. The United States was obliged, in turn, to maintain gold prices within 1 percent of $35 an ounce. Except for a transitional arrangement permitting a one-time adjustment of up to 10 percent in par values, members could change exchange rates thereafter only with the approval of the Fund. The Articles stated that such approval would be given only if the country's balance of payments was in "fundamental disequilibrium"—a term that has never been clearly defined.

Quotas and IMF Lending

Besides administering these Articles, the International Monetary Fund could also lend to member countries in balance-of-payments deficit from its own holdings of gold and foreign exchange. On joining, each member subscribed gold and its own currency in relation to its quota. Each member's quota took into account the economic importance of that member in the world economy. In one sense, the lending operations of the Fund resembled Keynes's International Clearing Union, but the obligation of surplus countries to lend to deficit countries was limited. Each member's obligation to lend to deficit countries was limited to the size of its quota in the Fund and no more. The Bretton Woods system contained the fatal flaw that Keynes had worked so hard to avoid. The burden of adjustment had to be borne entirely by deficit countries, while surplus countries continued without restraint to accumulate income-earning assets denominated in foreign currencies. The asymmetry of the adjustment process eventually caused the collapse of the Bretton Woods system in the early 1970s.

The Postwar Dollar Shortage

The Marshall Plan   One of the main concerns expressed by Keynes and other European representatives at the Bretton Woods conference of 1944 was that postwar reconstruction would be severely constrained unless Europe's international reserves, completely exhausted to finance the war, could be replenished. The dollar shortage predicted by the Europeans did indeed materialize after the war was over. The Lend-Lease program ended in 1945 and its termination led to a rapid depletion of European and Japanese foreign exchange reserves. In the two years 1946–1947 the rest of the world used about $6 billion of its gold and dollar reserves to finance its deficit with the United States. Threatened with the loss of reserves, they were faced with the choice between deflation and devaluation. The United States solved Europe's balance-of-payments problems by providing billions of dollars to Europe under the Marshall Plan, formally known as the European Recovery Program. Between mid-1948 and mid-1952 the United States provided $11.6 billion in the form of grants and $1.8 billion in the form of loans to Europe. These funds averted the dollar shortage and allowed European countries to avoid both deflation and, to a large extent, devaluation. After a general devaluation of European exchange rates during September 1949 (ranging from $30\frac{1}{2}$ percent for the British pound to 12.3 percent for the Belgian franc), no further depreciation of European currencies occurred until August 1957, when France, saddled with an increasingly costly war in Algeria and the political unwillingness to impose restrictive monetary policies on an inflationary economy, devalued the franc by 20 percent.

Balance-of-Payments Deficits in the 1950s   During the 1950s Europe and Japan rebuilt their industrial bases and substantially improved their balance of payments. From 1952 to 1965 the United States ran a balance-of-payments deficit in every year except 1957. To a large extent, however, those balance-of-payments deficits played a beneficial role in the new international payments system. Member countries of the International Monetary Fund had to hold reserves of dollars or gold to support their currencies during periods of balance-of-payments deficits. A major weakness in the Bretton Woods arrangement was that it failed to provide for a systematic increase in world reserves of dollars and gold as world trade grew. The Fund subscriptions created a once-and-for-all increase in world reserves, but the Fund could not continue to create world reserves (as would have Keynes's International Clearing Union through the creation of bancors). The only way the rest of the world could increase its foreign exchange reserves was through U.S. balance-of-payments deficits.

Redistribution versus Increase in International Reserves   In order to increase their foreign exchange reserves, foreign countries had to maintain undervalued currencies to generate balance-of-payments surpluses. This meant that the United States had an overvalued currency and a balance-of-payments deficit. However, the effect of U.S. deficits on world reserves depends critically on how the rest of the world wants to hold those reserves. If foreign countries purchased gold from the United States at $35 an ounce, total world reserves would not increase. The increase in foreign countries' reserves would be offset by a drop in U.S. reserves. On the other hand, if foreign central banks held dollars as reserves rather than gold, total world reserves would increase. Foreign countries' reserves would go up, but U.S. reserves would not go down.

United States Creates International Money in the 1950s

Central banks did hold most of their reserves in the form of dollars rather than gold. In essence, the United States assumed the role of a world central bank. Foreign central banks deposited their purchases of dollars in special accounts at the Fed with instructions that they be invested in U.S. government securities. These dollar assets were an attractive way of holding reserves because they earned interest, whereas gold did not. Of the $8.5 billion increase in world reserves in the years 1949–1959, $7 billion consisted of dollar liabilities to foreign central banks. The use of dollar liabilities as international reserves came to be known as the *key currency* reserve system. During most of the 1950s the U.S. balance-of-payments deficit basically reflected the dollar's role as the key currency. Foreigners wanted dollar liabilities as reserves. However, in 1958 they decided that they had accumulated enough dollar reserves and the gold drain began.

The Gold Drain

Suez Crisis in 1956

In 1956 Britain, France, and Israel invaded Egypt to retake the Suez Canal, which had just been seized by Egypt's leader, Abdul Gamar Nasser. The United States pressured for a cease-fire, which materialized only after the Suez Canal had been blocked by sunken ships. The resulting disruption of oil supplies from the Middle East produced a temporary surge in U.S. oil exports to Europe. In 1957 the United States ran its first balance-of-payments surplus since 1951.

Balance-of-Payments Deficits on Current Account

A combination of events brought an end to the era of the dollar shortage. The reopening of the Suez Canal in 1958 sharply reduced European imports of U.S. oil. Moreover, the new Common Market drastically altered trade patterns by decreasing internal tariff barriers and increasing external tariffs against U.S. exports. In addition, France, which had already devalued in 1957, devalued the franc again in late 1958 to ensure that it would enter the new Common Market with an undervalued currency. These developments sharply reduced U.S. exports, while imports continued to rise. As a result, the current account deteriorated dramatically from a surplus of $3.5 billion in 1957 to deficits of $5 million in 1958 and $2.1 billion in 1959. This deterioration in the current account balance on top of capital outflows and large military expenditures abroad created large balance-of-payments deficits for the United States.

Foreign Central Banks Convert Dollars into Gold

Between 1958 and 1961 the United States ran balance-of-payments deficits totaling over $10 billion. This time foreign central banks were not willing to finance the U.S. payments deficit by accumulating dollar reserves. They demanded gold for approximately two-thirds of the payments deficit. The U.S. gold stock fell from about $23 billion in 1957 to less than $17 billion in 1961.

Restrictive Monetary Policy in 1959 to Deter Gold Drain

Fear of continued gold outflows prompted the Fed to switch to a restrictive monetary policy before the economy had completely recovered from the 1957–1958 recession. The discount rate was raised in five steps from $1\frac{3}{4}$ percent in April 1958 to 4 percent in September 1959. The resulting decline in Federal Reserve credit together with gold outflows caused the money supply to decline at an annual rate of more than 2 percent from the summer of 1959 to the summer of 1960. This decline in the money supply heralded the 1960 recession.

Continued Gold Drain Despite 1960 Recession

The 1960 recession reduced U.S. imports while rising incomes abroad stimulated exports. The result was a dramatic turnaround in the U.S. current account balance to a surplus of $1.8 billion in 1960. Despite this improvement in the current account, however, the gap between high interest rates of a booming Europe and low interest rates of the United States in recession caused a sharp increase in capital outflows, resulting in continued payments deficits and gold outflows.

Kennedy's Concern over Balance of Payments

Although the 1960 recession did improve the U.S. current account balance, it also contributed to the defeat of the Republican candidate in November. The balance-of-payments problem remained a major concern of the new Kennedy administration, however. Arthur Schlesinger once reported:

> The balance of payments remained a constant worry to Kennedy. Of all the problems he faced as President, one had the impression that he felt least at home with this one. He used to tell his advisers that the two things which scared him most were nuclear war and the payments deficit. Once he half-humorously derided the notion that nuclear weapons were essential to international prestige. "What really matters," he said, "is the strength of the currency. It is this, not the *force de frappe*, which makes France a factor. Britain has nuclear weapons, but the pound is weak, so everyone pushes it around. Why are people so nice to Spain today? Not because Spain has nuclear weapons but because of all those lovely gold reserves." He had acquired somewhere, perhaps from his father, the belief that a nation was only as strong as the value of its currency; and he feared that, if he pushed things too far, "loss of confidence" would descend and there would be a run on gold. But he was determined not to be stampeded into restrictive domestic measures, and he brought steady pressures for remedies which would not block expansion at home. The problem perhaps constrained him more in foreign affairs. He thought, for example, that the continuing payments deficit gave France, with its claims on American gold, a dangerous international advantage; and at times he even briefly considered

doing things which would otherwise run athwart his policy, like selling submarines to South Africa, in the hope of relieving the strain on the balance of payments.[1]

International Competitiveness Improves in 1960s

The problem was not that the U.S. economy was uncompetitive with the rest of the world. In fact, the competitive position of U.S. industry as measured by unit labor costs was improving relative to most of its foreign competitors. Manufacturers' labor costs actually fell at an annual rate of 0.7 percent between 1960 and 1965, while the labor costs of U.S. competitors rose at rates of 2 to 6 percent a year. This improvement in the competitive position of U.S. industry was a principal factor accounting for the increase in the current account surplus from $1.8 billion in 1960 to a spectacular $5.8 billion in 1964.

Balance-of-Payments Deficit on Capital Account

It was the enormous outflow of capital that constituted the U.S. balance-of-payments problem. Short-term interest rates were higher in Europe than in the United States and hence short-term capital was drawn abroad. Just as serious was direct investment by U.S. firms in productive assets abroad. Changing trade patterns created incentives for U.S. firms to build factories behind the tariff walls of the new Common Market.

Monetary Policy Constrained by Balance-of-Payments Deficit

Kennedy had pledged during the 1960 election that he would "get the country moving again" with economic policies that would produce an annual growth in output of 5 percent. The Fed cooperated by switching to easier monetary conditions during the summer of 1960. This produced a dramatic recovery in 1961. In early 1962, however, the rate of monetary growth slowed and subsequently economic growth started to lose steam. The Fed shared the Kennedy administration's concern with the weakening economy but was also worried about the balance-of-payments deficit. The United States already had a balance-of-payments deficit of $2.24 billion in 1962.

Expansionary Monetary Policy and Capital Outflows

If the Fed accelerates the rate of monetary growth, the immediate effect is an excess supply of money. As individuals attempt to reduce their money balances, they create an additional flow demand for bonds that causes interest rates to drop, as shown in Figure 23.1a. Lower interest rates then induce foreigners to borrow in the United States and U.S. residents to lend abroad. These capital outflows constitute a supply of dollars, as shown in Figure 23.1b. Moreover, lower interest rates also increase expenditures on goods and services. If some of these expenditures are for foreign goods and services, the additional imports increase the supply of dollars even more. This creates a policy dilemma. An acceleration in the rate of monetary growth for the purpose of stimulating economic growth would at the same time worsen the balance of payments.

[1]Arthur Schlesinger, Jr., *A Thousand Days: John Kennedy in the White House* (Boston: Houghton Mifflin, 1965), pp. 654–655.

Figure 23.1   The Effect of an Acceleration in Monetary Growth on the Balance of Payments

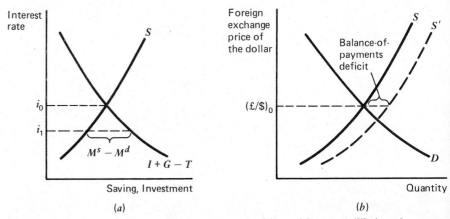

(a)   (b)

Figure 23.1a shows saving and investment schedules with an equilibrium interest rate of i_0. The immediate effect of an acceleration in monetary growth is to produce an excess supply of money. This excess creates an additional flow demand for bonds which depresses the interest rate to i_1. As the interest rate drops, foreigners borrow in U.S. financial markets and U.S. residents buy foreign financial assets. The resulting capital outflow increases the supply of dollars to the foreign exchange market, as shown in Figure 23.1b, causing a balance-of-payments deficit.

Fiscal Stimulus to Investment Raises Interest Rates

Kennedy's solution to this policy dilemma was to create tax incentives for investment at home. In 1962 he accelerated the rate at which businesses could depreciate their investments for tax purposes and introduced a 7 percent investment tax credit applicable only to investment in the United States. Since these tax incentives increased the profitability of investment, the marginal efficiency of investment schedule shifted to the right, as shown in Figure 23.2a. To the extent that the tax incentives reduced tax revenue, the government deficit also increased slightly. Even though the rise in after-tax income probably shifted the savings schedule to the right, the net effect was to raise the equilibrium interest rate from i_0 to i_1. Higher interest rates, however, induced foreigners to purchase U.S. financial securities and U.S. residents to borrow abroad. These capital inflows added to the demand for dollars, as shown in Figure 23.2b, and created an improvement in the balance of payments.

Expansionary Monetary and Fiscal Policies, 1962–1964

By using a policy mix of an expansionary monetary policy combined with tax incentives to investment, Kennedy was able to avoid the dilemma of choosing between economic growth and the need to prevent a worsening in the U.S. balance-of-payments deficit. The tax incentives set off an investment boom in 1963 and 1964. The demand for funds to finance that

Figure 23.2   The Effect of Accelerated Depreciation and the Investment Tax Credit on the Balance of Payments

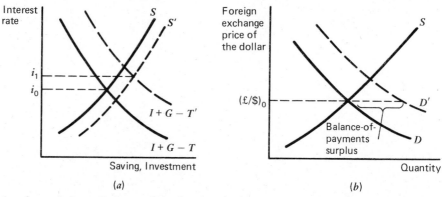

Accelerated depreciation and the investment tax credit increase the profitability of investment. To the extent that they reduce tax revenue they also increase the government deficit. The combined effect is to shift the $(I + G - T)$ schedule to the right in Figure 23.2a. To the extent that some of the increase in after-tax income resulting from these tax changes is saved, the saving schedule also shifts to the right. The net effect is an increase in the equilibrium interest rate from i_0 to i_1. This increase in interest rates produces capital inflows which increase the demand for dollars in the foreign exchange market as shown in Figure 23.2b. The result is to create a balance-of-payments surplus.

investment boom pushed interest rates up, despite an acceleration in the rate of monetary growth. As a result, Kennedy succeeded in stimulating economic growth without worsening the U.S. balance of payments.

Interest Equalization Tax of 1964   On July 18, 1963, Kennedy took one of his last actions to curb the outflow of capital. In a special message to Congress, he proposed an Interest Equalization Tax of 1 percent on foreign securities sold in the United States. A few months later Kennedy was dead and the presidency had passed to Lyndon Johnson. Congress finally passed Kennedy's tax cut legislation and the Interest Equalization Tax in 1964.

1966 Balance-of-Payments Surplus   Credit demands in 1965 were intense as the financing needs of the continuing investment boom collided with a sharp increase in government borrowing to finance the loss of revenue from the tax cut and the increase in military expenditures associated with the buildup in Vietnam. When the Fed suddenly slowed the rate of monetary growth in 1966, interest rates zoomed up. This rise in U.S. interest rates relative to those of foreign countries, especially Japan, sharply reduced capital outflows. In fact, 1966 was the first year since 1957 that the United States had a balance-of-payments surplus.

Figure 23.3   Interest Rates and the Balance of Payments, 1966–1969

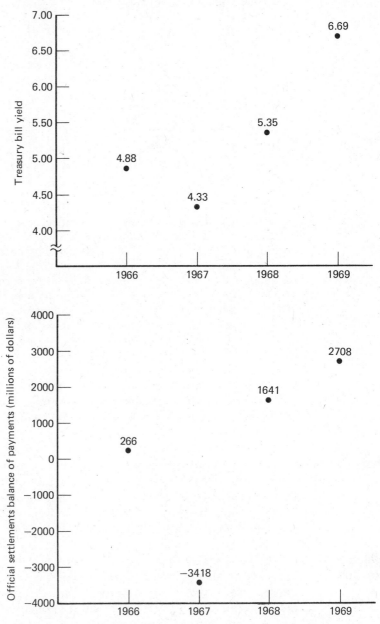

Source: International Financial Statistics, 23(12), December 1970, p. 344.

Monetary Expansion and the 1967 Balance-of-Payments Deficit

In early 1967 the Fed switched to an expansionary monetary policy. During 1967 and 1968 the money supply increased at the extremely rapid rate of 7.3 percent a year. As shown in Figure 23.3*a*, interest rates followed the typical pattern discussed in Chapter 15—first falling and then rising to even higher levels—after this acceleration in the rate of monetary growth. Immediately after the acceleration in the rate of monetary growth, interest rates fell sharply. This drop in interest rates relative to those abroad increased capital outflows, and the balance of payments registered a deficit of $3.4 billion in 1967, as shown in Figure 23.3*b*.

1968–1969 Balance-of-Payments Surpluses

However, as economic recovery raised income and the demand for money, interest rates started to rise. By 1968 the rate of inflation had begun to accelerate, reaching 6 percent by the end of the year. Widespread expectations of continuing inflation pushed interest rates to record levels in 1969. As interest rates in the United States rose relative to those abroad, the resulting reversal of capital outflows produced a strong improvement in the balance of payments, with the United States showing balance-of-payments surpluses of $1.6 billion in 1968 and $2.7 billion in 1969.

Inflation Creates Balance-of-Payments Deficits in 1970 and 1971

Although the inflation associated with the acceleration in the rate of monetary growth in 1967 and 1968 raised the level of nominal interest rates and thus improved the balance-of-payments capital account, it sowed the seeds of a continuing deterioration in the trade balance. Under a fixed exchange rate system, a country that has a higher rate of inflation than its trading partners will experience a decline in the relative price of traded to nontraded goods and a deterioration in its trade balance. From a surplus of $6.8 billion in 1964, the U.S. merchandise trade balance had deteriorated to a deficit of $2.7 billion in 1971. By 1970, financial markets had become fearful that further deterioration in the trade balance would force a devaluation of the dollar. Once such expectations became widespread, even high interest rates in the United States could not compensate for the financial risk of devaluation. Capital outflows created balance-of-payments deficits of $9.8 billion in 1970 and $29.8 billion in 1971.

The Breakup of the Bretton Woods System

Dollar Convertibility

The United States had an obligation under the Articles of the Bretton Woods Agreement to peg the price of gold at $35 an ounce. Although it had been illegal for U.S. citizens to own gold since 1933, foreigners could buy U.S. gold reserves at $35 an ounce because the United States guaranteed that it would intervene with gold sales if the price on private markets rose above $35. This meant that private speculators could become a potential threat to the U.S. gold stock. Besides meeting obligations to foreign central banks, the United States would also have to supply gold to private speculators who were betting on a devaluation of the dollar in terms of gold.

Speculation Accelerates Gold Drain in 1967–1968

U.S. balance-of-payments deficits had already caused a sharp decline in U.S. gold reserves. The gold stock fell to less than $12 billion by the end of 1967. Of that, all but about $2 billion was being held as backing against Federal Reserve notes; the Fed was required by law to hold a 25 percent gold cover against these notes. Private gold markets appeared to behave as though only the surplus over the legal cover was really available for sale. With the gold drain approaching $1 billion a month, speculators sensed the possibility of an imminent increase in the price of gold. This expectation accelerated the drain of U.S. gold into the hands of foreign speculators. The U.S. Senate frantically passed legislation removing the gold cover in early 1968.

United States Suspends Private Gold Sales in 1968

This legislation allowed the entire gold stock to be used to defend the convertibility of the dollar into gold at $35 an ounce, but the hemorrhage of U.S. gold into private hands continued. By March 1968 speculation against the dollar had reached enormous proportions, with gold losses approaching $500 million on some days. On March 17 the United States announced that it would no longer sell gold in the private market. It continued to honor its commitment to buy and sell gold in transactions with other central banks at $35 an ounce, but the price of gold in the private market was no longer pegged. Thus, the gold market was divided into a two-tier price system: fluctuating prices in the private market and a fixed $35 an ounce for official monetary transactions. The two-tier gold market insulated the U.S. gold stock from foreign speculators, but the balance-of-payments problem remained.

Balance-of-Payments Surpluses in France, Germany, and Japan

Of course, every deficit must have a surplus elsewhere to offset it. The surplus offsetting the U.S. balance-of-payments deficit was shared by West Germany, Japan, and France. To keep their currencies from appreciating, these countries had to buy dollars in the foreign exchange market. Most of these dollars were used to purchase U.S. treasury bills, but foreign central banks had the option of buying gold from the United States at $35 an ounce. Since 1958 every Secretary of the Treasury had spent part of his time traveling in Europe to persuade foreign central banks to hold their reserves in dollar liabilities rather than gold. West Germany and Japan went along with these U.S. requests, but France did not.

France Converts Dollars into Gold

General Charles de Gaulle regarded the holding of dollars as an involuntary transfer of savings to the United States which would help finance American imperial military and economic activities around the world. De

Gaulle personally opposed the war in Vietnam and felt that holding dollar reserves helped finance that war. His decision to convert France's dollar holdings into gold also reflected growing French opposition to the U.S. "takeover" of European industry. In 1967 Jean Servant-Schreiber published a best-selling book in France entitled *Le Défi Americain* (*The American Challenge*) that warned of an economic takeover of Common Market economies by U.S. corporations. De Gaulle insisted that the economic invasion by U.S. corporations was due "not so much to the organic superiority of the United States as to dollar inflation that it is exporting to others under the cover of the gold standard." If Americans wanted to buy French assets, De Gaulle would make them pay in gold.

Excess Dollar Supply and Forced Foreign Saving

There was a lot of truth in De Gaulle's analysis of the U.S. balance-of-payments problems. A U.S. balance-of-payments deficit meant that there was an excess supply of dollars in the foreign exchange market. Under the Bretton Woods system of fixed exchange rates, the central banks of the surplus countries (West Germany, Japan, and France) were required to buy up any dollars in excess supply. If the foreign central banks allowed the purchase of dollars to increase high-powered money, the U.S. inflation would simply be exported to their countries. In order to prevent imported inflation, the central banks of the surplus countries had to sterilize the purchases of dollars with offsetting open market sales of domestic securities. The central banks of Germany and Japan, which held their reserves in dollar liabilities of the U.S. government, were, in effect, borrowing in their own capital markets in order to acquire U.S. government securities. In fact, from 1966 to 1973 all the increase in federal debt found its way into the portfolios of monetary authorities, with the Fed absorbing $43 billion and foreign central banks buying $51 billion of the debt. Without these central bank purchases of U.S. government securities, that government debt would have had to be absorbed by the private sector in the United States, crowding out competing borrowers of loanable funds. The sterilized purchases of dollars by foreign central banks were essentially involuntary transfers of foreign savings to U.S. capital markets, which lowered U.S. interest rates. This involuntary inflow of foreign savings thus made it cheaper for U.S. corporations to expand their operations at home and abroad. It also made it possible for Americans to finance additional purchases of goods and services and minimized the economic sacrifices involved in fighting the war in Vietnam. To some degree, the United States could have guns *and* butter.

French Balance-of-Payments Deficit after 1968 Student Revolt

De Gaulle continued purchasing gold from the United States until 1968. In May of that year Danny le Rouge led a student uprising at the Sorbonne University in Paris which almost toppled the De Gaulle government. Eventually, the students were joined by workers in a general strike which succeeded in paralyzing the French economy. De Gaulle finally gave in to their demands, and the wage explosion which followed completely eliminated France's cost advantage in international trade. From April 1968 to April 1969 hourly wage rates in manufacturing rose almost 17 percent. By the second quarter of 1969 France had a trade deficit of $2.7 billion. Fears of a devaluation of the franc caused speculators to sell francs, further aggravating the French balance-of-payments deficit. Instead of buying gold, France was now compelled to seek financial help from the United States and to sell half the gold accumulated through the 1960s to prevent the franc from depreciating against the dollar.

Franc Devalued and Mark Revalued in 1969

De Gaulle regarded a devaluation of the franc as a sign of national weakness and refused to devalue. However, the political fortunes turned against him and he resigned in April 1969. The new government, faced with massive reserve losses, devalued the franc by 12½ percent on August 8, 1969. Two months later the German mark was revalued by 9.3 percent. With this realignment of European exchange rates, speculators now turned their attention to the dollar.

Special Drawing Rights in 1970

One of the more ironic aspects of the dollar's decline was U.S. support for the creation of Special Drawing Rights (SDRs). The SDR concept bore a striking resemblance to Keynes's bancors. It essentially turned the International Monetary Fund into a world central bank able to create international reserves as would have Keynes's International Clearing Union. The United States was on the verge of becoming a chronic deficit country, just as Britain had been in 1944. Now it was the United States that favored an arrangement that would *oblige* surplus nations to lend foreign exchange to deficit countries. A modified U.S. proposal was put into effect on January 1, 1970.

Monetary Expansion and Balance-of-Payments Deficit in 1970

Thanks to an extremely restrictive monetary policy which pushed up interest rates to record levels, as well as to the disastrous French balance-of-payments deficit, the Nixon administration was not plagued by balance-of-payments problems during its first year in office. In fact, the United States had a balance of payments surplus of $2.7 billion in 1969. In 1970, however, the balance-of-payments position changed dramatically. In January 1970 Nixon replaced William McChesney Martin as chairman of the Federal Reserve Board with Arthur Burns. Shortly thereafter, the Fed shifted to an easier monetary policy. Three-month treasury bill rates fell from almost 8 percent in January to less than 5 percent by the end of the year. Although the current account improved as a result of the 1970 recession, which reduced demand for imports, capital flowed to the higher interest rates in Europe and the payments deficit ballooned to $9.8 billion.

Balance-of-Payments Deficit Explodes in 1971

In 1971 the United States experienced its first deficit in merchandise trade of this century. Where once the trade surplus had been sufficient to finance U.S. overseas military programs and capital outflows, now there was a trade deficit which required financing too. The official settlements deficit—the amount of unwanted dollars purchased by foreign central banks—was an incredible $29.8 billion in 1971. In addition to the current account deficit of $1.4 billion, capital outflows caused by investor uncertainty about the dollar contributed another $28 billion to the balance-of-payments deficit. Despite these huge purchases of dollars, foreign central banks were very restrained in their demands for gold from the United States. Even though central banks abroad purchased more than $21 billion unwanted dollars in the first nine months of 1971, the United States lost only $840 million of its gold reserves. Nevertheless, the U.S. government was worried. If foreign central banks demanded gold, the United States would not be able to maintain convertibility of the dollar into gold, except by re-establishing the par value of the dollar at a price substantially above $35 an ounce.

Overvalued Dollar Reduces International Competitiveness

In addition to threatening the convertibility of the dollar into gold, the overvalued dollar also made it extremely difficult for U.S. traded goods industries to compete internationally. Labor costs were rising as workers increased their wage demands to keep up with inflation. While the non-traded goods industries could pass those higher labor costs on in higher prices, the traded goods industries could not. If they raised their prices, they would lose their markets to foreign competition. The producers of traded goods put increasing political pressure on the Nixon administration to do something about the overvalued dollar. Meanwhile, Congress was introducing several pieces of legislation, such as the Burke-Hartke bill, which would sharply increase tariffs.

Europe and Japan Refuse to Revalue

European and Japanese central banks were reluctant to let their currencies appreciate too far against the dollar. European and Japanese export industries enjoyed their competitive advantage in world markets because of the overvalued dollar, and they used all the political muscle they had to resist a revaluation of their currencies. So long as they refused to let their currencies appreciate against the dollar, the United States could not devalue. Under the Articles of the International Monetary Fund, responsibility for pegging exchange rates rested with foreign central banks. The United States had the sole responsibility for pegging the dollar price of gold. If Japan and Europe continued to maintain their current exchange rates to the dollar, a devaluation of the dollar against gold would leave traded goods' producers no better off than they had been before

Germans Stop Dollar Purchases in May 1971

In May 1971 the international monetary system of fixed exchange rates broke down under the strain of U.S. balance-of-payments deficits. On May 5, after the West Germans had purchased $1 billion during the first hour of trading, the Germans stopped supporting the dollar. The floating of the mark was followed by revaluations of the Swiss franc and the Austrian schilling. Despite these revaluations of European currencies, however, the dollar remained in a precarious position. In mid-May France and Belgium demanded gold from the United States, reducing the U.S. gold stock to only $10.6 billion. This triggered a sharp rise in gold prices on private bullion markets.

United States Suspends Dollar Convertibility in August 1971

Finally, on Sunday evening, August 15, 1971, President Nixon dropped a bombshell on U.S. trading partners. In a televised speech, Nixon announced a radically new economic program to deal with the overvalued dollar. Included in the program were: a 90-day freeze on wages and prices to break inflationary expectations, an import surcharge of 10 percent, and suspension of the convertibility of dollars into gold. Since the United States no longer honored its obligation to the International Monetary Fund to sell gold at $35 an ounce, Nixon had put the world on a dollar standard. The president acknowledged that "this action will not win us any friends among the international money traders. But our primary concern is with American workers, and with fair competition around the world." The 10 percent surcharge on imports was characterized as a "temporary action" designed to pressure other countries into appreciating their currencies so that "American products will not be at a disadvantage because of unfair exchange rates. When the unfair treatment is ended, the import tax will end as well. . . . The time has come for exchange rates to be set straight and for the major nations to compete as equals. There is no longer any need for the United States to compete with one hand tied behind her back." Having urged central banks to accumulate dollar reserves for over two decades, the United States was now telling the world to let the dollar drop in value, making those dollar-denominated reserves worth less.

Smithsonian Agreement of December 1971

In the months that followed the decision to close the gold window, John Connally, Nixon's new Secretary of the Treasury, used the leverage of the 10 percent import tax to negotiate a new set of exchange rates. What finally came out of this power play was the Smithsonian Agreement of December 18, 1971, which officially devalued the dollar by an average of 12 percent against the currencies of 14 major industrial countries. The official price of gold was raised to $38 an ounce. President Nixon proclaimed that this was "the most significant monetary agreement in the history of the world," but the truth was that the United States needed a bigger devaluation than it got. The 12 percent devaluation was not sufficient to eliminate the excess supply of dollars on the foreign exchange market. The U.S. balance-of-payments deficit was still over $10 billion in 1972. In early 1973, partly in reaction to the unprecedented expansion in the U.S. money supply during 1972, private speculators sold large amounts of dollars in the foreign exchange market. Foreign central banks purchased about $10 billion in the first three months of the year alone—compared with a U.S. deficit of $10.4 billion for the whole year of 1972—in an attempt to support the dollar. When this massive intervention failed to stabilize the dollar, even after an additional devaluation of the dollar in February, fixed exchange rates were abandoned.

Generalized Floating Starts in March 1973

On March 16, 1973, the finance ministers of the European Common Market announced that they would let their currencies float against the dollar. Japan had already let the yen float against the dollar on February 12. The European communique agreed:

> . . . in principle that official intervention in exchange markets may be useful at appropriate times, to facilitate the maintenance of orderly conditions, keeping in mind also the desirability of encouraging reflows of speculative movements of funds. Each nation stated that it will be prepared to intervene at its initiative in its own market, when necessary and desirable, acting in a flexible manner in the light of market conditions and in close consultation with the authorities of the nation whose currency may be bought or sold.

In other words, the dollar was on a managed float.

Monetary Policy Independence under Floating

The breakup of the Bretton Woods monetary order occurred because of a shift in political preferences towards increased monetary autonomy. The fixed exchange rate system interfered with the pursuit of domestic monetary policy objectives. Because a flexible exchange rate system can protect domestic traded goods industries from being priced out of world markets as a result of inflation, it permits much greater freedom for national monetary policies.

Devaluation and the Trade Balance

The devaluation of the dollar in 1971 had the immediate effect of raising the relative price of traded goods in the United States. An increase in the relative price of traded goods makes traded goods more profitable to produce but more expensive to consume. As these economic forces tend to increase the supply of traded goods and reduce demand, the trade balance measured in physical quantities improves. However, the trade balance enters the balance of payments not as physical quantities, but measured in dollars—the trade deficit in quantities times the price of traded goods. Since quantities of traded goods that are supplied and demanded respond only slowly to an increase in the relative price of traded goods, but the price of traded goods rises almost immediately after a devaluation, a country with an existing trade deficit usually experiences a further deterioration in the domestic currency value of its deficit following a devaluation before any improvement takes place. This phenomenon is referred to as the J-curve effect.

The J-Curve for the U.S. Current Account

This J-curve pattern is quite apparent in the data for the U.S. current account, shown in Figure 23.4. The current account deficit was $2.9 billion in 1971, the year of the devaluation. The deficit widened to $8.6 billion in

Figure 23.4   U.S. Balance of Payments on Current Account, 1971–1973

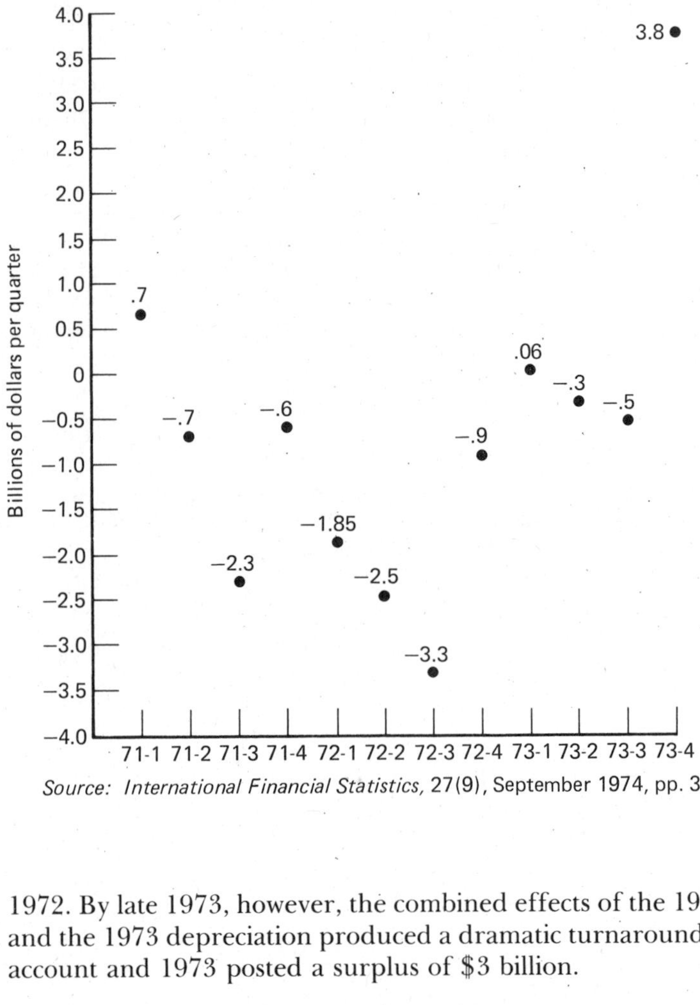

Source: *International Financial Statistics*, 27(9), September 1974, pp. 374–375.

1972. By late 1973, however, the combined effects of the 1971 devaluation and the 1973 depreciation produced a dramatic turnaround in the current account and 1973 posted a surplus of $3 billion.

Floating Exchange Rates and the Energy Crisis

Dollar Depreciation and Appreciation in 1973

After the floating of the dollar in March 1973, the dollar depreciated until early July, when its price bottomed out at a level which on a trade-weighted basis was 21.2 percent below its pre-Smithsonian par value. It then strengthened through the rest of the year to reach a level only 17 percent below its pre-Smithsonian price by the end of the year. One of the reasons for the strengthening dollar in late 1973 was the improvement in the U.S. balance of payments on current account.

Oil Shock and Trade Deficits

The quadrupling of oil prices by OPEC in early 1974 was probably the most severe shock to the international monetary system since World War II. This extraordinary rise in OPEC oil prices had a tremendous effect on the balance of payments of oil-importing countries. Imports from OPEC countries to the United States rose by $12.2 billion in 1974. If OPEC had spent all this oil revenue on U.S. goods and services, nothing would have happened to the trade balance. However, the oil states could not absorb such a massive intake of goods. The increase in U.S. imports from OPEC was offset slightly by a $2.9 billion rise in U.S. exports to OPEC, but the deterioration in the U.S. trade balance with OPEC was still an incredible $9.3 billion. This more than accounted for the shift in the aggregate trade balance from a $700 million surplus in 1973 to a deficit of $5.9 billion in 1974.

Petrodollars Recycled

The rise in oil prices increased the OPEC countries' current account surpluses from about $4 billion in 1973 to $66 billion in 1974. By definition, the current account balance of the rest of the world deteriorated by about $62 billion in 1974. The huge current account deficits of the oil-importing countries were financed by a "recycling" of "petrodollars." The OPEC countries used much of their additional oil revenue to buy financial securities from or make loans to the oil-importing countries. Although the oil-importing countries were going into debt, there were no imbalances between the supply of and demand for their currencies on the foreign exchange market. The increased supply of non-OPEC currencies on the foreign exchange market caused by the huge oil imports was offset by an increased demand for these currencies created by the purchase of financial securities by OPEC.

OPEC Investment in U.S. Assets

In 1974, OPEC countries invested about $11 billion in the United States, more than offsetting the deterioration of the U.S. current account balance with OPEC of $9.3 billion. This created a net upward pressure on the value of the dollar. The dollar did not actually rise in value because this upward pressure was offset by an outflow of capital from the United States to other oil-importing countries that borrowed heavily in U.S. capital markets to finance their own oil imports.

Balance-of-Payments Deficit in 1974

In 1974 the U.S. official settlements balance-of-payments deficit was $11 billion. To a large extent, these increases in dollar holdings by foreign central banks reflected the accumulation of reserves by the OPEC countries. In essence, OPEC countries were depositing their oil revenue in U.S. money markets and the United States was acting as a financial intermediary by lending those deposits to other oil-importing countries.

OPEC Influence on Exchange Rates

Although the OPEC countries provided the funds to finance the current account deficits of the oil-importing countries, the recycling of the petrodollars put OPEC in a position to dictate foreign exchange rates. Those countries that received capital inflows from OPEC greater than their current account deficits with OPEC experienced upward pressure on the value of their currencies in the foreign exchange market. Those countries receiving capital inflows from OPEC less than their current account deficits with OPEC experienced downward pressure on the value of their currencies.

Dollar Strengthens in 1975 and 1976

The dollar actually strengthened on the foreign exchange market during 1975 and 1976, as capital inflows from OPEC and private foreign investors were attracted by a favorable investment environment in the United States and the U.S. current account surplus. This strengthening of the dollar was due primarily to a fairly restrictive monetary policy. After increasing at an annual rate of 7.2 percent during 1972 and 1973, the money supply slowed to 5 percent during the 1974–1976 period. However, the election of Jimmy Carter in November 1976 brought this period of monetary restraint to an end.

Carter and the Collapse of the Dollar

Easy Monetary Policy in 1977–1978

The Carter administration wanted a more rapid expansion of the money supply to reduce unemployment, and the Fed complied. Although Arthur Burns continued to preach monetary restraint, thus incurring the wrath of the White House, he let Carter have an extremely expansionary monetary policy. From the third quarter of 1976 to the third quarter of 1978 the money supply accelerated to an annual rate of 8 percent.

Inflation and Flight from Dollar Assets

This acceleration in the rate of monetary growth brought the period of dollar strength to an end. Since the acceleration in monetary growth leads to higher rates of inflation, purchasing power parity necessitates a depreciation of the dollar against currencies with lower inflation rates, as shown by the line *PPP* in Figure 23.5. However, in the short run, the liquidity effect of an excess supply of money reduces real rates of interest and causes capital outflows. As a result of these capital outflows, the exchange rate actually falls by more than that required by purchasing power parity.

Negative Real Interest Rates in the United States

As shown in Table 23.1, real rates of interest in the United States not only dropped significantly following the acceleration of monetary growth in 1977, but also remained negative for the remainder of the 1970s. By early 1977 real rates of interest in the United States were considerably below those abroad. For example, short-term interest rates were about $4\frac{1}{2}$ percent in both the United States and Germany, but prices were rising about $2\frac{1}{2}$ percentage points faster in the United States than in Germany. Since interest rates on dollar assets no longer compensated for the difference in inflation rates, investors began to unload their dollar assets and purchase

Figure 23.5   Effects of an Acceleration in the Rate of Monetary Growth under Floating Exchange Rates

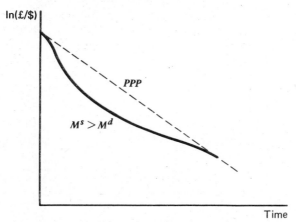

The dashed line *PPP* represents the path of exchange rates if purchasing power parity holds. The foreign exchange price of the dollar will depreciate at a rate equal to the difference between the U.S. rate of inflation and the world rate. However, while a disequilibrium excess supply of money exists, real rates of interest will be depressed, inducing capital outflows. These capital outflows will cause the exchange rate to fall by more than that required for purchasing power parity.

assets denominated in Japanese yen, German marks, and Swiss francs. In the third quarter of 1976, the last quarter before the acceleration in monetary growth, $800 million of capital flowed into the United States from foreign investors. From the fourth quarter of 1976 to the third quarter of 1977 capital flowed out of the United States at a rate of about $5 billion a quarter.

Table 23.1   Realized Real Rate of Return on 30-Day Treasury Bills

Date	Real Interest Rate
1976	0.26
1977	−1.55
1978	−1.70
1979	−2.59
1980	−1.03
1981	5.30
1982	6.42

Source: Updated from Zvi Bodie, "Commodity Futures as a Hedge Against Inflation" *Journal of Portfolio Management,* 9(3), Spring 1983, Table 1, p. 13.

Carter Ignores Weakening of the Dollar in 1977

Initially, Carter showed little concern for the weakness of the dollar. He claimed that current account deficits simply reflected the fact that the U.S. economy was recovering faster from the 1974–1975 recession than the economies of the United States's trading partners. The solution to the dollar problems, from Carter's viewpoint, was to persuade the surplus countries, especially Germany and Japan, to switch to expansionary monetary policies in order to stimulate their economies. Carter made it clear that U.S. recovery would not be sacrificed out of concern for the weakness of the dollar. In fact, on June 24, 1977, Secretary of the Treasury Michael Blumenthal actually asked the Germans and the Japanese to let their currencies appreciate against the dollar in order to stimulate U.S. exports.

Carter's Fight with the Fed Accelerates Capital Flight

Despite the fact that the money supply was growing at the fastest rate since 1972, Carter's Council of Economic Advisers openly criticized the Fed during the fall of 1977 for its moves to raise short-term interest rates. Indeed, the Council argued that the money supply should grow even more rapidly. When this confrontation between the Carter administration and the Fed became public, the flight from the dollar intensified. With the announcement that Carter would replace Arthur Burns with G. William Miller, a man more sympathetic to White House policies, capital outflows increased to almost $14 billion a quarter. In the last four months of 1977 the dollar fell 8.8 percent against the German mark and 9.6 percent against the Japanese yen, despite massive purchases of dollars by the German and Japanese central banks. From the fourth quarter of 1976 to the third quarter of 1977, foreign central banks purchased approximately $5 billion per quarter. This support of the dollar increased during the fourth quarter of 1977 and the first quarter of 1978 to over $13.5 billion a quarter. However, even this massive intervention could not stop the sharp decline of the dollar.

Intervention to Support the Dollar in 1978

By the beginning of 1978 Carter decided that the dollar had fallen enough. On January 4 the Treasury and the Fed announced that they would intervene in the foreign exchange market to support the dollar. To implement this new policy, the Treasury announced that it had negotiated a $2 billion swap line with the German central bank to supplement existing Federal Reserve credit lines with foreign central banks. As its contribution, the Fed raised the discount rate from 6 to $6\frac{1}{2}$ percent. These actions temporarily arrested the fall of the dollar, but by early February the dollar had resumed its downward trend. After using up almost three-quarters of the original $2 billion German swap line, the Treasury had to ask for an additional $4 billion on March 13. This renewed commitment to an active defense of the dollar, combined with a further increase in the discount rate to 7 percent in May, succeeded in generating a modest recovery of the dollar during April and May.

Figure 23.6 Exchange Rates, 1975–1982

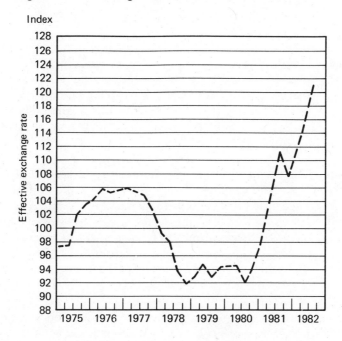

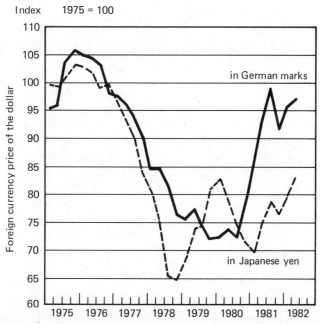

The effective exchange rate index is a weighted average of the exchange rates between the dollar and 17 other major currencies.

Source: Federal Reserve Bank of St. Louis, *International Economic Conditions,* January 24, 1983, p. 2, and *Federal Reserve Bank of New York Quarterly Review,* 7(2), Summer 1982, p. 2.

Dollar Continues to Decline in 1978

By early summer 1978, however, the dollar was again under widespread selling pressure. News that the money supply had increased at an annual rate of 9.3 percent during the second quarter and that inflation had reached double digits sent the dollar plummeting. Altogether, from the fourth quarter of 1976 to October 1978 the dollar fell 47 percent against the Japanese yen and Swiss franc and 27 percent against the German mark, as shown in Figure 23.6.

U.S. International Competitiveness Improves in 1977–1978

The decline of the dollar dramatically increased the competitive position of U.S. producers of traded goods. From the end of 1976 to August 1978, wage rates rose about 13 percent in Japan. After adjusting for the 43 percent fall in the value of the dollar in terms of yen, Japanese wage rates increased by approximately 60 percent in terms of dollars. Even though German wage rates were constant in marks, in terms of dollars they went up by almost 30 percent. During the same period, U.S. wage rates went up only 13.6 percent. Given this sharp increase in foreign labor costs, the price of imported goods rose dramatically. The availability of imports limits the prices that domestic producers of traded goods can charge for their products. The sharp rise in foreign labor costs allowed U.S. producers of traded goods (especially steel, textiles, aluminum, and automobiles) to raise their prices and increase sales at the same time. The relative cost advantage of U.S. producers permitted them to capture larger shares of world markets. Likewise, the rise in the relative price of traded goods induced domestic consumers to substitute nontraded for traded goods, thus dampening the demand for imports.

J-Curve Response in 1978 but Trade Balance Improves in 1979

During 1978 the volume of exports did increase much faster than the volume of imports. Nevertheless, prices of traded goods initially adjusted substantially more than quantities, thus causing the dollar value of the deficit to worsen. This J-curve effect operated with a vengeance during the last half of 1977 and the first quarter of 1978, when the current account deficit ran at an average annual rate of $20.4 billion, as shown in Figure 23.7. However, by early 1979, differences in the relative costs of production had induced sufficient changes in domestic production and consumption of traded goods to improve the current account drastically. Despite the Iranian oil shock, which pushed the price of OPEC oil up 42 percent, the current account showed a surplus of $1.6 billion during the first half of 1979.

Carter's 1978 Anti-Inflation Program Discounted

By autumn 1978 the Carter administration had undergone a change of heart about its economic priorities. The unemployment rate had fallen from 7.8 percent at the end of 1976 to 5.8 percent in October 1978, but inflation (as measured by the consumer price index) had accelerated from 4.2 percent during the last quarter of 1976 to over 10 percent. Public opinion polls now showed that inflation was the number one concern of the

Figure 23.7 U.S. Balance of Payments on Current Account, 1976–1979

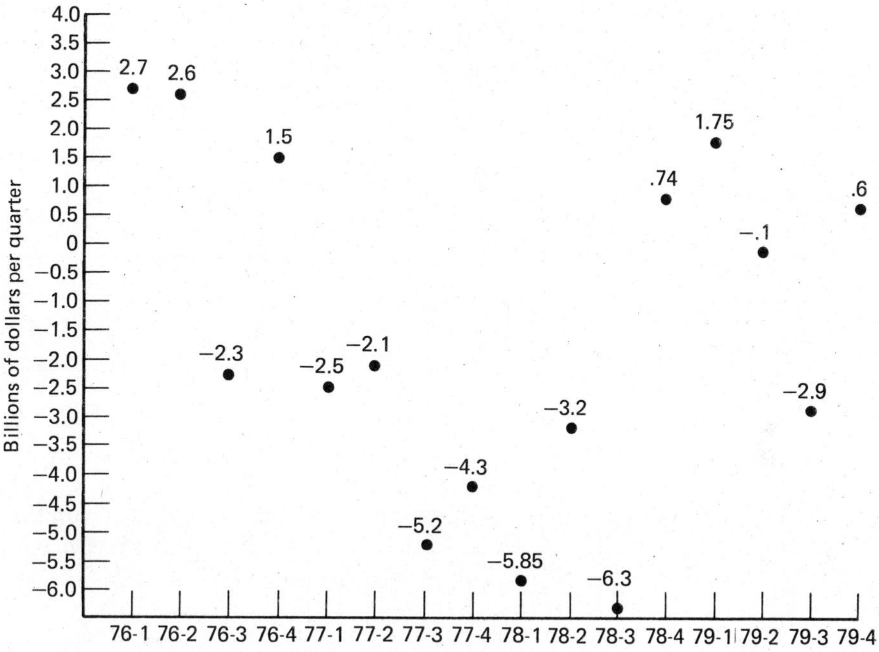

Source: *International Financial Statistics,* 32(12), December 1979, pp. 404–405; and 33(9), September 1980, pp. 404–405.

American people. Carter responded to these fears on October 24, 1978, by offering a new anti-inflation program of fiscal restraint. There was to be an immediate freeze on the hiring of federal employees to reduce the payroll by an estimated 20,000 employees during 1979. The centerpiece of his anti-inflation program was a set of voluntary wage and price guidelines: a 7 percent voluntary restraint on increases in wages and benefits and a profit-margin constraint on profits. The foreign exchange market reacted negatively towards the Carter program and during the following week the dollar dropped sharply.

Defense of the Dollar in 1978
Threatened with a new run on the dollar that would intensify domestic inflation, Carter authorized Blumenthal to put together a plan to defend the dollar. On November 1 Blumenthal announced that the Treasury had put together a $30 billion currency support package. The United States asked the International Monetary Fund for $5 billion in SDRs, the Treasury authorized the sale of $10 billion in foreign currency-denominated government securities, and swap lines were increased by $6 billion with the Germans, $5 billion with the Japanese, and $4 billion with the Swiss. Blumenthal also announced that the United States would sell 1.5 million ounces of gold each month for an indefinite period of time. The Fed's

contribution to the defense of the dollar was an increase in the discount rate from 8½ to 9½ percent, the biggest jump since 1933. Moreover, in a remarkable departure from tradition, it was Treasury Secretary Michael Blumenthal, not Federal Reserve Chairman G. William Miller, who announced the boost in the discount rate.

Monetary Restraint Increases the Value of the Dollar in Early 1979

These actions succeeded in slowing the rate of monetary growth. After growing at an annual rate of 8.2 percent from the fourth quarter of 1976 to the fourth quarter of 1978, the money supply slowed to an annual growth rate of only 4.7 percent from November 1978 to February 1979. This slowing of the rate of monetary growth in the face of double-digit inflation produced a downturn in the economy during the second quarter of 1979. However, the dollar did stage a strong recovery on the foreign exchange market. As real interest rates rose in the United States, capital flows were reversed. During the first five months of 1979 there were net capital inflows in excess of $30 billion. By April the dollar had risen 17 percent against the Japanese yen, 8 percent against the German mark, and 14 percent against the Swiss franc. The dollar would have been even stronger had there not been large sales of dollars by foreign central banks. During the first half of 1979 foreign central banks' dollar holdings in the United States fell by over $18 billion and the United States was able to repay all its swap liabilities to foreign central banks by May.

Accelerated Monetary Growth in Mid-1979 and Capital Outflows Resumed

The Fed did not stick to its commitment of monetary restraint, however. As soon as the first signs of an economic downturn appeared, the Fed abandoned monetary restraint and produced a virtual explosion in the rate of monetary growth. During the second quarter of 1979 the annual rate of monetary growth accelerated to 10½ percent. The Fed's capitulation in the face of a relatively small increase in the unemployment rate convinced investors that the Fed could not withstand political pressures for monetary stimulus. Capital outflows resumed.

Dollar Collapse in Mid-1979

By June 1979 interest rates were falling in the United States despite double-digit inflation but were moving up in Germany and Japan. The dollar started to slide again, despite intervention by U.S. and foreign central banks which ran as high as $500 million a day. By late July the dollar had fallen more than 6 percent against the mark since the beginning of June. It was against this background that Carter named G. William Miller the new Secretary of the Treasury to replace Michael Blumenthal, and appointed as chairman of the Federal Reserve Board Paul Volcker, president of the New York Federal Reserve Bank and one of the most outspoken advocates of monetary restraint in the Federal Open Market Committee. This change in the leadership of the Fed briefly restored confidence in the dollar. However, Volcker's honeymoon lasted only a little more than a month. In September 1979 the dollar weakened dramatically against the German mark, despite heavy intervention by central banks to support the dollar. On September 18 Volcker pushed through an increase in the discount rate from $10\frac{1}{2}$ to 11 percent against the publicly announced opposition of three of the seven governors. However, this modest rise in the discount rate at a time when the money supply was increasing at an annual rate of $9\frac{1}{2}$ percent did nothing to dampen speculation against the dollar.

October 1979 Defense of the Dollar

On October 5, 1979, Volcker returned to Washington after attending the Belgrade meeting of the International Monetary Fund and placed a conference call to the presidents of the Federal Reserve Banks requesting an emergency meeting of the Federal Open Market Committee the next morning. At that emergency meeting the Board of Governors announced that the discount rate was to be raised to a record 12 percent and that a marginal reserve requirement of 8 percent on bank Eurodollar borrowings was to be imposed. The Federal Open Market Committee voted to place greater emphasis on controlling the growth in the monetary aggregates and less emphasis on keeping short-run movements of the federal funds rate within a narrow preset range. After these policy actions, the money supply slowed to an annual rate of growth of less than 5 percent from September 1979 to January 1980.

Tight Monetary Policy in 1980

In February 1980 the money supply started to grow again at double-digit rates. This time the Fed acted quickly to restrain monetary growth by raising the discount rate to 13 percent. Then on March 14 a 3 percentage point surcharge was added to the 13 percent discount rate for large commercial banks which were frequent borrowers from the Fed. In addition, at the request of the Carter administration, the Fed introduced a credit restraint program which imposed a 15 percent marginal reserve requirement on specific kinds of consumer lending. As a result of these actions, the money supply declined at an annual rate of over 5 percent from February to May.

The Dollar Appreciates in Early 1980

In the wake of this slowdown in the rate of monetary growth, market interest rates rose sharply, exceeding past records by sizable margins. As short-term interest rates rose in the United States, the interest rate differential in favor of dollar-denominated assets widened and the value of the dollar increased. Between September 28, 1979, and April 7, 1980, the dollar rose 16 percent against the Japanese yen, 13 percent against the German mark, and 20 percent against the Swiss franc.

Fed Supports the Dollar

By early April 1980 economic activity began to weaken. This, along with the imposition of the credit control program, caused a sharp decline in interest rates beginning in early April. This fall in U.S. interest rates eliminated the interest differential in favor of the dollar and the dollar dropped precipitously. The Fed bought over $1 billion in the foreign exchange market between April 8 and April 23, but even this intervention could not prevent the trade-weighted value of the dollar from declining 6 percent during that two-week period. This intervention in the foreign exchange market, together with open market sales of government securities, caused bank reserves to fall by $1.5 billion from April 23 to May 14. As a result, the money supply dropped, greatly exacerbating the decline in economic activity.

Expansionary Monetary Policy and Dollar Declines in Mid-1980

In May 1980 the Fed reversed its policy of monetary restraint and injected reserves into the banking system. From the end of May until election day in November, the money supply rose at an annual rate of 16 percent—the most rapid rise during any six-month period in the previous two decades. Short-term interest rates, responding to this sharp acceleration in the rate of monetary growth, fell more than 8 percentage points below their April peaks. With the United States still facing an underlying rate of inflation of about 10 percent, the real rate of return on short-term securities denominated in dollars became negative by about 2 percent. In contrast, short-term real interest rates in Germany and Japan were generally positive. By late June the dollar had given up all the gains it made in the October 1979–April 1980 period.

Reaganomics and the Dollar

Fiscal Incentives to Investment

The fortunes of the dollar changed radically with the election of Ronald Reagan. The centerpiece of Reagan's economic program was the Economic Recovery Act of 1981. This new legislation represented the most comprehensive change in the federal tax laws since the Kennedy tax cut in 1964. Tax rates were reduced in three steps, providing a cumulative tax cut of 23 percent by 1984. The act also provided significant tax incentives for capital formation. Business firms investing in new machinery and equipment were given a 10 percent investment tax credit and allowed to depreciate their investment in five years. Firms investing in cars, trucks, and research hardware received a 6 percent investment tax credit and were allowed to depreciate their cost over three years.

Fiscal Investment Incentives and the Exchange Rate

The accelerated depreciation provisions, the investment tax credits, and the tax rate reductions contained in Reagan's new legislation resembled closely Kennedy's tax policies in the early 1960s. However, Kennedy's tax policies were undertaken when exchange rates were fixed. Since Reagan's tax cuts were initiated under a floating exchange rate system, the international effects were very different. In order to analyze these effects, consider Figure 23.8. Accelerated depreciation and the investment tax credit increase the profitability of investment and thus increase the amount of

Figure 23.8   The Economic Effects of the Economic Recovery Tax Act of 1981

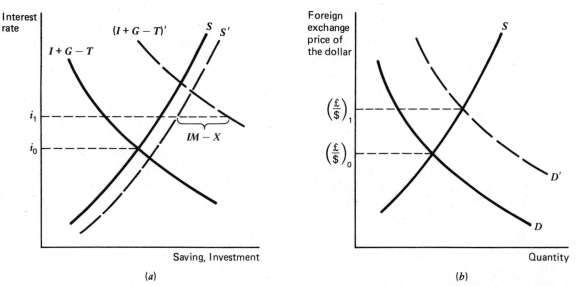

(a) (b)

The investment stimulus, together with the increase in the government debt, will shift the $(I + G - T)$ schedule to the right in Figure 23.8*a*. Since individuals will save part of the increase in after-tax income, the saving schedule will also shift to the right. However, the net effect will be to raise interest rates. This increase in interest rates will attract capital inflows and shift the demand schedule for dollars in the foreign exchange market to the right in Figure 23.8*b*. Equilibrium takes place at an exchange rate $(£/\$)_1$, where capital inflows are offset by the current account deficit, and an interest rate i_1, where $(I + G - T) - S$ equals the current account deficit.

investment that can be undertaken profitably at any interest rate. This investment stimulus, together with the increase in the government deficit resulting from the loss of tax revenue, shifts the $(I + G - T)$ schedule to the right, as shown in Figure 23.8*a*. Although some of the increase in after-tax income may be saved, shifting the saving schedule to the right also, the net effect of the tax legislation is to raise interest rates. This increase in interest rates attracts capital inflows and thus increases the demand for dollars in the foreign exchange market, as shown in Figure 23.8*b*. With floating exchange rates, the increase in the demand for dollars appreciates the dollar from $(£/\$)_0$ to $(£/\$)_1$. This appreciation in the foreign exchange price of the dollar reduces the relative price of traded goods and produces a current account deficit. The foreign exchange market thus comes into equilibrium when the current account deficit exactly offsets capital inflows. However, this implies that flow equilibrium will occur at the interest rate i_1 where $(I + G - T) - S$ is equal to the current account deficit.

Monetary Restraint, Fiscal Stimulus, and the U.S. Balance of Payments

The combination of the Economic Recovery Tax Act of 1981, large increases in defense expenditures, and a restrictive monetary policy that held monetary growth to only 5 percent in 1981 pushed real rates of interest to their highest levels in the postwar period. After being negative for much of the 1970s, real rates of interest rose to 5.30 percent in 1981 and to 6.42 percent in 1982, as was shown in Table 23.1. With real rates of interest significantly lower abroad, funds came pouring into dollar-denominated assets and the dollar soared to its highest value in more than a decade. From the third quarter of 1980 to June 1982 the foreign exchange price of the dollar rose over 30 percent, as was shown earlier in Figure 23.6.

Even after the Fed switched to an expansionary monetary policy in July 1982, real rates of interest remained at historically high levels. Moreover, most other industrial countries followed the lead of the United States and accelerated their monetary growth rates as well in 1982. Thus, despite the rapid growth in the money supply since July 1982, the foreign exchange price of the dollar remained at about the same levels reached in the summer of 1982 for at least a year.

Figure 23.9　U.S. Balance of Payments on Current Account, 1980–1982

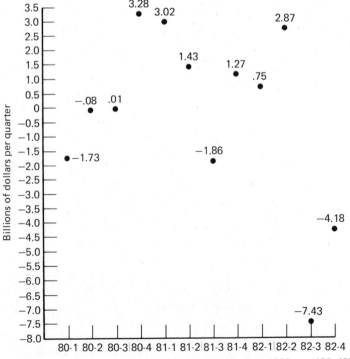

Source: *International Financial Statistics*, 36(6), June 1980, pp. 436–437.

Strong Dollar Hits Traded Goods Industries

By reducing the price of traded goods, the extraordinary appreciation of the dollar contributed to the impressive reduction in the inflation rate during 1982. However, it also took a terrible toll on the traded goods industries in the United States. The steel and automobile industries suffered huge job losses as imports captured large shares of domestic markets. After running current account surpluses of $1.5 billion in 1980 and $3.9 billion in 1981, the current account turned around dramatically in 1982, running deficits averaging $23.2 billion a year in the last two quarters of the year, as shown in Figure 23.9.

Summary

1. The postwar dollar shortage in Europe was alleviated by U.S. aid under the Marshall Plan.

2. U.S. balance-of-payments deficits in the 1950s increased international reserves for the world as a whole because the dollar was a reserve asset.

3. Continued balance-of-payments deficits caused an oversupply of dollars, and foreign central banks began converting dollars into gold.

4. The Fed raised interest rates in 1958–1959 to deter the gold drain.

5. The deficit on capital account improved U.S. international competitiveness and the current account exhibited large surpluses in the first half of the 1960s.

6. Kennedy used fiscal policy to stimulate investment in 1962–1964. This raised interest rates and hence did not worsen the balance of payments as would have any monetary stimulus.

7. Higher nominal interest rates caused by accelerating inflation improved the balance of payments in 1968–1969. Continued inflation, however, caused balance-of-payments deficits in 1970–1971. Increasing risk of devaluation caused speculative capital outflows.

8. A two-tier gold market was established when the United States suspended gold sales in the private market in 1968. Sales of gold at $35 an ounce were confined to foreign central banks wanting to convert official dollar holdings.

9. The United States supported the creation of Special Drawing Rights in 1970.

10. After monetary expansion in 1970, the balance-of-payments deficit soared in 1971. The United States suspended convertibility of the dollar in August 1971.

11. Exchange rates were generally floated in 1973. The dollar fell and U.S. international competitiveness improved dramatically.

12. OPEC investment in U.S. assets produced a capital account inflow that offset the current account deficit with OPEC countries. This actually strengthened the dollar in 1975 and 1976.

13. Expansionary monetary policy in 1977–1978 produced accelerated inflation and a capital outflow. The United States intervened to support the dollar in 1978, but its value continued to decline.

14. The capital outflow of 1977–1978 improved U.S. international competitiveness and the current account improved in 1979.

15. The dollar collapsed in mid-1979 as investors feared increased inflation. Monetary policy was tightened after October 1979 and the dollar appreciated in early 1980.

16. Fiscal investment incentives and restrictive monetary policies raised real interest rates in 1981 and 1982. The dollar appreciated because of capital inflows, and traded goods industries in the United States were hit severely by foreign competition.

Questions

1. What was the postwar dollar shortage and how was it alleviated?
2. How did U.S. balance-of-payments deficits in the 1950s increase total international reserves?
3. What was the gold drain and why did it start?
4. How did Kennedy stimulate the economy without worsening the balance of payments?
5. Why did expansionary monetary policy in the second half of the 1960s at first improve the balance of payments (1968–1969) and then worsen it (1970–1971)?
6. How was the two-tier gold market established in 1968?
7. Why did the United States support the creation of Special Drawing Rights in 1970?
8. What was Nixon's reaction to the soaring balance-of-payments deficit of 1971?
9. How did OPEC affect the value of the dollar?
10. Why did the dollar collapse in 1978 and 1979?
11. Why did the dollar appreciate in 1981 and 1982?
12. What was the domestic impact of the dollar's appreciation in 1981 and 1982?

Index